Katherine,

Thank you for you service
at Sunset. May the Lord
continue to bless you life.

Jeff

Who's Afraid of the Holy Spirit?

An Investigation into the Ministry of the Spirit of God Today

M. James Sawyer and Daniel B. Wallace, eds.

Biblical Studies Press
Dallas, Texas

Trademark and Copyright Information

Table of Contents

Foreword

Josh McDowell

The ministry of the Holy Spirit has been hotly contested for the better part of a century. And the debate has split the Christian community into two camps: charismatics and cessationists. Each side of the debate has hardened its stance and dug in its heels, particularly with reference to the "sign gifts." But the issues run deeper than this.

Charismatics sometimes accuse their cessationist brothers and sisters of quenching the work of the Spirit. Sadly, that is often the case. But as the essays in this book show, not everyone who believes the sign gifts died in the first century acts as if the Holy Spirit did, too!

Cessationists often accuse charismatics of focusing too much on the ministry of the Holy Spirit. But, practically speaking, many cessationists confine the work of the Spirit to the pages of scripture. Some who speak of a "personal relationship" with Christ act as if scripture is some sort of replacement for the personal presence of the Spirit. They have forgotten that scripture is a means rather than an end. It's a means to a *relationship.*

Oh, how God longs for a relationship with you! But a personal, intimate, vital relationship with the God of the universe demands more than right beliefs! It requires the transformational experience of God's very presence. The editors call this experience *pneumatic* Christianity.

This fascinating book is both broad and deep. Wrestling with topics not normally considered in books on the work of the Spirit, the authors of these essays address creativity and the arts, discerning God's will, the history of the church, creating a worshiping community, the relationship between scholarship and the ministry of the Spirit, and so much more! In addition, they show us a glimpse of the African-American church and the dynamic role culture plays in the manifestation of the work of the Spirit. And they take a powerful look at the work of the Holy Spirit in the non-western world, unveiling a dynamic virtually unknown in the west.

Both cessationists who long for more in their relationship to God and charismatics who may think they have cornered the market on the Spirit's ministry will learn much from this innovative book.

The essays that follow are thought provoking and heart stirring. They call you to think more broadly and deeply about the ministry of the Spirit. They challenge you to set aside your fear of losing control. And they exhort you to entrust yourself to the powerful, personal presence of the living God. I join the authors in urging you to embrace *pneumatic* Christianity. After all, it's *biblical* Christianity.

Josh McDowell

Foreword

Wayne Grudem

This is a remarkable book. I came away thinking that there is much more common ground than I had realized between thoughtful, Bible-based cessationists and thoughtful, Bible-based Pentecostals, charismatics, and other evangelicals who believe the miraculous gifts of the Holy Spirit continue today.

I do not mean to say that the authors have given up their view that miraculous gifts of the Holy Spirit ceased with the death of the last apostle (around 90 A.D.). But several of the authors affirm (1) that miracles certainly continue today; (2) that the Holy Spirit often bears witness to us and guides us through subjectively perceived instincts, feelings, and thoughts in addition to his guidance through the words of the Bible; (3) that the Holy Spirit's work in bringing us to Christian maturity will often result in strongly felt, positive emotions (such as love, joy, peace); (4) that proper study of the Bible should be carried out while we are continually conscious of an ongoing personal relationship with God; (5) that the proper goal of all academic study of the Bible is a changed heart that results in increased love for God and other people; (6) that among cessationists, scholarly research, seminary study, and pastoral activity have too often degenerated into a cold rationalism characterized by an unbiblical fear of emotions and fear of loss of control (which prohibits the Holy Spirit from acting in ways we did not plan for), and (7) that this rationalism can actually lead to spiritual defection among those most highly trained by such a system. I can only applaud such claims. In fact, I would only add that the danger of pursuing rationalistic scholarship devoid of any awareness of a personal relationship with God is not confined to cessationist circles but constantly challenges all Christian scholars who live and work in today's post-Kantian and largely anti-Christian culture.

I did not agree with everything in this book, but I agreed with most of it. I hoped that some of it would affirm even more about the Holy Spirit's work. And I disagreed with small parts of it here and there.

My overall expectation is that the book will be widely welcomed among many in the cessationist tradition who have believed and practiced many of the things discussed in this book but have been hoping for some biblically-based, academically credible leaders to provide this kind of theologically sound argument for "progressive cessationism" (my term for what I read in this book), and thereby to give them encouragement to be open to the Holy Spirit's work in various ways today. This may include being much more sensitive to the Holy Spirit's moment-by-moment guidance through the day, or praying with more expectant faith for the Holy Spirit's miraculous work, or allowing times of personal and corporate prayer and praise to be much more filled with exuberant joy or sorrowful weeping in response to the Holy Spirit's presence, or talking openly with others about the Holy Spirit's work in one's life without fear of being accused of doctrinal error or dangerous subjectivism. If these things happen more frequently in cessationist circles (indeed, in all evangelical circles!), I am sure the authors would be thankful to God, and I believe that God also would be pleased with such indications of a deeper personal relationship with himself.

Because the book is so diverse, it is difficult to write an adequate foreword without saying something brief about each of the various chapters, so that is what I have attempted to do in the appendix entitled "Response."

Wayne Grudem
Research Professor of Bible and Theology
Phoenix Seminary, Phoenix, Arizona
October 2, 2005

Preface

The origins of this book came in the early 1990s when both of us editors (Jim Sawyer and Dan Wallace) were facing trauma in our lives and in the lives of our families—traumas that our rationalistic theological training had left us unequipped to deal with. The propositions of our theology left us cold, and failed to speak vitally to the pain we each felt. Independently, as scholars trained in the evangelical cessationist tradition we came to grips with the spiritual sterility of that tradition. As we shared our personal "war stories" we discovered similar trajectories in the development of our understanding of the reality and necessity of the personal and existential work of the Holy Spirit in our lives. Doctrine and biblical knowledge alone simply did not cut it.

Out of our conversations, the sharing of the pain and reflection on our background, the idea for a book addressing our concerns was born. While not embracing what we consider to be the excesses of Pentecostalism, the charismatic movement, and the Third Wave, we have embraced what we have tentatively called *pneumatic Christianity.* We contend that the way evangelical cessationism has developed was reactionary and reductionistic. Rather than focus upon scriptural images of the Holy Spirit as a presence deep within the soul of the believer, cessationism has reactively denied experience in opposition to the Pentecostal overemphasis upon experience, which at times supplanted the revealed truth of scripture. In one sense this volume is not intended to be programmatic; rather it is exploratory. One theme that surfaces numerous times throughout the essays is the issue of control. As a group we have individually and independently recognized that we really are not in control of our lives. The place of control belongs to God alone. Our attempts for control can be a subtle grasp at self-deification. The fear of loss of control, we are convinced, has driven much cessationist literature.

In another sense it *is* programmatic in that it marks a departure from the way many in the cessationist camp think. In this respect, it is much closer to the way charismatics think. The difference, then, is in the details. But the big picture for both charismatics and pneumatics is the same: God is in control; we aren't.

In short, our tradition framed the issue wrongly. It threw out the proverbial baby with the bathwater. The Pentecostal/charismatic tradition has focused on the sign gifts of the Spirit. We have become convinced that the ministry of the Spirit is far wider and deeper but more subtle than even the Pentecostal/charismatic tradition envisions it. Consequently the essays of this volume explore, however tentatively, an attempt to steer a middle ground between the sterile cessationism that essentially locks the Spirit in the pages of scripture, and an anything-goes-approach that has characterized parts of the Pentecostal/charismatic/Third Wave movements.

The contributors to this volume come from different backgrounds: two are Anglican, one is Chinese, one is African-American, two are Baptist, one is Presbyterian, and several others come from the Bible Church tradition. We would emphasize that as a group we do not represent a unified position on the nature of the ministry of the Spirit, but we are united in asserting the vital personal presence of the Holy Spirit in our lives. We have different emphases, perspectives, and concerns. We do not all agree with one another in every point. While we all agree that hard cessationism is inadequate, some are far closer to the Pentecostal/charismatic/Third Wave tradition while others are closer to the traditional cessationist position.

Finally, it is our prayer that evangelicals would interact with the points raised in these essays. We hope that men and women of God will be touched by what is written here, and that there will be renewal in the church.

Contributors

Dr. Richard E. Averbeck (B.A. Calvary Bible College, Kansas City. M.Div., Grace Theological Seminary, Ph.D. Annenberg Research Institute (formerly Dropsie College), M.A, biblical counseling from Grace Theological Seminary.) is professor of Old Testament Studies and Biblical Counseling at Trinity Evangelical Divinity School (1994-). He is also the Director of the Spiritual Formation Forum. His publications include contributions to *The Dictionary of Biblical Theology*, *New International Dictionary of Old Testament Theology and Exegesis*,

Dictionary of the Old Testament: Pentateuch, Spiritual Formation: An Evangelical Perspective; and chief editor of *Life and Culture in the Ancient Near East*.

Dr. Gerald Bray (B.A., McGill University, M.Litt., D. Litt., University of Paris-Sorbonne) is an ordained minister of the Church of England and taught theology for many years at Oak Hill College in London. Since 1993 he has been the Anglican Professor of Divinity at Beeson Divinity School, Samford University, Birmingham, Alabama. He is the author of numerous books, including *The Doctrine of God; Biblical Interpretation: Past & Present; Creeds, Councils and Christ; Personal God;* and *Documents Of The English Reformation* as well as numerous articles. He is also the editor of the Anglican journal "Churchman".

Dr. David Eckman (Th.M., Ph.D., Golden Gate Seminary) specializes in the Old Testament, and Spiritual Formation. He has pastored for a decade and a half and has served as Executive Vice president for Western Seminary. Presently is Associate Professor at Western Seminary's Northern California Campus and Co-Founder and Director of *Becoming What God Intended Seminars* (www.whatGodintended.com). He has written the *Guideposts Commentary on the Minor Prophets*, and *Becoming Who God Intended* and has contributed to the *New King James Study Bible*.

Dr. Reg Grant (B.A, SMU, Th.M, Ph.D., Dallas Theological Seminary) is Professor of Pastoral Ministries at Dallas Theological Seminary where he teaches courses in preaching, drama, voice, creative writing and creative radio production. His publications include *STORM: the Surprising Story of Martin Luther* as well as contributions to numerous books and articles. Several of his films have won major film festival awards including "Top Educational Film in America"; two have won Emmys. He currently hosts the radio program *EarSight,* a daily devotional program. He serves on the advisory board for Nest Entertainment, and on the board of directors for Probe Ministries.

Dr. Jeff Louie (Th.M., Ph.D. Dallas Theological Seminary) is an ordained minister and has been in pastoral ministry for twenty years, six years at Chinese Bible Church of Oak Park, IL (1984-1990) and for the past fourteen years as Senior Pastor at Sunset Church in San Francisco, CA. He also serves as adjunct professor at Western Seminary's Northern California Campus.

Dr. James I. Packer (M.A., D.Phil. Oxford University) has had a long and distinguished career in ministry including several years service as assistant minister at St. John's Church in Birmingham, England; Senior Tutor at Tyndale Hall, Bristol (1955-61); Warden of Latimer House, Oxford (1961-1970); Principal of Tyndale Hall Bristol (1970-72); Associate Principal, Trinity College, Bristol, (1972- 1979). He has served at Regent College Vancouver since 1979, beginning as Professor of Systematic and Historical Theology (1979-1989), Sangwoo Youtong Chee Professor of Theology (1989-1996), Board of Governors' Professor of Theology (1996-). His numerous writings include: *Fundamentalism and the Word of God, Evangelism and the Sovereignty of God, Knowing God, Keep in Step with the Spirit, Christianity the True Humanism, A Quest for Godliness, A Passion For Faithfulness The Redemption and Restoration of Man in the Thought of Richard Baxter*. His *Collected Shorter Writings* are available in four volumes, and a selection of his articles has been published as *The J.I. Packer Collection*. He is also an Executive Editor of Christianity Today.

Dr. Willie O. Peterson, (B.A., Dallas Baptist College, Th.M., Dallas Theological Seminary, D. Min., Western Seminary) has broad ministry experience over the past two decades including fourteen years as Senior Pastor of Bethel Bible Fellowship in Carrollton, Texas, Assistant Director for the Doctor of Ministry Studies at Dallas Theological Seminary, and Vice President and National Field Director of the Urban Evangelical Mission in Dallas, Texas. He also has a recognized International Conference Speaking ministry covering Africa, Europe, Southeast Asia and India.

Dr. Timothy J. Ralston (Th.M., Ph.D., Dallas Theological Seminary) lives in Dallas, Texas, where he serves as Professor of Pastoral Ministries at Dallas Theological Seminary. A member of the North American Academy of Liturgy, he is a specialist in worship and Christian spirituality. He is recipient of the Henry C. Thiessen (Th.M.) and William F. Anderson (Ph.D.) Awards in New Testament Studies at Dallas Theological Seminary.

Dr. M. James Sawyer, (B.A., Biola University, Th.M., Ph.D., Dallas Theological Seminary) has taught Theology, Church History and Historical Theology for more than twenty years. He is Professor of Theology and Church History at Western Seminary's Northern California extension (1989-). His publications include numerous articles and books including, *Taxonomic Charts of Theology and Biblical Studies, Charles Augustus Briggs and Tensions in Late Nineteenth Century Theology,* and *The Survivor's Guide to Theology* and co-author of *Reinventing Jesus?* His non-academic ministry experience includes Youth for Christ, and mission work in South America. He is also regularly involved with the "Perspectives on the World Christian Movement."

Dr. Donald K. Smith (B.S., M.S., M.A., Ph.D., University of Oregon) was for twenty-one years Distinguished Professor of Intercultural Communication and Missiology at Western Seminary in Portland, Oregon. He is presently Dean of WorldView Institute (a graduate level international living-and-learning community). For 30 years a missionary evangelist, journalist and educator in Africa, based in South Africa, Zimbabwe, and Kenya, Dr. Smith was founder of Daystar University in Nairobi. His experience includes teaching, editing, publishing, developing literacy materials in African languages, anthropological research, evangelism, preaching and supervising Bible translation programs in more than 40 languages. His books, *Creating Understanding* and *Make Haste Slowly,* are used widely in missions training. Through WorldView Institute he continues an extensive overseas ministry, focusing on emerging Third World mission societies and leadership of national churches.

Dr. Daniel B. Wallace (Th.M., Ph.D., Dallas Theological Seminary) has taught New Testament for over two decades. His *Greek Grammar beyond the Basics: An Exegetical Syntax of the New Testament* (Zondervan, 1996) is used in more than two-thirds of the schools that teach intermediate Greek. He has written one other textbook and has several more in progress, as well as more than a score of articles in theological journals. Recently his scholarship has shifted from syntactical and text-critical issues to more specific work in John, Mark, and nascent Christology. His postdoctoral work includes work on Greek grammar at Tyndale House in Cambridge, England, textual criticism studies at the Institut fuer neutestamentliche Textforschung in Muenster, Germany, as well as work at Tuebingen University. He is also on pastoral staff at Stonebriar Community Church in Frisco, Texas, and senior New Testament editor of the NET Bible.

Introduction:

Who's Afraid of the Holy Spirit? The Uneasy Conscience of a Non-Charismatic Evangelical

Daniel B. Wallace

Through the experience of my son's cancer, I came to grips with the inadequacy of the Bible *alone* to handle life's crises. I needed a existential experience with God. I got in touch with my early years as a charismatic and began reflecting on how the Holy Spirit works today. I saw scripture in a new light and began wrestling with the question, If the Holy Spirit did not die in the first century, what in the world is he doing today? This essay offers eleven theses that begin to explore answers to that question.

This message was originally delivered as the presidential address of the Evangelical Theological Society's Southwest Regional meeting in the spring of 1994, held at John Brown University in Arkansas. It was modified further for publication in *Christianity Today*, appearing in the September 12, 1994 issue. It has now been thirteen years since my son's cancer, the event that was the catalyst for this original essay. He is doing fine—so fine in fact that he wrestled on varsity in high school for four years and was co-captain his last two. He is now finishing up his bachelor's degree at the University of Texas in Austin.

Introduction

I am a cessationist. That is to say, I believe that certain gifts of the Holy Spirit were employed in the earliest stage of Christianity to *authenticate* that God was doing something new. These "sign gifts"—such as the gifts of healing, tongues, miracles—*ceased* with the death of the last apostle. This is what I mean by "cessationism." Some cessationists might style themselves as "soft" cessationists whereby they mean that *some* of the sign gifts continue, or that the sign gifts may crop up in locations where the gospel is introduced afresh,[1] or that they are presently agnostic about these gifts, but are not a practicing charismatic. For purposes of argument, I will take a hard line. In this way, anything I affirm about the Holy Spirit's ministry today should not be perceived as being generated from a closet charismatic. I wish to address some concerns that I, as a cessationist, have concerning the role of the Holy Spirit today among cessationists.

While I still consider myself a cessationist, the last few years have shown me that my spiritual life had gotten off track—that somehow I, along with many others in my theological tradition, have learned to do without the third person of the Trinity.

But this did not hinder my academic work. Mine had become a cognitive faith—a Christianity from the neck up. As long as I could control the text, I was happy. I lived in the half-reality that theological articulation is valid only if it is based on sound exegesis and nothing else. Like the proverbial frog in the slowly simmering pot of water, I did not sense that I was on the way to self-destruction.

Thirteen years ago, the Almighty suddenly and graciously turned up the heat. He provided me with a wake-up call to get me out of the pot. I am sharing my testimony in hopes that many others who are in cauldrons of their own making might realize the danger—and get out.

This article has two parts. First, a personal testimony. I wish to relate to you, at some length, who I am and how God is working in my life. Second, I have **eleven** theses to put on the table—theses that have to do with our deficiencies in how we relate to the Holy Spirit. Many of these, as well as several others, have been fleshed out by the authors for this book. It is our prayer that this volume will be a stimulus to move other cessationists to take more seriously the ministry of the Holy Spirit today. In short, we are asking a fundamental question that all cessationists must ask themselves: If the Holy Spirit did not die in the first century, what in the world is he doing today?

My Spiritual Journey

I grew up in a conservative Baptist church in southern California. I was converted at age four when I attended Vacation Bible School in the summer of 1956. My brother, at the ripe old age of five and a half, led me to Christ. Ironically, he was not a believer at the time. A dozen years later I was instrumental in bringing him to the Savior.

I grew up in the church. My youth was characterized by timidity: I was a Clark Kent with *no* alter ego. I was afraid of life, afraid to explore, afraid to question *out loud*. In spite of this—or, perhaps because of this, I was a leader in the youth group. But I had questions that would not go away—questions about whether I had had an authentic Christian experience. At age sixteen I was in the midst of a life-threatening crisis: should I or should I not ask Terri C. out for a date? Because of the turmoil in my soul, I quickly agreed when a friend invited me to a charismatic revival at Melodyland in Anaheim, California. The house was packed; several thousand were in attendance. The speaker said some things that disturbed me intellectually. When he gave an altar call, I was ready to go forward and give him a piece of my mind. As I got up out of my seat, the Holy Spirit grabbed my heart and said, "No, this is not the reason you're going forward. You need to get right with God." Now, he did not speak audibly to me. These words are not to be put in red letters. But as I rose, before I took one step, I was overwhelmingly convicted of my own sin. The Spirit of God was definitely in that place.

As I came forward, four or five hundred other people streamed forth to the center stage. With hundreds of people there, I was quite amazed when the speaker, microphone in hand, selected me. "Why have you come forward, young man?" he queried. "I came to rededicate my life to Christ," I answered. It was a good thing that the Holy Spirit changed my heart before my lips got in gear!

That night, January 6, 1969, was the major turning point in my life. I still celebrate it as my spiritual birthday (since the exact date of my conversion at age four was and still is a bit fuzzy).

Before I left Melodyland that night, a man invited me to visit his fellowship in Huntington Beach. I joined the group and became a charismatic. The group was vibrant in worship, courageous in evangelism. My faith was alive. My prayer life was thriving. And, for the first time in my life, I gained courage.

I would pray for hours daily, asking God to grant me the gift of tongues. After a weeknight meeting, when one of the "apostles" (apostle Bob, I believe[2]) discovered that I had not spoken in tongues, he asked if I had been baptized in the Spirit. When I answered in the negative, he laid his hands on me and did the job right there on the sidewalk. Observing that nothing had changed, he doubted my salvation.

So I quietly left the group. In the coming months, I fellowshipped at Calvary Chapel, where the neo-charismatic movement finds its origins. Finally, and quite naturally, I left the charismatic movement altogether. I had seen the abuses, and noticed that many things did not measure up to scripture. But my zeal for God was not quenched. I was a part of the Jesus movement as a non-charismatic. I continued to pray, evangelize, and read my Bible. In fact, there was a long stretch of time in which I read my New Testament, cover to cover, every week. I saw God's hand in everything. And the Lord granted me a measure of courage that was not and is not *naturally* mine.[3] Although I had left the charismatic movement, it took me a long time before I replaced my passion for Jesus Christ with a passion for the Bible.

Because of my interest in spiritual things, I decided to attend a Christian liberal arts college. I attended Biola University, married a beautiful Irish lass[4] right out of college, and came to Dallas for more theological training.

Through the years, after going to a Christian college and a cessationist seminary, I began to slip away from my early, vibrant contact with God. My understanding of scripture was heightened, but my walk with God slowed down to a crawl. I took a defensive and apologetic posture in my studies of scripture. In the last several years, I began questioning the adequacy of such a stance—recognizing, subconsciously at least, that it did not satisfy my deepest longings.

Joe Aldrich, the president of Multnomah Bible College, once told me, "It takes the average seminary graduate five years to thaw out from the experience." For most seminary graduates, I suspect, that thawing out may come through the natural course of events. But it took several crises before the Lord started warming me up again. The one that really put on the afterburners was what happened to my son, Andy, thirteen years ago—when he was eight years old.

In December 1991, Andy was kicked in the stomach by a school bully. He developed stomach pains that persisted for quite some time. His personality changed. He was no longer the happy little comic; he was somber, scared, and tired. Two months later, through a providentially-guided indiscretion, Andy left the bathroom door open when my wife walked by. She saw something that horrified her: his urine was brown. That same day, she took him to our family physician. This began a series of doctors and specialists. None of them had a clue as to what was wrong. Finally, he was admitted to Children's Hospital on April 20, 1992, scheduled for a kidney biopsy.

Before the biopsy was to be performed, a sonogram was conducted. We had anticipated a blood clot on the kidney, but the sonogram revealed that something more was present. Perhaps it was a tumor. *One* physician suggested exploratory surgery instead of a biopsy. This sounded crazy to me! Cut my "Beaker"[5] open! We agreed, grudgingly, to this procedure.

The surgery took place on Wednesday, April 22. That's when the nightmare began. One of the physicians prepped us ahead of time:

Mr. and Mrs. Wallace, I wouldn't be overly worried about this operation. What the sonogram revealed may still be just a blood clot. And if it's not a blood clot, then, most likely, it's a benign tumor. And if it's not benign, then it is probably a Wilm's tumor. This is a congenital kidney cancer found in children. It's treatable and curable. However, if it's not a Wilm's tumor, there is the very slight possibility that what your son has is renal cell carcinoma. But that is such a rare cancer in children that the likelihood is quite remote.

As the hours during and after the surgery wore on, we found ourselves getting hit with wave after wave of dreaded news. Andy, indeed, had renal cell carcinoma (RCC). And it was not just the normal type—which was lethal enough. Andy had the more potent strain of RCC. By 1992, less than *ten* children ever diagnosed worldwide had lived beyond two years with this strain of RCC. Apart from radical surgery, it's virtually untreatable and incurable, as far as medical science knows.

There was good news through all this, news of a providential character, news which gave us hope that our son would live. First, the bully who kicked Andy in the stomach probably saved his life. Only in one third of the cases of RCC is there bloody urine. The other symptoms are usually a *mild* stomachache and an occasional low-grade fever.[6] That kick to the stomach probably triggered the bloody urine. Second, the one physician who insisted on exploratory surgery instead of a biopsy also saved his life. RCC is so potent a cancer that every case on record in which a biopsy was performed resulted in the death of the patient. In the midst of wondering, of confusion, of crying out to God, I could still see his hand in all this.

Andy's kidney was removed in the surgery and he went through various grueling tests in which his body was probed for any remnants of cancer. The bone marrow test was the most traumatic. My brave wife held Andy in her arms for 20 minutes as this little boy clutched her, screaming in her ear, "Make them stop, Mommy! Make them stop!" Six days of testing produced no trace of cancer.

RCC in children is so rare that Andy's case was the first one reported in the United States since 1984. Globally, he was the 161st child ever diagnosed with it. There are no support groups. Before Andy left the hospital, a team of ten physicians could not decide whether to administer chemotherapy. It would strictly be a preventive measure, but with RCC, prevention is everything. If the cancer metastasizes again, he will die (as far as statistics reveal). No child has yet survived a return of RCC. The choice was ours whether or not to go with chemotherapy.

We decided to go with chemotherapy, because the risk of not doing it, wondering whether that might kill him, was too great to bear. I cannot adequately describe what the next six months were like—for Andy, for me and his mother, for his three brothers. But I can tell you that I was in an emotional wasteland. I was angry with God and I found him to be quite distant. Here was this precious little boy who was losing his hair, and losing weight. At one point he weighed only *forty-five* pounds. His twin brother at that time weighed eighty-five pounds. Andy was so weak that we had to carry him everywhere, even to the bathroom.

Through this experience I found that the Bible was not adequate. I needed God in a personal way—not as an object of my study, but as friend, guide, comforter. I needed an existential experience of the Holy One. Quite frankly, I found that the Bible was not the answer. I found the scriptures to be helpful— even authoritatively helpful—as a guide. But without *feeling* God, the Bible gave me little solace. In the midst of this "summer from hell," I began to examine what had become of my faith. I found a longing to get closer to God, but found myself unable to do so through my normal means: exegesis, scripture reading, more exegesis. I believe that I had depersonalized God so much that when I really needed him I didn't know how to relate. I longed for him, but found many community-wide restrictions in my cessationist environment. I looked for God, but all I found was a suffocation of the Spirit in my evangelical tradition as well as in my own heart.

Eleven Theses

It was this experience of my son's cancer that brought me back to my senses, that brought me back to my roots. And out of this experience I have been wrestling with practical issues of pneumatology.

I want to offer eleven suggestions, eleven challenges—eleven theses if you will—that deal with areas in my own life that God is addressing. I don't yet have

95 of them—and this isn't the Schlosskirche of Wittenberg. But I hope and pray that this essay will help other cessationists avoid the traps I fell into.

(1) Although the sign gifts died in the first century, the Holy Spirit did not. Cessationists can affirm that theologically, but pragmatically we act as though the Holy Spirit died with the last apostle. This is my fundamental thesis, and it's well worth exploring. What can we, as cessationists, affirm that the Holy Spirit is doing today? What did Jesus mean when he said, "My sheep listen to my voice" (John 10:27)? What did Paul mean when he declared, "all who are led by the Spirit are the sons of God" (Rom 8:14)? What did John mean when he wrote, "You have an anointing from the Holy One" (1 John 2:20)? I am increasingly convinced that although God does not communicate in a way that opposes the scriptures, he often communicates in a non-verbal manner to his children, giving them assurance, bringing them comfort, guiding them through life's rough waters. To deny that God speaks verbally to us today apart from the scriptures is not to deny that he communicates to us apart from the scriptures.

(2) Although charismatics have sometimes given a higher priority to experience than to relationship, rationalistic evangelicals have just as frequently given a higher priority to knowledge than to relationship. Both of these miss the mark. And Paul, in 1 Corinthians, condemns both. Knowledge puffs up; and spiritual experience without love is worthless.

(3) This emphasis on knowledge over relationship can produce in us a bibliolatry. For me, as a New Testament professor, the text is my task—but I made it my God. The text became my idol. Let me state this bluntly: *The Bible is not a member of the Trinity.* One lady in my church facetiously told me, "I believe in the Trinity: the Father, Son, and Holy Bible." Sadly, too many cessationists operate as though that were so.

One of the great legacies Karl Barth left behind was his strong Christocentric focus. It is a shame that too many of us have reacted so strongly to Barth, for in our zeal to show his deficiencies in his doctrine of the Bible we have become bibliolaters in the process. Barth and Calvin share a warmth, a piety, a devotion, an awe in the presence of God that is lacking in too many theological tomes generated from our circles.

(4) The net effect of such bibliolatry is a depersonalization of God. Eventually, we no longer relate to him. God becomes the object of our investigation rather than the Lord to whom we are subject. The vitality of our religion gets sucked out. As God gets dissected and trisected (in the case of you trichotomists), our stance changes from "I trust in" to "I believe that."

(5) Part of the motivation for depersonalizing God is an increasing craving for control. What I despised most about charismatics was their loss of control, their emotionalism. We fear that. We take comfort in the fact that part of the fruit of the Spirit is "self-control." But by this we mean "do all things in moderation"—including worshiping God. But should we not have a reckless abandon in our devotion to him? Should we not throw ourselves on him, knowing that apart from him we can do nothing?

Instead, as typical cessationists, we want to be in control at all times. Even when it means that we shut God out. It is this issue of control that kept a good friend of mine a cessationist so long. Now, as a member of the Vineyard movement, he is quite happy: he acknowledges that he never was in control in the first place. In the midst of what I consider to be a heterodox shift on his part, there is nevertheless this honest breakthrough with God.

(6) God is still a God of healing and miracles. As a cessationist, I can affirm the fact of present-day miracles without affirming the miracle-worker. God is still a God of healing even though I think his normal *modus operandi* is not through a faith-healer. The problem with some charismatics is that they believe that God not only can heal, but that he must heal. That is one reason why, up until fairly recently, charismata has been a movement among Arminians. A few years back, I contracted a bizarre form of viral encephalitis. I went to hospital after hospital, finally ending up at the Mayo Clinic. At one hospital, a Christian friend came to visit me. She prayed for me in a long, drawn-out ritual, *commanding* God to heal me! For her, God was simply a tool, an instrument wielded by the almighty Christian. If her faith (or my faith) was strong enough, God had to heal me. That's the way the genie works.

At the same time, the problem with many non-charismatics is that although they claim that God can heal, they act as if he won't. We often don't believe in God's ability—we don't really believe that God *can* heal. This can take various forms. I might not pray for someone because of my understanding of God's sovereignty: "Whatever's going to happen is going to happen, and there's nothing I can do to change God's mind." Hence, we can excuse our lack of prayer on a belief in God's sovereignty. Or we might take the opposite view: "God really is not powerful enough to do this sort of thing. Sure, he can perform miracles but they're few and far between. He's probably already hit his quota for the year, so why bother with prayer?"

Thus, the problem with some charismatics is a denial of God's sovereignty; the problem with some non-charismatics is a denial of God's ability or goodness or both. And neither group is being completely honest with God. Neither is submissively trusting him.

(7) Evangelical rationalism can lead to spiritual defection. I am referring to the suffocation of the Spirit in post-graduate theological training, as well as the seduction of academia. Most seminary professors can think of examples of gifted young students we have mentored who seemed to have lost all of their Christian conviction in an academic setting. For many of us, this recollection is terribly painful. How many times have we sent Daniels into the lions' den, only to tell them by our actions that prayer won't do any good?

One particular instance is very difficult for me to think about. One of my brightest master's students two decades ago went on for doctoral work at Oxford. His seminary training prepared him well in exegesis. But it did not prepare him well in prayer. Some years ago I caught up with him and discovered that he was not only confused about his evangelical heritage, he was even questioning the uniqueness of Jesus. This student had suppressed part of the arsenal at his disposal: the witness of the Spirit, something non-believers can't touch. To this day I wonder how much I contributed to this man's confusion and suppression of the Spirit's witness.

It is not the historical evidences *alone* that can lead one to embrace the resurrection as true. The Spirit must work on our hearts, overcoming our natural reticence. When our graduates go on for doctoral work, and forget that the Spirit brought them to Christ in the first place, and suppress his witness in their hearts, they are ripe for spiritual defection. We need to be reminded—especially those of us who live in an academic setting—that exegesis and apologetics are not the sum of the Christian life.

I speak not only from the experience of my students. In my own doctoral program, while seriously grappling with the evidence for the resurrection, I suddenly found myself in an existential crisis. I was reading in biblical theology at the time, wrestling with those two great minds, Rudolf Bultmann and Karl Barth. I was impressed with the fact that as strong as the historical evidence is for the resurrection, there is and always will be a measure of doubt. Evidence alone cannot bridge the gap between us and God. As much as I wanted the evidence to go all the way, I couldn't make it do so. At one point there was real despair in my heart. I had gotten so sucked in to the cult of objectivism that I forgot who it was who brought me to faith in the first place. Only when I grudgingly accepted the fact that *some* faith had to be involved—and *that* through the Spirit's agency—could I get past my despair. The non-verifiable elements of the faith had become an embarrassment to me, rather than an anchor.

(8) Many of the power brokers of evangelicalism, since the turn of the century, have been white, obsessive-compulsive males. Ever since the days of the Princetonians (Hodge, Warfield, Machen, et al.), American non-charismatic evangelicalism has been dominated by Scottish Common Sense, post-Enlightenment, left-brain, obsessive-compulsive, white males. This situation reveals that we are suppressing a part of the image of God, suppressing a part of the witness of the Spirit, and that we are not in line with historic Christianity.[7] The implications of such demographics are manifold. Three of them are as follows.

- The white evangelical community needs to listen to and *learn* from the black evangelical community. I find it fascinating that the experience of God in the black *non*-charismatic community is quite different from that in the white non-charismatic community. In many ways, it resembles the white charismatic experience more than the white cessationist experience of God. A full-orbed experience of God must take place in the context of community. And that community must be heterogeneous. If, as has been often stated, 11 o'clock Sunday morning is the most segregated time in America, then something is desperately wrong with the Church.

- The Holy Spirit does not work just on the left brain. He also works on the right brain: he sparks our imagination, causes us to rejoice, laugh, sing, and *create*. Few Christians are engaged and fully committed to the arts today. Where are the hymn writers? Where are the novelists? Painters? Playwrights? A very high-powered editor of a Christian magazine told me a few years back that he knew of only one exceptional Christian fiction writer. What are our seminaries doing to encourage these right brainers? What is the Church doing to encourage them?[8]

• We men have failed to listen to the women in our midst—and this failure is related to our not hearing the voice of the Spirit. If the *Imago Dei* is both male and female, by squelching the valuable contribution of women, we distort that very image before a watching world.

(9) The Holy Spirit's guidance is still needed in discerning the will of God. The rationalism in our circles makes decision-making a purely cognitive exercise. There is no place for prayer. There is no room for the Spirit. I believe there is a middle ground between expecting daily revelations, on the one hand, and basing decisions solely on logic and common sense on the other. I may not receive revelations, but I do believe that the Spirit often guides me with inarticulate impulses.

(10) In the midst of seeking out the power of the Spirit, we must not avoid the sufferings of Christ. This is the message of the Gospel according to Mark: the disciples could not have Christ in his glory without Christ in his suffering. Too often when we decide that it's a good thing to get to know God again, we go about it on our own terms. Again, I speak from personal experience.

Some time back, one of my students died of cancer. Another was about to die. I began urging students at the seminary to pray for God's intervention. The Lord did not answer our prayer in the way we had hoped. Brendan also died. My own pain was increased when I saw his three small children paraded in front of the mourners at his memorial service.

Through the deaths, tragedies, and suffering that seem to be "par for the course" of being a Christian, and seem to abound for the seminary family, I have learned about suffering and honesty with God. I questioned God—and still do. Out of my pain—pain for these students and their families, pain for my son, pain for myself—has come honesty and growth. I have moments when I doubt God's goodness. Yet I do not doubt that he has suffered for me far more than I will ever suffer for him. And that is the only reason I let him hold my hand through this dark valley. In seeking God's power, I discovered his person. He is not just omnipotent; he is also the God of all comfort. And taking us *through* suffering, not out of it, is one of the primary means that the Spirit uses today in bringing us to God.

(11) Finally, a question: To what does the Spirit bear witness? Certainly the resurrection of Christ. How about the scriptures? A particular interpretation perhaps? Eschatological issues? Exegetical issues? Don't be too quick to answer. Some of this needs rethinking… In fact, my challenge to each of us is this: reexamine the New Testament teaching about the Holy Spirit. Don't gloss over the passages, but wrestle with what they mean. If the Spirit did not die in the first century, then what in the world is he doing today?

In conclusion, to my charismatic friends, I say: We must not avoid suffering as though it were necessarily evil, for we cannot embrace Christ in his resurrection apart from embracing him in his death. To my cessationist friends: We must not anesthetize our pain by burying our heads in the text, as if a semi-gnostic experience of the Bible will somehow solve the riddle of our misery. And to my son I say: I love you, Andy. And I am grateful for all that you, in your childlike faith, taught me about life and about God.

The Holy Spirit in the Hebrew Bible and Its Connections to the New Testament

Richard E. Averbeck

Understanding the OT terms "Holy Spirit" and "the Spirit of God (or the LORD)" and the theology associated with them depends on grasping the significance of the fact that, in about 40% of its occurrences, the Hebrew word "spirit" (*ruakh*) basically means "wind or breath," not "spirit." The NT word (*pneuma*) is also used in this way on occasion. And when these Hebrew and Greek words mean "spirit," the reference is often to the human "spirit." Furthermore, certain passages draw out the correspondence between the Spirit of God and the human spirit, and the importance of God's work through this correspondence (e.g., 1 Cor. 2:10-12). The Spirit of God is the person of God that vivifies the spirit of people to God (Ezek 37; Rom 8:16). The baptism of the Spirit shifts the metaphor from "wind" to "water," the point being that physical purification by water has a corresponding reality in the purification of the human spirit through the Holy Spirit (Matt 3:11; John 1:32-34; Ezek 36). Similarly, like physical water, one can drink of the Spirit as water that gives life to the human spirit (e.g., John 7:37-39). The Holy Spirit did all of these things for both Old and New Testament believers, so in this sense the Holy Spirit not only indwells NT believers, but also did something similar in the lives of OT believers.

The goal of this essay is to examine the foundations of the biblical teachings about the Holy Spirit in the Hebrew Bible (Old Testament). Although along the way I will mention most of the important ways the term "spirit" (Hebrew רוּחַ, *ruakh*) is used in the Hebrew Bible, it is not my intention to provide an exhaustive or even comprehensive review of the uses of the term. There are a number of good surveys of various kinds already available to the reader.[1] Instead of that, I intend to highlight and investigate certain expressions and specific contexts in which the term "spirit" occurs in the Old Testament and their importance for expressions and patterns found in the New Testament, specifically as it relates to our Christian understanding and experience of the Holy Spirit. The focus will be on the Old Testament patterns of expression and some of the most important passages in which they occur, but we will also follow them through into the New Testament to the degree that is possible in this short paper.

"Holy Spirit" in the Old Testament

The term "Holy Spirit" actually occurs only three times in the Hebrew Bible. The expression itself is literally " your (God's) Spirit of holiness" (רוּחַ קָדְשְׁךָ, *ruakh qodᵉshkha*), but the Hebrew language often creates adjectival expressions by means of what is known as the construct genitive relationship between words (i.e., the construction "the...of..."; so the "Spirit of holiness" = "the Holy Spirit"). In these three instances, therefore, the LXX (the Greek translation of the Hebrew Bible) renders this expression with the same combination of Greek words that the New Testament uses for what we translate as "Holy Spirit" in the English versions (i.e., in Greek the noun πνεῦμα [*pneuma*] "Spirit" with [it is usually only followed by the adjective in anarthrous constructions] the adjective ἅγιον [*hagion*] "Holy").

The first occurrence is in Ps 51:11[13], when David prays in penitence to the Lord, "Do not reject me! Do not take your *Holy Spirit* away from me!".[2] The two other occurrences are in Isa 63:10 and 11, where the Lord refers to the Israelites as those who had grieved his Holy Spirit by rebelling against him even though he had so graciously delivered them in the days of old:

But they rebelled and offended his *[H]oly Spirit,*

so he turned into an enemy

and fought against them.

His people remembered the ancient times.

Where is the one who brought them up out of the sea,

along with the shepherd of his flock?

Where is the one who placed his *[H]oly Spirit* among them…

Isaiah 63:14 then refers back to the "[H]oly Spirit" in vv. 10–11 as "the Spirit of the LORD" who had given them rest in the days of old. The latter expression and its interchangeable counterpart "the Spirit of God" (compare, for example, 1 Sam 10:6 with 10:10) occur a total of about 94 times in the Hebrew Bible;[3] that is, if one includes instances where "the (my, your, his) Spirit" clearly refers to "the Spirit of the LORD/God" in the context.

Of course, in the Jewish tradition the Holy Spirit referred to in the Hebrew Bible is not taken to be the third person of the "Trinity," so in such passages the Hebrew word is translated "spirit," not capitalized "Spirit."[4] In general, the Jewish view is that "the spirit of God referred to in the Bible alludes to His energy (Isa 40:13; Zech 4:6)."[5] Accordingly, it is recognized that "the divine origin of the spirit" is implied by the term "his (the LORD's) spirit of holiness" (רוּחַ קָדְשׁוֹ, *ruakh qadᵉsho*), "Yet this does not mean that the holy spirit was regarded as a hypostasis distinct from the divine presence (*shᵉkina*)."[6] In other words, according to the Rabbis, although the "spirit of God" is of divine origin, this does not mean that there is a "Holy Spirit" as a divine person. On the contrary, the holy spirit is a mode of the one and only God's self-expression in word and action.

As Christians we insist that we too believe in only one God (we are monotheists), but articulate this in terms of the tri-unity of the one God— Father, Son, and Holy Spirit—the Trinity (see, for example, the baptismal formula in Matt 28:19, "baptizing them in the name of the Father and the Son and the Holy Spirit"). This is as it should be, but that does not mean we have no difficulties with our understanding of the "Trinity." Specifically with regard to the Holy Spirit, there has been no small debate in two areas that are of special concern in the present essay: (1) the degree of revelation of the *person and divinity* of the Holy Spirit in the Old Testament as compared to the New Testament (compare, for example, the Jewish view outlined briefly above), and (2) the *work* of the Holy Spirit *in the life of the believer* in the Old Testament as opposed to the New Testament, regarding the Holy Spirit's "regenerating" and especially "indwelling" of believers in the Old Testament.[7]

Wind, Breath, and the Spirit of God and People

Any meaningful understanding of the Holy Spirit of God in the Bible will need to begin with an understanding of the term "spirit." The various ways *ruakh* ("spirit") is used in the Hebrew Bible contributes a great deal to our understanding of the revelation of the person and divinity of the Holy "Spirit" in the Old Testament and in the New. To begin with it is important to realize that out of the 378 occurrences of the term "spirit" in the Old Testament it actually means "wind" or "breath," not "spirit," about 140 times (the exact number depends on how one reads certain passages). Thus, almost 40% of the time *ruakh* refers to the literal *movement of air* in: (1) natural weather (e.g., Gen 3:8; 1 Kgs 18:45; Ps 1:4; Eccl 1:6, 14, etc.; note also the "four winds" for the four compass directions, Jer 49:36), which is, of course, under the control of God and sometimes a means through which he acts in the world (e.g., Gen 8:1; Exod 10:13; Num 11:31), or (2) "air breathing" animate beings, mankind and animal (e.g., Gen 6:17; 7:15), or (3) even metaphorically for God's "breath" as expressed through the "wind" of nature (e.g., Exod 15:8; cf. 14:21-22, 29).

Wind, Breath, and the Human Spirit

The connection between "wind" and "breath" seems natural to us even today and appears, for example, in our common expression for having the "wind [actually the 'breath'] knocked out" of a person (through a physical "blow" of some kind). The link between "wind/breath" and "spirit," however, is not so transparent to us. The linguistic data suggest that *in the Bible the link between "wind" and "breath" clearly extends also to "spirit."* In other words, it is easy for us to see the connection between wind and breath simply by reference to the "movement of air" that they have in common, but in the Hebrew Bible both wind and breath are just as closely related to "spirit." This is apparent from early in the canon, extending all the way through it; it is also extremely important to our understanding of the nature of "spirit" and, therefore, the Holy "Spirit." The connection to Greek *pneuma* is there for us in such words as *"pneum*onia," and even for English "spirit" we have words like *"a*spirate" and *"a*spirator" (cf. also "aspiration," etc.), but it is not explicit to us on the surface of our language as it is in the Bible.

Compare, for example, Gen 2:7 "the LORD God formed the man from *the soil* [עָפָר, *'afar*] of the ground and breathed into his [i.e., the man's] *nostrils* the *breath* (נְשָׁמָה, *nᵉshamah*) of *life*...," with Genesis 7:22b, where all mankind and land animals "in whose *nostrils* was the *breath* [*nᵉshamah*] of the *spirit* [*ruakh*] of *life*, died" (NASB) in the flood (except those on the ark of course). The former verse refers only to man and links "breath" (*nᵉshamah*) to "life," but the latter refers to both man and air-breathing land animals and, above all, links "breath" to "spirit" (*ruakh*) and then to animate "life." Moreover, according to Eccl 3:19–21, both animals and people "have the same breath [or 'spirit,' *ruakh*]" (v. 19), and "Who really knows if the spirit [or 'breath,' *ruakh*] of man ascends upward, and the spirit of the animal goes downward to the earth?" (v. 21). By and large, the English versions translate *ruakh* as "breath" in v. 19, but, for example, NET, NIV, and NRSV switch to "spirit" in v. 21 while NASB retains "breath." Whatever one makes of the theology in this passage (i.e., the relationship between people and animals), it is not sound method to shift from one translation to the other in these verses when the same word is being used and the topic has not changed. The point is that we have trouble with this in the English versions precisely because in our language we do not see the natural link between "wind/breath" and "spirit" in the same way and to the same degree as the ancients did when they used the term *ruakh*.

Hebrew *ruakh* is often used for elements of the human "spirit" in scripture (ca. 120 times). As such, it refers to vitality of life (e.g., Gen 45:27; Josh 5:1; 1 Kgs 10:5; Isa 38:16), moral and spiritual character (e.g., positive: Isa 26:9; Mal 2:16; and negative: Isa 29:24; Ezek 13:3), capacities of mind and will (e.g., Exod 28:3; Job 20:3 lit. "the spirit of my understanding"; Pss 51:10 [12], 12[14]; 77:6 [4]), and various dispositions or states of the human person and personality (e.g., Num 5:14 "spirit" = feelings, suspicions; Judg 8:3 "spirit" = anger, resentment; Prov 16:18–19 "low of spirit" = humble, but "high spirit" = prideful; 17:22 "a crushed spirit" = discouraged, depressed; Eccl 7:8 "long of spirit" = patient; Prov 14:29 "short of spirit" = quick-tempered; etc.).

Toward the end of Ecclesiastes, at the climax and conclusion of the book, we find the same term used for the immaterial component of a person as opposed to the material in terms that recall Gen 2:7 (cited above): when a person dies "*the dust* [*'afar*] returns to the earth as it was, and *the spirit* [*ruakh*] returns to God who gave it" (Eccl 12:7; cf. Ps 146:4; Isa 42:5). Similarly, but in a context where we once again see the close connection between "spirit" (*ruakh*) and "breath" (*n^eshamah*), Elihu says, "If God were to set his heart on it, and gather in his *spirit* and his *breath*, all flesh would perish together and human beings would return to *dust*" (Job 34:14–15). God is the one "who forms *the human spirit* within a person" (Zech 12:1), so it naturally returns to him at death.

Breath, Spirit, and the *Person* of the Spirit of God

On at least one occasion David expressed his trust in God in the midst of life-threatening circumstances by exclaiming, "Into your hands I commit my spirit; redeem me, O LORD, the God of truth" (Ps 31:5[6] [NIV]). David was entrusting his spirit to God for deliverance from death. Jesus drew upon this expression at the point of death on the cross, entrusting his spirit to God in death, "Father, into your hands I commit *my spirit* [*pneuma*]" (Luke 23:46).[8] Here Jesus, like David before him, was referring at least to his human spirit (if not also the Holy Spirit), so we have the Old Testament concept of the "human spirit" coming into the New Testament even in regard to the Son of God himself. Jesus was as fully human as he was divine. The parallel passages in Matthew and John simply refer to the fact that at this point Jesus "gave up his spirit" (Matt 27:50; John 19:30). Interestingly, Mark 15:37 puts it this way: "And Jesus uttered a loud cry, and *breathed* his last" (Greek ἐξέπνευσεν [*exepneusen*]; note the root *pneuma* ["spirit"] in this verb).

This shows that, as in the Old Testament, in the New Testament also there is a close connection between "spirit" and "breath" or "breathing." When the "spirit" of a person departs their physical body dies because it no longer "breathes." The same idea appears, for example, in Jas 2:26, "For just as the *body* without the *spirit* is dead, so also faith without deeds is dead." Even in life one can refer to the combination of "body" (*soma*, or "flesh" *sarx*) and the "spirit" (*pneuma*) as making up the whole person (e.g., 1 Cor 7:34; 2 Cor 7:1; Col 2:5, and the combination of body, flesh [as embodied sin], and spirit in 1 Cor 5:3–5), although other combinations can also be used (see, e.g., "soul and body" in Matt 10:28 and "spirit, soul, and body" in 1 Thess 5:23). Moreover, like in the Old Testament, the "spirit" is the seat of human character as well as capacities and dispositions. For example, it can be treated as the seat of intuition (Mark 2:8), discouragement or internal despair (Mark 8:12), joy (Luke 1:47 // with "soul" in v. 46), intense affection (John 11:33), an internal sense of being in one form or another (2 Tim 1:7, a spirit of fear, as opposed to a spirit of power, love, and self-discipline), and so on. When referring to the human spirit, therefore, *ruakh* ("spirit") can refer either to an immaterial element of the human person or personality, or to the whole of the immaterial person.

The point is that there is a great deal of continuity from the Old Testament on into the New Testament in regard to the concept of "spirit" (including "breath" and "wind," see more on the latter below). For purposes of our discussion here, it is absolutely essential to observe that this continuity extends also to "the Spirit of God." Perhaps one of the best places to see this is in 1 Cor 2:10b–12:

> For the Spirit searches all things, even the deep things of God. For who among men knows the things of a man except the man's *spirit* [lit. *the spirit of the man*] within him? So too, no one knows the things of God except *the Spirit of God*. Now we have not received the *spirit* of the world, but *the Spirit who is from God*, so that we may know the things that are freely given to us by God.

The grammatical structure of the expression "the spirit of man" in v. 11 corresponds to that of "the Spirit of God" later in the same verse.[9] This correspondence provides one of the most obvious, simple, and helpful ways of approaching the subject of God's Spirit in the Old Testament in relation to the Holy Spirit in the New Testament. *Just as people have a "spirit," so does God.*

We will discuss the activities of the Spirit of God in the next major section of this essay. For now our concern is with the nature and divinity of the God's Spirit. As noted above, the expression "the Spirit of God/the Lord" and its pronominal equivalents (e.g., "my Spirit") occur many times in the Hebrew Bible, while "Holy Spirit" occurs only three times. In the New Testament the situation is very different, almost reversed. "The Spirit of God/the Lord" occurs only about 25 times, but "(Holy) Spirit" over 150 times. At least on one level it seems most natural that since "the spirit of man" fits his nature as human, similarly, "the Spirit of God" fits God's nature as divine.

This may seem simplistic, but the New Testament actually sets the precedent for it in certain passages, one of the most important being 1 Cor 2:11 in its context (cited above), where the very point of the argument depends on seeing the correspondence and relationship between the Spirit of God and the spirit of man. The "spirit" of the man knows the deep things of the man, that is, his thoughts (v. 11a). Similarly, the "Spirit" of God knows the deep things of God (v. 10b), that is, his thoughts (v. 11b). Moreover, the way we come to understand "the things that are freely given to us by God" by his grace through faith in Jesus Christ (v. 12b; cf. vv. 1–9) is by receiving the Spirit of God in our human "spirit" (v. 12–13; cf. v. 10a). Having the Spirit, we are "spiritual" and "have the mind [νοῦς (nous)] of Christ" (v. 16b).

Compare also, for example, Rom 8:16, where we again find that "The *Spirit* [of God; see the context] himself bears witness to *our* [human] *spirit* that we are God's children." Moreover, in both the Old and the New Testaments God has set his Spirit "in" and "among" his people for guidance and empowerment (see the New Testament passages just cited and compare Gen 41:38; Num 27:18; and note esp. the term "Holy Spirit" in Isa 63:11–12 with "the Spirit of the LORD" in v. 14). This makes it possible for us to "grieve the Holy Spirit" of the LORD/God through various forms of rebellious misbehavior (Isa 63:10; cf. esp. Eph 4:30). As a human person's spirit can be grieved, so can the Spirit of God who dwells in our human spirit and among us (see more on the matter of "indwelling" later in this essay).

So it seems we can think about our subject in the following way from the point of view of certain passages in scripture. The spirit of a human person is distinguishable from his or her body. The spirit is the person whether embodied or not. If in this sense the spirit of a person is the person, then the Spirit of God is God. If the human spirit separates from the body, the body dies (to be resurrected later), but you still have the person in the form of his or her spirit.

The Spirit of God is God, one of the divine persons of the Godhead. Moreover, if and when the Spirit of God occupies the human spirit of a person, that person is made alive to God on the level of her or his spirit. The close relationship between "breath" and "spirit" as translations of the same Hebrew word suggests that if a person has "breath" they are alive physically and if they have the Spirit of God they are alive spiritually. The Spirit of God is the person of God who vivifies the spirit of people to God. The analogy is not perfect, of course. For example, the scriptures are not suggesting by this analogy that God the Father somehow corresponds to our physical body. "God is spirit, and the people who worship him must worship in spirit and truth" (John 4:24). Nevertheless, on certain points at least we can reason back by analogy from a biblical understanding of the human person as a way of approach to a good biblical understanding of the person of God, especially in terms of the "Spirit" of God as a divine person, the Holy Spirit.

Wind, Spirit, and the Nature of the Spirit of God

If one of the explicitly biblical perspectives from which to approach an understanding of the Holy Spirit of God is through comparison and contrast with the human spirit of people, then another is through the nature and effects of "wind." We have already referred to several passages in the Old Testament where *ruakh* means "wind." Conceptually, "wind" is closely related to "breath," since they both involve the movement of air, and both of them are closely related to "spirit" because if a person stops "breathing" their life "expires" and the person's body gives up their "spirit." In turn, "spirit" also sometimes refers to that which constitutes the unique nature of a particular person—their individual personal vitality and personality, character, dispositions, and so forth. In the latter sense, the term also applies to the Spirit of God. I am not suggesting that Hebrew *ruakh* always means all these things, but that it can potentially mean any of them.

The close connection between "wind" and "spirit" comes to the forefront immediately at the beginning of the Bible. In Gen 1:2b we read that the "the Spirit of God [רוּחַ אֱלֹהִם, *ruakh 'elohim*] was moving over the surface of the waters" before the beginning of God's creative words in verse 3 (see "And God said…" through the chapter). Some have treated *'elohim* here as an adjective (i.e., its superlative use) meaning "mighty" or "terrible" so that the whole expression means "a mighty wind" or "terrible storm." However, there is no other instance in the Old Testament where *rûaḥ 'elohim* or any of its equivalents mean anything other than "the S/spirit of God/the LORD" or "the wind of God/the LORD." Moreover, the adjectival use of *'elohim* is foreign to this chapter where the term is used so many times to mean "God," and, in fact, serves as the primary focus throughout the chapter both conceptually and structurally. See Gen 1:1a, "In the beginning God …," and recall the repeated formula, "And God said…," beginning in verse 3 and running through the whole chapter as the common introduction to each creative movement of God.

The NRSV translates "a wind from God swept over…" rather than the NIV "the Spirit of God was moving over…," reflecting both the ancient Near Eastern background in which cosmologies sometimes include wind in the creative process, and some translations and discussions in the history of interpretation of Gen 1:2.[10] The rendering "wind of God" finds support in Gen 8:1b, where God "caused a wind to blow over the earth and the waters receded" after the waters of the flood had covered the earth. The context is similar to Gen 1:2 where waters are also covering the earth and God intends to cause them to recede in the following verses so that the dry ground might appear (later, on the third day of creation). Consider also the watery context in Exod 14:21–22, 29 where the Lord enabled Israel to cross the Reed Sea on dry ground by sending a strong east "wind" (*ruakh*) to drive the waters back. The poetic account in Exod 15 refers to this wind as a "blast" (*ruakh*) from the Lord's nostrils that piled up the waters (v. 8), and then he "blew" again with his "breath" (*ruakh*) to drown the Egyptian army with the same waters (v. 10). There are also a few instances in which the expression "the *ruakh* of the LORD" refers his "breath" or "wind" (e.g., Isa 40:7; 59:19). Moreover, the next occurrence of *ruakh* in the canon after Gen 1:2 is 3:8 in reference to the Lord God "walking in the garden in the cool [lit. 'to the wind'] of the day."

However, we also need to take seriously the fact that the vast bulk of occurrences of "the *ruakh* of the LORD/God" in the Old Testament refer to God's "Spirit" understood as the person of God that corresponds to the human "spirit" in people (see the reflections on this biblical analogy in the previous section above). Consider, for example, the third occurrence of *ruakh* in the canon (after Gen 1:2 and 3:8), where the Lord says, "My Spirit will not contend with man forever" (Gen 6:3 [NIV]). "Wind" would make no sense as an English rendering for *ruakh* in this context, and there are many like it. This must be taken into consideration in the translation and interpretation of Gen 1:2. It is especially significant that this is the third and last of the three clauses of verse 2 describing the condition of the earth before God's repeated pronouncement of creative words beginning immediately in verse 3. Some have argued that since "the Spirit of God" does not appear anywhere else in this chapter, therefore, translating "the wind of God" suits the focus on forces of nature throughout the chapter. However, translating "the Spirit of God" corresponds to the focus on God "speaking" (i.e., "breathing out" his pronouncements) throughout the chapter. In other words, the latter rendering would provide a more natural lead into the "And God said…" sequence of the chapter, beginning immediately after this clause.[11]

In any case, it seems to me that our problem in handling Gen 1:2 arises in the first place because we tend to think that "wind" and "Spirit" are mutually exclusive. In my opinion, there is no reason that *ruakh* in Gen 1:2 cannot be a reflection of the power of God present and ready to work through "wind" in this watery environment (cf. Gen 8:1 and Exod 14:21–22 and 15:8–10 cited above) as well as the work of the "Spirit" of God in shaping the creation through pronouncements (Gen 1:3ff), both at the same time (i.e., an instance of *double entendre*). As I have already explained and illustrated above, there is a very close connection between *ruakh* as wind/breath (i.e., the movement of air) and *ruakh* as (human) "spirit" or "Spirit" of God in the Hebrew Bible.

The Old Testament passage in which this stands out most clearly is Ezek 36–37. The well-known vision of the valley of dry bones in Ezek 37:1–14 begins with "the Spirit of the LORD" transporting the prophet to the valley (v. 1).[12] Of course, the dry bones represent the house of Israel as a whole, and the real question is whether or not there was any hope for Israel in the future (v. 11). A valley of dry bones suggests not, but God has something to say about that. As the vision goes, God tells Ezekiel to prophesy that God "will make breath (*ruakh*) enter" them so that they "will come to life" (v. 5). Ezekiel prophesies as he has been instructed and the bones rattle, come together, and receive from the Lord flesh and life-giving "breath" (*ruakh*) from "the four winds" (i.e., the four *ruakh*; vv. 7–10).[13] Note the link between "breath" and "wind" here. Finally, in the interpretation of this vision in vv. 11–14 God says that he will bring the people of Israel back to the land (i.e., out of their graves, vv. 12–13) in accord with the promise that, "I will put my Spirit (*ruakh*) in you and you will live" (v. 14). So here the "Spirit" of God is identified with the "breath" and the four "winds" of the vision. The oracle begins with "the Spirit of the LORD" transporting the prophet to the valley of dry bones and ends with the "Spirit" reviving the people (i.e., the dry bones) to bring them back from exile (i.e., the valley of dry bones) into the land of Israel.

This combination of wind, breath, and spirit extends also into the New Testament where its importance for understanding of the Spirit of God is maintained. For example, in his well-known "born again" (or perhaps better, "born from above") encounter with Nicodemus in John 3,[14] Jesus uses the wind/spirit correspondence to explain the nature of spiritual birth: "What is born of the flesh is flesh, and what is born of the Spirit is spirit" (v. 6), and especially, "The *wind* [*pneuma*] blows wherever it will, and you hear the sound it makes, but do not know where it comes from and where it is going. So it is with everyone who is *born* of the *Spirit* [*pneuma*]" (v. 8). We will say more about this passage below. What concerns us presently is the fact that Jesus rebuked Nicodemus for being "Israel's teacher" and not understanding the significance of the nature of "spirit" and the "Spirit" of God in spiritual birth into the kingdom of God (vv. 9–10). Later in the same Gospel we read that Jesus "breathed on them [i.e., his disciples] and said, 'Receive the Holy Spirit'" (John 20:22). It is as if his breathing on them was the means by which he passed the Holy Spirit over to them.

The dependence on the Ezek 37 imagery of wind, breath, and Spirit is hard to miss in John 3 and 20. Similarly, in Acts 2, "the blowing of a violent *wind*" accompanies the filling of the Holy Spirit on the day of Pentecost (vv. 2–4). Again, in 2 Pet 1:21b, Peter affirms that the Old Testament prophets "*carried along by the Holy Spirit spoke from God*" when they articulated the word of God we now know as the Old Testament. As many have observed, the verb "carried along" (Greek φερόμενοι [*pheromenoi*] from the verb φέρω [*pherō*]) is the same verb as that used for a boat being "driven along" by the wind in Acts 27:15. The main point is this: God's Spirit is like the wind.

We need to take this biblical analogy seriously in both understanding the nature of God's Spirit and in welcoming and engaging with his work. Wind is a mysterious and powerful force. We cannot always predict what it is going to do, and it is not under our control. The same is true of God. We cannot always predict what he is going to do, and he is not under our control even if he has told us what he is going to do. He is God. We are not. All this is true also of the Spirit of God. However, although we cannot completely understand and control the Holy Spirit, we can draw upon his power. Using the analogy of a ship driven by the wind (see above), we can "put up the sails" in our lives and thereby take advantage of the blowing of the Spirit in and through our lives. We are empowered by the Holy Spirit as long as we have our sails up.

Putting up the sails begins, above all, with being "born" of the Spirit into the kingdom of God (John 3). It continues through continuing attentiveness to God in our lives on various levels and in all sorts of ways, including, for example, the serious study of the scriptures that the Spirit himself "inspired" (see 2 Tim 3:16, "Every scripture is inspired by God [*God-breathed* (θεόπνευστος, *theopneustos*)]"; cf. 2 Pet 1:21 cited above), the practice of "unceasing" prayer (1 Thess 5:17), loving involvement with other believers (see, e.g., the fruit of the Spirit in Gal 5:16, 22–24), giving witness in the world to the truth and effectiveness of the gospel (Acts 1:8), and so on. The more we are attentive to God in all the various dimensions of our lives, the more we invite the Holy Spirit to empower us by "putting up our sails," to the degree these things are true of us, to that degree we live our lives by the power of the Holy Spirit.

Water, Spirit, and Transformation by the Spirit of God

Another whole set of biblical images associated with the Holy Spirit are those that in some way have to do with water. The vision of Ezek 37 is actually an extension of the previous oracle in Ezek 36:22–38, in which the Lord promised to respond to the rebellious defilement of the nation and their profaning of his holy name among the nations. This is his promised response:

I will *sprinkle you with pure water* and you will be clean from all your impurities; I will purify you from all your idols. I will give you a new heart, and I will *put a new spirit within you*; I will remove the heart of stone from your body and give you a heart of flesh. *I will put my spirit within you*; I will take the initiative and you will obey my statutes and carefully observe my laws. Then you will live in the land I gave to your fathers; you will be my people, and I will be your God (Ezek 36:25–28).

Three points in this passage are especially important to our present discussion. First, the Lord promised to "cleanse" the nation from their all their "impurities" and "idols" by sprinkling (actually "splashing") the people with "pure water." Second, the Lord promised to change their human spirit by putting within them "a new spirit." Thus, he will change their "heart" from being hard like stone (non-responsive) to being soft like human flesh and, therefore, responsive to God's touch. The third point is actually closely related to the second. The Lord promised to put his "spirit *within* [the midst of]" them and thereby move them to follow the Lord's covenant law (v. 27). This, of course, is the essence of putting "a new [human] spirit *within* [the midst of]" them (v. 26).

Water Purification and Baptism with the Spirit

It is important to observe the close pattern of parallels between this passage and what Jesus said to Nicodemus in John 3:5–6, "I tell you the solemn truth, unless a person is born of *water* and *spirit*, he cannot enter the kingdom of God. What is born of the flesh is flesh, and what is born of the *Spirit* is *spirit*." The combination of water, spirit, and Spirit here recalls the same elements in Ezek 36:25–27 (cited above) and the relationship between them. Water is mentioned first because purification from impurity and infidelity is the necessary environment for revival of the heart and spirit of people by the work of God's Spirit. Ezekiel was both born as a priest and called to be a prophet (Ezek 1:1–3), and the two offices come together here. In Ezekiel's day Israel needed both purification by water and vivification by the Spirit. John the Baptist was also both born a priest (Luke 1:5, 57–66) and called to be a prophet (Matt 3:1–4; 11:7–15; note especially the quotations from Isa 40:3 in Matt 3:3 and Mal 3:1 in Matt 11:10, and compare John's lifestyle with Elijah, Matt 3:4; 11:7–8; and 2 Kgs 1:8).

The connection of John 3 back to John 1 is important here. John the Baptist came to prepare the people for the Messiah, and he did this through water purification, a baptism of repentance (John 1:24–28; cf. Matt 3:2, 8, 11; Mark 1:4–5; Luke 3:3, 8). But the Son of God himself would be the one who would "baptize with the Holy Spirit" (John 1:33b). The Jewish leaders had sent "priests and Levites" (v. 19) to question John about who he was (vv. 19–23) and the purpose of his baptismal water purification practices (v. 25). Of course, this would be natural since priests and Levites were the ones responsible for such purifications in Israel (cf., e.g., Lev 14 with Matt 8:4). John's ministry continued along this line of "ceremonial washing," over which disputes sometimes also arose between John's disciples and other Jews (see, e.g., John 3:25).[15]

John the Baptist made the connection between his own ministry and that of Jesus through a theologically creative metaphorical parallel between his own baptism "with water" (John 1:31) and Jesus' baptism "with the Holy Spirit" (John 1:33). I am aware of no precedent for this analogy (water baptism > Spirit baptism) in the Old Testament or intertestamental literature.[16] John seems to have coined the term as a graphic image that would serve to both compare and contrast his own ministry with that of Christ. People of the day were accustomed to ritual washings with water, but "washing with the Holy Spirit" was another matter. Even if the expression itself derives from John the Baptist, nevertheless, the idea behind it is Ezekiel's prophecy of the Spirit of God transforming the spirit of people from death to life in the same context as God cleansing his people by washing them with clean water (Ezek 36:25–27 with 37:13–14). This is clear from the correspondences between John 3 and Ezek 36:25–27 outlined and explained above.

The metaphorical image of "baptism with the Holy Spirit" caught on in the New Testament and came to serve as a pivotal theme of continuity from the Gospels into Acts and the Epistles. *The metaphor takes the idea of purification of the human body through physically washing with water and extends it to purification of the human spirit through spiritual washing with the Holy Spirit.* This constitutes the pivotal shift from the water baptism of John to the Spirit baptism of Jesus that John the Baptist was so concerned to emphasize (see, e.g., Matt 3:11 and John 1:32–34). Similarly, when Jesus himself met with the apostles immediately before his ascension (Acts 1), in anticipation of the day of Pentecost (Acts 2), he once again called their attention to the importance of the link between John's baptism with water and his own baptism with the Holy Spirit: "John baptized with water, but you will be baptized with the Holy Spirit not many days from now" (Acts 1:5), and "you will receive power when the Holy Spirit has come upon you, and you will be my witnesses in Jerusalem, and in all Judea and Samaria, and to the farthest parts of the earth" (Acts 1:8).

Although the term "baptism of the Holy Spirit" is not used in the record of Philip's ministry in Samaria, nevertheless Acts 8 emphasizes the importance of maintaining a direct connection between baptism "into the name of the Lord Jesus" (Acts 8:16) and receiving "the Holy Spirit" (Acts 8:15, 17). Peter recalled Jesus' baptismal teaching in Acts 1:5–8 when he was asked to explain and justify the water and Spirit baptism of the first gentiles (Acts 11:15–16; cf. 10:44–48). Similarly, Paul came to the believers in Ephesus when they had been baptized with John's "baptism of repentance" (Acts 19:4) but not yet "into the name of the Lord Jesus." Therefore, they had not received the Holy Spirit (vv. 2, 6). In fact, they had not yet "even heard that there is a Holy Spirit" (v. 2b). The phraseology here recalls John 7:39. Jesus had once again used a water motif to speak of "the Spirit, whom those who believed in him were later to receive." John adds further, "For the Spirit had not yet been given [lit. 'for (the) Spirit was not yet'], because Jesus was not yet glorified."

Pouring, Drinking, and the "Indwelling" of the Holy Spirit

This brings us to the Holy Spirit's "indwelling" of believers. Clearly, according to Paul there is no being a Christian without being "baptized by the Holy Spirit." As he puts it in 1 Cor 12:13, "for in one Spirit we were all baptized into one body. Whether we are Jews or Greeks or slaves or free we were all made to drink of the one Spirit." In Acts 19 Paul immediately led the Ephesian disciples (v. 1) to faith in Jesus, "baptized" them "into the name of the Lord Jesus," and laid his hands on them so that "the Holy Spirit came on them" (vv. 4–6). We have already observed that, as a motif, "baptism" in (with, or by) the Holy Spirit is new in the New Testament, but we have also seen that it is based on the combination of divine promises in Ezek 36:25–28. God promised that he himself would purify Israel with clean water (cf. the water baptism of John the Baptist) and, in association with that, put a new (human) spirit in them by putting his Spirit in them to vivify their spirit (see also Ezek 37:14; cf. the Spirit baptism of Jesus).

Paul's other image of the Spirit in 1 Cor 12:13 calls up another whole set of expressions in the Old Testament that serve as background for the New Testament teaching of the indwelling Holy Spirit. He writes: "we were all made to drink of the one Spirit." There is a very real difference between using water for purification (i.e., baptism) and drinking it. Likewise, baptism in (with, or by) the Holy Spirit is quite another thing from "drinking" of the Holy Spirit. We have already discussed the person(ality) of the Holy Spirit based on the comparison to the human spirit (he is personal and manifests the divine nature of God). We have also investigated the nature of the Holy Spirit as (life-giving) "breath" and mysterious yet empowering "wind." Furthermore, we have already begun our discussion of the Holy Spirit as "water" with the remarks above on the Spirit's baptism that cleanses the human spirit.

On the latter point the connection back to Ezek 36–37 binds cleansing from impurities with vivification of the human spirit by God putting his "Spirit" there (Ezek 36:25–27 and 37:14). This combination of divine activities constitutes the regenerating and renewing of peoples' hearts and lives about which both the Old and New Testaments speak.[17] In Ezekiel's terminology it changes the heart from a "heart of stone" to "a heart of flesh" (Ezek 36:26). Jeremiah refers to the same essential thing with a different image when God speaks through him, "I will put my law within them and write it on their hearts and minds" (Jer 31:33). Again, this is what Moses means when he says, "Circumcise then your heart, and stiffen your neck no more (Deut 10:16 [NIV]; cf. 30:6, Lev 26:41; Jer 4:4; 6:10 [lit. "ears are uncircumcised"]; 9:25–26; Ezek 44:7). Paul applies this to saving faith in Rom 2:28–29, where he refers to "circumcision is of the heart *by the Spirit*" (see also Phil 3:3; Col 2:11; and implied elsewhere, e.g., Eph 2:11). There is no "circumcision of the heart" without the work of the Spirit of God in the heart/spirit of the person involved. This is true no matter whether we are talking about the Old Testament or the New.

God has always wanted the same thing from everyone and, according to passages like those cited just above, his resources have always been available and at work to bring this about in the lives of believers whether in Old or New Testament days. The scriptures talk about this in all sorts of different ways and illustrate it through various kinds of metaphors, a few of which are listed above. Therefore, when God spoke through Ezekiel looking forward to a future day when this would take place in Israel, he was not suggesting that this kind of work in the hearts of people had never been seen before in anyone's life. What he was saying is that there was a day coming when God will restore Israel as a nation, bringing them back from exile to reoccupy the land. This would require a work of the Spirit of God changing their hearts and, historically, it took place when they were restored to the land after the Babylonian exile.

This is not the place to deal with all the historical and spiritual factors that bear on Israel's restoration from their captivity in Babylon and the work of Holy Spirit in that instance (see, e.g., Hag 2:5 and Zech 4:6). The point is that this kind of work of the Holy Spirit took place before the time of Ezekiel and at the time of the restoration that Ezekiel predicted. It also continued after the restoration into New Testament times when John the Baptist, Jesus, Paul, and others drew upon Ezekiel's words to explain and illustrate the work of the Holy Spirit in the lives of Christians. Consider, for example, all the background concepts Paul draws upon in Titus 3:5–6, where he writes that God "saved us not by works of righteousness that we have done but on the basis of his mercy, through the *washing* of the new birth and the *renewing of the Holy Spirit*, whom he *poured out* on us in full measure through Jesus Christ our Savior" (cf. also Eph 5:26–27). There is no regeneration anywhere or anytime without the pouring out of the Holy Spirit.

Finally, we come to the matter of the outpouring and indwelling of the Holy Spirit in the Old and New Testaments, about which there has been no small amount of disagreement. This is especially the case regarding whether or not the Holy Spirit indwelt Old Testament believers like he does New Testament believers (for the latter see especially Rom 5:5, 8:9; 11, 1 Cor 2:12; 6:19–20; Gal 4:6; 1 John 3:24; 4:13). On the one hand, it seems difficult to suggest that regeneration could take place in the Old Testament without the Holy Spirit indwelling the believer. On the other hand, some passages in the New Testament, especially in the Gospel of John, seem to suggest that indwelling began in the New Testament at Pentecost. For example, as Jesus put it to the apostles in John 14:17, the Holy Spirit "resides *with* you and will be *in* you." There are several difficulties in this verse even on the text-critical level,[18] but as the NET reads it there appears to be a suggestion that there will be a shift from the Holy Spirit being "with" them while Jesus was still with them to the Holy Spirit being "in" them after he leaves.

This accords well with the normal understanding of John 7:37–39:

> On the last day of the feast, the greatest day, Jesus stood up and shouted out, "If anyone is thirsty, let him come to me, and let the one who believes in me drink. Just as the scripture says, '*From within him will flow rivers of living water.*'" (Now he said this about the Spirit, whom those who believed in him were going to receive, for *the Spirit had not yet been given* [lit. 'for [the] Spirit was not yet'], because Jesus was not yet glorified.)

The context is the "Feast" of Tabernacles, at which there was traditionally a water-pouring ceremony (cf. Zech 14:8, 16–18).[19] Jesus took the opportunity to pronounce that the one who believes in him will have "streams of living water" flowing "from within him" (cf. Jesus with the woman at the well in John 4:10, 14). John the apostle, in turn, explains that Jesus was referring to the Spirit of God, whom such believers would later receive. The reason they had not yet received the Spirit was because this was to happen only after Jesus had been glorified, which is the point of John 14:17 (cited above), and, in fact, "the Spirit was not yet" (a literal translation).

Now, John could not mean by this explanation that there was no Holy Spirit in existence yet because he had already made much of the Holy Spirit's presence and work earlier in his Gospel (see especially John 1:32–34 and 3:5–8, and the discussion above), and had even recorded Jesus' rebuke of Nicodemus for not knowing about these things (John 3:9–10). Even if John was not fully aware of and did not understand the Old Testament background of the Holy Spirit at the time Jesus made this statement, certainly by the time he wrote his Gospel and made the explanatory comment we are considering here, he had experienced the work of the Holy Spirit in his own life (see especially Pentecost) and learned of the Spirit's activities in Old Testament days. By that time he knew that it is not true that the Holy Spirit "was not yet" in existence in Jesus' day, so that cannot be the correct interpretation of John 7:39. The same may be true of the similarly-worded remark in Acts 19:2, when the disciples at Ephesus said, "we have not even heard that there is a Holy Spirit," although at that time they may have been functioning at the same level of ignorance about the Holy Spirit as Nicodemus was in John 3.

The most natural way to understand the intent of these passages is to say that in the days of Jesus the Holy Spirit was not yet active in the lives of believers in the way that he would be after Jesus was glorified, starting on the day of Pentecost (Acts 2). Some would extend the argument back to the whole Old Testament period as well, although it is difficult to understand how this makes sense in light of Ezek 36:27, "I will put my Spirit within you," unless one makes it to be entirely eschatological into the future beyond the restoration from the captivity (see the problem with this approach discussed above), or exclusively collective, referring to God putting the Holy Spirit "in the midst of" Israel as a nation, not "within" individuals. It is true that the pronoun "you" is plural in Ezek 36:27, but the same is true of the whole passage, including the references to changing their heart (v. 26) and so on. One can hardly speak of changing the heart a nation without changing the heart of the people who make it up. Moreover, the New Testament writers did not read the passage this way. They allude to it on both communal and individual levels (see, e.g., 2 Cor 3:3–6 and, again, the personal individual remarks of Jesus to Nicodemus which so clearly draw upon Ezek 36).

In reality, there is probably a combination of things going on here. First, there is the Jewish tradition about the cessation of the time of prophecy with the last of the Old Testament prophets.[20] There is evidence for this tradition of "the quenched Spirit" in intertestamental and rabbinic literature, as well as Josephus, perhaps based on Old Testament passages such as Ps 74:9, Zech 13:2–3, and Mal 3:1, 4:5–6. This suggests that, at least in part, the point of the passages about the lack of the indwelling work of the Spirit in the days of Jesus arises from the fact of the cessation of prophetic activity since the Old Testament prophets. This does not necessarily mean that there was a complete lack of prophetic activity (see, e.g., Luke 1:67 and 2:25–32), but perhaps the time from the last Old Testament prophets to the time of Jesus was like the time of Eli's decline: "Word from the LORD was rare in those days; revelatory visions were infrequent" (1 Sam 3:1; contrast vv. 19–21).

The second point is related to the first. The fact of the matter is that, from Pentecost forward, the indwelling of the Holy Spirit is closely tied to his prophetic work. Peter explained the activities of the Spirit at Pentecost by citing

Joel 2:28–32a (3:1–5a in Hebrew). Peter's quotation of the first two verses reads this way (Acts 2:17–18):

> "And in the last days it will be," God says, "that I will *pour out my Spirit* on all people,
> and your sons and your daughters *will prophesy*,
> and your young men will see visions,
> and your old men will dream dreams.
> Even on my slaves, both men and women,
> I will *pour out my Spirit* in those days, and *they will prophesy*."

"Pouring out" of the Spirit (like water) is associated, therefore, with the prophetic activity of the Old Testament. In Ezek 39:29, the last verse of the section that includes Ezek 36–37, God uses the same expression to refer to his commitment to transform and restore Israel: "I will not hide my face from them any longer, *when I pour out my spirit* on the house of Israel, declares the Sovereign LORD." There are other expressions used for the same thing, but they all associated this kind of Spirit-activity with the institution of prophecy. Consider especially Num 11:29b, where Moses says, "Oh that all the LORD's people were *prophets*, that the LORD would *put his Spirit* on them!" (cf. also 1 Sam 10:10–13 and many other places).

The point of Joel 2 as well as Peter's quotation of it in Acts 2 is that there will be a difference in the last days (i.e., the days since Pentecost). Namely, Moses would have his wish come true. The Lord did "put his Spirit on" all his people, and they all became prophets. The same has been true of all born-again (from above) Christians since that day until now. We have all received the Holy Spirit into our lives by whom we have been cleansed (i.e., baptism of the Holy Spirit, 1 Cor 12:13a) and of whom we drink as he wells up within us (1 Cor 12:13b). All believers are called to be prophets and, therefore, proclaimers of the gospel. This is indeed new in the New Testament. Jesus even hinted at this early in his ministry: "Blessed are you when *people* insult you and persecute you and say all kinds of evil things about you falsely on account of me. Rejoice and be glad because your reward is great in heaven, for they persecuted the prophets before you in the same way" (Matt 5:11–12).

That brings me to a third point. The coming of the Holy Spirit into our lives today brings with it the accomplished work of Christ in his life, death, burial, and resurrection. This also is new compared to Old Testament believers. The indwelling of the Spirit is, of course, metaphorical. If we cut open our bodies we will not find the Holy Spirit visible there. He inhabits our human spirit, which is immaterial by nature, just as God is (John 4:24). This means that what he brings with him into our lives is the full force of "the things freely given to us by God" in Christ Jesus (1 Cor 2:12). Yes, there is "indwelling" in the Old Testament, but not in this way and to this degree of the fullness of God's salvation plan accomplished. The Holy Spirit now can bring all this to bear upon us, and that is his very purpose as Paul observes in 1 Cor 2:12.

Summary and Conclusion

There are some things that are completely new about the work of the Holy Spirit in the New Testament compared to the Old Testament. The Holy Spirit as the agent of Jesus' conception through Mary springs to mind immediately. But much of what is there in the New Testament already has its roots sunk deep into the soil of the Old Testament. What I have written here is something of a phenomenology of the Holy Spirit based in the Old Testament. It is true that the term "Holy Spirit" only occurs three times in the Old Testament, but "the Spirit of God" occurs many times and we see the latter pattern in other terminology as well, for example, "the Spirit of Christ."

Our understanding of the person(ality) of the Holy Spirit finds its base in the comparison to the human spirit (he is personal and manifests the divine nature of God). The nature and power of the Holy Spirit is based in the fact that he is (life-giving) "breath" and mysterious yet empowering "wind." Like water, he is also the one who cleanses our hearts (baptism of the Holy Spirit) and constantly provides water for us to drink as we carry out our prophetic ministry in the Church and in the world. Some of this is new in some ways in the New Testament, but the foundations for them are laid in the Old Testament. The implications of all these images are not always clear in the Old Testament, and sometimes not even in the New Testament in certain places, but they are there nevertheless.

The Witness of the Spirit in Romans 8:16: Interpretation and Implications

Daniel B. Wallace

A comprehensive examination of the usage of συμμαρτυρέω in Greek literature, as well as other exegetical evidence, leads to the conclusion that this verb means "bear witness *to*" in Rom 8:16. The passage thus is affirming that the Holy Spirit has an ongoing witness to our inner being. One implication of this is that we have assurance of salvation not just because of the word of God but also because of the testimony of the Spirit to our hearts. There are also implications for perseverance of the saints and for believers working at the highest levels of scholarship (e.g., it is dangerous to think that mere exegesis will give one certainty; ultimately, a vibrant relation to God through the Holy Spirit must be at the heart of loving God with one's mind).

Introduction

B y way of introduction to the discussion of Rom 8:16, I want to talk about a larger issue. Consider this introduction as the saddle burr.

The Church at the beginning of the 21st century is facing several crises, many of them of its own making. Among these are the crisis of the Spirit and the word. Non-charismatic evangelicals typically give their allegiance to the word; charismatics, to the Spirit. It's like being back in Corinth: "I'm of Paul"; "I'm of Apollos"; "I'm of the Bible"; "Yes, but I'm of the Holy Spirit." This is not just an issue of authority, but even of how one defines what it is to be a Christian, both individually and communally. The name says it all: "Bible Church"; "Holy Ghost Cathedral of Praise." One church spends the majority of its time studying the Bible; another spends most of its time praying and singing. One church sees Christianity through primarily cognitive lenses; the other, through emotional lenses.

Perhaps I have exaggerated the portrait just a bit. Still, it is true that we have two very different brands of evangelical Christianity today. Ironically, both brands, I believe, *mimic* culture. The first is, to some degree, a product of the Enlightenment in which reason reigns supreme. This is true even in many so-called "Bible churches." "Bible" becomes a synonym for a particular *set* of interpretations about the Bible. Sometimes in our zeal to be biblical we forget what it means to be spiritual. Truth is prized more than love; interpretation takes the place of application. (And too often there are particular pet views that are unshakeable, in spite of the evidence to the contrary.) One lady in my church touched the heart of the problem when she facetiously declared, "I believe in the Trinity—the Father, Son, and Holy Bible."

The second brand of evangelical is more a product of postmodernism—even before postmodernism was in vogue: personal experience reigns supreme. Ironically, many who were leaders in the Bible church movement are now spearheading the signs and wonders movement.

Now that I have succeeded in stepping on *everybody's* toes, let me proceed. The topic of this essay is "The Witness of the Spirit in Romans 8:16." I will offer both an interpretation and several implications from this text. I may be wrong in both. I don't live in a vacuum either. Culture has impacted me, too—although I'm sure that it has *not* impacted me as much as it has impacted you: I'm from southern California, where there is precious little culture!

I ask you to hear me with an open mind and an open heart. We are all creatures of our culture; we are driven by our own presuppositions. As Bultmann noted, half the battle in exegesis is being able to ask the right questions, being able to challenge our own presuppositions. (Whatever Bultmann's faults were—and they were legion—he *did* know how to ask the right questions.) The other half, though, is bowing to the evidence, rather than manipulating the data. After all, virtually all heterodoxy is based on what is possible, not on what is probable.

The question that this passage raises is this: What is our authority today? What is it that guides us and to which we subject ourselves? What gives us comfort and assurance? On what do we base the assurance of our salvation? Is it the word? Or is it the Spirit? Or is there some symbiotic relationship between the two that deserves exploring?

Put another way, Is our faith totally objective? Is Christianity only a logical and empirical reality, or is there not a mystical element to it as well? The answer that I will propose is not new, but it is increasingly being abandoned, especially among cessationists today.

Interpretation

Romans 8:16 reads simply αὐτὸ τὸ πνεῦμα συμμαρτυρεῖ τῷ πνεύματι ἡμῶν ὅτι ἐσμὲν τέκνα θεοῦ. There are two possible translations at the crucial juncture. Either "The Spirit himself bears witness *with* our spirit that we are God's children," or "The Spirit himself bears witness *to* our spirit that we are God's children."

Grammatically, the issue is simply this: Is τῷ πνεύματι (*tō pneumati*) a dative of association ("*with* our spirit") or a dative indirect object ("*to* our spirit")? Exegetically and theologically, the issue may be far deeper: If a dative of association is in view, then our spirit joins God's Spirit in bearing witness that we are God's children, that we are saved. But *to whom* is this witness made? Many argue that such a witness is made to ourselves (thus, "the Spirit bears witness along with our spirit *to us* that we are God's children"). On the other hand, some argue that such a witness is made to *God*. In this construct, there is no witness of God's Spirit *to us*. Rather, both "spirits" testify *Godward*; both are advocates of our status before the great Judge.

If, on the other hand, a dative indirect object is in view, then God's Spirit is testifying *to* our spirits, that is, to *us*. In this case, believers are the *recipients* of the testimony of the Spirit.

The first view (what we will call the *associative* view) *may* imply that the Spirit has nothing to do with the believer's assurance of salvation.[1] This is especially the case if the witness is *Godward*. The second view (what we will call the *indirect* view or *indirect object* view) certainly implies that the Spirit's testimony to the believer is an important aspect of assurance. The first view allows one to claim assurance based directly on the objective data, the word. The second view opens the doors to a soft mysticism, suggesting that though the word is essential to assurance, God's Spirit is also essential to offer such comfort.

Arguments for "with our spirit"

Scholars are divided on this issue, even evangelical scholars. However, it seems that the predominant view is the dative of association view ("with our spirit"). Most translations take this view. Thus, "with our spirit" is the reading of the AV, ASV, NASB, RSV, NRSV, ESV, NKJV, HCSB, NIV, TNIV, JB, NJB, and Moffatt. It is also adopted by many commentators today such as Stifler, Shedd, Hendricksen, Dunn, Fitzmyer, Schreiner, probably Moo, and possibly Stuhlmacher. Others, too, seem to be in favor of this view.[2]

The most cogent argument for this view is found in Gordon Fee's massive work, *God's Empowering Presence: The Holy Spirit in the Letters of Paul.* He argues as follows: To take the dative as an indirect object is an "unnecessary expedient that abandons Pauline usage for the sake of a prior theological concern that is not involved here."[3] He draws the negative conclusion that "This means that those who make much out of the concept of 'the inner witness of the Spirit' are probably also missing Paul's point."[4]

The main arguments for the associative view are as follows:

1. In keeping with *Deut 19:15*, two witnesses are needed to establish the truth of a matter. Thus, the Holy Spirit and our spirit must give a combined testimony to confirm our salvation.[5]

2. To argue that the Spirit bears witness *to* our spirits seems to presuppose that the *moment of salvation* is in view. But the present tense (συμμαρτυρεῖ, *summarturei*) argues against this; this is an activity that is ongoing in the life of the believer. Hence, "to our spirit" cannot be the meaning of the text here.

3. The *verb itself* suggests an associative idea: it is μαρτυρέω (*martureō*) prefixed by the preposition σύν (*sun*). Such verbs regularly take datives of association.[6]

Arguments for "to our spirit"

The indirect object view is not without its representatives. For the most part, English translations are against it,[7] but other translations (such as the Vulgate[8] and Luther's Bible[9]) are often for it. As well, several notable scholars have adopted this view, such as Luther, Calvin, Leenhardt, Godet, Hodge, Strathman (in *TDNT*), Morris, Murray, and Cranfield. The view is well represented, though more so among older, Reformed works than recent writers.

I think that this is the correct view. I wish to first interact with the arguments mentioned above; then, offer some further evidence on behalf of the indirect object position. The arguments are as follows.

1. To see *Deut 19:15* as part of the background of this verse is unnecessary. It seems to presuppose that the Spirit's testimony is not good enough if offered by itself. This also presupposes that *our* testimony, in combination with the Spirit's, *is* good enough! But elsewhere in the NT a single testimony is often acceptable, especially one offered *by God*.[10] Indeed, the vast bulk of texts in which the Spirit bears witness rest the claim made on that witness alone; no other witness is necessary.[11]

Further, *if* a second witness is sought in this text, there is a better candidate than our own spirits. Paul uses the verb μαρτυρέω only twice in Romans, only once prior to chapter eight. In what is his central passage on justification, 3:21–26, he notes that "the righteousness of God has been *witnessed* by the Law and the Prophets."[12] This righteousness is applied to "all who believe" (3:22). There, the justified state of the believer is witnessed by the scriptures; here, it is witnessed by the Spirit. It is precisely this twofold testimony—that of the Spirit and the word—offered at two key junctures in Romans, that constitutes the basis of the believer's assurance.

But I do not think that that is Paul's point here. I do not think that he is looking back five chapters to find a second witness. Let me repeat: the necessity of having a second witness is based on two assumptions: (1) that συμμαρτυρέω (*summartureō*) means *bear witness together with*, and (2) that the Spirit's testimony is inadequate to confirm the truth of our salvation. The first of these assumptions is probably wrong, and the second is not in the picture here. But even if the first assumption is correct, this does not mean that "our spirit" needs to be that second witness.

2.   It is erecting a straw man to say that the indirect object view only applies to the *moment of conversion*. To be sure, it does apply to that moment. But it also applies later. We should give the present tense, συμμαρτυρεῖ, its full force. But as such, it is rather broad. The present tenses in this chapter that refer to the Spirit consistently are used of the entire time period from regeneration to glorification. Note for example:

- "You, however, are not in the flesh but in the Spirit, if indeed the Spirit of God *dwells* [οἰκεῖ, *oikei*] in you. Now if anyone does not *have* [ἔχει, echei] the Spirit of Christ does not belong to him" (v. 9)

- "the Spirit… *lives* [οἰκεῖ] in you" (v. 11)

- "all who *are led* [ἄγονται, *agontai*] by the Spirit are the sons of God" (v. 14)

- "the Spirit *helps* [συναντιλαμβάνεται, *sunantilambanetai*] us… the Spirit *intercedes* [ὑπερεντυγχάνει, *hupentugchanei*] for us… the Spirit *intercedes* [ἐντυγχάνει, *entugchanei*] on behalf of the saints" (vv. 26, 27)

It is self-evident from these verses that the Spirit's inner witness is part of the process of sanctification and encompasses the time from the spiritual cradle to the physical grave. Is not his intercessory ministry true for our entire lives, from the time we were converted? Does he not dwell in us from day one?

3.   The *lexical argument* is the most compelling—namely, that σύν- prefixed verbs take datives of association. This is, *prima facie*, what the text is speaking about. This is the view that even first-year Greek students learn. But we need to

nuance our view of the syntax here. Specifically, there are five problems with this assumption.

First, even if a σύν- prefixed verb does take a dative of association, this does not mean that it cannot take an indirect object or some other dative use. In my *Greek Grammar beyond the Basics: Exegetical Syntax of the New Testament*, I note that "not every dative following a σύν- prefixed verb is a dative of association…"[13] A dozen examples are listed to prove the point, but several more could be mentioned as well.[14]

Second, a number of σύν- prefixed verbs have lost their associative force in Koine Greek. Sometimes the compound verb is weakened, becoming synonymous with the simple verb. At other times, the prepositional prefix functions much like other prepositional prefixes, viz., to intensify or strengthen the force of the verb. Students of Greek are well aware of examples such as κατεσθίω (*katesthiō*) as an intensification of ἐσθίω (*esthiō*, "to eat" becomes "to devour"). This same kind of transformation occurs with σύν- prefixed verbs on occasion. Thus, for example συμβαίνω (*sumbainō*) means "happen to," not "go with" as in "it has *happened to them* [συμβέβηκεν αὐτοῖς, *sumbebēken autois*] according to the true proverb, 'a dog always returns to its vomit'" (2 Pet 2:22).[15]

Third, the standard lexicon of the Greek New Testament, Bauer-Danker-Arndt-Gingrich's *Greek-English Lexicon of the New Testament and other Early Christian Literature* (known as BDAG), says that συμμαρτυρέω is an intensified verb. BDAG note that as early as the sixth or seventh century BC "the prefix σύν- [on this verb] has in the highest degree the effect of strengthening" the force of the verb.[16]

Fourth, although this particular verb occurs only three times in the NT (and not at all in the LXX), all of its occurrences are in Romans. (Remarkably, it is more frequent than μαρτυρέω in this book!) In its two other occurrences, it most likely has the force of intensifying the force of the verb;[17] in the least, the evidence offers no comfort to the associative view. For example, Rom 9:1 reads, "My conscience bearing me witness [that] I am not lying" (or, "my conscience bearing witness *to* me [that] I am not lying").[18]

Fifth, in light of the paucity of usage within the NT coupled with BDAG's insistence that the prepositional prefix of this verb strengthens the basic force of the verb, an examination of its usage elsewhere is called for. Remarkably, most of those who argue for the associative view simply assume a meaning for this verb without examining the evidence—or, it seems, without interacting with BDAG. Before we look at the data, the parameters of our investigation need to be delineated.

One of the fundamental problems with this verb is that in certain contexts the meaning of "bear witness with" someone can mean *almost* the same thing as "bear witness to" someone. This is one of the reasons why there is confusion in Rom 8:16. For example, even in the indirect object view, there are various permutations:

(1) "bear witness to" a jury or a judge

(2) "bear witness to" the truth, act, opinion, etc.

(3) "bear witness to" the defendant, either for/on behalf of (*dativus commodi*) or against (*dativus incommodi*) him; this also shades off into "assure."

The first of these would be a pure indirect object usage: the jury or judge is neutral and is hearing the case. The second kind of bearing witness is a confirmation of the truth, etc. This would certainly not involve an associative idea unless that which bears the truth-witness is also cut from the same cloth, or if truth is personified. The third permutation, that of bearing witness to, for, or against a defendant is the kind of indirect usage I see in Rom 8:16. It is thus *also* a dative of interest.[19] But this is the closest of the three permutations to an associative idea. So, how can we distinguish the two in other texts?

There are some guidelines that can be used. First, if the meaning fits in with (1) or (2) above, then the verb obviously does not carry an associative notion. But in instances where a dative of interest could be detected, other tests need to be employed. We suggest two. First, we need to compare συμμαρτυρέω with μαρτυρέω. If the latter could be substituted for συμμαρτυρέω without an alteration in the meaning, then συμμαρτυρέω will be regarded as having an intensifying force. If, however, the substitution would alter the sense, then συμμαρτυρέω is considered to bear an associative idea. It should be noted at the outset that μαρτυρέω regularly occurs with dative indirect objects that sometimes shade off into *dativus commodi* or *dativus incommodi*, but *not* with datives of association.[20] *The mere presence of a dative substantive with* συμμαρτυρέω, *therefore, is not a sufficient basis for taking the dative as associative since dative substantives frequently occur with* μαρτυρέω.[21]

Second, when the verb occurs *without a dative* substantive in the context, this semantic situation will usually indicate that the verb is an intensifying form of μαρτυρέω. There will be some rare exceptions to this (such as cryptic expressions in poetry as in Sophocles, *Electra* 1224), but the vast bulk of σύν—prefixed verbs that bear an associative nuance are found with an explicit dative of association in the context.[22] The parameters are thus clear.

Συμμαρτυρέω is, by any standard of measurement, a rare word. It occurs in extant Greek literature, from Homer to AD 1453, certainly no more than 200 times. A search of TLG, the published volumes of the *Oxyrhynchus Papyri*, Tebtunis papyri, and the digitized collections of papyri from Duke University and the University of Michigan—a grand total of more than 60 million words of Greek literature[23]—revealed only 164 instances.

I have not examined every instance in detail, but can at least offer some representative texts.[24] These will be listed diachronically within two groups: instances in which a dative substantive is found, instances in which no dative substantive is found with the verb.

The relevant data are included in an endnote.[25]

In sum, I have found συμμαρτυρέω predominantly to take dative indirect objects rather than datives of association.[26] BDAG's statement that "the prefix σύν– [on this verb] has in the highest degree the effect of strengthening" the force of the verb is largely vindicated. At the same time, some of the texts were ambiguous, and most likely, some that were not examined could possibly display an associative force. Nevertheless, the *prima facie* lexical assumption—viz., that since the verb here is prefixed by σύν– it must take a dative of association—is clearly wrong. The lexical argument, then, though plausible on its face, seems to fall apart upon closer scrutiny. Along these lines, it may be noteworthy that Fee does not even raise the lexical issue, but prefers to argue against the indirect object view by insisting that it is only a theologically-motivated interpretation without substance. Just the opposite seems to be the case.

In addition to these three counter-arguments, a few others may be put forth on behalf of the indirect object view.

4.　　The associative view involves too many complications. If, for example, the *Godward* associative view is adopted (viz., that our combined testimony is to God), then we have a couple of problems. First, where else does the Bible promote such a radical *inequality* in the co-witnesses? (This would be like Walter Cronkite and some three-year-old concurring on the details of a newsworthy event.) In particular, the Holy Spirit's witness does not require a second opinion. Our testimony is unnecessary. To suggest otherwise is like saying, "God says—and I can back him up on this…"! Second, as Cranfield notes, "What standing has our spirit in *this* matter? Of itself it surely has no right at all to testify to our being sons of God."[27] In the context our spirit especially seems to have little say. The self-doubts expressed in Rom 7—whether that chapter is autobiographical or of a more universal nature—stand in bold relief to Rom 8. Whatever else chapter 7 is saying, it is arguing that the unaided inner self is defeated by sin and makes no contribution to sanctification. But thanks be to God that the law of the Spirit of life has set us free!

5.　　So much for the Godward witness. But if the dual witness is *manward*, there is another problem. If "our spirit" refers to our "inner person," as almost all commentators take it, then what is the difference between "our spirit" and "ourselves"? If there is no real difference, what does it mean that "the Spirit bears witness with our spirit to ourselves"? Does this mean that we witness to us? This sounds as if the responsibility to convince myself of my salvation is myself. This interpretation, of course, is refuted on its face.

6.　　Positively, we can argue from two vantage points: context and correlation. The *context* of Rom 8 involves especially two themes—assurance of salvation and the role of the Holy Spirit in the believer's sanctification. These two are not unrelated. The assurance offered seems to come from two sources: inner testimony and external fruit. The one, in fact, seems to be the prerequisite for the other. Notice the following verses:

- Verse 4—"so that the righteous requirement of the law may be fulfilled in us, who do not walk according to the flesh but according to the Spirit."

- Verse 9—"You, however, are not in the flesh but in the Spirit, if indeed the Spirit of God lives in you."

- Verse 14—"For all who are led by the Spirit of God are the sons of God."

- Verse 23—"we ourselves also, who have the firstfruits of the Spirit, groan inwardly as we eagerly await our adoption, the redemption of our bodies."

- Verses 25–27—"But if we hope for what we do not see, we eagerly wait for it with endurance. In the same way, the Spirit helps us in our weakness, for we do not know how we should pray, but the Spirit himself intercedes for us with inexpressible groanings. And he who searches our hearts knows the mind of the Spirit, because the Spirit intercedes on behalf of the saints according to God's will." *Paul is stressing in these verses, it seems, that though **we** might waver, the Spirit does not. The Spirit helps us in our weakness and our doubts.*

- Paul concludes with vv. 31–39 in which he evidently is arguing against doubts that are caused by our own inner turmoil as well as by external forces. Verses 31–34 ask the repeated question, "If God is for us, who can be against us?" (v. 31). Verses 35–39 ask the question, "Who will separate us from the love of Christ?" The accusation of condemnation is something *felt* on the inside. The defense is also internal: because we are in Christ *and* because he is in us, we stand secure before God.

- In this great chapter it seems that the Spirit produces the assurance we so desperately need. Because we have the Spirit, we have hope. Yet even in our hope, he helps our weakness and intercedes for us. Because we have the Spirit, we bear fruit for God. The order is significant: The Spirit dwells in us, thus enabling us to live for God. We can have assurance of our salvation the moment we are converted, and as much as our own hearts try to condemn us, the Spirit intercedes.

7. Finally is the argument from *correlation*. To see the Spirit of God working on our hearts, sustaining our belief both in God and in our relationship to him, is a theme found elsewhere in the NT. This theme suggests an inaugural fulfillment of Jer 31. As new covenant believers, the Spirit of God has come to reside in us. We *each* know God immediately. Thus, in Heb 10 the author picks up the prophecy of Jer 31 and essentially argues that God places knowledge of himself

within us when he forgives our sin. The author begins the OT quotation in v. 15 with an introductory statement that *looks like it was lifted right out of Rom 8:16*: "And the Holy Spirit also witnesses to us" (μαρτυρεῖ δὲ ἡμῖν καὶ τὸ πνεῦμα τὸ ἅγιον.) Thus, in both passages we are told that the Spirit bears witness and that there is something placed within us by God in relation to securing our salvation. This is no accident; it is part of the NT authors' understanding of the new covenant.

The connection might be even stronger. Paul begins the eighth chapter of Romans by ringing the chimes of freedom that the Spirit has wrought for us: "For the law of the life-giving Spirit in Christ Jesus has set you free from the law of sin and death." But he does not develop this idea of the *law* of the Spirit further; rather, he replaces it with talk of the Spirit directly. Indeed, the Spirit gets top billing in this chapter, just like the law received it in the previous chapter. Why, then, does Paul begin with "the *law* of the Spirit"? In the least, he is certainly connecting his argument to chapter 7, perhaps as a kind of rhetorical bridge. But there may be more; it is distinctly possible that Paul has in mind Jer 31:33: "I will put my law within them and write it on their hearts and minds." The internal witness of God in one's heart is here proclaimed; the law written on the heart, the law of the new covenant, indeed seems to be the Spirit himself.[28]

As well, the whole of 1 John stresses the role of the Spirit in our assurance. First John 3:20 is right to the point—"if our conscience [Greek: *heart* (καρδία, *kardia*)] condemns us, that God is greater than our conscience [Greek: *heart* (καρδία)]." This is perfectly in keeping with what I believe Paul is saying in Rom 8:16. The associative view has an anthropological-hamartiological problem at this point: if our heart condemns us, in what sense could it be a witness to God on our behalf?[29]

In preparing for this essay, I came across a statement by Gregory of Nyssa which also implicitly links 1 John 3:20 with Rom 8:16. In one place he comments on Paul's great pneumatological confession:

> For it is necessary, according to the oracle of Paul, that the Spirit of God should testify to our spirit, but not that our spirits should be approved by our judgment. For he does not say, "The one who commends himself is approved, but the one whom the Lord commends is approved."[30]

It is evident that Gregory's understanding of συμμαρτυρέω in Rom 8:16 is similar to ours—and that the link of Rom 8:16 with 1 John 3:20 was already done centuries ago.

To sum up: Rom 8:16 should be translated "The Spirit himself bears witness *to* our spirit that we are God's children" because of sound lexical, contextual, and biblico-theological reasons. Further, to take it otherwise leaves too many loose ends and raises more questions than it answers. Although to be sure some of the arguments are on better footing than others, it seems to me that the most probable exegesis of this passage (not just what is possible) is that there is an inner witness of the Spirit which prompts in the believer that filial response of "Abba, Father!" leading him to the assurance of salvation.

Some Implications

1.   Obviously, the main implication has to do with *assurance of salvation.* We know that we are saved because of the testimony of scripture *and* because of the inner witness of the Spirit. I know I am a child of God not just because the Bible tells me so, but because the Spirit *convinces* me so. The present tenses in relation to the Spirit in Rom 8 are used predominantly to suggest an ongoing state from regeneration to glorification (thus, customary presents). Because of the Spirit's witness I have assurance at the front end *and* throughout my life. But the Spirit sustains in me not just belief, but fruit. Because he dwells in me, he can prompt me to good works. The cause-effect relationship here must be carefully noted: I am assured of my salvation, first, because the Spirit indwells me. Thus, I can have such assurance before I do *any* good works for God. But as I continue, because of the Spirit's presence and power, I will persevere. My saved status thus receives *confirmation* by my works.

2.   *For perseverance of the saints:* There are some today who argue for eternal security, but against the perseverance of the saints. This viewpoint, in its most rigorous form, argues that the perseverance doctrine makes assurance based on works and thus cannot offer such assurance at the point of conversion. This view also argues that even if a person believed only for a short time, and then *stopped* believing, he is still saved. In order to sustain this argument, one has to deny the inner witness of the Spirit. The only assurance is the objective word. This, to me,

smacks of rationalism. It is a view that, ultimately, finds its roots in the Enlightenment, not in the revealed word.

The Spirit not only assures our hearts that we are saved; he also *sustains* that belief. True believers continue to believe because the Spirit energizes that faith. And he does more: he also energizes the fruit that results from that faith. Thus, the position that we can be eternally secure *without* persevering seems to embrace both a weak view of sin (in that we have the ability to sustain belief without the Spirit's aid) and, consequently, a defective pneumatology.

3. *How* does the Spirit bear witness to our spirits? Certainly, he works on our hearts to convince us of the truth of scripture. But there is more. His inner witness is both immediate and intuitive. It involves a non-discursive presence that is recognized in the soul. This at least is the position of Calvin and the Reformers, and I can find nothing to contradict this either in Rom 8 or in my own experience. Indeed, except for periods of heightened rationalism in church history (such as we faced in the 20th century, with its still lingering effects), this seems to be the steady opinion of the majority of orthodox theologians.[31] Thus, the inner witness of the Spirit is *supra*-logical, not sub-logical—like the peace from God that surpasses all understanding. There are elements of the Christian faith that are not verifiable on an empirical plane. This makes them no less true.

4. *For conflict in the academic realm:* If the witness of the Spirit that I am a child of God is intuitive, then it is outside the realm of that which is objectively verifiable. This does not make it any less true. We are too much sons of the Enlightenment when we deny intuition and internal apprehensions any value. When you fell in love, what scientific means did you use to verify the state of your heart? None. As every mother tells her child, "You just know." It's an apt analogy because it is one of the last vestiges of the pre-Enlightenment era that we still affirm. No one challenges it because there are no scientific means for determining whether a person is in love. Yet, we send bright young students, armed with an M.Div. or Th.M. from an evangelical seminary, into battle at secular schools, telling them only, "Trust your exegesis." Too many have become spiritual casualties because they suppressed the inner witness of the Spirit. Liberal theology can tamper with the meaning of the text and plant seeds of doubt about historical proofs. If I am trusting *only* in historical evidences, not realizing that

there is still a step of faith involved, I have already lost the battle. Don't misunderstand: we need to contend for the basic tenets of the faith with all the logical and empirical tools at our disposal. But by themselves, these evidences are not capable of proof. The noetic effects of sin are so powerful that without the Spirit's aid, we, too, will begin to doubt. Doctoral students and academicians, more than anyone else, need to maintain a warm heart for God *precisely* because of the academic rigor of their chosen field. An academic life gives one no excuse for a lack of piety. Indeed, if it is to be for God's glory, piety must be at the heart of that breathless pursuit of truth. We simply cannot risk giving God a partial offering: we cannot give him our minds while holding back our hearts.

The Spirit and Community: A Historical Perspective

Gerald Bray

This essay surveys the ways in which Spirit-led community has been understood at different times in Christian history. After explaining the basic principles of medieval Christendom, it examines the ways in which Protestantism has developed a doctrine of the invisible church, which is manifested in visible ecclesiastical institutions to varying degrees. It concludes with a challenge to Evangelicals to re-examine their basic assumptions in an effort to find new ways to build Spirit-led communities today.

The Biblical Background

Any discussion of the historical relationship between the doctrine of the Holy Spirit and ideas of community must obviously begin with the New Testament, which records how the Christian Church began and in the process lays down the basic principles that have provided the general guidelines for subsequent developments. Of course, a historical perspective on this must consider how the New Testament was actually used in apostolic and sub-apostolic times, not what can be read out of it today. To say that the early Church made a selection of its inheritance and emphasized some things more than others is not to claim that it somehow failed in its mission, nor is it to say that that pattern must be the norm for all time. Without passing judgment on the first Christians, it is only reasonable to suppose that in any generation there will be certain tendencies and biases in biblical interpretation which are difficult to classify as right or wrong in an absolute sense, but which are no longer held today in quite the same way. The modern reader need only consider what the apostle Paul says about celibacy (for example), and compare it with the practice of the modern Protestant churches, to realize just how true this is.

For the early Church, the most noticeable work of the Holy Spirit in building the Christian community was undoubtedly the way in which he was seen to have broken down the barriers between Jews and Gentiles, making them both one in the body of Christ. To many of us, who do not normally think of religion as an aspect of ethnicity, this does not seem especially striking, but the evidence of the New Testament suggests that it caused a major upheaval at the time, particularly among Jewish Christians, who were not always prepared to welcome outsiders. We should not forget, for example, that Paul's epistle to the Romans was occasioned by this very thing, and that it is in this context that his argument for justification by faith alone is set. Furthermore, the means by which the Spirit achieved this unity was baptism: "For in one Spirit we were all baptized into one body. Whether we are Jews or Greeks or slaves or free we were all made to drink of the one Spirit" (1 Cor 12:13), or again: "making every effort to keep the unity of the Spirit in the bond of peace. There is one body and one Spirit, just as you too were called to the one hope of your calling, one Lord, one faith, one baptism" (Eph 4:3-5). Whatever we may think of baptism today, we probably do not assume that it will be the means of breaking down social and economic barriers. But for the first Christians, to be baptized in the Spirit was to put off the old man, with its ethnic and social limitations, and to become a new creation in Christ. From the very beginning, Christians were aware that they constituted a new society, a community which was in the world but not of it.

This awareness had very practical implications for the way in which Christians were expected to live. They were no longer subject to the provisions of the Jewish law, but this did not excuse them from having to develop their own distinctive lifestyle, one which would reflect the indwelling presence of the Holy Spirit. To put on Christ meant to cease living as the other Gentiles lived (Eph 4:17-32). To achieve this, the first requirement was a new attitude, according to which people would seek to be like God in true righteousness and holiness. Christians were told, for example, that they must tell the truth, and not try to deceive one another. They were called to "put away every kind of bitterness, anger, wrath, quarreling, and evil, slanderous talk" (Eph 4:31). Instead of that, they were to "be kind to one another, compassionate, forgiving one another, just as God in Christ also forgave you" (Eph 4:32). This radical change of behavior was the direct result of the fruit of the Spirit at work in the lives of believers (Gal 5:22), and it made a deep impression on contemporaries. "See how these Christians love one another" (cf. *Epistle to Diognetus*, 1) was a common remark among pagans, even if Christians themselves (like modern readers of Paul's epistles) were often more aware of their failings in this area than of their successes.

Another factor which distorts our perception of the early Church is that today, when we read the New Testament, we tend to apply the language of holiness, predestination, and election to individual believers first, and only secondarily to the community. But this was not the way it appeared to the first Christians, who never used the word "saint" (ἅγιος [*hagios*], used substantivally) in the singular in the NT, except generically (as in "every saint" in Phil 4:21). They believed that they were a holy nation, a special people, God's chosen ones. The responsibility of the individual was to conform to this pattern. so that he or she would be considered as worthy representatives of the group. Holiness was not just a sign of separation from the world; it was also the mark of belonging to the new community being forged by the Holy Spirit.

Within this community, the leaders were to behave in exactly the opposite way to what was found among pagans. They were to be humble, to be servants of all, and to outdo one another in love and service. Hospitality was a particularly important part of this; Christians met in each other's homes, and welcomed missionaries and other travelers who were about the Lord's business. Incidentally, this duty of showing hospitality remained extremely important for centuries, even after Christianity had become the dominant religion and it was no longer possible for individuals to practice it on the same scale. When that happened, the duty of hospitality devolved on the official representatives of the Church—the clergy and (above all) the monastic communities. The *hospital*, as its name suggests, had its origin in this very tradition. The Christian Church was meant to be a caring community, demonstrating the love of the Spirit in practical and social ways.

One of the most intriguing features of this community building was the way in which the Holy Spirit gave different gifts to different members of the Church, for the mutual edification of the body. Modern readers of the New Testament are only too familiar with 1 Cor 12-14, which is the main passage dealing with this subject, but once again it is important to recognize that there is a key difference between the way most of us read that passage and the way it was understood by the early Christians. Today, we start with individuals and their gifts, and try to figure out how they can best be harmonized in a functioning community. But the early Christians began with the community and its needs, looking for the gifts to be given as and when they were required for the common good. It was because speaking in tongues made the smallest contribution to the common good that it was regarded as the least (i.e., the most dispensable) of the gifts, which is not what we usually find today in charismatic circles. When the exercise of particular gifts caused conflict, the answer given by the early Church was not "you in your small corner and I in mine," as it often is today, but "what makes for the upbuilding of the body?" The apostle Paul did not hesitate to tell people to refrain from exercising their gift if it was going to provoke dissension in the congregation!

The Experience of Catholic Christendom

As the Church expanded and became an established part of the wider society, it was inevitable that some of the features that characterized its early years would undergo a transformation. We have already seen what happened in the case of hospitality, which became institutionalized during the middle ages, though the ideal was never abandoned. As numbers increased and Church members were no longer close friends, worship services became more ritualized, with the result that spiritual principles like the maintenance of peace came to be symbolized by specific gestures. Human nature being what it is, there were many occasions when these gestures were very hollow, and eventually such ritualism fell into disrepute because of the hypocrisy that surrounded it. But it should not be forgotten that to a large extent this was the inevitable fruit of growth and that those who developed these ways of expressing fundamental Christian principles were trying to preserve them in a new situation, not wanting to abandon or corrupt them. After the fall of the Roman Empire in the West, the Church became the framework in which society generally functioned. That created a situation in which, on the one hand, it was very difficult for non-Christians to function normally, and on the other hand, it was almost impossible for the Church to maintain its high standards of community life. On the first point, Western European society came to accept that membership in it was defined by baptism. Jews, being unbaptized, were excluded from it, and were often forced to live in ghettos, when they were not expelled altogether. Heretics and schismatics were regarded then as rebels would be today, and they were persecuted accordingly. The Reformation did not really change this situation, at least not in the short term, which explains why independent Protestant congregations were often persecuted by Protestant state churches, as well as by Catholic ones. In Great Britain, for example, there was no legal toleration of non-state churches until 1689, more than 150 years after the Reformation, and members of those churches did not acquire full civil rights until 1828-29, more than 50 years after the American revolution had introduced religious freedom, based on the complete separation of Church and state, into the thirteen colonies.

On the second point, the medieval Church did what it could to maintain standards, even though its success was often patchy at best. For example, the

Church tried to introduce something called "the truce of God," which forced warring armies to cease fighting during times of special religious observance. Ideally, of course, Christian Frenchmen should not have been fighting Christian Englishmen at all, but the Church was never able to stamp out warfare altogether. It did, however, manage to impose certain standards of treatment for hostages and captured prisoners, and it was occasionally able to prevent an outbreak of hostilities by timely arbitration. This may all seem a long way from the New Testament command to keep the unity of the Spirit in the bond of peace, but it gives some idea of the complications that arose when the attempt was made to apply such principles across an entire society, in which everyone was expected to be Christian.

As far as its internal life was concerned, the Church institutionalized the work of the Holy Spirit in ways which can be classified under three headings—authority, doctrine and ministry. Of these three, authority was the most fundamental. The Bible was the Church's main constitutional document, given by the Holy Spirit for the government of the Christian commonwealth. If something was laid down as mandatory in scripture, then it had to be applied in the Church, though this was not as simple a matter as it might seem. Much of the Bible was interpreted allegorically, and large parts of it were hard to codify for general consumption, even if its basic principles were clear enough. How, for example, do you go about loving your neighbor in a feudal society? As time went on therefore, it was inevitable that a subsidiary body of law would appear which would fill in gaps left by scripture and apply its teachings to new situations. This law emanated primarily from the great Church councils, though the decretals of popes and the sayings of the major Church fathers were also accorded normative authority. By the thirteenth century there was a large and functioning body of so-called canon law, which contemporaries regarded as a gift of the Spirit to the Church, enabling it to maintain order in an increasingly complex society.

The interpretation of this body of law was entrusted to the clergy, and particularly to the bishop of Rome, whose position in the Church became ever more exalted as time went on. It would be no exaggeration to say that in the medieval Church, discussion of the spiritual gifts concentrated very largely on the papacy, which came to be perceived as the repository of the Spirit's charismatic teaching authority. All other ministries had to be validated by the papacy in order to function legally, a system which inevitably made reform very difficult, since any criticism at the grassroots level would in some sense be an attack on the supreme head of the whole organization. Ordination came to be regarded as a sacrament in which the Holy Spirit was given to the ordinand to enable him to exercise the spiritual gifts needed for his ministry. The personal character and spiritual life of the clergyman were secondary considerations, because his spiritual power was a gift exercised in the context and by the license of the institutional Church, not something bestowed on him as an individual. Few things, in fact, were harder for the medieval Church to cope with than the assertion that a man (or a woman) was inspired by God outside the framework of the Church. Joan of Arc may have been an extreme case, but the accusation that she was inspired by the devil was logical, given the presuppositions of the system. It was no accident that the prophetic voice could only be heard on the fringes of the institutional system, and that as time went on suppressing it was often the only way the institution could continue to function. Thus we find that whereas Francis of Assisi was eventually able to make his voice heard in the early thirteenth century, 150 years later John Wycliffe was silenced, and the same thing (or worse) would have happened to Martin Luther if he had not managed to break the mold altogether.

In matters of doctrine, the medieval period was also a time of growing systematization, as can be seen from the work of men like Thomas Aquinas, which is very different in style and presentation from that of the fathers of the early Church. Once again, this was perceived by contemporaries as the work of the Holy Spirit, which helped Christians absorb the challenge presented by the rediscovery of Aristotelian philosophy. That systematization of this kind often led theologians to discuss questions which scripture did not touch (such as the temperature of hellfire) and which later generations were to make fun of, must not detract from the essential aim of the exercise, which was to preserve the body of Christ and extend its mission to every corner of human life and interest. A system has to be all inclusive for it to work, and if it leads to theological speculation which goes beyond what is wise or well founded, that is a small price to pay for the benefit of security which it offers to those who accept it. The middle ages initiated this development, but it would be idle to suppose that it is dead today—many churches, not least those of a conservative Protestant type, have a similar devotion to systematization which characterizes their theology, and a similar tendency to speculate theologically beyond what the evidence warrants in the interests of consistency.

In the wider sphere of Church discipline, authority in matters of doctrine was also given to Church councils, and (in the West) it was eventually located in the papacy. A conflict between these two conceptions of authority divided the Eastern from the Western Church in the eleventh century, and that division has never been overcome. Four hundred years later, a similar conflict broke out in the Western Church, but the popes of the time were able to neutralize the trend towards conciliarism, which proved to be too unwieldy and inefficient a system to be able to function effectively, and by 1450 the movement towards a declaration of papal infallibility in matters of faith and morals was well underway, even if it was not to be proclaimed officially until as late as 1870. All of this process, it must be repeated, was regarded by those involved in it as the ongoing work of the Holy Spirit in the Church, and interpreted by them as a necessary evolution in the context of the Church's growth and expansion.

The Reformation

The increasing inflexibility of the medieval system, coupled with a series of crises in the institution of the papacy which greatly undermined its effectiveness and its prestige, prepared the way for a massive overhaul of the Church's structures. This was actually attempted on several occasions, and by 1500 almost everybody agreed that far-reaching change was necessary. It is tempting to see the Reformation as the housecleaning of the corrupt medieval Church, but this is too simplistic an explanation of it. Luther and his followers were not just interested in putting the system right; they were fired by a different vision of what the Church was all about. It was this that ultimately lost them the support of humanistic reformers like Erasmus and produced a split in the medieval organization that has never been healed.

At one level, the Reformation produced relatively little change in the Church. It remained an institution which was theoretically coterminous with civil society, and it was not possible for any individual to participate fully in that society if he or she did not belong to the officially recognized local church. A break with the papacy meant no more than a transfer of the authority previously granted to the pope to the secular ruler, who became responsible for Church government and even for establishing doctrine. Even when religious toleration was eventually—and grudgingly—granted by the secular authorities, the position of the state church was not substantially altered, and in countries where a religious establishment remains, that position is still more or less in effect today. This creates an anomalous situation in which it is accepted that the Church may be governed by people who do not belong to it, even in the most formal of senses. But few Christians are comfortable with the idea that the Holy Spirit would work through unbelievers in order to establish the worship and doctrine of the Church, and this particular, if admittedly unintended, result of the Reformation has become an embarrassment to those who are forced to live with it.

But at the same time there has been a different dynamic at work within Protestantism, which has helped even the Protestant state churches to avoid the kind of polarization between Church and state which characterized many Catholic countries for much of the nineteenth and twentieth centuries. This is the view that the Church is essentially an invisible community, or as the Anglican Book of Common Prayer expresses it, *the mystical company of all faithful people.* Once this view took hold, the institutional Church could be regarded as an external shell, a vehicle which might be useful for the mission of the Church in the world, but which was not essential to its existence. The doctrine of the invisible Church is a key tenet of the Reformation, and sets Protestants apart from other Christians in ways which are not always fully recognized. Protestantism, for example, can fragment (as it has) into an apparently endless number of denominations without losing its fundamental unity. However great the rivalry between Presbyterians and Baptists (to take but one example) may sometimes be, there is always a sense in which they are prepared to work together in interdenominational organizations like the Bible Society and so on. In many cases, parachurch societies have had a greater influence on the spiritual formation of church members than the denomination to which they happen to belong. Even in places where denominationalism does not really exist, such as the Lutheran countries of Scandinavia, it is still true that the most lively groups in the church have drawn their spiritual sustenance from so-called inner missions, evangelistic organizations which seek to convert people who are nominally church members, but whose beliefs and level of commitment leave a good deal to be desired.

Furthermore, it cannot really be said that this belief was not one that emerged gradually as Protestantism developed; in essence, it can be found from the very beginning. For example, the Lutheran Augsburg Confession of 1530 says in Article 8: "Though the Church be properly the congregation of saints and true believers, yet seeing that in this life many hypocrites and evil persons are mingled with it, it is lawful to use the sacraments administered by evil men according to the voice of Christ: *The scribes and Pharisees sit in Moses' seat...* (Mt 23:2)." It is obviously not true that the intention of the Article is to support the ministry of unworthy men, but the tension which it reveals between the ideal and the real is so great, and expressed in such strong language, that it is hard to imagine how anyone with even the slightest degree of reforming zeal could possibly live with such a situation for long. The Article in effect gives an open invitation to those who take their faith seriously to seek to root out the hypocrites—after all, Jesus did not exactly tolerate the activities of the scribes and the Pharisees, and after his death and resurrection, the newly-formed Church moved out of their orbit altogether!

In England, slightly later, we find Article 20 of the Forty-two Articles of 1553 (recycled as Article 19 of the Thirty-nine Articles of 1571), which states: "The visible Church of Christ is a congregation of faithful men in which the pure Word of God is preached and the sacraments be duly administered..." It is obvious that although the emphasis is placed on the visible Church, the way in which that is recognized depends entirely on spiritual principles which derive essentially from the invisible body of Christ. Once again, there is an implicit invitation to make the visible community conform to these spiritual principles. It is true that a subsequent Article (27 in 1553; 26 in 1571) provides for the spiritual inadequacies of the Church's ministers, and reminds us that their work is not compromised by their failings because they are the servants of Christ, but the emphasis is clearly on the need to ensure that the ministry be as blameless as possible. It is in this sense that Article 24 of 1553 (23 in 1571), which says that only properly ordained persons should be permitted to minister in the congregation, must be understood. Although it certainly upheld the authority of the visible Church, the underlying understanding was that only suitable men would be chosen and appointed in the first place. That is not made clear in the Article, but it is perfectly obvious from the Ordinal (1550), on which the Article was based.

As the doctrine of the primacy of the invisible over the visible Church began to sink in, many Protestants came to the conclusion that a large percentage of Church members were not really Christians at all. Baptism could no longer be understood as entry into the Christian community in anything but a formal sense. If it was accompanied by faith, then fine, but even so it was the faith which counted, not the sacramental rite. Without faith, baptism was at best a waste of time and at worst blasphemous. The same applied, *mutatis mutandis*, to all the other sacraments and rites of the Church. Even ordination meant nothing without the unction of the Holy Spirit, with the result that Protestants have grown used to a situation in which many official pastors are reckoned to be spiritually dead (or even heretical) by a sizeable proportion of the Church's membership, while other people who are officially laymen are accepted as Spirit-anointed preachers and teachers. In exceptional cases, it can even happen that someone like Billy Graham, for example, may acquire the status of a pan-Protestant spokesman without any official recognition at all. This occurs because a sufficiently large percentage of Protestants agree that Billy Graham has received a spiritual gift of preaching, teaching, and evangelism to which the official recognition of the institutional Church has nothing further to contribute.

Given this situation, it is hardly surprising that the work of the Spirit in building community is a problem for Protestants in a way that Catholics and Eastern Orthodox find hard to understand. As far as they are concerned, the pattern of the institutional Church is the work of the Spirit, which overrules the inadequacies and sinfulness of particular individuals. Protestants place little faith in the institution of the Church, with the result that the charismatic credibility of the individual minister or Church member acquires much greater weight. A Catholic priest who falls into notorious sin only rarely shakes anyone's faith in the Church, but a Protestant evangelist who falls in the same way can have a much more devastating effect on his followers. As far as most Protestants are concerned, a preacher who does not lead a holy life does not preach in the Spirit, and they are quite prepared to abandon such people to their own devices and look for spiritual sustenance elsewhere.

The Puritan Tradition

The existential situation of the Protestant churches more or less since the time of the Reformation is well known, and it has contributed strongly to what may loosely be called the Puritan tradition. Its classical doctrinal formulation is the Westminster Confession of Faith (1647), whose Chapter 25 has this to say about the Church: "The catholic or universal Church, which is invisible, consists of the whole number of the elect that have been, are, or shall be gathered into one, under Christ the head thereof; and is the spouse, the body, the fullness of Him that filleth all in all. The visible Church, which is also catholic or universal under the Gospel (not confined to one nation, as before under the law), consists of all those throughout the world that profess the true religion, and of their children, and is the kingdom of the Lord Jesus Christ, the house and family of God, out of which there is no ordinary possibility of salvation." Here it is perfectly obvious that the invisible Church defines the visible one, and indeed, it is hard to see precisely what the difference between them is. In principle, there is not meant to be any difference at all, and if there are unworthy members of the visible Church, then it is presumably the duty of the Church's ministers to convert them (if possible) or, if not, to discipline and root them out.

The essence of Puritan ecclesiology is that the Holy Spirit is the author and sustainer of the Christian community, which does not exist without him. Outward forms and symbols may have their uses, but if they do not reflect an inner reality they can and therefore must be dispensed with, because then they have become deceptive and even blasphemous. Certainly, any individual believer would be justified in abandoning such things, and might even be urged to do so by those who think that an ungodly ministry or congregation can do them nothing but harm. At a deeper level, Puritans of this type are always ready to pick up and go, because in their heart of hearts they know that the perfect Church does not exist here on earth. The best they can do is to minimize the corruption they find, and remain within a particular fellowship as long as it does nothing which might offend their sensibilities. Experience, however, shows that offense of this kind is given fairly often, and so it is not unusual for churches to split from time to time, with members who are not satisfied with the spiritual tone of the community going off to found a purer one. These people will naturally assert that the Holy Spirit is responsible for their actions, and the history of Protestantism contains enough examples of successful schism to give a certain plausibility to this claim. To take but the most prominent example, how many Anglicans would dare to say that Methodism is a wicked schism that has never been blessed by God? It is not the purpose of this chapter to debate the theological foundations for such beliefs, but rather to look at the historical consequences that they have had. For better or for worse, it is in the Anglo-Saxon world that Puritanism (in the sense outlined above) has developed most extensively. It first appeared in the sixteenth century, when it was largely an attempt to reform the Church of England along more purely Calvinist lines. As such it was a pressure group within the Church, rather than a theological challenge to its existence. However, that began to change in the late 1580s when some of the more radical Puritan types started to preach what is now known as separatism. They believed that the visible Church could never be reformed as it should be, and that the only answer was for the saints to leave it and establish their own communities. After a number of false starts, and not a little persecution from the authorities, a group of these separatists took the final plunge and left England altogether—for the New World. Arriving in what is now Massachusetts, they set about trying to establish a model Christian commonwealth, in which the power of the Holy Spirit would be fully manifested in every aspect of life.

The subsequent history of that experiment is sufficiently well known to give us pause. Even in New England, where every colonist was meant to be a saint, a perfect society could not be established. It soon became necessary to institute a system of surveillance, so that deviations from the accepted norm could be rooted out. Those who could not (or who would not) conform to expectations were imprisoned, expelled, or simply encouraged to leave. Not surprisingly, most of those who suffered in this way were convinced that they were the true carriers of the Spirit, and that their persecutors had betrayed the original vision. A similar, if somewhat less dramatic, process occurred in England, especially after the triumph of Oliver Cromwell in 1649. Under his commonwealth government, the rule of the saints proved to be just as onerous as it did in New England, and it had the same fissiparous results. By the time it ended, the godly were divided into a dozen sects, each of which claimed to be in possession of the real truth.

The Puritan experiment in government was a disaster, but at least it proved that their vision of the Church was incompatible with political stability as long as the Church was expected to play an important role in secular life. In the long run, one of the most important results of their failure was to be the separation of Church and State in America and the granting of freedom of worship in Britain. This went a long way to resolve the problem of outside interference in the Church's internal affairs, but of course it did nothing to solve the Puritan dilemma. For in spite of what some extremists tried to claim, the corruption of the Church was not the result of its state connection. It was an internal problem, rooted ultimately in the sinfulness of every human being, and manifested in the lack of discipline and spiritual lethargy that were evident to any careful observer (and remember that most Puritan ministers were specialists in the art of careful observation). Some extremists were moved to think that human sinfulness could be done away with, and this produced the doctrine known as perfectionism. Even as great a man as John Wesley was tempted by this, and towards the end of his life he apparently came to believe that he had had a second blessing from God which enabled him to be totally free from sin.

Few have ever been tempted to go quite that far, but other solutions to the problem have been canvassed, and some of them can scarcely be regarded as more orthodox than that. One of the most common of these has been the tendency to target certain things, like outward dress and behavior, as signs of holiness, and to confine one's interest to them. For example, conservative Protestant churches have spent an enormous amount of time and energy fighting the evils of dancing, drinking, smoking, card-playing and so on, on the assumption that such activities betray a community which has rejected the guidance of the Holy Spirit. Whether true holiness can ever be made visible is doubtful, but most Christians in the Puritan tradition have acted as if this were both possible and necessary. Secular critics never tire of condemning the hypocrisy of this, pointing out (for example) that many of these so-called fundamentalists will invest in the stock market but campaign vigorously against bingo on the ground that the latter is gambling. On a more serious level, it is not difficult to demonstrate that churches of this kind have often been very strong in areas of the world where there has been open and scandalous social injustice—in the American South for instance, or in South Africa. When this sort of thing happens, the impression is given that the only way holiness can be achieved is by defining it so narrowly that large areas of human life are simply left out of account.

Another way of dealing with the problem, which is usually connected with the sort of moralism just outlined, is what has come to be called revivalism or restorationism. The two things are not identical, but they are closely related and belong to the same theological frame of mind. The underlying belief is that the Holy Spirit descends on God's people at periodic intervals in order to convict them of their backsliding and bring them back to him. Historically speaking, there is no doubt that religious revival has frequently taken place. And everyone would agree that it has left strong traces in its wake. The entire Evangelical movement is ultimately the product of the great eighteenth-century revival, and churches in the Methodist and holiness traditions owe their origins to this phenomenon. Restorationism merely takes this idea one stage farther, claiming that the Holy Spirit periodically inspires Christians to recover the Church as it was in the New Testament, and the churches which are founded as a result of this conviction are naturally—in the eyes of those who belong to them—the only ones in which the Spirit is truly at work today. That these bodies are in reality little different from any other conservative church, being distinguished only by an exceptional degree of conservatism in certain selected areas (e.g., the passive role of women, the rejection of instrumental music, etc.) is immediately obvious to outsiders, including many who would be otherwise sympathetic to their general position. But this does not seem to make much impression on the restorationists themselves, who are convinced by their own experience that the Holy Spirit has created their communities in a special way for a particular purpose. Often indeed, they refer to each other as Christians, brethren, or believers, on the implied assumption that others who are not of their persuasion do not really count. This is the authentic spirit of Puritanism taken to its logical extreme. Most conservative Protestants do not go that far, but anyone who has been touched by the Puritan spirit will feel the pull of this approach, and will either be attracted to imitate it to some degree or to combat it as a major threat to a more moderate (and fundamentally more compromising) position.

Conclusion: The Evangelical Dilemma

Our survey of historic Protestantism has revealed that the Reformation distinction between the visible and the invisible church, and its clear preference for the latter, which in effect is allowed to become the yardstick by which the purity of the former is measured, has produced a strong Puritan tendency which has manifested itself in different ways over the years but which reflects what is essentially a single approach to the question of the Holy Spirit and community. That is to say that the ideal Church is one in which the Holy Spirit's sovereignty is revealed, not only in the preaching and teaching ministry, but also in the life and behavior of the membership. However much it may be denied by those who hold this position, there is really no room in such a vision for weaker brethren—those who cannot live up to the required standard ought not to be there at all. If by some fluke weaker brethren actually make it into the Church, they can only be evangelized, disciplined and (if all else fails) thrown out. They cannot be tolerated, for the simple reason that a little leaven leavens the whole lump, and if some people are allowed to get away with lower levels of commitment it will not be long before the entire Church goes the same way. This is what is supposed to have happened in the late middle ages, it is what has certainly happened more recently to the mainline Protestant denominations, and it is what will inevitably happen to anyone who tries to relax the traditional standards. Most Evangelicals today, whether they like it or not, are to some degree inheritors of this approach to spiritual life in the Church community. Even those who reject and deplore it are chiefly noticeable for the fact that they go out of their way to break the taboos they have grown up with—they seldom if ever present a viable or attractive alternative to what they perceive to be wrong.

All this presents us with a dilemma. On the one hand, we are committed to an ecclesiology which gives more importance to the invisible Church than to the visible one. This principle is undoubtedly right as far as it goes because man is basically a spiritual being, created in the image and likeness of God, and the gospel is essentially a spiritual message—of conviction of sin and of redemption by the shed blood of Christ. But on the other hand, we are also committed to making the invisible visible in the world—as a witness to those who do not believe. This witness has a dual purpose, which is to glorify God and to win others for Christ. Experience has shown that attempts to produce a spiritual community by exclusion do not work, and are more likely to have the opposite effect on outsiders from the one intended. But if we fail to preach that a Spirit-filled Church must demonstrate the fruits of the Spirit we shall soon fall back into the very ritualism and institutionalization which the Reformers revolted against. How then can we achieve purity and holiness without becoming narrow and legalistic? How can we receive and accept spiritual blessings without condemning those who have not shared our experience and without splitting the Church? Can there ever be a purely Evangelical church, or are Evangelicals better off being prophetic voices in mixed churches of a broader theological complexion? And if we choose to go that route, where do our first loyalties lie— to other Evangelicals or to the non-Evangelical elements in our own denominations?

These are the challenges which face us today as we look for ways of building a Spirit-filled community life. They arise from the past, but it has to be confessed that history is not all that encouraging to those who may be trying to resolve the dilemma outlined above. We have to admit that keeping the unity of the Spirit in the bond of peace has never been easy, and it has seldom been achieved for long outside the confines of fairly narrow groups. What we now need is to ask ourselves whether this is the only kind of viable fellowship which is possible in a fallen world, or whether there is a way in which as Evangelicals we can demonstrate that we really were all baptized by one Spirit into one body.

The Witness of the Spirit in the Protestant Tradition

M. James Sawyer

This essay traces the historical articulation of the Protestant doctrine of the Witness of the Spirit as an immediate pre-reflective personal experience in the heart of the believer from its initial articulation by John Calvin to the present day. Include in this survey are the doctrine's reconceptualization by the Puritans, the return to Calvin's emphasis in the teaching of Wesley and Edwards followed by a survey of the nineteenth century debate over the doctrine between the Princetonians on the one hand and Charles Briggs and Abraham Kuyper on the other. It concludes that contemporary evangelicalism has succumbed to the same type of rationalism as characterized the Princetonians and in the process has stripped the doctrine of its existential viability.

In the medieval period the assurance of the presence of God was cut off from the ordinary believer and held captive by the Roman Catholic magisterium and in the sacerdotal system. The Bible was proclaimed to be the word of God on the authority of the Church, and it was the Church that mediated God's presence to the believer through the sacraments. God the Father was utterly transcendent, and Jesus Christ was the righteous Judge of the earth. Communication from and communion with God was in a practical sense mediated through the church hierarchy.

God, the Reformers thundered in response, was not bound by men. The authority of his word was not vouchsafed by human authority. He himself took the initiative in assuring the believer of the shape and veracity of his word. In so asserting, the Reformers challenged directly the pretentious assertions of late medieval Catholicism and contended that the word of God has authority over the Church, rather than the Church having authority to declare what is the word of God. Likewise, the Reformers declared that God the Holy Spirit witnessed *directly* to the heart of the believer giving assurance that that believer is in fact saved, regenerate, and a child of God. Thus was born the doctrine known today as the *Witness of the Spirit*, or the *Internal Testimony of the Holy Spirit*.

The doctrine of the Spirit's witness as it has developed historically has a two-pronged application: first, witness to the divine origin and veracity of the scriptures, and second, witness to the reality of the individual believer's experience of salvation. These emphases are sometimes at wide variance, yet both aspects are treated under the rubric of the *witness of the Spirit*. The purpose of this study is historical, not exegetical. It is to survey the doctrine of the *witness of the Spirit* from the time of the Reformers down to the present day, noting various emphases, understandings, and applications of the doctrine by various selected individual theologians, and to conclude with some contemporary observations.

Calvin, the Reformers, and the *Witness of the Spirit*

The Reformers did not invent the doctrine of the witness of the Spirit as is sometimes charged. It is found in some form in the patristic period, most notably in Augustine.[1] With reference to the Spirit's witness to scripture, justification for the doctrine was found in such passages as 1 Cor 2; John 16:13–

15; 1 Thess 1:5; and 1 John 2:20, 27. With reference to the Spirit's testimony concerning the believer's salvific relationship with God, Paul's testimony in Rom 8:16 stated the doctrine explicitly, albeit in nascent form: "The Spirit himself bears witness to our spirit that we are God's children." They also found the doctrine obliquely referenced and inferred from numerous other passages.[2]

John Calvin, the first theologian to develop the teaching of the witness of the Spirit, speaks at length of that witness under two separate headings, the immediate testimony of the Spirit to the heart of the individual that the canon of scripture is the word of God, and the activity of the Spirit touching the hearts of men and women to give assurance of their new status before him as his children.

The Witness of the Spirit to the Word

Calvin and the other Reformers[3] did not found their doctrine of canon-determination upon human authorship, nor upon the authority of the Church but upon the witness of the Spirit.

The Reformers had rejected out of hand the Roman Catholic contention that the Church determined the canon by its own authority. Calvin and the Reformed confessions were agreed that the determining principle of canon was in the intrinsic nature of Holy Writ itself. Calvin stated:

> But a most pernicious error widely prevails that Scripture has only so much weight as is conceded to it by the consent of the Church. As if the eternal and inviolable truth of God depended on the decision of men....
>
> For, as God alone is a fit witness of Himself in His Word, so also the Word will not find acceptance in men's hearts before it is sealed by *the inward testimony of the Spirit*. The same Spirit, therefore, who has spoken by the mouths of the prophets, must penetrate into our hearts, to persuade us that they faithfully proclaimed what had been divinely commanded.[4]

Calvin explicitly rejected any attempt to build a faith in the scriptures upon evidence as an approach which amounted to "doing things backwards."[5] Instead, he rested all assurance upon the inward testimony of the Holy Spirit working on the heart of the believer. Thus, scripture was "self-authenticated; hence, it is not right to subject it to proof or reasoning. And the certainty it deserves with us, it attains by the testimony of the Spirit."[6] He eschewed the necessity of any rational proofs since the majestic character of the scriptures themselves displayed in the heart of the believer a certainty more convincing than any human argument. Calvin's lead was followed by the Reformed confessions in this matter.

The Second Helvetic Confession stated:

> We believe and confess the Canonical Scriptures of the holy prophets and apostles of both Testaments to be the true Word of God and to have sufficient authority of themselves, not of men....[7]

The Gallican Confession similarly testified:

> IV. We know these books to be canonical, and the sure rule of our faith, not so much by the common accord and consent of the Church, as by the testimony and inward illumination of the Holy Spirit, which enables us to distinguish them from other ecclesiastical books.
>
> V. We believe that the Word contained in these books has proceeded from God and receives its authority from him alone, and not from men.[8]

So too, the Westminster Confession stated with reference to canonical authority:

> IV. The authority of the holy Scripture, for which it ought to be believed and obeyed, dependeth not upon the testimony of any man or church, but wholly upon God (who is truth itself), the Author thereof; and therefore is to be received, because it is the word of God.
>
> V. We may be moved and induced by the testimony of the Church to a high and reverent esteem of the holy Scripture; and the heavenliness of the matter, the efficacy of the doctrine, the majesty of the style, the consent of all the parts, the Scope of the whole (which is to give all glory to God), the full discovery it makes of the only way of man's salvation, the many other incomparable excellences, and the entire perfection thereof, are arguments whereby it doth abundantly evidence itself to be the word of God; yet, notwithstanding, our full persuasion and assurance of the infallible truth, and the divine authority thereof, is from the inward work of the Holy Spirit, bearing witness by and with the Word in our hearts.[9]

This is not to say that all testimony was subjective, rather that there was a twofold Divine witness. God witnessed to himself objectively in the pages of scripture and the Holy Spirit witnessed subjectively to the heart of the believer. This doctrine rooted itself deeply in the Protestant tradition generally.[10]

Thus, Calvin and the other Reformers built the doctrine of the witness of the Spirit to the word in opposition to Catholic claims of authority over the scripture. In the context of the debate with Catholicism the Spirit was declared to be sovereign in assuring of God's provenance of the written word. But this was only one prong of the dynamic of the Spirit's witness. The other had direct reference to the believer's immediate relationship to God as Father.

The Witness of the Spirit in Salvation

The doctrine of salvation is developed at great length by Calvin in book three of the *Institutes*. It is here that one sees the pastoral heart of the Geneva reformer and the lengths to which he went to ground the believer's salvation in the experience of the presence of God in his/her life. Calvin insists that assurance is of the essence of faith and a *sine qua non* of salvation. He assails those who would rob the believer of the immediate assurance of the presence of God and replace it with an assurance mediated by any so-called evidences of grace which could be found in the life.

> Not content to undermine the firmness of faith in one way alone, they assail it from another quarter. Thus they say that even though according to our present state of righteousness we can judge our possession of the grace of God the knowledge of final perseverance remains in suspense. A fine confidence of salvation is left to us, if by moral conjecture we judge that at the present moment we are in grace, but we know not what will become of us tomorrow! The apostle speaks far otherwise: "I am surely convinced that neither angels, nor powers... will separate us from the love by which the Lord embraces us in Christ [Rom 8:38–39]. They try to escape with the trifling solution, *prating that the apostle had his assurance from a special revelation.* But they are held too tightly to escape. For there he is discussing those benefits which come to all believers in common faith, not from those things he exclusively experiences.[11]

This position which Calvin assails is what Berkhof has labeled "pietistic nomism" which is in opposition to the Reformers and the apostles.[12] Berkhof has noted that the Reformers in opposition to Rome sometimes stressed assurance as the *most important element* of faith. Both Calvin and the Heidelberg catechism saw assurance as belonging to the essence of faith. While

> Pietistic Nomism asserted that assurance does not belong to the very being, but only the well-being of faith; and that it can be secured, except by special revelation, only by continuous and conscious introspection. All kinds of "marks of the spiritual life" derived not from Scripture but from the lives of approved Christians became the standard of self-

examination. The outcome proved, however, that this method was not calculated to produce assurance, but rather to lead to everlasting doubt, confusion and uncertainty.[13]

Calvin similarly observed that *"faith implies certainty."*[14] He observed of those who deny this truth:

> Also there are very many who so conceive of God's mercy that they receive almost no consolation from it. They are constrained with miserable anxiety at the same time as they are in doubt with whether he will be merciful to them because they confine that very kindness of which they seem utterly persuaded within too narrow limits. For among themselves they ponder that it is indeed great and abundant, shed upon many, available and ready for all; but uncertain whether it will ever come to them, or rather they will come to it.... Therefore it does not so much strengthen the spirit in secure tranquility as trouble it with uneasy doubting. But there is a far different feeling of full assurance that in the Scriptures is always attributed to faith. It is this which puts beyond doubt God's goodness clearly manifested for us [Col. 2:2; 1 Thess 1:5; cf. Heb 6:11 and 10:22]. But this cannot happen without our *truly feeling its sweetness and experiencing it* ourselves. For this reason, the apostle derives confidence from faith and from confidence, in turn, boldness. For he states: "Through Christ we have boldness and access with confidence which is through faith in him... By these words he obviously shows that there is no right faith except when we dare with tranquil hearts to stand in God's sight. This boldness arises only out of a sure confidence in the divine benevolence and salvation. This is so true that the word faith is often used for confidence.[15]

Calvin speaks to the same issue of confidence before God based upon the individual believer's "essential righteousness" noting that such an approach cannot but "...deprive them [believers] of a lively experience of Christ's grace."[16] The net effect is "To enfeeble our assurance of salvation, to waft us above the clouds in order to prevent our calling upon God with quiet hearts after we, assured of expiation, have laid hold upon grace."[17]

McGrath has observed that "For the Reformers it was necessary to know that one was a Christian, that the Christian life had indeed begun, that one had been forgiven and accepted by God—and on the basis of that conviction, the living of the Christian life, with all its opportunities, responsibilities and challenges, could proceed."[18]

In many places Calvin explicitly references the witness of the Spirit in the life of the believer, heaping scorn upon those who would deny the experiential aspect of his ministry or suspend assurance of salvation upon something other than the Spirit's immediate witness:

> But they contend that it is a matter of rash presumption for us to claim an undoubted knowledge of God's will. Now I would concede that point to them only if we took upon ourselves to subject God's incomprehensible plan to our slender understanding. But when we simply say with Paul: "We have received not the spirit of this world, but the Spirit that is from God..." by whose teaching "we know the gifts bestowed on us by God" [1 Cor 2:12], how can they yelp against us without abusively assaulting the Holy Spirit? But if it is a dreadful sacrilege to accuse the revelation given by the Spirit either of falsehood or uncertainty or ambiguity, how do we transgress in declaring its certainty?
>
> But they cry aloud that it is also great temerity on our part that we thus dare to glory in the Spirit of Christ. Who would credit such stupidity to those who wish to be regarded as the schoolmasters of the world, that they so shamefully trip over the first rudiments of Christianity? Surely, it would not have been credible to me, if their extant writings did not attest it. Paul declares that those very ones "who are led by the Spirit of God are sons of God..." [Rom 8:14].[19]
>
> Paul teaches that God is called "Father" by us at the bidding of the Spirit, who alone can "witness to our spirit that we are children of God" [Rom 8:16]. Even though these men do not keep us from calling upon God, they withdraw the Spirit, by whose leading he ought to have been duly called upon. Paul denies that those who are not moved by the Spirit of Christ are servants of Christ [cf. Rom 8:9]. These men devise a Christianity that does not require the Spirit of Christ. He holds out no hope of blessed resurrection unless we feel the Spirit dwelling in us [Rom 8:11]. These men invent a hope devoid of such a feeling.
>
> Yet perchance they will answer that they do not deny we ought to be endowed with the Spirit; but that it is a matter of modesty and humility not to be sure of it.[20]

Elsewhere Calvin testifies further of the experience of the Spirit:

> "Now we know," says John, "that he abides in us from the Spirit whom he has given us." [1 John 3:24; 4:13.] And what else do we do but call Christ's promises into question when we wish to be accounted God's servants apart from his Spirit, whom he has declared he would pour out upon all his own people? [Isa 44:3; cf. Joel 2:28.] What else is it, then,

than to do injury to the Holy Spirit if we separate faith, which is his peculiar work, from him? Since these are the first beginnings of piety, it is a token of the most miserable blindness to charge with arrogance Christians who dare to glory in the presence of the Holy Spirit, without which glorying Christianity itself does not stand! But, actually, they declare by their own example how truly Christ spoke: "My Spirit was unknown to the world; he is recognized only by those among whom he abides" [John 14:17].[21]

For they imagine that people who are touched by no fear of God, no sense of piety, nevertheless believe whatever it is necessary to know for salvation. As if the Holy Spirit, by illumining our hearts unto faith, were not the witness to us of our adoption! And yet they presumptuously dignify that persuasion, devoid of the fear of God, with the name "faith" even though all Scripture cries out against it. We need no longer contend with their definition; our task is simply to explain the nature of faith as it is set forth in the Word of God. From this it will be very clear how ignorantly and foolishly they shout rather than speak about it.

I have already touched upon part; I shall later insert the rest in its proper place. I now say that nothing more absurd than their fiction can be imagined. They would have faith to be an assent by which any despiser of God may receive what is offered from Scripture. But first they ought to have seen whether every man attains faith by his own effort, or whether through it the Holy Spirit is witness of his adoption. Therefore they babble childishly in asking whether faith is the same faith when it has been formed by a superadded quality; or whether it be a new and different thing. From such chatter it certainly looks as if they never thought about the unique gift of the Spirit. For the beginning of believing already contains within itself the reconciliation whereby man approaches God. But if they weighed Paul's saying, "With the heart a man believes unto righteousness" [Rom 10:10], they would cease to invent that cold quality of faith. If we possessed only this one reason, it would have been sufficient to end the dispute: that very assent itself — as I have already partially suggested, and will reiterate more fully — is more of the heart than of the brain, and more of the disposition than of the understanding. For this reason, it is called "obedience of faith" [Rom 1:5]...[22]

For Calvin it is not too much to say that the witness of the Spirit is tied up with faith itself. He sees faith as engendered by the Spirit, who continues to speak to the heart of the believer once he has come to faith. Clearly, faith is not mere *assensus* or *notitia* but a vital *fiducia* and is inexorably linked to the work of the Spirit.

The Puritans' Development of the *Witness of the Spirit*

When one turns his attention from the Geneva Reformer and the early Reformation conceptions of the ministry of the Spirit, especially with reference to salvation and the assurance that the believer is to have in his confidence before God, to the later Puritans, one finds a decided shift in emphasis. The Puritans continued the emphasis of Calvin and other Reformers on the necessity of the witness of the Spirit, and applied it especially to the doctrine of salvation; however there is now an emphasis of a Spirit-given assurance as being a *fruit of faith* rather than endemic to the very nature of faith itself.

The concept of the witness of the Spirit was not denied. Rather, the immediate internal testimony was seen as being given later in the Christian life rather than at its outset. Some of the Puritan writers go so far as to call the experience of the immediate direct supra-rational witness of the Spirit as a "new conversion." Packer summarizing the Puritan position says, "Assurance is the conscious fruit of supernatural enlightenment and cannot exist till it pleases God to give it."[23]

Rather than the immediate direct experience of the presence of the Spirit and grace of God as Calvin taught, the Puritans saw assurance as coming only gradually (except in unusual cases). The convert was required to *think and hope* with reason that he was a believer, but he had *no direct evidence* of this fact without until such time as he received supernatural assurance through a post-conversion experience dawned in his consciousness.[24]

Goodwin, one of the great Puritan writers on the subject, describes the two means open to the believer as to assurance:

> The one way [what the Puritans called the practical syllogism] is *discoursive,* a man gathereth that God loves him from the effects [i.e., marks of regeneration], as we gather that there is fire because there is smoke. But the other way is *intuitive...* it is such a knowledge as whereby we know that the whole is greater than the part... There is light that cometh and overpowereth a man's soul and assureth him that God is his and he is God's and that God loveth him from everlasting.[25]

Similarly, Sibbs says the "the Spirit doth not always witness... by force of argument from sanctification, but sometimes immediately by way of presence; as the sight of a friend comforts without help of discourse."[26] The point here is not that the Puritans denied the concept of the witness of the Spirit, rather that they redefined it in contradistinction to the position taken by Calvin. And that redefinition in some ways directly contradicted the perspective of the Geneva Reformer, for it made assurance based on "essential righteousness." Rather than feeling the direct evidence of the love of God being shed abroad in our hearts, the Puritans contended that this direct evidence is not normally given immediately. Rather they see the norm of the witness as being indirect, and coming from inference of the *practical syllogism*.

Contrast this mentality with Calvin who notes that "a man cannot seriously apply himself to repentance without knowing himself to belong to God."[27] Likewise, he contends that "no one is truly persuaded that he himself belongs to God unless he has first recognized God's grace."[28] In context this is clearly an immediate experience rather than a rational reflection on truth.

The English-speaking Calvinistic tradition emphasized works as the basis for assurance and down-played building the Christian life upon the direct experience of an individual's acceptance before God. The immature believer was, in their minds, normally cut off from any *direct* assurance. Assurance was to be discovered through the *reflex action* or the *practical syllogism*. Bell has observed that in the Scottish Presbyterian tradition it was clearly taught that the Christian is justified by a direct act of faith which apprehends the imputed righteousness of Christ. However, knowledge that he has done so is to be seen only indirectly in light of self-examination. This "reflex act of faith" was said to be more spiritual than the simple direct apprehension of Christ as Savior.[29] This perspective stands in stark contrast with the mentality of Calvin and the early Reformers. As Packer has observed: "The heart of the biblical gospel was to them [the Reformers] God's free gift of righteousness and justification… This justification was to them not a theological speculation but a *religious reality* [an experience], apprehended through prayer by revelation from God via the Bible."[30]

Calvin insisted upon the "witness of the Spirit" as a vital aspect in the assurance of salvation. This "witness" involves a personal communion with God. Isaac Dorner, reflecting Calvin, argued that spiritual truth made a demand on the soul if certainty were to be attained. Thus, certainty and assurance of spiritual truth were qualitatively different in nature than certainty of all other knowledge.

Faith became the *principium cognescendi.* This faith was a product of the personal experience of the presence of God and the medium of his presence. "…[F]aith has a knowledge of being known by God, and of its existence because of God, and in such a way that it knows God as the one self-verifying and self-subsisting fact…"[31] Thus faith offers a divinely-assured certainty since it involves a genuine reciprocal divine communion attested in the human soul. This is not mysticism in the classic sense of the term. Rather God, as a person, reaches out to directly touch the soul of the individual and give certain knowledge of himself.

In contrast to this perspective Packer notes that, for the Puritans, "man cannot come to know any spiritual object except by the use of his mind."[32] The full assurance spoken of in scripture is achieved by a rational reflection and meditation on the exposition of scripture.

The *Witness of the Spirit* in the First Great Awakening

John Wesley

In the context of the First Great Awakening in America and the Evangelical Revival in England, John Wesley picked up on vital Reformed themes seen particularly in Calvin, developed them, and then formally integrated them into his theological method. Particularly, Wesley advocated and further developed Calvin's doctrine of the *witness of the Spirit* in the heart of the believer. He insisted with Calvin, and against the Puritan perspective, that the witness of the Spirit is a personal experience *prior* to rational reflection.

In his understanding, the witness of the Spirit functioned in two areas. First, as assurance of salvation, the Spirit speaks directly to the human heart, giving a guarantee that the individual is in fact adopted into the family of God. The second area of the Spirit's witness is in the ongoing relationship that the believer has with God, especially at the moment of entire sanctification. This is not just an initial momentary emotional feeling, but a genuine ongoing personal relationship. He says that faith is a divine supernatural evidence or conviction of things not seen, not discoverable by our bodily senses. In this experience the Spirit takes truth that is known rationally and makes it personal. For example, to the question, "But how do you know that you are sanctified, saved from your inbred corruption?" Wesley answers,

We know it by the witness and fruits of the Spirit. First, by the witness, for, when we were justified, the Spirit witnessed to our spirit that our sins had been forgiven; even so, when we were sanctified He witnessed that we had been washed... the latter witness of the Spirit is just as clear and firm as the former.[33]

While the witness of the Spirit was an internal experience, Wesley denied that it was mystic because it retained the subject-object relationship. There was no melding of the human personality with the divine; rather the individual was touched by God the Spirit in such a way as to give assurance of his/her personal relationship with God. He unambiguously defined the witness thus:

By the testimony of the Spirit, I mean, an inward impression on the soul, whereby the Spirit of God immediately and directly witnesses to my spirit, that I am a child of God; that Jesus Christ hath loved me, and given himself for me; that all my sins are blotted out, and I, even I, am reconciled to God.[34]

Wesley explicitly denied the route taken among some of the Puritans with reference to the *practical syllogism*, insisting instead that the witness of the spirit could not possibly arise out of rational reflection; rather it must by its very nature be prior to such reflection.

4. "Because ye are sons, God hath sent forth the Spirit of his Son into your hearts, crying, Abba, Father." *Is not this something immediate and direct, not the result of reflection or argumentation?* Does not this Spirit cry, "Abba, Father," in our hearts the moment it is given, antecedently to any reflection upon our sincerity; yea, to any reasoning whatsoever? And is not this the plain natural sense of the words, which strikes any one as soon as he hears them? All these texts then, in their most obvious meaning, *describe a direct testimony of the Spirit.*

5. That the testimony of the Spirit of God must, in the very nature of things, be antecedent to the testimony of our own spirit, may appear from this single consideration: We must be holy in heart and life before we can be conscious that we are so. But we must love God before we can be holy at all, this being the root of all holiness. Now we cannot love God, till we know he loves us: "We love him, because he first loved us." And we cannot know his love to us, till his Spirit witnesses it to our spirit. Till then we cannot believe it; we cannot say, "The life which I now live, I live by faith in the Son of God, who loved me, and gave Himself for me." Then, only then we feel our interest in his blood, And cry, with joy unspeakable, Thou art my Lord, my God! Since, therefore,

the testimony of his Spirit must preach the love of God, and all holiness, of consequence it must precede our consciousness thereof.

6. And here properly comes in, to confirm this scriptural doctrine, the experience of the children of God; the experience not of two or three, not of a few, but of a great multitude which no man can number. It has been confirmed, both in this, and in all ages, by "a cloud" of living and dying "witnesses." It is confirmed by your experience and mine. The Spirit itself bore witness to my spirit that I was a child of God, gave me an evidence hereof, and I immediately cried, "Abba, Father!" And this I did, (and so did you,) before I reflected on, or was conscious of, any fruit of the Spirit. It was from this testimony received that love, joy, peace, and the whole fruit of the Spirit flowed. First, I heard, Thy sins are forgiven I Accepted thou art! — I listen'd, and heaven sprung up in my heart.[35]

However this denial of the practical syllogism did not signal a denial of indirect evidence in helping the believer to establish confidence in his relationship with God. Rather, he explicitly taught that the indirect witness of the Spirit, which would correspond to the *practical syllogism*, or the *reflex action*, must of necessity *follow* the direct testimony of the Spirit. In following this path, Wesley again followed Calvin who permitted looking at one's life for evidence of salvation only after one was fully assured of his relationship with God by means of the direct testimony of the Spirit.[36] Wesley says,

And it is not questioned, whether there is a testimony of the Spirit; but whether there is any direct testimony; whether there is any other than that which arises from a consciousness of the fruit of the Spirit. We believe there is; because this is the plain natural meaning of the text, illustrated both by the preceding words, and by the parallel passage in the Epistle to the Galatians; because, in the nature of the thing, the testimony must precede the fruit which springs from it; and because this plain meaning of the word of God is confirmed by the experience of innumerable children of God; yea, and by the experience of all who are convinced of sin, who can never rest till they have a direct witness; and even of the children of the world, who, not having the witness in themselves, one and all declare, none can know his sins forgiven.[37]

So stridently did Wesley promote this doctrine that he even claimed that justification by faith would have to be denied were the direct testimony of the Spirit to be denied.

8. Every one, therefore, who denies the existence of such a testimony, does in effect deny justification by faith. It follows, that either he never

experienced this, either he never was justified, or that he has forgotten, as St. Peter speaks, του καθαρισμου των παλαι αυτου αμαρτιων the purification from his former sins, the experience he then had himself; the manner wherein God wrought in his own soul, when his former sins were blotted out.

And the experience even of the children of the world here confirms that of the children of God. Many of these have a desire to please God: Some of them take much pains to please him. But do they not, one and all, count it the highest absurdity for any to talk of knowing his sins are forgiven? Which of them even pretends to any such thing? And yet many of them are conscious of their own sincerity. Many of them undoubtedly have, in a degree, the testimony of their own spirit, a consciousness of their own uprightness. But this brings them no consciousness that they are forgiven, no knowledge that they are the children of God. Yea, the more sincere they are, the more uneasy they generally are, for want of knowing it, plainly showing that this cannot be known, in a satisfactory manner, by the bare testimony of our own spirit, without God's directly testifying that we are his children.[38]

When emphasizing the immediate experience of the Spirit, or a Spirit-given certainty, the question that arises is how do experience and scripture interrelate. Wesley always viewed religious experience with skepticism. He was particularly wary of visions, dreams, and the like, and insisted that scripture must have priority in judging the validity of such personal experiences. Experience cannot stand in opposition to the Bible. On the other hand he recognized that experience can and does confirm scripture. But even here he draws the distinction between the emotional feeling and a settled conviction. Emotions can wax and wane but heart-settled conviction will not waver. He in practice did not use experience as an independent authority to confirm the truth of scripture but as a test as to the viability of various proposed interpretations of scriptural passages. He also recognized that the Spirit deals in different ways with different people.[39]

Jonathan Edwards

With Wesley, Edwards was a great preacher of the First Great Awakening. And like Wesley, he had a keen interest and fervent awareness of the necessity and reality of the witness of the Spirit in the life of the believer as an immediate experiential presence. He at various times makes mention of the work of the Spirit. A couple of examples will suffice to show his essential agreement with

Wesley as to the nature of the witness, and his continuity with the Reformers in linking the witness of the Spirit to confirming the truth of the word of God. Edwards notes,

> And it seems to be necessary to suppose that there is an immediate influence of the Spirit of God, oftentimes, in bringing texts of Scripture to the mind. Not that I suppose it is done in a way of immediate revelation, without any use of the memory; but yet there seems plainly to be an immediate and extraordinary influence, in leading their thoughts to such and such passages of Scripture, and exciting them in the memory. Indeed in some, God seems to bring texts of Scripture to their minds no otherwise than by leading them into such frames and meditations as harmonize with those Scriptures; but in many persons there seems to be something more than this...[40]

In speaking of one of his parishioner's experiences of the Spirit, Edwards testifies again to the immediate nature of the witness of the Spirit in confirming the truth and divinity of scripture.

> She had sometimes the powerful breathings of the Spirit of God on her soul, while reading the Scripture; and would express her sense of the certain truth and divinity thereof. She sometimes would appear with a pleasant smile on her countenance; and once, when her sister took notice of it, and asked why she smiled, she replied, I am brim-full of a sweet feeling within.[41]

Thus, with both Edwards and Wesley there is an insistence on the immediate nature of the witness of the Spirit. Neither one follows the Puritan lead of insisting on the practical syllogism in gaining assurance of salvation. For both, the evidence of the Spirit is an immediate supra-rational experience in the soul, not unrelated to the word, and not to be conceived as mysticism.

The Witness of the Spirit in the Late Nineteenth Century

The Princetonians and Charles Briggs

When attention is turned to the late nineteenth century, one again finds reference and appeal to the doctrine of the witness of the Spirit, but with a different twist than one sees in Wesley or the Puritans, or even in Calvin. In part this is due, I believe, to the very different context of the late nineteenth century from the sixteenth through the eighteenth centuries. The context was one of the rise of biblical criticism (which threatened received orthodox formulations and defenses), and also the wedding of conservative American orthodox theological formulations to Scottish Common Sense philosophy. This gave rise to an anti-mystic approach that viewed with suspicion all claims to certainty in matters of faith not grounded in rational processes. The focus of the *witness of the Spirit* was with reference to the word as it was during the Reformation. But we find in the literature a sharp division over the way that God and his word are to be recognized as seen in the approaches espoused by Princetonians, and their infamous opponent Charles Augustus Briggs.

Perhaps the best way to illustrate the concept of the witness of the Spirit in the thought of the Princetonians is to survey their method of canon-determination. The Princetonian explanation of the canon-determination process was made in the context of the Roman Catholic claim that the Church had determined the canon. In this the Princetonians mirrored the concerns of the Reformers. However the approach taken stood in sharp contrast to the Reformers. In contrast to Rome, Charles Hodge contended that the principle for canon-determination in the Old Testament was that those books, and only those, which Christ and his apostles recognized as the written word of God, were entitled to be regarded as canonical.[42]

This recognition was accomplished in two ways. First, those books that the New Testament cited as scripture were to be afforded canonical status. Secondly, Hodge contended that when the New Testament referred to the Sacred Book of the Jews *as a volume*, it recognized all the writings contained therein as inspired and authoritative. The only thing to be determined was the extent of the books that the Jews regarded as inspired. On this point Hodge was adamant: "...there can be no reasonable doubt. The Jewish canon of the Old Testament contained all the books and no others, which Protestants now recognize as constituting the Old Testament Scriptures."[43] This criterion relegated the Old Testament Apocrypha to uninspired status. It is curious, however, from a methodological perspective that Hodge, having already played his trump card, so to speak, then referred to the *intrinsic content* of the apocryphal books as further evidence of their spurious nature.

Turning to the New Testament, the principle of canon-determination was equally as simple. The criterion was solely apostolicity, which was defined as either apostolic authorship or apostolic sanction. The logic behind this single test was simple. "The Apostles were the duly authenticated messengers of Christ, of whom He said, 'He that heareth you, heareth me.'"[44] Thus, at least in the New Testament, the question of canon was established solely upon the question of human authorship. A. A. Hodge followed his father's lead, asserting:

> We determine what books have a place in this canon or divine rule by an *examination of the evidences* which show that each of them, severally, was written by the inspired prophet or apostle whose name it bears, or, as in the case of the gospels of Mark and Luke, written under the superintendence and published by the authority of an apostle. This evidence in the case of the sacred Scriptures is of the same kind of historical and critical proof as is relied upon by all literary men to establish the genuineness and *authenticity* of any other ancient writings…. This is (a) Internal,—such as language, style and the character of the matter they contain; (b) External,—such as the testimony of contemporaneous writers, the universal consent of contemporary readers, and corroborating history drawn from independent credible sources.[45]

Warfield, too, concurred with this line of reasoning.

> We rest our acceptance of the New Testament Scriptures as authoritative thus, not on the fact that they are the product of the revelation-age of the church, for so are many other books which we do not thus accept; but on the fact *that God's authoritative agents* in founding the church gave them as *authoritative to the church which they founded….* It is clear that prophetic and apostolic origin is the very essence of the authority of the Scriptures.[46]

Thus, at least in principle, the wedding of canon to human authorship was complete. This wedding placed the Princetonians in the curious position of reliance upon the discipline of higher criticism, a discipline which they disavowed, in order to establish the canon. With reference to the concept of the witness of the Spirit, Warfield turned the Reformers' perspective on its head. Rather than appeal to the witness of the Spirit in any direct and authoritative fashion he asserted "…that the inspired Scriptures as such may be determined for faith, there is need, besides the witness of the Holy Ghost, of an *external criterion.*"[47] Elsewhere, Warfield explicitly denied that the witness of the Spirit was in any sense direct and supra-rational, insisting that the Spirit works in giving assurance only through rational evidence. Any concept of direct supra-rational assurance was dismissed as "mystic." In so doing he reduced the concept of the witness of the spirit to a sanctified rationalism.[48]

Charles Briggs criticized this wedding of canon to human authorship as a theological novelty.[49] He argued that the Reformers had not founded their doctrine of canon determination upon human authorship, but upon the witness of the Spirit.

The Reformers had rejected out of hand the Roman Catholic contention that the Church determined the canon by its own authority. Calvin and the Reformed confessions were agreed that the determining principle of canon was in the intrinsic nature of Holy Writ itself as witnessed by the Holy Spirit.[50] God witnessed to himself objectively in the pages of scripture and the Holy Spirit witnessed subjectively to the heart of the believer. As Briggs stated:

> ...other testimony is valuable and important, yet, the decisive test of canonicity and interpretation of the Scriptures is God Himself speaking in and through them to His people. This alone gives us the *fides divina*. This is the so-called formal principle of the Reformation, no less important than the so-called material principle of justification by faith.[51]

Clearly the Reformers themselves as well as the Reformed Confessions envisioned the word of God as being sealed to the heart by the testimony of the Spirit alone, rather than by the deducing of proof of apostolic authorship. Briggs' attack on the Princetonians at this point was justified and accurate.

The Princetonians, however, remained unimpressed by Briggs' arguments. C. W. Hodge's reaction to Briggs' article, "Critical Theories of Sacred Scripture in Relation to Their Inspiration: The Right, Duty, and Limits of Biblical Criticism," in the *Presbyterian Review*, is illustrative of the Princetonian perspective on the necessity of *rational* certainty in the establishment of the authority of the Bible as divine authority: "...that the canon is determined subjectively by the Christian feeling of the Church, & and not by history, & that it is illogical to prove first Canonicity, & then Inspiration, ...*then you have given away the whole historical side of the argument of the Apostolic origin of the Books & of Christianity itself.*"[52] Certainty of validity of the canon as the word of God, for the Princeton theologians, was established by rational and historical proofs without recourse to the doctrine of the witness of the Spirit in any vital way.

Briggs' approach to certainty with reference to the biblical text specifically and in matters of faith generally marked a radical departure from that of Princeton. He objected that reasoning powers gave the soul only "probability, not certainty,"[53] and therefore, were not adequate to establish divine authority. Reason could only give a human authority.[54] His approach reflected that of the Westminster Confession. Certainty was not to be achieved by rational demonstration, but by the inner witness of the Spirit.[55]

Briggs allied himself with the Westminster Confession and Calvin, charging that the Princetonians were those who had departed from the Confession by basing their doctrine of assurance on rational proofs rather than on the divine testimony in the heart of the believer.[56] He moved certainty from the realm of the objective and verifiable to the realm of the subjective, assurance by the Spirit.

Assurance of truth for Briggs rested upon the testimony of the Spirit. The Spirit did not, however, work in a vacuum. He bore witness to the infallible divine truth found in scripture.[57]

The *witness of the Spirit* to the word became for Briggs the watchword of canonical determination. The real question of canon was the question of divine authorship. The historic Protestant position as espoused by Briggs saw human authorship as insignificant in canon-determination. As Luther had said, "What if Moses didn't write the Pentateuch?" The real issue became, "Was it written by God and witnessed by the Spirit?"

This would seem to open the door for every man to determine his own Bible. Not so, replied Briggs:

> Criticism takes from every denomination of Christians and from tradition and from the theologians their spurious claims to determine the Canon of Holy Scripture for all men; but it does not give that authority to any individual man. It puts the authority to determine His Holy Word in God Himself. It teaches us to look for the divine evidence in the Holy Scriptures themselves. It tells us to open our minds and hearts and submit ourselves to the message of the Divine Spirit and accept the Bible God has made for us. But it does tell every man to make up his own mind as to the authority of the writings which are said to belong to Holy Scripture. It endorses the right of private judgment in this matter as in all others. It makes the divine authority of the Canon, and of every writing in the Canon, a question between every man and his God.[58]

He proposed a threefold program for canon-determination, built upon the "rock of the Reformation principle of the Sacred Scriptures."[59] The first principle of canon-determination was the testimony of the Church. By examining tradition and the early written documents, he contended that *probable evidence* could be presented to men that the scriptures "recognized as of divine authority and canonical by such *general consent* are indeed what they claim to be."[60]

With reference to the Protestant canon this evidence was unanimous. This evidence was not, however, determinative. It was only "probable." It was the evidence of *general consent*, although given under the leading of the Spirit. It was from this general consent that conciliar pronouncements were made. It did not, however, settle the issue, since divine authority could not be derived from ecclesiastical pronouncement or consensus.

The second and next higher level of evidence was that of the character of the scriptures themselves. Their character was pure and holy, having a beauty, harmony, and majesty; they evidenced a simplicity and fidelity to truth; they gave exalted conceptions of man, God, and history. The scriptures also breathed piety and devotion to God; they revealed redemption and satisfied the spiritual longing within the soul of man. All these features served to convince that the scriptures were indeed the very word of God.

The third and highest principle of canon determination was that of the witness of the Spirit. Here he moved to the center of the "Protestant Principle." He stated, "The Spirit of God bears witness by and with the particular writing or *part of a writing*, in the heart of the believer, removing every doubt and assuring the soul of its possession of the truth of God."[61]

Briggs saw the witness of the Spirit as threefold. As noted above, the Spirit bore witness to the particular writing. Secondly, the Spirit bore witness "by and with the several writings in such a manner as to assure the believer"[62] that they were each a part of the one divine revelation. This argument was cumulative. As one recognized one book as divine, it became easier to recognize the same marks in another of the same character. A systematic study of the scriptures yielded a conviction of the fact that the canon was an organic whole. The Holy Spirit illumined the mind and heart to perceive this organic whole and thus gave certainty to the essential place of each writing in the word of God.[63]

Third, the Spirit bore witness "to the Church as an organized body of believers, through their free consent in their various communities and countries to the unity and variety of the… Scriptures as the complete and perfect canon."[64] This line of evidence was a reworking of the Historical argument but strengthening it with the "vital argument of the divine evidence."[65] Whereas before, the Church testimony was external and formal, whenever the believer came to recognize the Holy Spirit as the guiding force in the Church both in forming the canon and its recognition, "then we may know that the testimony of the Church is the testimony of the divine Spirit speaking through the Church."[66]

Summarizing Briggs' method of canon-determination: first, the logical order began with the human testimony as probable evidence to the divinity of scripture. This testimony brought the individual to esteem the scriptures highly. When he turned to the pages of scripture itself, they exerted an influence upon his soul. Finally, the divine testimony convinced him of the extent of the truth of God, at which point he shared in the consensus of the Church.[67]

Abraham Kuyper

When one moves from the American scene to that of the Netherlands during this same period, one finds, perhaps surprisingly, in the theology of Abraham Kuyper an articulation of the concept of the witness of the Spirit to the word very similar to that of Briggs. Kuyper insists that the "mysticism of the Spirit is indispensable to the theologian."[68] But this mysticism is not without an objective ground. That is found in the word of God.

> Now however, the influence of this reality operates upon theology in a threefold way: First, materially, by the provision of matter which it brings to theology; secondly, by the influence of the Church, so far as that Church propels its confession as a living witness; and thirdly, in the theologian personally, inasmuch as his own spiritual experience must enable him to perceive and understand what treasures are here at stake. Coordinated under one head, one might say that the Holy Spirit guarantees this organic articulation through the agencies of the Holy Scripture, the Church, and the personal enlightenment of the theologian.[69]

Failure to maintain these three factors in tension leads either to a rationalism that attacks the very heart of theology, or to a sentimentalism that dissolves into either mysticism or pietism.

With the Reformers and Briggs, Kuyper understood the witness of the Spirit as being personal, directed to the personal *ego*.[70] However, in contrast to others heretofore examined, Kuyper emphasizes the corporate nature of the witness of the Spirit in the Church in a way that it has not heretofore been seen. It is this corporate witness which serves to hold in check a rampant individualism by which every individual might determine his or her own canon.[71]

Kuyper's discussion cites the same three factors as does Briggs in the same order as the method by which canonical certainty is to be achieved, but while Briggs limits his discussion particularly to the shape of the canon, Kuyper ultimately extends the concept to the theological enterprise generally.[72]

Concluding Observations

The *witness of the Spirit* is explicitly taught by Paul in Rom 8:14–16, "For all who are led by the Spirit of God are the sons of God. For you did not receive the spirit of slavery leading again to fear, but you received the Spirit of adoption, by whom we cry, "Abba, Father." The Spirit himself bears witness to our spirit that we are God's children." The apostle John likewise states, "By this we know that we reside in God and he in us: in that he has given us of his Spirit" (1 John 4:13) The Protestant tradition has consistently affirmed in principle the doctrine of the witness of the Spirit, yet the explanation and implications of the doctrine have been widely misunderstood. As this brief survey has shown, the concept of the Spirit's direct work on the heart of the individual has always been recognized, although the Puritans would withhold that evidence until later in one's spiritual life as one achieved maturity.

As I observe conservative evangelicalism today I find a curious situation. With reference to the Spirit's witness to the word, in our doctrine of canon the concept is conspicuous by its absence. A number of years ago I wrote an article entitled, "Evangelicals and the Canon of the New Testament."[73] In that article I argued for a recognition of the place that the Spirit plays in our certainty as to the shape of the canon. One reviewer rejected out of hand the whole line of argument as being subjective. Another individual commented, "How does this differ from the Mormon's burning in the bosom?" What neither reviewer seemed to grasp was that my argument was simply a plea for a return to the historic Protestant position with reference to our doctrine of canon.

As we turn our attention to the doctrine of the *witness of the Spirit* in salvation we are again faced with a curious situation. One debate that has continued for years within the Evangelical Theological Society is that of Lordship Salvation. Those associated with the free grace position consistently deny that the witness of the Spirit is an experience in the heart of the believer.[74] However, many of those who assert the Lordship position also deny in a very practical sense the vitality of the Spirit's immediate witness and deny that certainty of salvation is possible in this life. Instead they propose a contemporary version of the *practical syllogism* as the only means of knowledge that one is in fact saved.[75]

These incidents are, I believe, illustrative of the rationalism that has infected our circle of evangelicalism. We have seen abuses of the subjective and experiential. These abuses have elicited a reaction, not just against the abuses themselves but also against the foundations out of which the abuses arose. This reaction has had the effect of squeezing the Holy Spirit out of his rightful place in the life of believer and in the Church.

The Ministry of the Spirit in Discerning the Will of God

J. I. Packer

The Holy Spirit is given to all Christians to transform them by his teaching, making them into God-focused thinkers and equipping them to discern his will and make decisions accordingly. They do this by rational reflection on their life-situation, helped by wise and godly advice, within the parameters that the Word of God establishes. The idea that the superior path in matters of guidance is to wait passively before God for direct promptings to action to come into one's mind is a mistake. So is the superstitious notion that failure to discern the specifics of God's vocational guidance sentences one irrevocably to a second-best life, with no restoration possible.

In the English-speaking Western evangelical world the words "guidance" and "will of God" have become labels for a pastoral problem that has come to loom large in public discussion, because for many believers it has been a source of intense personal anxiety. This problem has the shape of an ellipse with two foci. Focus one is the question of the God-pleasing way to make decisions, particularly about such major matters as whom to marry, where to live, what career to follow, how many children to plan for, what church to join, and so on. There is agreement that God's guidance should be sought in making decisions, but uncertainty as to how one does this. Focus two is the question of how we should deal with inward impressions, suggestions, promptings and urges that come to us unbidden, sometimes as we try to work our way through problems of decision, sometimes, it seems, as we try to evade them, and sometimes, as we say, out of the blue. Evangelicals are aware that these impressions might be the voice of God, and also that they might not; so how may we tell whether promptings we feel are products of our own disordered imagination (wishful thinking or obsessive fear), or Satanic proposal, like the ideas put into Jesus' mind in the wilderness temptation, or monitions from God on which we should act? On this two-pronged problem of discerning the will of God at least three dozen books[1] have been written at a popular level during the past half-century, and the fact that they have all found buyers shows how widespread concern about this matter has become.

The present essay aims to explore the ministry of God's Holy Spirit in relation to this problem. In light of all that has been written on it already I do not think I shall be found saying anything notably new. But I shall attempt to demonstrate that the problem is regularly discussed in too narrow terms, isolating it from God's total ministry to his Church on earth in a way that is biblically improper, and that makes it both more difficult in itself, and more threatening to sensitive souls, than ever it ought to be. If I can show this, the labor of composition will be well worthwhile.

I open my argument with some general observations on the transforming and enlarging of personal consciousness and individual experience that the ministry of the Holy Spirit in the human heart brings about. This is basic to every mode of spiritual discernment, and every quest for it.

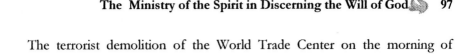

The terrorist demolition of the World Trade Center on the morning of September 11, 2001, has led many to speak of it, with good reason, as a day that changed the world. But there was another day that changed the world, in a much deeper and more far-reaching way: that was Pentecost morning in the year 30 or thereabouts, when shortly before nine o'clock Jesus of Nazareth, God's glorified and enthroned Christ and the world's cosmic Lord, poured out the Holy Spirit on his disciples gathered in Jerusalem (Acts 2:1–41). For it was then that the new covenant ministry of the divine Spirit was initiated, and that ministry—maybe I should say, the Church in the power of that ministry—has done more to change the world than any other force since history began.

Jesus, as recorded in John's Gospel, had already declared what this new ministry would involve. It would not be the world's first acquaintance with the Spirit of God, who had already (so the Old Testament tells us) been active in creation, providence, revelation, gifting for leadership, and renewing of hearts. But this would be the opening of a new era, all the same, with the Spirit adding a new role to the work he was doing already. Jesus would send the Spirit as "another Paraclete" (Helper, Supporter, Counselor, Comforter, Encourager, Advocate—παράκλητος [*parakletos*] has a wider range of meaning than any one English word can cover), to be not just "with" but "in" his disciples for ever (14:16–17). Through his coming Jesus himself, now absent in body, and his Father with him, would come and reveal themselves to disciples in a personal and permanent way, in a communion of love (14:18–23). As teacher, the Spirit would enable the apostles to recall and grasp what they had heard from Jesus, and would add more to it (14:26; 15:26; 16:13). Thus the apostles would come to see the full truth about Jesus' glory (16:14) and so be qualified to bear faithful witness to him (15:27). Then through that witness the Spirit would convince people everywhere of the Christian facts (16:8–11; 17:20) and bring them through new birth to the living faith in Christ that marks entry here and now into God's kingdom (3:1–15). Hereby the Spirit would engender in life after life the joy and influence that Jesus pictured as "living water" in flow out of the believer as a temple of God (7:37-39, cf. 4:10–14; Ezek 47:1–5).

In this is foreshadowed all of Paul's presentation of the Spirit's ministry to individuals (illumination, incorporation into Christ, certification, jubilation, moral transformation, final glorification: see 2 Cor 3:14–4:6, cf. 1 Cor 2:9–15; 1 Cor

12:13, cf. Rom 8:9–13; Rom 8:14–17, cf. Gal 4:4–6; Eph 1:13–14; Rom 14:17, cf. 15:13; Gal 5:22–25; 2 Cor 3:18). And what is said here also anticipates both Paul's further teaching about the Spirit's ministry to the Church (incorporating and indwelling, gifting and upbuilding: see 1 Cor 3:16; 12:6–31; Eph 2:19–22; 4:4–16), and Luke's fascinating and fascinated narrative in Acts of the Spirit's initiating and empowering activities in the Church's first generation. The New Testament view, first to last, is that since Pentecost the Holy Spirit, as the executive of the Trinity and Jesus' personal agent, has been constantly at work forming the new human family, which is the Church, by re-making sinners in and through Christ in the manner described. Ministry of the gospel is new covenant ministry, and new covenant ministry communicates the life-giving Spirit to this effect (2 Cor 3:6).

Now all that has been said above has experiential implications that revolutionize the workings of our minds. Paul signals this when he writes:

> [Christ] died for all so that those who live should no longer live for themselves but for him who died for them and was raised. So then from now on we acknowledge no one from an outward human point of view. Even though we have known Christ from such a human point of view, now we do not know him in that way any longer. So then, if anyone is in Christ, he is a new creation; what is old has passed away—look, what is new has come! (2 Cor 5:15–17)

We hear much today of altered states of consciousness induced by new age techniques of meditation; it would be well if more attention were paid to the altered state of mind into which new creation by the Spirit brings believers. This new consciousness begins as a permanent pervasive awareness of the inescapable reality, heart-searching presence, and saving love of our holy sovereign God, with a sense that we ought to pray to him, live to him, and seek to please him in all that we do, and at every turn of the road. Then, within this basic framework, Paul speaks directly of "the renewal of your mind." He does this in a truly foundational statement about discerning the will of God. That statement runs as follows.

> Therefore I exhort you, brothers and sisters, by the mercies of God, to present your bodies as a sacrifice—alive, holy, and pleasing to God—which is your reasonable service. Do not be conformed to this present world, but be transformed by the renewing of your mind, so that you

may test and approve what is the will of God—what is good and well-pleasing and perfect. (Rom 12:1-2)

"The mercies of God," in this passage, are the blessings to previously lost sinners that Rom 1–11 has been spelling out. "Bodies" are the readers' whole selves. "Holy" means dedicated by man and accepted by God. "Spiritual worship" (so RSV, ESV; NET, KJV, etc. have "reasonable service" here) is the life of God-glorifying homage that we owe to our divine Rescuer, history's mighty Lord, the God of the doxology of Rom 11:33–36. "Conformed to" means shaped by, and "this present world" means the existing order of things (culture, heritage, conventions, assumptions, expectations). "Transformed," the verb from which comes our word "metamorphosis," means changed in both outward style and inward character; it is the verb Paul used in 2 Cor 3:18, where the KJV's "changed form glory to glory" renders exactly what he wrote. "Don't let the world around you squeeze you into its own mould, but let God re-mould your minds from within," was J. B. Phillips' luminous rendering of what verse 2 is saying. "Mind" (νοῦς, *nous*) here signifies all that the Bible means by "heart": namely, the dynamic core of our personhood out of which flow the desires, instincts, tastes, loves, and fears that determine our goals, purposes, mindsets, plans, attitudes, aversions, schemes, excitements, boredoms, and so forth. This is mind, not just as a power of reasoning, but as an index of character. "Test and approve" precisely translates a Greek verb for which English has no one-word equivalent. The "will of God" is what will please him for each person to do in each situation (that is the thought that the words "good" and "well pleasing" and "perfect" are underlining). We are to discern God's will for our actions by *testing* (that is, thinking through and comparing) the options and alternatives that are open to us. What Paul sees, and tells us, is that only those whose minds have been re-made by the Holy Spirit thorough one-time regeneration leading to ongoing sanctification will be able to make this discernment adequately. The verbs in verse 2 are in the present tense, signifying continuous or repeated action: the renewal of our mind is to be a continuous process, and the discerning of God's will is a task to be repeated whenever fresh choices need to be made.

But without this renewal, no matter how much thinking we do, and however correct our theological formulations, personal discernment of the will of God will not take place. For the will of God covers not only what we do outwardly as performers, but also how and why we do it from the standpoint of our motives and purposes. If these inner aspects of action are not as they should be we fall short of the *perfect* (that is, in the Greek, the fully-fashioned and complete) *will of God*, as did the Pharisees in Jesus' day. Those who are not yet new-created in Christ and indwelt by his Spirit can neither conceive nor achieve the attitudinal rightness (love to God and neighbor: Matt 22:34–40) and the motivational rightness (the "glory," that is, the display and praise of God: 1 Cor 10:31) that make behavior acceptable in God's sight. This is because, to cite Phillips' paraphrase again,

> the unspiritual man simply cannot accept the matters which the Spirit deals with—they don't make sense to him, for, after all, you must be spiritual to see spiritual things. The spiritual man, on the other hand, has an insight into the meaning of everything, though his insight may baffle the man of the world...we who are spiritual have the very thoughts of Christ! (1 Cor 2:14–16).

"Thoughts" there is *mind* in the Greek, the same word as in Rom 12:2, meaning thoughts shaped and driven by desires of the heart. When in regeneration the Holy Spirit unites us to the risen Christ, our hearts are remade in the image of his, so that we too, like him in the divine-human unity of his personhood, constantly desire to love and obey and please and honor and exalt and glorify the Father. Accordingly, in our Christian lives we will be dominated and driven (and if we misbehave, accused) by this overmastering, ineradicable desire, that the Spirit has planted within us. And our thoughts, like Jesus' own, will embody and express this purpose, and enlist all our creativity and power of imagination and relational capacities in its service. So to live is now our nature. Our blind eyes have been opened, our deaf ears unstopped, and we have tasted the good word of God; our hard hearts have been softened, and our hostility to God's law (that is, his across-the-board instruction on how to please him) has been turned into a love of it. We are conscious of being people who now know God and are known by him in a life-giving relationship. We are new and different creatures, responding to God and reacting to people and things in a new way that was not part of our lives before. In a word, our experience has been changed. And it is out of this decisive experiential transformation, through the present help of the indwelling Holy Spirit, that discernment of the will of God in each specific case is born.

The Holy Spirit and the Path of Discernment

The gnawing evangelical anxieties about guidance that the three-dozen books mentioned above are addressing did not enter into the practice of discernment for decision-making among evangelicals of the older school. Informed by biblical theology and narrative, soaked in the biblical text itself, aiming always at the best for God's cause and others' good, and confident in God's promise of guidance to the humble and prayerful (see Pss 5:8; 23:2–3; 25:8–9; 32:8–9; Jas 1:6), they sought to be made wise, prudent, and judicious, men and women of good judgment. They asked that God would thus enable them to see each time the course of action for which there was most to be said as they reviewed facts, took advice, measured their personal resources, surveyed circumstances, and calculated the consequences of possible choices. Bruce Waltke models this older practice when he writes:

> When I wonder about which job offer to take, I don't go through a divination process to discover the hidden message of God. Instead I examine how God has called me to live my life; what my motives are; what He has given me a heart for; where I am in my walk with Christ; and what God is saying to me through Hs word and His people.[2]

There are in this, to be sure, pitfalls, all the direct result of being the sin-spoiled creatures that we are, immature, prejudiced, out-of-shape, and as yet imperfectly sanctified. We need to be aware of how choices may go wrong.

Our understanding of scripture can be incomplete and twisted, particularly when we live in anti-theological and pagan cultures and belong to churches that, for whatever reason, do not preach and teach the entire Bible.

What we think of as our godly desires, which may indeed have their roots in the prompting of the Holy Spirit, can nonetheless be self-centered, self-serving, and self-indulgent to a far greater extent than in our naïve self-ignorance we suspect. Zeal for God, however intense, is no substitute for self-knowledge, and lack of self-knowledge can lead into fanatical craziness.

Our ability to measure our own gifts and potential constantly proves deficient, the more so the younger and more inexperienced we are. Either we undervalue what we can do, feeling that something is beyond us when in fact we could handle it well, or we overvalue our powers, assuming (for example) that because we can talk steadily for long periods we must have a teaching or preaching gift. (Let it clearly be said: no one has a teaching gift unless people actually learn something from him, nor has anyone a preaching gift unless people actually meet God under his ministry.) And it is regularly beyond the power of consciously gifted people to tell whether they have the character qualities needed to sustain their gifts in useful exercise.

Awareness of the reality of these pitfalls burns into the mind the need to distrust emotionally-charged impressions and to take advice from those we recognize as wise, tough-minded, and godly, and most importantly from persons who know us well. The Holy Spirit regularly guides us in discernment for decision-making via the judgments of others.

A case study of decision-making in the life of a great evangelical of the old school, the Englishman John Charles Ryle (1816–1900), expository preacher and writer, evangelical leader, and first bishop of the diocese of Liverpool, will bring some of this into focus.[3]

Ryle's father's bank suddenly went bankrupt in 1841, when Ryle was 25, headed for public life, and a converted Christian of four years' standing. Reared in the lap of luxury, he now found himself virtually penniless. He sought ordination, not because he wanted to be a clergyman (he didn't) or felt an inner constraint to become one (he felt none), but because it was the only profession open to him that would give him an immediate salary. The evangelical bishop who was willing to ordain him saw his Oxford degree and lively Christian experience as adequately qualifying him for the clergyman's role. (This, then, was a decision based on Ryle's circumstances and a bishop's judgment of his fitness.) Having won his spurs as a minister in two brief underpaid posts, Ryle accepted an invitation to a rural pastorate with a stipend sufficient for a married man, and there wooed the first, followed after her death by the second, of his three wives. His guiding light here was to choose as a spouse someone he could thoroughly respect: *"the great thing I always desired to find was a woman who was a real Christian, who was a real lady, and who was not a fool."*[4] His actual discernment, as he applied this principle of wisdom, did not fail him, but the bad health of both his first and second wives drained his resources, and fifteen years after his first marriage he found himself a widower with five children, and a poor man once more. (Good decisions do not always bring the good consequences that we hope for.) A move to a larger, better paying parish and a third marriage led to nineteen years of happy and fruitful ministry there. This however was eventually interrupted, early in 1880, by the invitation to become dean of the cathedral at Salisbury, presumably as a light and honorific job for his old age (he was almost 64), and so a new decision had to be made.

He did not want to go.

> Flesh and blood were utterly against it [he wrote to a friend]. But *almost* every one of 16 men I consulted said, "You ought certainly to go for the sake of Christ's cause in the Ch(urch) of E(ngland)."—So who was I that I could withstand? I had prayed for light and signs of God's will, and this was all I got. If three men had said "Refuse," I would have refused...But...I am a soldier. The Captain of my salvation seems to say, "these are your marching orders." I have nothing to do but to *obey*. Pray for me. My heart is very heavy.[5]

So, discerning from advice received what he ought to do, though against his own desire, he told his people he was leaving them, and got ready to move. But then, within weeks, out of the blue, and requiring immediate decision for political reasons, came the call to Liverpool. To that call Ryle, having already adjusted to leaving the place he liked most, was able to say a responsible "yes" on the spot— actually, on the platform where he had just dismounted from the train and been confronted for the first time with the offer. (This appears as two-stage circumstantial guidance: had God not first led Ryle to commit himself to leave his comfortable pastorate, he would have been in no position to utter that instant "yes." But as it was, he needed only a split-second comparing the depressing prospect of Salisbury with this new challenge, and his mind was made up.) Ryle thus, it would seem, concluded himself called by God to be Liverpool's first bishop. And over a period of twenty years, despite his age, he proved himself to be the man for the job, giving the diocese an infrastructure and personnel that made it the most evangelical in doctrine, and evangelistic in practice, anywhere in the Church of England.

Was Ryle led by the Holy Spirit in his discernments of the will of God? Surely he was. Were these discernments the product of inner voices or impressions, freak coincidences, private revelations, or any such thing? No; they were the rational fruit of having a biblical value-system and a heart for God, for his gospel and for his glory; and of seeking wisdom, noting circumstances, taking advice, and not letting the merely good elbow out the best. By these means the Holy Spirit gave Ryle discernment for his decisions, and we should expect that he will use the same means with the rest of us.

This is the moment for pointing out that God in the Old Testament, and Christ specifically in the New, are set forth as *shepherding* the holy flock and each individual within it (see Pss 23; 77:20; 78:52; 80:1; John 10:11–16, 25–30; Heb 13:20; 1 Pet 5:4). Shepherding means caring for, watching over, protecting and preserving, guarding and guiding the sheep as they feed and travel to their many places of pasture. Giving us discernment of his will is only part of the Shepherd's work ordering our lives as he leads us home to glory. The Father, the Son, and the Spirit shape our circumstances, overrule our advisers, and sustain our overall sense of spiritual realities and theological truths, as well as prompting the brainwork that processes the factors that yield the discernments needed for decisions. The idea that at some point in the decision-making we are left to fend for ourselves is a mistake, and a troublesome one, as we shall shortly see.

The Holy Spirit and Defects in Discernment

How is it then that in this matter of discerning the will of God errors get made? Well, how in God's world do human mistakes ever get made? Here we face, as so often, the mystery of created freedom in a world governed by its sovereign Maker and Master. This is a *both…and*, a state of things in which two seeming incompatibles coexist and it is beyond us to know how what is the case can be. It is a situation best labeled, in echo of Kant, an *antinomy*. The fact that we can and do err and sin does not overthrow God's controlling lordship, any more than that controlling lordship turns us into robots, destroying our self-determining individuality so that we are no longer moral agents answerable to God. This is how things are. So in every part of life intellectual and behavioral lapses actually occur; and we must not be surprised to meet them. We now examine two common mistakes relating to our Spirit-given discernment of the will of God: the first, about man's passivity, and the second, about God's plan.

(1) The error about man's passivity.

In the movement led by the magnetic Frank Buchman through the middle decades of the last century, which at various times was called Buchmanism, First Century Christian Fellowship, the Oxford Group, and Moral Re-Armament, it was the rule to have a daily "quiet time" in which one practiced what is nowadays called listening prayer. That is, one reviewed one's ongoing life before one's divine Watcher and noted what practical ideas about things to do and not to do, people to deal with, tasks to tackle and so forth, broke surface in one's mind. These thoughts, writes Garth Lean, "became known, in the verbal shorthand of Buchman and his friends, as 'guidance,' though neither he nor they considered that all such thoughts came from God."[6] To avoid potentially vicious self-deception, these thoughts were always to be tested by whether they embodied absolute honesty, purity, unselfishness, and love, whether they squared with the Church's teaching and experience and the mind of others seeking guidance this same way, and whether they were actually practicable. So far, so good; none of this is off center. But in the world of simplistic and somewhat loosey-goosey pietism where this practice was developed the thought-processes comparing alternatives that discernment ordinarily requires were not stressed. Expectations of immediacy in guidance became unhealthily high, while the mental passivity that was cultivated—the fallowness of the mind, as we might call it—led inevitably to an increasingly narrow and undoctrinal mindset, the outcome of which was Moral Re-Armament's drift into multifaith moralism to further its political agenda. This was not a fruitful way to go. Small wonder that Buchmanism is now a thing of the past.

But the legacy of this once influential movement seems to be fourfold:

First, it has given the word "guidance" universal label status among evangelicals for all that is involved in discerning the will of God. This continues.

Second, it has reinforced already widespread expectations of being admonished for action by a direct "word from the Lord," either through what Pentecostals describe as prophecy, or through a contrived sign ("putting out a fleece"), or through some striking factual coincidence or new notion springing from words of scripture, or through some private inner revelation by dream, voice, or intrusive thought. This also continues.

Third, it has encouraged a murky pride, elitism, and sense of superiority among those who have thought they were receiving, or had received, divine guidance in the supra-rational way that has just been outlined. This still appears.

Fourth, it has generated, and continues to generate, anxiety, depression, and paralysis of action in some who have sought guidance this way without receiving it, and now are either marking time as still they wait for it, or are blaming themselves for not seeking it seriously enough and viewing themselves as relegated to the ranks of second-class Christians—a form of anxiety and inner bleakness that links up with a further condition at which we shall look in a moment.

In saying this, and calling for appropriate brainwork to discern God's will, I do not mean to imply that only persons of high intelligence, trained minds, and academic excellence can hope to discern the will of God. Paul prays that God would fill the Colossians

> with the knowledge of his will in all spiritual wisdom and understanding, so that you may live worthily of the Lord and please him in all respects: bearing fruit in every good deed, growing in the knowledge of God (Col 1:9-10).

"Spiritual," the qualifier of wisdom and understanding, means precisely "given by the Holy Spirit," and the Spirit is no respecter of persons when it comes to education or brain power. In similar vein, Paul prays that the Philippians' love

> may abound even more and more in knowledge and every kind of insight so that you can decide what is best, and thus be sincere and blameless for the day of Christ, filled with the fruit of righteousness that comes through Jesus Christ to the glory and praise of God (Phil 1:9-11).

"Decide" here is the same word as "test and approve" in Rom 12:2. All Christians have minds, and they are not to be left lying fallow; all are to put the minds they have to work in the discernment process.

The nature of the brainwork involved is clear from James Petty's analysis of the Spirit's role in divine guidance.

1. The Spirit illuminates the connection between God's word and our lives.

2. He does this by personalizing and particularizing (applying) the will of God for us…

3. The result of the Spirit's work is not so much a "message from God" as it is a provision of "discernment and wisdom" granted for specific situations and progressively built into Christians as a character trait.

4. Though it is wisdom from God, it also becomes our wisdom…From God's perspective it is a direct gift, supernaturally given by the Spirit. From our perspective, it is our renewed mind enabled by God to see as Christ sees. It is our wisdom, yet it is God's. It is Christ's mind, yet it is given to us as ours. Scripture sees it both ways and so should we.[7]

Christians may not make rules for God. It is clear that on occasion God has bypassed reason, giving discernment of his will in a direct and immediate way, just as has been claimed, and it is not for us to deny that he may do so again. But God makes rules for Christians, and it is equally clear that we have no business expecting to discern his will save by Spirit-led reasoning in the manner described. The exception should not be mistaken for the rule. "Let your mind alone" (the title of one of James Thurber's extravaganzas) is not the way of wisdom for discerning God's will. Passivity of mind, valued and cherished, will keep us from spiritual discernment rather than lead us to it.

(2) The error about God's plan.[8]

That God has a comprehensive, foreordained purpose and plan for all of world history, form the greatest events to the smallest, and that this includes a specific, detailed intention for the life of every human being, is to my mind beyond doubt: the Bible is clear on it. That his intention, once you become a Christian, is comparable to an itinerary drawn up for you by a travel agent, where everything depends on you being in the right place at the right time to board the plane or train or bus or boat or whatever and where the itinerary is ruined once you miss one of the preplanned connections, is, by contrast, a sad misconception. It is, however, a common view, and has bitter implications. If, on this view, your discernment fails and you get your guidance wrong on some key matter, a substandard, second-best spiritual life is all that is open to you. Though not perhaps on the scrap heap, you are certainly on the shelf, having lost forever much of your usefulness to God. Your mistake sentences you to live and serve your Lord as a second-rate Christian.

What is wrong with this idea? Three things, at least.

First, it is a speculation—in plain English, a guess, a fancy, indeed a fantasy, and a morbid one at that. There is nothing in scripture to support it.

Second, it assumes that God lacks the wisdom or the will or the goodness or the power to put us back on track when we have slipped. But this is false, and to think otherwise is unbelief. The grain of truth in this view is that bad choices have bad consequences, from which we cannot expect to be totally shielded and with which, therefore, we may now have to live, as Jacob had to live with the limp he got fighting God at Jabbok and David had to live with the family troubles he brought on himself by his marital rovings. But the idea that God cannot or will not forgive and restore when transgressors and wanderers confess their follies and repent of them, flies in the face of scripture. Ponder the implications of Solomon's prayer in 1 Kgs 8:27–53, and 2 Chr 6:18–40, and the testimonies in Pss 32 and 85:1–3, the promise in 1 John 1:9, if you doubt that.

Third, this idea ignores clear lessons from Bible biography. Scripture shows us servants of God making great and grievous mistakes in seeking to discern God's will for their actions—Jacob beggaring his brother and fooling his father; Moses killing the Egyptian; David numbering the people; Peter boycotting Gentile Christians at the meal table, for instance—yet none was thereafter demoted to second-class status. And if God restored David after his adultery with Bathsheba and taking out of Uriah, and Peter after his threefold denial of Christ, we should not doubt his readiness to restore Christians who acknowledge that they failed badly in their endeavor, or perhaps by their reluctance, to discern the will of God.

The source of this mistake about God's plan appears to be a streak of legalism, linked it seems with classic dispensational theology, that found its way into evangelical teaching on the Christian life at the turn of the nineteenth century when dispensationalism was riding high and the older evangelical theology was at a discount. This was the era in which life-occupations were graded on a strict scale of value and desirability (first and best, overseas missionary; second, ordained pastor; third, physician and nurse; fourth, schoolteacher; fifth, money-maker to support evangelical enterprises, and so on), and holiness teachers proclaimed a double standard, urging that it was better, though not necessary, to choose to be a spiritual Christian rather than remain a carnal one. And much was made of Paul's warning that the "wood, hay, stubble" of the careless Christian's life would be incinerated in a "judgment of works"—"If anyone's work is burned up, he will suffer loss, but he himself will be saved, but only as through fire" (1 Cor 3:15). Most of this legalism is now defunct, and it is to be hoped that the frightening and really blasphemous mistake about the plan of God that we have been looking at will perish with it.

Last Word

Finally, it needs to be said that the ultimate purpose of God for every Christian is character-transformation and growth into the full image of Jesus Christ; and therefore that the Holy Spirit's work of imparting wisdom for the discerning of God's will, case by case, is part of that larger enterprise for which our sanctification is the usual name. What God wants for us is not simply a flow of correct discernments in the choices we make, but that we become discerning persons in ourselves, as Christ was a discerning person before us. "Wisdom in the Old Testament" writes Bruce Waltke, and in the New Testament this is equally the case, "is a character trait, not simply thinking soberly. People with wisdom have the character whereby they can make good decisions."[9] But the people with wisdom are those in whom the word of Christ dwells richly (see Col 3:16), and these are the people who heed the summons: "just as you received Christ Jesus as Lord, continue to live your lives in him, rooted and built up in him" (Col 2:6-7). He is the wisdom of God, the Lord of glory, the good shepherd, and his people's life and hope. So studying the Spirit's works in our discerning of God's will should bring us to the place where with Charles Wesley we sing:

> Captain of Israel's host, and Guide
>
> Of all who seek the land above,
>
> Beneath thy shadow we abide,
>
> The cloud of thy protecting love;
>
> Our strength, thy grace; our rule, thy word;
>
> Our end, the glory of the Lord.
>
> By thine unerring Spirit led,

> We shall not in the desert stray,
>
> We shall not full direction need,
>
> Nor miss our providential way;
>
> As far from danger as from fear,
>
> While love, almighty love, is near.

Let Wesley's lyric be the bottom line, and the last word, and the constant song of all our hearts.

The Spirit's Role in Corporate Worship

Timothy J. Ralston

The Holy Spirit assumes a vital role in Christian worship as the sign of God's work through Christ. The Spirit confirms God's covenant relationship, a prerequisite for acceptable worship. His presence creates the worship sanctuary, forming the bounds of its community and unifying its members. By convicting of sin, he ensures the integrity of the covenant worshipers and with his gifts he strengthens them to serve one another. Emphasizing the experience of the worshiper as the evidence of the Spirit depreciates his more significant functions, often leading to misunderstanding, pragmatism, narcissism and an idolatry of self rather than the worship of God.

Introduction

L isten to any circle of Christians talking about their church these days and one subject always comes up: worship.

That's good! Worship is a central emphasis of the Bible from Genesis to Revelation. Adam and Eve were commissioned to "serve" in the Garden, God's first sanctuary on the earth. The patriarchs marked their journeys by their devotion at God's altar. For forty years Israel used the tabernacle as its compass when marching and as the center for its bivouac. Once Israel had a king, Solomon's Temple became the perpetual reminder that God, not the king, had the preeminent place in the nation. Worship dominates the themes of joy and lament in Israel's Psalter, the prophets' indictments, the Old Testament summary to love God with our whole being (Luke 10:27), and the apostle Paul's description of sanctification (Rom 12:1). History's final response to Jesus (Phil 2:9-11), the visions of heaven's activities (Rev 4:1–5:14), and history's end (Rev 21:26) are filled with worship. It's the motive behind the Father's mission in the world (John 4:23). God created and redeemed us so that he might receive worship from his creation. Worship is the goal of God's work.

If the worship of God has been a priority for God's people, churches across America seem to have taken this emphasis seriously. Newspapers advertise "praise and worship" churches. Billboards invite passers-by to "dynamic," "contemporary," and "fresh" worship services, all of which are taken as evidence of "Spirit-filled" worship. Paul asserts that Christians "worship by the Spirit of God" (Phil 3:3) through whom our prayers ascend to the Father (Eph 2:18). It all sounds so biblical.

But what do *we* mean with these labels? Unfortunately, what they mean to the average Christian today is a *style* of worship, things like an "upbeat" tempo, extended periods of congregational singing, a service where we move from song to song with little or no break in the flow of the music, a strong rhythm (accentuated perhaps by clapping or physical movement in the congregation), more contemporary musical arrangements and accompaniment (keyboards, synthesizers, guitars, drums, etc.). To some it denotes a preference for one kind of music (short, memorable, simple words and tunes) over another (often classified as "stuffy old hymns" which use more traditional tunes or speak with more complex poetry filled with archaic language). Even those who object to defining the Holy Spirit's role in worship this way may still assume that when the Holy Spirit presides over corporate worship the worshipers will have greater exuberance and emotion, spontaneous or unplanned acts will occur in the service, or the service itself will proceed without a preplanned order.

Great danger lurks here. Popular descriptions are theological sandbars. They can shift our focus from God's inspired objective statements about his role in our worship to prejudices formed by the feelings aroused through a particular style of music or service. The Holy Spirit's role in corporate worship becomes a function of our response rather than an objective theological reality. We miss the more basic and important roles that the Holy Spirit assumes whenever God's people gather to worship. The Old Testament provides many examples of God's condemnation and rejection of worship that forgot or ignored his expectations. Even if we offer worship with the sincerest of motives, we overlook what God says at our peril.

Today we speak of individual worship (such as practiced in personal devotions) and corporate worship (such as we experience in a church "worship service"). This distinction is relatively new among Christians. Biblically and historically, personal acts of worship were merely one end of the spectrum; corporate acts of worship at the other. So-called "personal" worship was but a stepping-stone to worship offered within the gathered community of God's people. Personal worship was insufficient in itself to honor God as he desired. In the early centuries of the Church an overemphasis on personal (or "private") worship was considered characteristic of the heresy of Gnosticism! But the importance and characteristics of corporate worship are no longer widely understood, assumed, or even taught today among American evangelical Christians. It's time to recover the significance of corporate worship and a biblical understanding of the superintending ministries of the Holy Spirit within it.

Worship, the Covenant, and the Spirit

Any discussion of corporate worship must start with a prerequisite taught by both Old and New Testaments: God only accepts worship offered within a covenant framework. Any legitimate definition of worship that aspires to be biblical must first acknowledge that worship is defined as a celebration of one's covenant relationship with the Holy Lord God. The term "covenant" simply describes an explicit relationship between two parties, in this case God and human beings. The relationship has clearly defined prerequisites and commitments. Sometimes both parties to the covenant must keep all the commitments for the covenant to remain in force (a "conditional" covenant) while at other times God promises to uphold the covenant with no mention being made of the other party's responsibilities (an "unconditional" or unilateral covenant).

Regardless of the nature of the covenant, the biblical words translated "worship" assume this prerequisite. Unlike the ever-popular English etymology of worship from "worth-ship"—ascribing worth to another—the Bible's own language presents a more complex picture which for convenience can be organized in three word-groups. The first word-group, the Hebrew *hishtakhavah* (השתחוה) and the Greek *proskuneō* (προσκυνέω), stresses submission to another. Translated by the term "worship" in our English Bibles, they describe "bowing down" or falling prostrate before another who is worshiped. This represents an ancient way of showing one's vulnerability and, therefore, submission to the one worshiped. Like other terms for obeisance, "worship" assumes that a relationship exists (or perhaps is sought) with a greater individual. Those who bow down, whether by choice (freely submitting) or by force (defeat by the other), indicate their acknowledged responsibility to live by the superior's will. When I worship, I am consciously stating to God that he is in control of all things that relate to my life.

A second larger word-group presents worship as service or obedience to another. It often has with priestly overtones: '*bad* (עבד), *latreuō* (λατρεύω), and *leitourgeō* (λειτουργέω) from which we get our English term liturgy. In each case the worshiper performs what God asks of him or her. Worship as service grows directly from worship as submission. If I submit to another's rule, then I am responsible to fulfill the wishes of the one I worship. Here we begin to see the unity between worship as "lifestyle" and worship as "praise" for both are ways in which I am doing what God asks of me. Paul calls our daily "living sacrifice" a *latreia* (λατρεία) or service to God (Rom 12:1). Similarly the more general term, godliness or *eusebeia* (εὐσέβεια), derived from the more specific worship term, *sebomai* (σέβομαι), stresses how one honors the deity in all things. Therefore, how I fulfill God's desires for my life in every aspect, fulfill my responsibilities as outlined in the covenant he has made with me, and remain in a right relationship with him is "worship." All of life reflects my worship of God. Hence, these two biblical word-groups for worship assume and stress a covenant relationship with God, both in submission (obeisance to God's will) and in service (obedience to God's commands).

The third word-group is often overlooked in worship studies: "remember." The Old Testament Hebrew word *zakar* (זכר) focused on God's promises for his people in their worship—the inauguration, obligations, continuing benefits, and future consummation of the covenant. Every festival, sacrifice, and memorial designed to promote the worship of God was instituted as a "memorial." "To remember" invoked the existence of a binding covenant, calling all to recognize and fulfill their responsibilities, joining with all who ever participated in the same covenant as a single community under God's rule. Passover was Israel's quintessential act of "remembering" (cf. Exod 12:14; 13:3, 9). It repeatedly affirmed God's unique act of covenant whereby he created Israel as a distinct people for himself (cf., e.g., Lev 11:45; 26:45; 2 Sam 7:23; Hos 11:1; cf. Matt 2:15). Jesus used the corresponding Greek term, *mimnēskomai* (μιμνήσκομαι) to describe the role of the cup within the Lord's Supper as the inauguration of the [new] covenant (Matt 26:28; Mark 14:24; Luke 22:20; 1 Cor 11:25). Consequently gathering around the bread and cup quickly became a defining purpose for Christians gathered to worship (Acts 2:42; 20:7; 1 Cor 11:17–34).

Why the Spirit in this discussion of covenant? Since Jesus Christ's ascension the Holy Spirit defines the scope of the covenant inaugurated by Christ and our participation in that covenant. He is the promissory note of God's covenant with humanity in this age (John 16:7–14; Eph 1:13–14). He takes up his residence in the believer at the moment of conversion (1 Cor 12:13). His indwelling presence, therefore, defines who is a member of Christ's Church, God's covenant community. He marks those individuals in the covenant through faith in Jesus Christ. The indwelling Holy Spirit is its sign and its seal. Corporate worship can only be offered to God by those who have an explicit relationship with God, evidenced by the Spirit's presence.

Beyond mere word-groups, God's stated priorities for and judgments of the Old Testament worshiper stress the relational basis of worship. God expected conformity to his covenant and only accepted worship from those who understood and wholeheartedly obeyed the requirements of the covenant he had made with them. God decreed that Israel gather to worship him "in the place that he would choose" and by the means he had dictated as part of the covenant (cf. Deut 12:5, 11, 14, 18, 26; 14:23, 24; 15:20; 16:2, 6, 7, 11, 15, 16; 17:8, 10; 18:6; 26:2; 31:11). No other site or means was acceptable to him, only that demanded by his covenant with his people. Further, the worshipers were living as God asked. They were fulfilling their role in the covenant or, as we say, they had a right standing within the covenant relationship. Their lives were marked by integrity within the covenant.

In such a relationship each party was well known to the other. Therefore, God rejected worship offered with a false view of God. Although their makers presented them as Israel's God, God rejected the golden calf of Aaron (Exod 32:1–10) and those of Jeroboam (1 Kgs 12:25–33; 13:1–3). He characterized such worship as that given to "demons" (Deut 32:15–18; Ps 78:54–64; Jer 23:13–15; Ezek 8:1–15). God did not give a worshiper "the benefit of the doubt" due to ignorance or graciously "change the address" of the offering, even if it only represented a less than proper understanding of who he is. Further, God rejected all corporate worship offered contrary to his demand including, for example, defective sacrificial animals (Mal 1:6–14) or blood offerings involving human beings (Ezek 8:16–18). He demanded that whatever was offered be exactly and only what he required. He rejected all worship offered without regard for personal sin. A violation of the covenant showed the absence of wholehearted submission and, therefore, disqualified any statement of "submission." Worship without concern for God's revealed pattern or offered without regard for personal integrity (holiness) and humility demonstrated a worshiper's failure to take seriously the person of God and the stipulations of a right relationship with him. Therefore, God coveted obedience above all (1 Sam 15:22–23; Pss 40:4–8; 51:16–17) and rejected the worship of the rebellious (Jer 23:10–12; Mic 6:6–8; Mal 2:13–17), worship offered with a wrong motive (such as Cain's self-centeredness shown by his reaction to God's acceptance of Abel (Gen 4:3–7), Saul's disobedient sacrifice to feed his own self-importance (1 Sam 15:3, 9, 12–15), or Israel's use of sacrifice as a divine bribe to preserve their self-indulgence (Isa 1:1–31). The Old Testament prophets proclaimed God's rejection of worship offered on "autopilot," dependent on the execution of the form alone for its spiritual value without any thought to one's integrity in the covenant requirements (Joel 6:20; 7:16–28; 14:14; Amos 4:4–5; 5:21–27). God expected his worshipers to be consumed by an attitude of integrity and the act of obedience.

Things don't change in the New Testament. Jesus criticized his contemporaries for their failure to fulfill God's requirements before worshiping (e.g., Matt 5:21–24; 6:1–24). To the Samaritan woman he defined New Testament worship as offered "in spirit and truth" (John 4:24). "In truth" describes the objective prerequisite of conformity to the revelation of God for humanity in worship (his holiness as the one true God and how he has revealed that he is to be worshiped). "In spirit" denotes the subjective prerequisite: the integrity and sincerity required of every worshiper. (John may intend a *double entendre here.* Jesus' use of "spirit" may include the work of the Holy Spirit, but the grammar of the passage and the explicit definition where the term is used elsewhere in John's Gospel leads most interpreters to construe the expression as a reference to the Holy Spirit in a secondary sense for the term here.) The author of Hebrews emphasized the same (Heb 10:5–7). Consequently both Old and New Testaments agree that God only accepts worship offered by a humble, committed servant under his covenant, a covenant that is qualified by the Holy Spirit's presence in our lives and in our worship.

Unfortunately many modern Christians have lost sight of this. While it's true that "Everyone can know God" (that is, the knowledge of God is accessible to anyone who genuinely seeks him), people conclude that "Anyone can worship God" (that is, God accepts worship offered by any person regardless of their spiritual status). This logic is flawed. It ignores the covenant prerequisite of worship. It also ignores the nature of relationship. Consider an analogy from modern media. You've watched a television program, have an emotional connection with the show, and think you know the actors. You may even believe you have a relationship with one of them (as some overzealous fans actually do). But try to get personally involved with them and you'll be very disappointed. First, they don't know you or have any reason to want to engage with you. There has been no basis for friendship. Second, they don't want you to relate to them as the characters they portray because it's not who they really are. They don't want friendship based on your ignorance or misperception. So chances are they will not receive your overtures. Similarly God isn't interested in the relationship assumed by corporate worship if it isn't true to what he really is or isn't made by someone with whom he has already established a covenant basis for the relationship. For the world today corporate worship that is acceptable to God demands the presence of the Spirit of God as the evidence of a relationship with God.

Worship, Community, and the Spirit

We've established the prerequisite of covenant to corporate worship. In the New Testament the presence of the Holy Spirit seals the covenant with the worshipers. The Holy Spirit's second function in worship is his creation of the worshiping community. Biblical covenants always involve a group. God redeems individuals, but his redemptive goal is the creation of a people, a community.

In the Old Testament God acted as he had promised, redeemed his people, and then brought them together into a community of persons in the covenant (Ps 106:4; Isa 11:12). For an Israelite to be judged by God took the form of isolation from the community. Individuals were sent out to be alone. People groups were dispersed. Those judged were now unable to gather for the worship God had stipulated. This explains in part the agonies of the Old Testament psalmist suffering in his solitude and isolation and provides the theological matrix behind "excommunication" as isolation from the church community, an extreme discipline in the New Testament.

By contrast every Israelite re-experienced community through the annual memorial "remembrances" of their covenant. "Remembrance" in the Old Testament spoke of the unity of all Israel in covenant. These remembrances proclaimed the unity of those under the covenant. This transcended the limitations of time and space. The covenant participants were re-united by each memorial celebration of the covenant. The Old Testament experience of unity was designed around geography. The covenant participants came together for these festivals, enjoying social proximity (as in themes of the ascent Psalms, particularly 122 and 133, sung at such festivals). In time Jerusalem became the single acceptable "high place" where the nation reemphasized its spiritual center. Even today these festival celebrations emphasize the unity of the Jewish community despite its worldwide dispersion.

For Christians this experience of community becomes reality through the Holy Spirit indwelling each covenant member. He unites believers into a single people, the community of Christ. At one level the Spirit connects the members of a local congregation together into a functioning whole. At a higher level he connects all believers, both as individuals and local communities to all others everywhere. He erases the separation of space and geography between each congregation. At the highest level the same Spirit bonds those who have been divided from the earthly community by death with their brothers and sisters yet living on the earth. He brings the Church scattered throughout time and space into an organic whole. His presence in our worship affirms that we are not alone. We become joined with a people that spans the globe and transcends time. In an age when God's covenant with humanity extends beyond the Old Testament ethnic and geographic boundaries of Israel, only the Holy Spirit makes "corporate" worship possible. Therefore, for those living in the light of the New Covenant, corporate worship that is acceptable to God assumes a covenant community that has been created and qualified by the Holy Spirit.

Worship, the Sanctuary, and the Spirit

The concept of community underlies a third aspect of the Spirit's role in corporate worship. In the Old Testament the Spirit's presence defined the "sanctuary" where God chose to set his throne. This location on the earth denoted the center of his community and his rule. During Israel's time this term applied to both the Tabernacle (e.g., Exod 25:8) and the Temple (e.g., 1 Chr 22:19). They served as God's "royal palace," the Holy Place as his "throne room," and the Ark of Covenant as his "throne." The overwhelming presence of the Spirit upon these structures at their completion affirmed their role (Exod 40:34–38; 2 Chr 5:13–14). (This foreshadows the New Testament's treatment of Old Testament priestly figures of Jesus Christ. When God's sanctuary is identified, its priest becomes paradigmatic for Christ. The first Adam "serves" the garden sanctuary as priest of the creation. Melchizedek is designated priest of Jerusalem, the city built on the sanctuary mount to which God directed Abraham and which was later designated as God's Zion sanctuary. The Aaronic priesthood, the most explicit symbol, serves the Tabernacle and Temple sanctuaries.)

Since the Holy Spirit indwells individual human beings today, Paul applies the concept of "temple" to individuals (2 Cor 6:14–18) and to the Christian community as a whole (1 Cor 3:16–17). Whenever believers gather in community, they form the earthly sanctuary in which God's rule is manifested and God's sacrifices are offered. The Spirit's presence in believers defines the boundaries of the true sanctuary by defining the worshiping community.

Very early on, Christians recognized this unique work of the Holy Spirit. Jesus' command to "remember" was instrumental in forming this theology. Used at the Last Supper, he invoked the Old Testament understanding of a covenant, its exclusive demands, and the fidelity of both parties. The celebration of this meal became central to Christian worship. Described as the "breaking of bread" in Acts (2:42; 20:7), the Eucharist became a focal point for corporate worship and soon functioned as the central act of Christian assembly. (Note the purpose statements in Acts 20:7 and 1 Cor 11:17–20, 33.) Christian and non-Christian sources from the first three centuries record Christians' weekly gatherings around two acts: the reading of the scriptures and the celebration of the Lord's Supper. Participation separated those in the church from those outside the holy community, a "eucharistic" community whose corporate identity was defined by the Lord's Supper. From earliest records through the Reformation we know of no Sunday—over 1500 years!—in which the Lord's Supper was not celebrated. Attendance in its weekly observance was obligatory even in times of extreme persecution. Like the synagogue, Christian communities took great care to identify those who were members of the covenant community through faith in Christ from those who only "observed" (whether unbelievers or not yet baptized). Before the observance of this rite the church publicly dismissed the unbaptized. They had not yet expressed unqualified faith in Christ in order to receive the promised Holy Spirit and were not considered members of the covenant. They were not allowed to participate in the community rite. Similarly, baptized believers under church discipline or involved in a time of penance were excluded. From the beginning, Christians took seriously the Holy Spirit's role as the definer of the sanctuary (the true worshiping community) and the validator of its offering.

Worship, Unity, and the Spirit

A fourth major consideration of the Holy Spirit's work in corporate worship extends from the preceding concepts of covenant, community, and sanctuary: he alone, the unique, active agent, fosters *functional* unity among the worshiping community. "Unity" refers to believers' common twofold allegiance: the Lordship of Christ over the community and relational harmony within the community. This commitment to unity is both a cognitive-volitional function that values being a harmonious whole and a practical expression of unity that wholeheartedly supports each despite our differences. It does not demand conformity or uniformity in thought or practice (as helpful as these might seem). The Old Testament prophets defined "righteousness" in relational terms. The Proverbs described "wisdom" within community functions. The New Testament presents "unity" as the complex of right relationships in the community. The significance of God's community transcends legitimate differences between individuals and even cultures. Consider spiritual gifts in the New Testament. Besides the biblical diversity of the gifts themselves, their expressions can be nuanced by cultural frameworks (i.e., ways in which one teaches another) and personality (i.e., extroverted or reflective styles). Yet all promote growth toward the corporate unity (Eph 4:11–16).

The Holy Spirit establishes the Church's unity ontologically because of his indwelling, defining the members of Christ's community. The expression of his ministry becomes the functional unity experienced between believers (1 Cor 12:4, 13; Eph 2:22; 4:3, 13; Phil 1:27) to complete the witness of Christ in the world (John 17:21–23).

Why unity? The first statements of unity among humanity represent a rebellion against God's order and rule. So God destroyed all life with a cataclysmic flood (Gen 6–9). Later at Babel God foresaw that the impulses and achievements of a sinful, unified humanity would only produce a similar rebellion against God's rule (Gen 8:21) requiring the same judgment. God thwarted humanity's unlimited capacity for rebellion by inaugurating linguistic divisions (Gen 11:1–9). These subgroups scattered over the earth as God had planned. Over time these geographical, racial, and cultural distinctions prevented humanity from achieving such unity again.

The Bible's vision, however, includes humanity's reunification once the problem of sin is eliminated. Through Christ believers have received the Spirit who provides the means to control the inborn selfishness and self-confidence ("flesh") that makes one vulnerable to rebellion against God (sin). God's people demonstrate the anticipated unity of God's people in the age to come. Corporate worship represents a radical, future-oriented ("eschatological") act. The unity of the worshiping church becomes a foretaste of the coming age when Jesus Christ rules over all and Christian unity brought through the Spirit becomes the primary evidence of Jesus Christ's deity and the credibility of God's promises through him (John 17:21–23).

This witness directly impacts corporate worship. Covenant fellowship in both Old and New Testaments finds its expression in eating together. Here the Lord's Supper presents a beautiful picture of setting aside our differences in obedience to God's rule. Consequently relational sins in the community invalidate the worship offered by the group (as Paul notes in 1 Cor 11:20). Acts of disunity contradict the testimony presented by eating together. It disregards God's mandate for the Church. It denies his eschatological goal. The hypocrisy of eating when we are divided by conflict brings the Spirit's judgment—sickness and death—upon the community, since all the members participate in the meal (1 Cor 11:30). Breaching the unity of the community through divisive talk or actions "grieves" the Spirit (Eph 5:29–32). The unity of believers under the rule and direction of the Holy Spirit functions as a prerequisite for the corporate worship that God accepts. It shows our submission to the Holy Spirit's work and our integrity under the new covenant. Without functional unity nurtured by the Holy Spirit there can be no acceptable corporate worship. Putting it another way,

"Worship that does not contribute to unity is not the worship embraced by Christianity."[1]

This pattern explains Jesus' injunctions concerning relational issues when making one's offering to God in worship (Matt 5:21–24; 18:15–20), the severe warnings against causing another member of the community to stumble, and the priority of unconditional, unlimited forgiveness (Matt 6:12–15; 18:21–25; Luke 17:1–3; Eph 4:32; Col 3:13). Worship and fellowship are inseparable. Authentic fellowship shapes obedient worship. To separate them represents a lethal assault on the nature of the Church. To build a church around any other focus or task (such as evangelism or education) may construct a respected institution but not the New Testament church as a worshiping community.

Worship, Integrity, and the Spirit

This introduces a fifth aspect of the Spirit's role in corporate worship: he preserves our integrity as community members in worship. He provokes and judges those things which violate the demands of the covenant, pollute the holiness of the sanctuary, disturb its communal identity, mar its functional unity, or disqualify its witness and offerings. His presence examines, reveals, and convicts us of our personal transgressions of God's standards. He prompts us to maintain our covenantal integrity before God, for without this our worship offering is disqualified. The Spirit preserves our identity as the pure, unified people whose worship will be accepted by God.

The Holy Spirit "empowers" our worship by these means. Under the covenant inaugurated with us by the ascended Lord Jesus Christ, worship without the Holy Spirit is not possible. His presence defines the members of the community. He forms the community itself as a sanctuary for the worship of the living God. He empowers each individual to contribute to the unity that alone testifies to the deity of the Savior. He provokes the purity of the community (both as a people and as a sanctuary). By these ministries he gives integrity to the worship offered by the corporate gathering of God's people and, therefore, its acceptability to God. Without these essential works of the Spirit of God, worship offered by people on earth in this age is not accepted by God.

Worship, Ministry, and the Spirit

Once we understand these foundational issues, we can focus on the spheres in which the Holy Spirit functions in corporate worship: the word, the sacraments (or ordinances), and the gifts. Many discussions begin here to find more tangible evidence of his presence, searching pragmatically for measurable results, and personal gratification they bring. But without exploring the prerequisite roles of the Spirit in corporate worship, all discussion of practical aspects is worthless.

Christians agree: The Spirit instructs us through the reading and exposition of the scriptures. The same Spirit who created the holy scriptures as he inspired its writers (2 Pet 1:20–21) illuminates its meaning and significance through its exposition (Rom 7:7; 1 Cor 2:4). Obviously this includes the meaning of a biblical text in its original context. Limiting his role to textual interpretation ignores two issues. First, any honest student of the scriptures quickly sees that those without the Spirit may reconstruct the literal-grammatical-historical meaning of the text just as well as those with the Spirit can. Secondly, New Testament references to "meat" and "milk" (1 Cor 3:1–23; Heb 5:11–6:12; 1 Pet 2:1–3) have less to do with the meaning of the scriptures than with their application. These suggest that illumination has more do with application than exegetical understanding. The Spirit directs our acts toward his goals of holiness and unity in community. He convicts us where we fail to live up to what we already possess. He enriches our worship according to his larger design for God's sanctuary on the earth.

The sacraments (or "ordinances" as some prefer to call them) constitute another visible presence of the Spirit in corporate worship. He informs the significance of baptism and the Lord's Supper as corporate acts of fellowship and worship. Both express spiritual integrity in community (corporate unity and purity). Baptism forms the act of entrance into the community. Participation in the Eucharist demonstrates fellowship within the community. The Holy Spirit enhances the participant's preparation. Each sincere worshiper opens himself to the Spirit, seeking his help to reveal personal or relational sin that have transgressed the covenant and thereby disqualified the offering. The Spirit provokes confession and repentance, maintaining the integrity of the rite for each individual and the community that celebrates it. We cannot participate legitimately in either rite without a conscious self-evaluation under the Spirit's direction.

The Spirit also functions within each celebration of baptism and the Lord's Supper. He activates the symbols' reality and significance to us. In baptism we experience our bond to Christ—his death to sin and resurrection to new life— through the Spirit. Our decision for baptism in water before the watching community leads us into the experience of the otherwise intangible realities of our cleansing and salvation. He invites us into the community of faith and presents the demand for a serious commitment to its ministry. Baptism gives the Holy Spirit a tangible means to impress upon us the reality of the exchange that occurred within us and the obligations it incurs upon us. In the Lord's Supper the Spirit gives us a witness of the unity and community of God's covenant people in the living Christ. Each decision to eat reinforces our identification with Christ in his works on our behalf. It challenges our cooperation with his work among us. As we partake of "the body and blood of Christ" the Spirit calls us to be one with our Savior, to sacrifice our interests for his as he did for the Father's. The Spirit's ministry makes sincere participation in either of these ordinances powerful acts of spiritual renewal. Our response to his work gives these ordinances their sacramental value, the tangible means to value and appropriate the significance of God's grace given to us by faith.

In addition to the word and the sacraments, the Spirit also provides enablement to individuals. In the New Testament the "gifts of the [Holy] Spirit" describe ministry-capacities dispensed by the ascended Christ to his Church for the growth of his community in unity and maturity, and made effective in the individual by the presence of the Spirit (Rom 12:6; 1 Cor 12:1–11; Eph 4:7–15; 1 Pet 4:10–11). Several of these enablements are exercised during corporate worship. We may debate the nature and identity of these gifts. Some argue that they represent capabilities apart from natural skill; others present them as the enhancement of latent, natural abilities. But the New Testament's primary thrust for their use emphasizes the humble submission of all of one's personal capabilities to God as sovereign bestowments for which each will answer to God: "For who concedes you any superiority? What do you have that you did not receive? And if you received it, why do you boast as though you did not?" (1 Cor

4:7). The Spirit superintends the distribution of these gifts to enhance the unity and growth of each community and the worldwide body of believers under the Headship of Jesus Christ. No exercise of a capacity, skill, or enablement should isolate one member from another or destroy the unity of his people. Community fractures contradict his divine function and oppose the purpose for which God gave these gifts. Division as a result of ministry reveals either the prostitution of a gift to self-centered ambition or the absence of the Spirit's enablement for the ministry. Paul labeled such self-serving ambition as "the flesh" (cf. Gal 3:19–21). Rather, every capacity possessed by every believer should be exercised "all for one and one for all!"

The Holy Spirit engages all members of the unified worshiping community in all the acts of corporate worship. He enables the general participation of the community as an expression of submission to the sovereignty of God (Eph 5:18–20; Heb 13:15; 1 Pet 2:5), particularly their prayers and hymns to God (Col 2:16; Eph 5:18–19; 6:18). He convicts the community as to their standing before God (1 Cor 14:25). The Spirit also works through the offerings to stimulate an attitude of joy and gratitude, but also the experience of conviction as he identifies the discrepancy between our behavior and God's truth as revealed in the reading and preaching of his word.

Once the worship has been offered by the community, the Spirit's presence empowers the legitimacy of these expressions made to the Father. This distinguishes true Christian worship as "trinitarian." A biblical approach to the Godhead assumes and presents the unique role of each member of the Trinity (Eph 5:20; 1 Thess 5:18; Rom 8:26; cf. Eph 2:18). Our worship expressions are directed to the Father, expressing appreciation for his works of creation and redemption. The worship is offered in the person of the Son, "in Jesus' name," an expression that speaks to the virtue of his ascended person and the authority he has conferred on those who are his. Our worship is legitimized by the Spirit's presence. He has bonded us to our Savior and guaranteed our salvation. It's not wrong to offer worship to Jesus Christ or the Holy Spirit, but the predominant theological pattern of New Testament worship teaches a functional trinitarian approach. This honors each member of the Godhead for a unique, individual role in the work of creation and redemption.

On this celestial level the Holy Spirit unifies and orchestrates the Church's offerings in many languages and forms into a coherent symphony. The Spirit who draws the line to define the worshiping community and connects all its members together into a single entity, draws all on earth into the cosmic chorus. He joins the redeemed of all ages, then adds them to the celestial voices of the angels who proclaim the glory of God. This image of praise as a coherent whole has prompted two different responses, both seeking universal conformity. Some standardize a form to enact the grand image of the Church corporate—always at worship in a common language. Standardized services throughout the Church fill each 24 hour-day with worship as the earth rotates through its many regions. Others like the Eastern Church's "Divine Liturgy" seek to imitate the images and commands of scripture concerning the worship of God so that their offering may be seamlessly integrated into the eternal chorus. But the New Testament offers no explicit liturgical order for the community and few explicit directions to exercise the priestly role in corporate gathering. We are commanded to read the scripture publicly (the words of scripture with a brief explanation as necessary), to celebrate the Lord's Supper, to offer prayers, to sing for mutual encouragement and admonition, and to make collections for the community's needs. Beyond this the New Testament gives considerable freedom to devise both an order of service and ways to express our praise under the direction of the Holy Spirit.

Finally, the Holy Spirit creates the bridge between worship and ethics. He strengthens believers to fulfill their covenantal obligations as affirmed in their worship. This connection appears in Isa 6, a passage that deals more with the consequences of the divine encounter than a liturgical pattern. Isaiah's vision of God and of the celestial worship that surrounded him (Isa 6:1–4) produced in the prophet a deep sense of inadequacy and sin (Isa 6:5) that was remedied supernaturally (Isa 6:6–7), followed by a commission to divine service (Isa 6:8–13).

Similarly Paul teaches that the Holy Spirit is the indispensable element required for personal sanctification. The Spirit strengthens believers to resist the flesh and live out God's standards in an evil world—standards that are most clearly displayed to believers in the context of expressing them back to God through acts of worship, our "spiritual worship" (Rom 12:1). Our obedience appears most eloquently and forcefully in corporate worship. An unbeliever who observes the community at worship should see the Spirit's expressions, convicting evidence of God's presence (1 Cor 14:24-25). Paul admonishes us to sing (in his day merely stylized speech or chant) for mutual encouragement and admonition (Eph 5:18-20). This expresses our behaviors (Eph 3–6) under the direction of the Holy Spirit's control over our lives (Eph 5:17). Worship and ethics are neither competitors nor isolated components of the Christian life. As authentic spirituality constantly drives us toward greater maturity, authentic worship drives us to a greater desire for our incarnation of his holiness.

Worship, Liberty, and the Spirit

This brings us to the last broad ministry of the Holy Spirit in corporate worship. Just as the Holy Spirit defines the community, unifies its members, equips its leadership, and empowers our participation to edify the community, the Spirit acts to ensure liberty within the community.

God's work displays both freedom and form. From Genesis to Revelation he demands order of his creation as an expression of his nature and character. Disorder, anarchy, and chaos offend his character and invoke his judgment, as illustrated by the chaos of languages at Babel (Gen 11:9). We, however, are seldom creatures of balance. We can so emphasize order and decorum that our activity degenerates into a formalism and rigidity that excludes God. Both freedom and form are necessary. Form assumes and fosters liberty and creativity of expression. Conversely freedom can beget new forms that speak in fresh ways.

God acts through human planning and ingenuity as well as apart from them. Therefore, both careful planning and spontaneity are appropriate. After planning we must always be open to the inbreaking of God's Spirit in our worship. In such ways the Holy Spirit can inform and direct the community—not as a "maverick" or an iconoclast, but as the source of order and liberty. The careful planning of corporate worship must always be open to the inbreaking liberty of the Spirit.

This inbreaking occurs at the level of service-leadership. Paul's teaching on spiritual gifts, their exercise in corporate worship, and the observation that "each one has a song, has a lesson, has a revelation, has a tongue, has an interpretation"

(1 Cor 14:26), may mean that the Holy Spirit empowers individuals to offer acts of worship not anticipated by the planners of the gathering. But such unplanned participation must conform to Paul's subsequent instruction concerning order (1 Cor 14:27–40). Each contribution must reflect the individual's giftedness (Rom 12:6-8; 1 Pet 4:10–11; 1 Cor 14:23–27). Participation must be under the individual's control so that it can be suppressed or channeled to a moment where its contribution is more appropriate (1 Cor 14:27, 30–33). The contribution made by the gift itself must be scrutinized by others for its significance to the community which has gathered for worship (1 Cor 14:29). Finally, if the exercise of one's gift does not contribute to the community's spiritual development the gifted one should remain silent (1 Cor 14:28). This assumes the gifted person can evaluate their ministry's impact on the community before exercising their gift and modify their ministry behaviors accordingly. This will avoid the potential for "chaos" and thereby reflect God's character and priorities.

This inbreaking also appears at another level. Biblical descriptions speak of both "required" elements, the minimal expectations of the worshiper (seen as the basic sacrifices or the tithe), and "spontaneous" elements, additional gifts reflecting one's desire to show a greater expression of the worshiper's obeisance and thankfulness (often described as freewill offerings). These spontaneous offerings go beyond the mere requirements of the form into the generous freedom of divine worship, but without any suggestion of social chaos or disorder in the act.

Does Paul's expression "sing with the spirit" (1 Cor 14:15) teach the Holy Spirit leads by spontaneous impulses? In the same verse he contrasts "my spirit" with "my mind," drawing a parallel between the act of "singing" with mind and spirit and the act of "praying" with mind and spirit. Earlier (14:14), he says "spirit" and "mind" within the worshiper are edified by a spiritual gift and the emphatic use of "my" draws attention to the worshiper rather than to the Holy Spirit. Therefore, his use of "spirit" (14:15) defines full-hearted engagement in the worship. Consequently the New Testament offers no explicit teaching that spontaneity is always the evidence of the Spirit's presence in corporate worship, only that the Spirit enables believers to contribute to worship leadership with divine enablements.

A focus on subjective engagement alone can also lead to flagrant abuse. We can ignore the Spirit's objective role and emphasize our subjective response, transforming worship into the idolatry of self. We begin to emphasize stylistic preferences over communal priorities. In a narcissistic age this abuse is endemic to both worship leaders and congregational participants. Leaders face a more subtle danger. Leading through our Spirit-given enablements, we invoke the Spirit before the community and begin to assume that our ministry makes the worship effective for its participants. Our identity gradually takes precedence over the Spirit's ministries. We prize the ability to help people "connect" with God in worship. God's presence comes at our beck and call. Shamans of the holy, we join with Simon the Sorcerer who thought of the Spirit as merely another tool to fulfill his own ambitions for the performance of his magic (Acts 8:9–23). We are sales managers, feeding the bankrupt self-interest of our audience rather than the sovereign God whom we profess to serve.

Dealing with Popular Terminology

Sometimes we use biblical language to describe the Spirit's roles during corporate worship. This inaccurate language may misrepresent his ministry, obscure a more accurate understanding, and even foster theological error.

Some use "the leading of the Spirit" to explain departures from the planned acts of worship. Biblically, "to be led by the Spirit" always describes the capacity to distinguish what is righteous, despite evil's frequent religious camouflage (Rom 8:14; Gal 5:18), a *moral* act. It's never used to denote a New Testament worship style known for the spontaneity of its execution.

Unfortunately we can impose severe constraints on worship behavior, demanding "decency and order" that often creates a severe predictability, boredom, or spiritual ignorance. The most immediate and pragmatic solution becomes the rejection of planning as unspiritual. But if God superintends all human agencies and if the Spirit indwells all believers, then carefully planned worship services are no less Spirit-directed than unplanned events. If we wish to use "led by the Spirit" to describe corporate worship, it should apply to the Spirit's direction of *all* worship and not just a specific style of worship.

What about "quenching the Spirit"? It gets used pejoratively to describe ignoring an inner impulse toward spontaneity in worship. Biblically this expression (1 Thess 5:19) appears in the context of an admonition to behave in ways that promote unity and purity within the community (1 Thess 5:12–22). The "prophetic utterances" (1 Thess 5:20) appear within a corporate context, so the focus remains the reception of prophecy by the community rather than a personal failure to follow one's impulses contrary or even without planning.

Finally, one often hears that "God dwells in the praises of his people." The popular explanation takes several forms: (a) God draws near to us as we sing (as if he was not present previously); (b) we experience God's presence as we sing (as if the subjective impression of God's presence was the *sine qua non* of corporate worship); (c) God validates the quality of our worship by the appearance of the Spirit through charismatic gifts, just as God's glory descended upon the Holy of Holies to validate Israel's claim to fellowship with God. These notions bear no relationship to the psalmist's meaning. The expression probably alludes to Ps 22:3. The psalmist cries out for deliverance. He speaks of how Israel's praises rehearse God's covenant faithfulness. This gives him confidence to trust God in his present circumstance. The misuse of this text misses the point of the psalm. More importantly, it risks making the omnipotent God subservient to our wishes and behaviors.

Perhaps the most popular expression is "the liberty of the Spirit" to describe a sense of freedom when one can act wholeheartedly or without constraint in the group. Here, too, its biblical meaning has been obscured. Paul uses it to define New Covenant life as opposed to Old Covenant life under the law of Moses (2 Cor 3:17; cf. 3:6). Our corporate worship occurs within the New Covenant; only in a covenant context does the term have significance. The Holy Spirit has the sovereign right to direct a worshiper to behave in ways that are "outside the box." Using this expression to describe one's emotional state during worship, or with the assumption that it describes a behavior that is normative for the Holy Spirit, risks associating the Spirit only with the unplanned or spontaneous, even the loss of the corporate order commanded by the Apostle Paul (1 Cor 14:40).

Anyone who has ever stood before a group to lead has had the experience that everything is going just right, that the audience is follows wholeheartedly.

The leader is "in the groove," experiencing "the liberty of the Spirit." Think of it as an aesthetic experience.

Aesthetic experiences (whether aroused by music, words, acts, or a combination of these) often arouse powerful emotions. Feelings and emotions are part of God's image. As a part of common grace they can nurture God's image as we respond to revelations of his character and priorities in art. They help us internalize and value what we experience, cope with our triumphs, repent of our shortcomings, even distinguish between what it true and what is false. They affirm our beliefs, encourage our perseverance, or convict us of our failure. When experienced in groups these feelings are even more powerful. Worship is art and we should expect it to arouse emotions. This "in the groove" feeling may be one sign of the Holy Spirit's work. But if anyone, Christian or non-Christian, can have this feeling, we must never assume that it is primary evidence for the Spirit's presence and work. This is nothing more than emotional narcissism. It ignores the biblical examples of agony and despair expressed by worshipers. True worship is both a personal and a corporate recommitment to God's rule, the decision to remain faithful to the covenant despite one's circumstances or feelings. The true joy of worship is to know that God is in control of our circumstances. We have no excuse for substituting emotional satisfaction for unreserved obedience.

Every audience provides feedback to its leader. People smile and nod when encouragement is given or beliefs are confirmed. Closed eyes and rapt faces reveal positive emotions. Conviction comes with discomfort or an averted gaze. Sometimes the feedback comes audibly. These encourage the leader to continue, to add, or to depart from his planned order. Leaders may use "leading," "liberty," and "quenching" as terms of convenience to describe their reaction to this experience.

Any misuse of biblical language should make us pause when we hear it. From the post-apostolic church through to present day, theologians have recognized, used, and taught the principle of *lex orandi lex credendi*.[2] This pithy summary teaches that worship functions as the *primary* source for a congregation's belief. Worship both states and teaches theology. Worship as theology is the primary means of spiritual formation for the believers who use its forms and language.

Even if these expressions can be used to describe an otherwise special moving of the Holy Spirit in corporate worship, they should not be considered normative to express the Spirit's activity in our worship. Language of convenience for one generation usually becomes the theology for the next and conviction for those following. One can see the logic behind James' admonition concerning the greater judgment for teachers!

Therefore, to guard the beliefs of those who follow us, it would be better if those who lead and teach corporate worship restricted this language to the biblical sense and be honest about the psychological dynamics of group leadership. If we are to have a coherent and biblically defensible theology of the Holy Spirit and corporate worship, we ought to be sure that our language will support it for those who will follow us.

Conclusion

For God's people worship is the highest vocation. It's the reason for our existence. We were created to honor God with our allegiance and obedience. Following the intrusion of sin we were redeemed and sanctified by God so that we might fulfill that calling. The Holy Spirit makes it possible for us to offer ourselves to God without reserve or condition. Under the new covenant the Spirit's presence identifies those who have chosen God's way through faith in Christ. He circumscribes this worshiping community, creating an earthly sanctuary of worship to the living God. He nurtures the unity that validates its divine Savior and its heavenly source by restraining our selfishness and endowing us with his strength. He inspired the word and illuminates it to guide our work. In the sacraments he assists us to express our identity and message. He breaks into our forms with liberty to refresh our message within the changing forms of history and culture.

With this in mind, it's easy to see where modern worship often makes three mistakes. First, we can overlook the objective aspects of his ministry in a desperate desire for an experience, as if this alone will validate the offering. We do the Spirit a disservice through our ignorance. Our poor vocabulary to describe the Spirit's ministries can confuse many. In time the theology of the Spirit will cease to reflect biblical priorities for his ministry. When we gather to enjoy musicians serenading us for our approval and refer to the passive, non-participative experience as a "worship concert," a subtle shift has occurred in our understanding. Worship's biblical community and its participative liturgy have been lost.

Secondly, growing emotional narcissism can breed means to ensure the desired response. The pragmatic evangelism born in the Second Great Awakening takes hold. Method dominates. We reduce the Spirit to the servant of our strategy, appearing according to our plan, validating our new theology of response. We become enamored by the effect of the art, the music, and enshrine them in carefully devised models.

Thirdly, seeking this desired end can lead the worshiper and the community to accept any means to the prize. Wanting the exciting, we emphasize the spectacular. Contrary to the Bible's directives concerning the Spirit's purpose and distribution of gifts, we individualize and democratize his enablements. The community of the gifts has been lost. The greater ministries of the Spirit have been ignored. True worship has been impoverished, bankrupted on the altar of biblical ignorance, social pragmatism, and human desire,

The ancient liturgies of Christendom always began by invoking the presence of God in the person of the Holy Spirit. Our forefathers understood this keystone truth: without the Holy Spirit neither God's presence nor the validity of their offering could be presumed. Only the presence of the Holy Spirit enables a congregation to respond to God as he desires and in ways appropriate to his covenant.

Is the Holy Spirit crucial to our corporate worship? Absolutely! Without him we cannot live the holy life that identifies us, qualifies us, informs us, and supports our work. Does the Holy Spirit "lead" corporate worship? Yes, *all* forms of worship, whether planned or unplanned, formal or casual, traditional or free, through the gifts he has given to God's people! Does the Holy Spirit have enough room to function as he may desire in our corporate worship? Probably not. But each week we have another opportunity to lower the barriers a little bit more.

Let our response be that of Richard Baxter, who, in *The Reformation of the Liturgy* (1661), encourages us to pray that the Holy Spirit would draw us to Christ, unite us in love, strengthen us in praise, confirm us in obedience, and seal us unto eternal life.[3]

God, People, and the Bible:
The Relationship between Illumination and Biblical Scholarship

Richard E. Averbeck

As a canonical text, the Bible has two horizons: first, the ancient authors (divine and human) intention in the text itself and, second, the modern reader as he or she engages in the study of the text. The authorial intention in the text itself carries the Holy Spirit's intended "meaning." Therefore, on the one hand, the "meaning" of the text shines forth from the author/text horizon. "Understanding," on the other hand, derives from the Holy Spirit's work of "illumination" on the horizon of the reader. This finds corresponding categories in modern speech-act theory. What we need to engage in is the kind of biblical scholarship in which the Bible is not only the subject of investigation, but the investigation itself turns back upon the scholar in a transforming way. This is what illumination is all about. There are three parts to this discussion: (1) the *intent* of biblical scholarship -- our goal in the study of the Bible is the transformed life of love from a pure, a good conscience and a sincere faith, (2) the *nature* of biblical scholarship -- our way of studying the Bible is that it is encounter with God as fully human person in submission to the Word, and (3) the *nurture* of biblical scholarship -- is through guiding people into a kind of reading of the Bible that corresponds to this intent and nature of biblical scholarship.

Let me begin by affirming that the Bible offers the *only* divinely revealed and, therefore, reliable foundation and guide for life and ministry. Jesus, who always spoke with authority (Matt 7:28–29; 28:18), said in the Sermon on the Mount: "everyone who hears these words of mine and puts them into practice is like a wise man who built his house on the rock" (Matt 7:24, NIV). Of course, Jesus was referring here specifically to his teachings in the sermon, but we know that our Lord intends that we should take all of the inspired word of God seriously, both Old and New Testament, and keep it *central* to the way we think about and respond to him as well as in our relationships and ministry to people. According to Ezra 7:6–10, for example:

> Ezra …was a scribe who was skilled in the law of Moses which the LORD God of Israel had given. The king supplied him with everything he requested, *for the hand of the LORD his God was on him*.… he arrived at Jerusalem, *for the good hand of his God was on him*. Now Ezra had given himself to the *study* [lit. "to seek"] of the law of the LORD, to its observance [lit. "do it"], and to *teaching* its statutes and judgments in Israel.

Similarly, Paul writes to Timothy in 2 Tim 2:14–15 telling him to "warn" people "not to wrangle over words," but instead, "make every effort" to gain approval from God by being "a proven worker who does not need to be ashamed, teaching the message of truth accurately".

If you love someone, you take what he or she says seriously. So it is with the word of God. The great *shema* of Deut 6 begins with the proclamation of one great principle: "Listen, Israel: As for the LORD your God, the LORD is one" (v. 4). Since that is the case, the first commandment constitutes the natural implication: there should be no divided loyalties. There is only *one* LORD, so "love the LORD your God with your *whole* mind, your *whole* being, and your *whole* strength" (v. 5; "and your whole strength" = literally, "with all your exceedingly," perhaps meaning "with all that you are and have"). The next verse comes to the main point I am trying to make here: "These words I am commanding you today must be *kept in mind*" (v. 6). If we truly love God, his word will be "kept in mind." His commandments are what we become preoccupied with. This naturally makes them that which we will talk about to our children in our various walks of life (v. 7), and we display his word in our public lives as well (vv. 8–9).

Of course, we could cite many such passages, and some will appear later in this article as we develop the two major discussions that make up the substance of this essay: (1) the Bible and human language and (2) the Bible and biblical scholarship. *My major purpose is to describe and encourage the kind of biblical scholarship in which the Bible is not only the subject of investigation, but the investigation itself turns back upon the scholar in a transforming way.* This kind of biblical scholarship takes place only when the Holy Spirit works powerfully in the scholar as he studies the very word that the same Spirit inspired (2 Pet 1:21, "men carried along by the Holy Spirit spoke from God").

Scholarly study of the Bible can be done either in a way that invites the Holy Spirit to do his transforming work through his word, or in a way that suffocates the work of the Spirit in the scholar's study, and in his or her life and ministry. When it comes right down to it, however, who among us does not want to have "the good hand of his God on him" as Ezra did? I will argue that this requires that we not only do good scholarship from an academic point of view, but that we do it with the kind of heart perspective that invites—yes, calls upon and welcomes—the Holy Spirit to do what he intends to do through his word in our study, our lives, and our ministries. This work of the Holy Spirit is sometimes called "illumination," the goal of which is to bring the word of God to bear so "that the eyes of" our "heart" may be "enlightened" (Eph 1:18; note "the Spirit of wisdom and revelation" in v. 17 [NIV]). We will say more about this later.

The Bible and Human Language

First we need to take a serious look at the current scholarly discussion of the Bible as *God's* word in *human* language. The hermeneutical issues that we face and the philosophical foundations that underlie them are important to my thesis that biblical scholarship done well will turn back on the scholar in a life-changing way. It is not my goal to deal with the standard hermeneutical concepts and exegetical procedures associated with historical-grammatical-literary interpretation of scripture (for example: grammar, semantics, syntax, historical backgrounds, literary genre, etc.). We have a number of fine textbooks on that subject.[1] As important as such issues and procedures are, the matters we need to deal with here run deeper and manifest themselves on three levels of scholarly discussion: (1) *distance* between the ancient author/text and the modern reader (2) the *nature* of language and text as a means of communicating meaning that a reader can understand, and (3) the *relationship* between meaning, understanding, and illumination.

Distance between Author/Text and Reader

Our first concern is the historical, cultural, and linguistic distance between the ancient author/text and the modern reader of the Bible. Of course, this problem arises in the reading of any ancient and/or foreign document. In the case of the Bible, however, the situation is further complicated by the distance between the divine author (God) and the human reader on ontological, intellectual, and moral grounds (Isa 55:8–9). These kinds of issues are related in one way or another to three main realities of the text: (1) there were human *authors* as well as a divine author, (2) there were ancient *readers* and there are modern readers, and (3) the Bible itself is a *text* (or perhaps we should say it is a canonical collection of text*s*)—it is literature, it is written in languages that are foreign to most of us, and, at the same time, it is the very word of God.

From a historical point of view there are two horizons in biblical interpretation: the world and worldview of the ancient author/text, as opposed to the world and worldview of the modern reader of the text.[2] Some would argue that the locus of meaning is in the intention of the original author(s). Others view the meaning of the text as that which arises in the understanding of the reader(s) in the process of reading and interpreting the text for today. In the latter case, the meaning of the text is regularly thought to be pluralistic because it arises from the world and concerns of the particular reader or group of readers. One person's world may vary considerably from that of another, so the interpretations may vary too, and often do.

Hermeneutically, in my opinion, the most satisfying resolution to this problem is to think in terms of fusing the two horizons (author/text and reader) by means of a hermeneutical spiral.[3] The modern interpreter naturally begins with his or her current horizon of understanding, which is actually a pre-understanding with which the reader necessarily approaches the ancient text. Pre-understanding is a good thing, but the more it has already been informed by previous well-accomplished readings of the text, the better it is.[4] In any case, the reader must respect the horizon of the ancient author/text lest he or she simply read his or her own horizon into the text and, therefore, learn and understand nothing from God's word.[5] As the reading begins the modern reader initiates a "dialogue with the text in which the text itself progressively corrects and reshapes the interpreter's own questions and assumptions."[6] Thus, the reader's pre-understanding becomes better informed as the dialogue proceeds in a spiral forward toward a relatively sound understanding of the meaning of the ancient author/text brought about through the cyclical interaction between the two horizons.

In the meantime, the reader's understanding of the impact that the true meaning of the ancient text has for his or her current situation also advances. The reader does not leave his own horizon behind but, instead, brings it with him into the engagement with the text. Here it helps to keep in mind that people from all times and places have always had to cope with essentially the same basic issues in life and death. There is common ground between us and the ancients. The cultures are different, but the basic human concerns have always been the same. Moreover, the image of God in people (Gen 1:26–28) lends us the capacity to hear God's concerns in the text and respond to them. In other words, we have common ground with both the God who inspired the writing of the Bible and the ancient authors and readers of the text. This makes it reasonable to assume that we can come to a meaningful understanding of the significance of the scriptures for our lives. We shall return to the importance of the Holy Spirit in transforming us through the reading of the text later in this essay.[7]

Language and Text, Meaning and Understanding

The second level of scholarly debate today in hermeneutics is even more fundamental than the first. It takes us deeper into the nature of language as language and the problems of "meaning" in texts and "understanding" of texts. Some of the most influential scholars in the fields of philosophy of language and literary theory have, in effect, turned language on its head. They emphasize the difficulties with "meaning" in language and texts, rather than the fact that, by definition, languages and/or texts normally serve as a means of communication. I am neither a philosopher nor fully trained in the theoretical foundations of modern literary theory. Nevertheless, this very "heady" discussion has had a profound effect on current biblical scholarship, especially through many of the new literary approaches to the Bible (e.g., deconstruction, reader-response, liberation hermeneutics, etc.). We live in a world and in a scholarly environment that has been deeply influenced by the questions about the nature of language, literature, and meaning raised in these disciplines, so biblical scholars dare not ignore them.[8]

My most helpful guide through this maze has been the writings of Kevin Vanhoozer, especially his recent book entitled *Is There a Meaning in This Text?*[9] It is widely recognized as an important book on language, meaning, and how the language of the Bible carries meaning about God and people, and about the Bible itself. It is about the history of the philosophy of language and the effects of modern literary theory on how people, especially biblical scholars, generally read and understand the Bible today. It is also especially significant for this essay that Vanhoozer includes in his book one of the most extensive and well-articulated treatments of the Holy Spirit's work of illumination available anywhere in recent theological literature.[10]

Basically, it all comes down to a certain "despair of language" that is at the core of postmodern thought about language as it relates to meaning and truth. The question is: Can we really speak of truth?[11] Premodern language theorists such as Plato, and the theologians who depended on their theories, such as Augustine, thought of words as *signifiers of reality*. "As words signify things, so things signify higher things," whether it be Plato's "eternal Ideas" or Augustine's allegorical interpretation or spiritually higher meaning of (figurative) language in the Bible.[12]

Modern language theorists (as opposed to both premodern *and* our contemporary postmodern theorists) break into two basic groups. The first group saw language as *information* about *subjective reality* (as opposed to empirical reality, see the next paragraph below). This was based upon Immanuel Kant's thesis that our mind does not actually know the world but shapes our perception of the world. Language, therefore, expresses our human subjectivity—our perceptions and experiences of the world—not the world directly. Our metaphysical ideas about ultimate reality beyond the material world are even more subjective, since the mind has no ability to penetrate beyond this world.[13] Theologically, Karl Barth accepted Kant's basic point of view and argued that, since God is so "wholly other," human language on its own can speak only of the world, not of God directly. The work of interpreting the words of the Bible only provides the occasion on which God may, through an event of his divine grace, disclose the word of God through the words of the Bible.[14]

Other modern language theorists were uncomfortable with such a subjective view of language. For them language is *information* about *empirical reality* (e.g., Bertrand Russell and Ludwig Wittgenstein in his early days). According to this view, one could take each individual empirically observable fact about the world and build a verifiable proposition about that fact. The logically-arranged combination of these verifiable propositions would then paint a logical picture of truth—of what we can know. This is called "logical positivism." Language, in the meantime, can say nothing about metaphysics; that is, the study of ultimate reality beyond what is empirically observable. The theological equivalent, according to Vanhoozer's analysis, is "biblical positivism," by which he means the biblical theological method of Old Princeton theologians such as Warfield and Hodge. While they all along denied the logical positivist dictum that one can say nothing about ultimate reality, nevertheless, from the point of view of the philosophy of language, their goal was to treat theology as an objective, inductive science by isolating and building propositions out of biblical facts one by one and then simply arranging them in a logical order.[15]

Postmodern language theorists return to Kant in the sense that they view all language as subjective, but they go further by arguing that language cannot get beyond itself to *any* reality outside of itself, *not even* the observable material world. They are committed to the indeterminacy of language. The structuralist view of language stands in the background here. According to the structuralists (e.g., Ferdinand de Saussure), a word in a language does not really represent anything outside of the language itself. Words are known only in relation to other words within the language system to which they belong. Poststructuralists (i.e., such postmodernists and deconstructionists as Jacques Derrida) go a step further when they argue that stable language systems do not exist. Every language is an ever-changing social construct, not really a means of expressing stable absolute truth. The possible meanings of words within texts or language systems change. So we find ourselves back at the "despair of language." Some postmodern theologians (e.g., Don Cupitt), therefore, do not think of theology as language about what really is. Instead, theologians should strive to speak creatively in order to generate meaningful human experience through the use of theological language.[16]

Can we turn this "despair of language" into a productive despair? Vanhoozer (following Paul Ricoeur and Ludwig Wittgenstein in his latter days) thinks so, and I agree, although being a biblical rather than a philosophical-systematic theologian, I would want to articulate the same answer in a different way. Much of what postmodernists observe about language and literature is indeed true, but there is another way of coming at the whole problem. The way forward is through language as communication. Language is not just a system of signs (semiotics), but a means of communication (semantics). We need to move away from a focus on words, to sentences and discourses that bear communicative purpose. Semiotics studies language as a system unto itself, but semantics and the pragmatics of language treat language in relation to the socially interactive communicative event it inherently serves. This involves both "intentions and conventions" and such is the stuff of "meaning."

Viewed in this way, language does "say something" in the context of the communicative event (it is "locutionary"), and because it says something it also "does something" (it is "illocutionary"; e.g., it warns, asserts, or promises). Moreover, the intention of language in the communicative event is to "make something happen" by addressing a person or group of persons (it is "perlocutionary"; e.g., it may simply inform, or it may persuade, encourage, or discourage). This, in turn, "invites a response" of some sort from the person(s) addressed (language is "interlocutionary"; e.g., the addressee[s] may agree, disagree, act, react, or simply respond with further discourse). Thus, "language is ultimately a medium of interpersonal interaction."[17]

Meaning, Understanding, and Illumination

This interpersonal communication occurs not only between people, but also between God and people. The Bible presents itself as a combination of the two, being intentional communication from divine *and* human authors to human readers, whom God himself created in his own image and likeness. The Bible "says something" and as such it "does something, makes something happen, and invites response," but how is the Holy Spirit involved in this process?

With his characteristic wit Vanhoozer writes: "The Spirit's work in interpretation is not to change the *sense* [of scripture] but to restore us to our *senses*" (emphasis mine).[18] His point is that the Holy Spirit's work of illumination is different from his work of inspiration, although he recognizes that the former is a natural extension of the latter: "the one who inspired scripture cannot contradict himself when he illumines it."[19] The difference is one of "meaning" versus "understanding," between the "objective" and "subjective" authority of scripture. Karl Barth collapsed the two into one, arguing that the Bible becomes the word of God only when the divine Holy Spirit makes it such for the reader in the act of reading.[20] On the contrary, in the process of inspiring the scriptures the Holy Spirit deposited a divinely intended meaning in the text (2 Tim 3:16–17) by driving the human writers along the course of divinely intended meaning (2 Pet 1:20–21). Put in terms of speech-act theory, the text itself is locutionary by virtue of the fact that it carries the Holy Spirit's intended "meaning"—it says something definite. Therefore, on the one hand, the "meaning" of the text shines forth from the author/text horizon.

"Understanding," on the other hand, derives from the Holy Spirit's work of "illumination" on the horizon of the reader.[21] Here is where the argument becomes a bit confusing. The question is whether or not illumination enlivens the illocutionary or perlocutionary dimensions of the text, or both, and where does the interlocutionary dimension of the text fit into the discussion of illumination? Vanhoozer never mentions the interlocutionary intent of the Bible in his discussion of the Holy Spirit's work in interpretation of the Bible. He argues that illumination is mainly perlocutionary, but also includes the illocutionary. The Spirit works to impress the reader(s) with the illocutionary force of the text and to promote obedience to its perlocutionary intent. Both are part of a proper "understanding" of the Bible, what Klooster calls "heart-understanding."[22]

We might compare this to the use of the Greek word γνῶσις (*gnōsis*) in 1 Pet 3:7, "Husbands, in the same way, treat your wives with consideration [lit. 'according to knowledge' (γνῶσις)] as the weaker partners and show them honor as fellow heirs of the grace of life. In this way nothing will hinder your prayers." This kind of knowledge or "understanding" involves more than cognitive understanding of spoken words. It includes hearing and understanding what is said, but it means that one also takes the words and the person seriously in a considerate way. It includes truly "knowing" one's wife as a person, and honoring and valuing her in a special way. She is to have a privileged place in her husband's life, a place of truly knowing and being known. Similarly, we are to take God at his word. We give him and his word a privileged place in our life. This is what it means to truly "understand" God and his word, and I would argue that this is what the Holy Spirit's work of illumination is about.

The best way of viewing illumination is to attach it to the reader's *acceptance* and *reception* of the meaning of the text rather than his or her intellectual grasp of what it says.[23] What I have in mind here are the principles of 1 Cor 2:14, "The unbeliever does not *receive* [i.e., embrace, welcome] the things of the Spirit of God, for they are foolishness to him. And he cannot *understand* them [lit. 'know' γινώσκω, *ginōskō*; cf. γνῶσις, *ginōsis*, and the remarks on 1 Pet 3:7 above], because they are spiritually *discerned* [i.e., evaluated, judged]." The point is that as an act of communication or a collection of such acts, the scriptures already have all the elements of a speech act built into them, just like any other literary composition. Hermeneutics as a discipline is not limited to principles of biblical interpretation, but extends to interpretation of all kinds of texts, ancient and modern.

The special problem with God's word is not with the scriptures themselves, but with our acceptance of what they say as true and our willingness to welcome that truth into our lives for impact on all levels: who we are and how we live. In short, the problem is that we are sinful down to the very core of ourselves. Therefore, we naturally resist scripture as an act of rebellion against the true God, whose divine intent was the reason for its composition on the first horizon and continues to be the divine purpose and goal of reading it on the second horizon. As Klooster puts it, "renewal of the heart in regeneration is the most radical form of illumination one experiences."[24] Taken in context, this regenerational illumination is what 1 Cor 2:14 is concerned about (see also 2 Cor 3:12–4:15 and compare John 3:19–21 and 1 John 1:5–7). Again, it is not so much a matter of perception of the meaning of sentences and paragraphs in scripture as it is the willingness of the reader to receive it.

This work of the Holy Spirit continues on into the Christian life as part of his sanctifying work in and among us. In Col 1:9–10 Paul writes about his prayers on behalf of the Colossian believers that God would fill them "with the knowledge of his will in all spiritual wisdom and understanding, so that you may live worthily of the Lord and please him in all respects: bearing fruit in every good deed, growing in the knowledge of God." Similarly, in the context of making reference to the Holy Spirit (Eph 1:13–14), he writes to the Ephesian believers that he has been praying for the "enlightening" of the "eyes" of their "heart" by "the Spirit of wisdom and revelation" so that they might "know him better." This includes knowing "the hope to which he has called" them, "…the riches of his glorious inheritance in the saints, and his incomparably great power for us who believe" (Eph 1:17–19).

First John 2:20–27 binds the "anointing" with the Holy Spirit at regeneration to the ongoing teaching of the Holy Spirit in the life of the Christian: "…the anointing that you received from him resides in you, and you have no need for anyone to teach you. But as his anointing teaches you about all things, it is true and is not a lie. Just as it has taught you, you reside in him" (1 John 2:27). There appears to be an echo here from the new covenant passage in Jer 31:31–34, where the Lord says, "I will put my law within them and write it on their hearts and minds. And I will be their God and they will be my people" (v. 33). Therefore, "'People will no longer need to teach their neighbors and relatives to know me. That is because all of them, from the least important to the most important, will know me,' says the LORD. 'All of this is based on the fact that I will forgive their sin and will no longer call to mind the wrong they have done'" (v. 34). On the one hand, one could be in the old covenant without having the law written on the heart; that is, without knowing the Lord. On the other hand, the nature of the new covenant is such that one will have the law written on their heart so that they know the Lord. No one will need to teach this to someone who has a new covenant relationship with the Lord.

John's point is similar: "…you have an anointing from the Holy One, and you all know. I have not written to you that you do not know the truth, but that you do know it, and that no lie is of the truth" (1 John 2:20–21). Therefore, no one needs to teach them that Jesus is the Son of God, nor the importance of abiding in him (vv. 22–24). Some teachers were trying to deceive them, but the anointing they have teaches them the truth and they need no one else to teach them these things as they continue to abide in Christ (vv. 26–27). Being in Christ brings with it the Holy Spirit's illumination that begins with the initial baptism in the Holy Spirit at the time of regeneration and continues to enlighten the eyes of their hearts about the things of Christ, as Paul puts it in Eph 1:17–18 (see above).

In light of all this, we should probably think of illumination as applying to the perlocutionary and interlocutionary dimensions of the text. The locutionary fact that the text says something and the illocutionary nature of what it says are both part of the text itself and, therefore, part of the Holy Spirit's work of inspiration, not illumination. These are the two parts of the "meaning" already accomplished in the text. For example, when Jesus says, "I tell you, unless your righteousness goes beyond that of the experts in the law and the Pharisees, you will never enter the kingdom of heaven" (Matt 5:20), he says something locutionary and what he says amounts to an illocutionary warning. The reader who perceives this has attained to a proper perception of the text. This does not require illumination by the Holy Spirit.

Whether the reader receives the perlocutionary force of Jesus' warning as meaningful for his or her own life and responds to the interlocutionary invitation to act on the warning, this is another matter altogether. The following antitheses (Matt 5:21–48) and, in fact, the whole Sermon on the Mount provide instruction and guidance for those who would take what Jesus said seriously and actively pursue a righteousness that does indeed surpass that of the Pharisees and teachers of the law. This is what the Holy Spirit's work of illumination is concerned with. The issue is not the "sense" of scripture but the need for us to come to our "senses."

I am not suggesting here that the work of the Holy Spirit in illumination has no effect on our "thinking." On the contrary, how we evaluate and respond to the word of God under the influence of the Holy Spirit constitutes a significant part of our thinking. My basic concern is that we distinguish between the qualities of textuality that make any text an act of communication, including the word of God, as opposed to the work of the Holy Spirit that enables us as sinners to receive what the Spirit's inspired scriptures say as meaningful and, in fact, authoritative for our own thinking and acting. I would also add that, ultimately, the fact that we receive the word of God as the guiding authority for our lives informs the ongoing development of our pre-understanding for approaching the biblical text anew. When all is said and done, the Holy Spirit's work of illumination has a "backlash effect" even on our perception of what the Bible says from a locutionary point of view and what it does by means of what it says from an illocutionary point of view. Illumination, therefore, helps us on both horizons (author/text and reader) even though its direct application is to the second horizon (the life of the reader).

The Bible and Biblical Scholarship

Our second major concern in this treatise is a natural extension of the first. We need to take the philosophical discussion of language and the biblical discussion of illumination articulated in the first section of this article and bring them to bear on the actual practice of biblical scholarship. The goal is to describe and encourage the kind of biblical scholarship in which the Bible is not only the subject of investigation, but the investigation itself turns back upon the scholar in a transforming way. There are three parts to this discussion: (1) the *intent* of biblical scholarship, (2) the *nature* of biblical scholarship, and (3) the *nurture* of biblical scholarship.

For some readers it may seem silly to go through the previous review and discussion of the history of the philosophy of language and new literary criticism (see above) only to come to the conclusion that the best way to read the Bible is as an act of communication. What else would it be? However, by following this line of thought we have accomplished three things. First, we have brought our discussion into contact with the core hermeneutical debates of our day. I hope the reader finds this helpful in his or her own engagement with the world of biblical scholarship today. What else is biblical scholarship about but the study of the Bible, especially its interpretation? Second, we have gone some distance toward putting pluralism in its proper place. One of the cultural effects of postmodernism is that language is indeterminate—it does not communicate a stable meaning and there is no such thing as absolute truth. Therefore, there can be no authoritative "metanarrative." That is, neither the Bible nor any other story can claim "to make sense of all other stories and the whole of reality."[25] But this is the very claim that the Bible does indeed make. I will return to this point in the conclusion.

Third, and most importantly for our present discussion, there is something very important to be gained for our topic by looking at the language of scripture as an act of communication, ultimately a divine act, but through human writers using human language. In summary, from this point of view, the text of scripture intends to make something happen in the heart of the reader that will bring about the appropriate response in the reader's life. This is, in fact, the arena in which the Holy Spirit's work of illumination takes place. This brings us to the issue of God's intention for us as we read the Bible, and that, in turn, is the most helpful point of departure for defining the divine purpose and perspective in biblical scholarship.

The Intent of Biblical Scholarship

What response does God himself intend to call forth from us through his self-revelation to us in his word? What impact does he intend to have on us as we study his word and on others through our teaching of it? From a biblical theology point of view, the best way to answer this question is through the use of what I have come to call "boil down" passages in the Bible. These are passages that come right out and say that they are "boiling down" the message of the Bible, or the goals and purposes of that message. In other words, there are occasions in the text when the text itself underlines the intended effect of biblical teaching on its readers. The Bible turns back upon itself. It is not surprising to find that many times the stated purpose has something to do with relationship between God and people, and between people. After all, the Bible is first of all and above all a relational book. God could be God without the Bible. People could be people without the Bible. The real reason for the existence of the Bible is the relationship between the two. We can put it this way: *if we come away from the Bible without relating well to God and people we have not read it well*. A spiritually formative approach to the Bible will have a profound relational effect on the scholar and through the scholar on his or her students.

The goal of our teaching. For example, according to the Apostle Paul there is *one* main goal for teaching God's word; namely, so that people grow to love better. In the first chapter of 1 Timothy Paul confronts a teaching problem in

Ephesus. There were those who were spreading "false teachings" having to do with "myths and interminable genealogies," were promoting "useless speculations rather than God's redemptive plan that operates by faith" (1 Tim 1:3–4). Paul had given Timothy a "command" to restrain them (v. 3), and in v. 5 he refers to this "command" as having a certain goal (Greek *telos*): "the aim of our instruction is love that comes from a pure heart, a good conscience, and a sincere faith." Paul then proceeds in vv. 6–7 to refer to these false teachers as those who "have strayed from these" principles; namely, the principles listed in the previous verse. In wandering away from these principles they have "turned away to empty discussion. They want to be teachers of the law, but they do not understand what they are saying or the things they insist on so confidently."

Good Bible teaching has as its goal "love"—the kind of love that comes only from "a pure heart, a good conscience, and a sincere faith." One could reach hither and yon for a biblical definition of love, but perhaps it is better to just stick with the context here and say that it is the kind of relational involvement with God and people that comes, first of all, from a "pure heart"—one cleansed of impurities (2 Tim 2:22). Second, it comes from a "good conscience"—a conscience that is not tainted with guilt, perversity, and ulterior motives. Thirdly, it comes from a "sincere faith"—an unhypocritical faithful walk with God. We dare not lose sight of this goal when we study and teach the Bible because if we do, then we have compromised the biblical integrity of our study from the point of view of what we are studying. Our scholarship loses its way.

The summary of the Law and the Prophets. We all know how easy it is to get caught up in controversy. We are so easily distracted from God's purposes even as we pursue those very purposes. It is instructive to observe that in 1 Tim 1:2–11 the real problem seems to have been how these false teachers were teaching the Old Testament law. We cannot go into the details of how they were misunderstanding the law and, therefore, misleading others in the way they were teaching it, but we know that the whole point of the law and the prophets was the same kind of love that Paul referred to in v. 5 as the goal of his own instruction. This is clear from the way Jesus summarized the law in the two great commandments. The Gospel of Matthew records it this way: "'Love the Lord your God with all your heart, with all your soul, and with all your mind.' This is the first and greatest commandment. The second is like it: 'Love your neighbor as yourself.' All the law and the prophets hang on these two commandments" (Matt 22:37–40).

Of course, this is not new in the New Testament. Jesus is quoting from the Old Testament itself and is suggesting this is the perspective from which we should understand all that is written there. If one does not get this out of their reading of the Old Testament then they have read it wrongly. Jesus says so!

My own experience in teaching the Old Testament is that many do not read it with this kind of understanding and effect in their lives. In some circles at least, there is a tendency to pit the Old and New Testaments against one another in some way. Jesus strenuously opposes this. The Old Testament was his Bible, and he had no intention of undermining its authority and importance through his life, death, or resurrection. Of course, various misunderstandings persist even today. Even the second great commandment itself is often misunderstood. I have heard people say that the second great commandment means that we need to learn to love ourselves so that we can love others. This turns the text on its head. The context in Lev 19 betrays this. The passage (vv. 15-18) reads:

> "You must not deal unjustly in judgment: you must neither show partiality to the poor nor honor the rich. You must judge your fellow citizen fairly. You must not walk about as a slanderer among your people. You must not stand idly by when your neighbor's life is at stake. I am the LORD. You must not hate your brother in your heart. You must surely reprove your fellow citizen so that you do not incur sin on account of him. You must not take vengeance or bear a grudge against the children of your people, but you must love your neighbor as yourself. I am the LORD. You would not want someone to pervert the

system of justice in such a way that you are treated unfairly, so don't do this to your neighbor. You would not want someone to slander you, so don't slander them either. You would not want someone to endanger your life, so don't endanger their life. You would not want someone to hate you or bear a grudge against you in their heart, so don't allow yourself to do that to them. Note the concern here for what is going on in one's heart. This is another common misunderstanding of the law. It is not just concerned about external behaviors, but also the activities of the heart. But the point I am making here is that the second great commandment is really essentially the same as the so-called "golden rule" in Matt 7:12, "In everything, treat others as you would want them to treat you, for this fulfills the law and the prophets."

We could go on about this passage, but the point here is that this is another "boil down" passage, and it comes down to the same basic underlying rationale for teaching the Bible as Paul did in 1 Tim 1:5. The goal of our instruction is love, and that was in fact the whole purpose of the law and the prophets from the start.

Faith and hope, with love above all. Similarly, one can turn to the transition and connection between 1 Cor 12 and 13. Paul summarizes the spiritual gifts and their significance, and then turns in another direction, saying, "And now I will show you a way beyond comparison" (1 Cor 12:31b). He immediately launches into a contrast between all things spiritual as opposed to love. He even concludes: "And now these three remain: faith, hope, and love. But the greatest of these is love" (1 Cor 13:13). How important is faith in Paul's writings? It is pivotal to the very gospel itself. How important is hope? Paul makes much of it for the life of the Christian (e.g., 1 Cor 15:19). But he still writes his praise song in 1 Cor 13 to love and gives it pride of place in relation to faith and hope (note also 1 Cor 8:1, "Knowledge puffs up, but love builds up").

The main point is this: love outweighs *any* knowledge, giftedness, or abilities we may have. By definition, if we do not love well we do not serve well no matter how well gifted we may be. This includes our giftedness as scholars. We all know that very gifted people have a lot of power, but that power can be used for either good or bad, whether in the Church or in the world. I in no way intend to diminish the importance of spiritual gifts, but I do sometimes get concerned about an overemphasis on spiritual gifts, as if they are what carries the ministry. The Holy Spirit has given these gifts to us for one reason and one reason only: so that we can use them to go love God and people. The spiritual gifts are neither an end in themselves nor the bottom line in ministry. The bottom line is how well we love. That is certainly clear from 1 Cor 13, and it is just as important for us as biblical scholars as anyone else.

The mark of the Christian. Finally, I turn to one more passage, John 13:34–35. Jesus said: "I give you a new commandment—to love one another. Just as I have loved you, you also are to love one another. Everyone will know by this that you are my disciples—if you have love for one another." Loving one another well is to be the distinguishing *mark* of the Christian and the Church. It is what makes us stand out as a community in the midst of this world. Unfortunately, the Church has not always been known for this in the world, and neither are Bible teachers and scholars. We too often lose track of the divine purpose as we pursue our study and our ministry.

If love is to be the goal of our instruction, if it is the summary on which all the law and the prophets hang, if it outweighs any giftedness we may have, even the gifts of the Holy Spirit, and if it is to be the distinguishing mark of the Church, then there is only one conclusion we can draw. Love is of primary importance in our lives as Christians, even as biblical scholars. In fact, it seems to me that one of the most important goals we could set for our scholarship is to bring the word of God to bear upon the people of God in such a way that they go forth and love God and people better. We as biblical scholars and teachers need to ask ourselves how well we are serving this expressed purpose of the Bible in the way we study and teach it. Not only "do *we* get it?" but are we keeping *others* focused on "getting it" by the way we do our scholarship and our teaching?

The Nature of Biblical Scholarship

This brings us to the nature of biblical scholarship. From time to time, we need to reassess ourselves and our scholarship in terms of what God has called us to do as scholars. Of course, each person has his or her own peculiar calling, but we also have a common calling to serve God and his Church well through our scholarship. I distinctly remember as a seminary student walking down a particular hallway one day thinking about God's call on my life and having it occur to me that perhaps God wants me to invest my life in helping the Church with the Old Testament. I thought, "the Church certainly needs some help here." It was a defining moment for me. Our scholarship is to be as much a mission as any other purposeful calling in the Church.

Here is where I would like to make a rather bold proposal. The fact that, as biblical scholars, we sometimes undo the divine intent of what we are called to do by the way we do it. Biblical scholarship is too often separated from simply being a good Christian who hears and responds to the work of God's Holy Spirit as we pursue our scholarship. One way of saying this is that *there is a problem with our hermeneutic—a serious problem* that keeps us from receiving the full impact of God and God's word in our lives as we are in the study. This, in turn, keeps us from teaching the Bible according to God's divine intention. We lose track of life in the study. As a result, we lose effectiveness in the lives of our students in the college or seminary classroom as well as in the church.

A simplistic or mechanical study of the Bible will not have the impact on us that God intends to have through his word. The common step-by-step process of first analysis, then synthesis, and finally application is inadequate and misleading. It does not yield the same kind of results as "meditation" on the word of God day and night, which is what the Bible calls us to in several places (e.g., Josh 1:8 and Ps 1:2). We need to come back to the question of the Holy Spirit in the study of the Bible and the nature of "illumination." I am suggesting that biblical scholarship that is worthy of the name will involve the full engagement of a scholar's spirit with the Holy Spirit in the process of studying the Bible. This means at least three things.

Taking God seriously in the study. First, *we need to take God himself seriously in the study by making our study an encounter with him.*[26] The most personally transforming activity we can engage in is worship. This is true even for us as scholars while we are doing our scholarship. What do I mean by making our study an encounter with him? I mean a sort of "practicing of his presence" in the study. True worship, true conscious practicing of God's presence, is the most transforming experience available to the Christian because it is the main way our heart (Hebrew לֵב, *lev*) gets turned around to go in a different direction. We are told in Prov 4:23, "Guard your heart with all vigilance, for from it are the sources of life." As is well known, the "heart" in Hebrew is a term that includes not only intellect but also attitudes, volition, perspectives on life, and the inner life overall. One mode and effect of worship is what one could refer to as "getting impressed with God." Putting it in those terms, one of our main problems in life and as scholars is that we are often impressed with the wrong things, something other than God himself.

We can know a lot and learn more without being transformed. Biblical transformation of the heart (mind, understanding, feelings, attitudes, motivations, etc.) takes place when we become so deeply impressed with God and his purposes in our lives that our will, our volition, becomes engaged in the ongoing process of change and growth. When what we are impressed with changes, then what we desire changes along with it. Deep and meaningful change takes place when the things that matter to us change, and that should be one of the major goals in our study of the Bible. We need to see God with the "eyes" of our "heart," as Paul puts it in Eph 1:18 (NIV). One thing is for sure, if we do indeed see God, like Isaiah in God's throne room, we will most certainly be impressed (Isa 6:1–4). That, in turn, will put the issues of our own lives and ministries in proper perspective as it did for Isaiah (Isa 6:5–8).

The Holy Spirit is directly involved in bringing about such encounters with God in our hearts and lives as part of his ministry of illumination. Consider especially 1 Cor 2, which is one of the most cited chapters in the Bible on the subject of the Holy Spirit and illumination. According to vv. 10–11, "the Spirit searches all things, even the deep things of God. For who among men knows the things of a man except the man's spirit within him? So too, no one knows the things of God except the Spirit of God." So the Holy Spirit knows the depths of God and a person's human spirit knows the depths of the person. According to v. 12, the divine Spirit is in direct and intimate contact with the human spirit of one who is in Christ: "we have not received the spirit of the world, but the Spirit who is from God, so that we may know the things that are freely given to us by God."

Paul takes this point further in Rom 8. The chapter begins with the fact that "there is therefore now no condemnation for those who are in Christ Jesus" (v. 1) and ends with what is virtually a hymn of thanksgiving to God that he will never condemn us; in fact, absolutely nothing in heaven or earth is "able to separate us from the love of God in Christ Jesus our Lord" (v. 39b; cf. all of vv. 31–39). Between the beginning and the end of the chapter there is a great deal said about the Holy Spirit, and once again the intimate connection between the Holy Spirit of God and the human spirit of a believer is expressed. This is especially clear in v. 16, "*The Spirit* himself bears witness to our spirit that we are God's children." We are God's adopted children, and this is truly something to rejoice about. This is the main thing among the gifts that "are freely given to us by God" (1 Cor 2:12b).

Yes, we struggle and groan in our fallenness in the midst of this fallen world, but the Holy Spirit helps us and even prays for us in the depths of our despair when we cannot even express it in words (Rom 8:17–27), so that through whatever happens, good or bad, we are conformed to the likeness of Christ (vv. 28–30). Then comes the hymn (vv. 31–39). So in spite of the pain of life we can still have our lives filled up with the Spirit, which will naturally lead us into worship of God (Eph 5:18–20).[27] This should be true in our study as much as anywhere else. I do not mean to suggest that all we ever do is rejoice and praise and give thanks. On the contrary, we often struggle as Rom 8 indicates. We will come back to this in the next section as it relates to the genuineness of worship. Nevertheless, in the midst of life the Holy Spirit continually works to help us see God's glory and grace with eyes of our heart, and to overwhelm us with that vision of God wherever we are and whatever we are doing, no matter what our circumstances may be for the moment.

Taking our humanity seriously in the study. Second, in addition to taking God himself seriously in our scholarship by seeing our study as an ongoing series of occasions for encounter with him, *we need to take our human nature and experience seriously by functioning as a fully human person in the study.* Our mind, will, emotions, attitudes, perspectives on life, personality, personal and interpersonal problems, background, and all the rest of what we are as a living breathing person need to be fully engaged as we study. I would argue that the most important exegetical and theological "tool" we have is our own "heart" as it has been shaped by our life experiences and especially by personal encounter with God himself. We have been taught and continue to use all sorts of tools in our study of the Bible. These include the biblical languages, various kinds of reference books, and so on. But the most important tool for reading and understanding the Bible is our heart.

We are not just a brain to be filled with data to manipulate, even biblical data. God did not write the Bible to computers. It was written to reach and impact people as they are—fully engaged in life on all the levels mentioned above. As we encounter God in all our humanness we are presenting our whole person to him for change, because what is real and deep within us is what is encountering him. I would argue that we should not "bracket out" or disengage with *anything* in our person or our lives while we are in the study *at any point* in the exegetical process. Doing this would amount to shutting that part of our life off from God in the midst of encountering him in his word.

By the nature of things, our knowledge of God through his Holy Spirit is intimately bound up with our knowledge of ourselves, that is, our human spirit. This is the so-called "double knowledge" that Calvin discusses in the first chapter of his *Institutes*.[28] Every first year Hebrew or Greek student knows that the major terms for the human "spirit" and the Holy "Spirit" are also common words for "wind" or "breath" in both the Hebrew Old Testament (רוּחַ, *ruakh*) and the Greek New Testament (πνεῦμα, *pneuma*). The existence of a human spirit in every person, and the affective nature of that human spirit, is clearly testified to in both the Old Testament (e.g., Jacob's revived "spirit" in Gen 45:27, and Ahab's sullen "spirit" in 1 Kgs 21:5) and the New Testament (e.g., Paul's gentle "spirit" in 1 Cor 4:21, and the "spirit" of power, love, and self-control rather than timidity in 2 Tim 1:7). In fact, one can argue from the Bible that it is precisely the presence of the immaterial "spirit" of a person that makes his or her material body alive as opposed to dead (Jas 2:26a, "the body without the spirit is dead"; see also Ps 31:5 echoed by Jesus on the cross in Luke 23:46, "Father, into your hands I commit my spirit!"). In other words, our human "spirit" consists of all that we are other than a physical body. When it is gone from our body we are physically dead but still a person.

We come to know God when we personally "receive" the Holy Spirit of God (who knows God deeply) in such a way that we experience the effect of the Holy Spirit's presence in our human spirit (which knows us deeply; 1 Cor 2:11–12). Thus, "we speak of these things [i.e., "what God has freely given us," v. 12b] in words not taught by human wisdom but taught by the Spirit, interpreting spiritual things to those who are spiritual" (v. 13 [NRSV]), for "we have the mind of Christ" (v. 16b). God is actually present "in" us and among us in the form of the third person of the Trinity (as well as the first and second persons [cf. John 14–16]). As Christians we are a temple of the Holy Spirit both individually, as a person of faith (1 Cor 6:19–20), and corporately, as a community of faith (1 Cor 3:9–17; cf. also Heb 3:6; 1 Pet 2:4–8; and especially Eph 2:19–22 and perhaps also 3:14–21).

We are called to "practice" the "presence of God" as persons of faith and as communities of faith, and that requires that our human spirit(s) be fully engaged in the process, whether it be in prayer, worship, Bible study, mission, or whatever. Our whole way of life is to be an act of worship (see, e.g., Rom 12:1), and this includes what we do as biblical scholars in the study. This is what it means to take God seriously in our study by making each occasion an encounter with him (see above). Similarly, taking our humanness seriously in the study of the Bible will require that we stay fully engaged as a fully human person as we study God's word. In a sense, our human spirit is the common ground on which we meet God in the person of, and through the presence of, the Holy Spirit. Of course, what we are saying here naturally raises the issue of objectivity and subjectivity in biblical interpretation.

Taking the Bible seriously in the study. Third, we not only need to take both God and our humanness seriously as we study, *we also need to take the Bible itself seriously by allowing the scriptures to have control in our study of it, not our own subjectivity.* We are by nature subjective, and that's okay, but we need to be *well informed in our subjectivity.* To be sure, one scholar's exegesis and interpretation of a particular passage may be different from that of another. This is a reality. We are fallen, so our scholarship is fallen too. The problem is that sometimes we confuse our humanness with our fallenness. We cannot separate the two in our present condition, but we can and must distinguish between them. There is nothing wrong with being human, but there is plenty wrong with being fallen. We do not want to eliminate any part of our humanness when we read and study the Bible, but one of the main purposes of reading the Bible is to transform our fallenness into godliness. As I have already argued, that is precisely the reason for the Holy Spirit's work of illumination.

So we dare not eliminate our humanness while studying the Bible. God wrote the Bible through fully human and subjective people in order to reach us as fully human and subjective people. As we engage in the study of the biblical stories, commands, parables, songs, letters, and so on, the Holy Spirit uses them to draw forth, scrutinize, and transform our drives, commitments, goals, attitudes, feelings, and beliefs. We cannot attain to absolute objectivity and, in my opinion, should not even try. But we don't just read things into the Bible from our own previous knowledge and experience either. Rather, as we become more and more well informed in our study of the Bible we have more to bring to the further reading of the text.

Moreover, if we have been fully engaged with God as a fully human person along the way, there is now passion for our life and ministry in the study as well as in the pulpit or behind the lectern. Then the exegetical tools become resources one is driven to use in his or her pursuit of God. Now the methods, techniques, and conceptual tools of historical-grammatical-literary interpretation become the servants they need to be in the pursuit of genuine understanding of God's word for our own lives and the lives of others. They make sense not only in the study but also in life outside the study.

At the end of the first section of this article I discussed the philosophical and hermeneutical relationship between meaning in the biblical text, understanding of the text, and the Holy Spirit's work of illumination in our engagement with God as we read and study the text. I attempted to define and describe *what illumination is about*. In this section we have pursued the biblical theology of *how illumination actually works*. I am suggesting that as we become *fully engaged on all three points of the triangle* between God, people, and the Bible (see the figure below), we put ourselves in a place and posture for the Holy Spirit to impact us personally and relationally as we study the text. He "illumines" (or "enlightens") our understanding, our attitudes, our perspectives on life, and our relationships. This is what illumination is, and this is how it works.

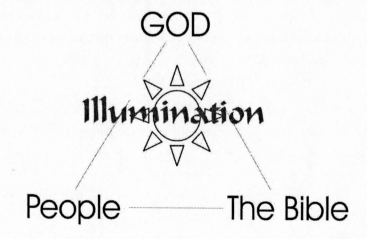

I have already argued that illumination is concerned with the impact of the text on how we think and how we live. In his work of illumination, the Holy Spirit intends to bring about a full-orbed experience of being impacted as a person by God while we are in the text. Yes, we need to diligently pursue the correct interpretation of the text in terms of its meaning (2 Tim 2:15). At least in some passages of the Bible this requires all the scholarly effort and finesse we can muster, all that we have available to us in terms of exegetical, conceptual, and intellectual tools for engagement with the text. The propositional statements and intent of scripture are of immense importance. Nevertheless, we must never lose track of the goal toward which the Holy Spirit is driving us. God is concerned not only about our intellectual grasp of his word, but the grip his word has on our hearts and our lives through the effective work of his Holy Spirit in our human spirit.

Many of the passages used in the discussion of illumination clearly point us in this direction. By way of review, take for example 1 Cor 2:10–16 where the Holy Spirit works in the human spirit so that we not only "know the things that are freely given to us by God" (v. 12) but also see the importance of these things for the way we live our lives (vv. 13–16). The message here is the simple gospel, "Jesus Christ and him crucified" (v. 2 [NIV]; cf. all of vv. 1–10), which is "the wisdom of God, hidden in a mystery" (v. 7) even though to "the man without the Spirit" it is a bunch of "foolishness" (v. 14 [NIV]). The whole thing looks different in the Spirit. It is the gospel that transforms us as the Holy Spirit brings its various truths to bear upon us, which are the things "freely given to us by God." Moreover, the gospel is always "good news" to everyone, non-Christian and Christian alike. Even if we are already true believers, there are always ways in which the impact and significance of the gospel still needs to be worked into our human spirit, and from there into every aspect of our lives.

Similarly, Eph 1:17–19 talks about "spiritual wisdom and revelation" associated with enlightening "the eyes of" the "heart." Col 1:9–13 talks about gaining the knowledge of God's will in spiritual wisdom and understanding so that we "live worthily of the Lord" and share in the light of the Kingdom of Christ.

In essence, we invite the Holy Spirit to have this effect in our lives by engaging well on all three points articulated above: *encountering* God as a fully human *persons* open to the impact of *God's word.* In terms of language as an act of communication, the Holy Spirit, who is the original divine author of scripture in the first place, takes his word and creates an act of communication on the spot by bringing his inspired text to bear on the heart and life of the reader.[29] When we purpose to study our Bible this way, application is no longer a last step after-thought taken up after we do all we can to "get the text right." Instead, application becomes central to our experience of the Bible even in our study through the Holy Spirit's work of illumination.

Let me emphasize here that I am not talking about a supposed distinction between academic study and devotional reading of the Bible. There can be different opinions on that. My point is that true biblical scholarship must not only concentrate on the Bible but on the expressed purposes of the Bible as God's revelation. Only this kind of scholarship is thoroughly biblical, and the Holy Spirit's work of illumination is absolutely required for those who wish to study it this way.[30]

The Nurture of Biblical Scholarship

All of this affects how we teach the text too. We need to nurture this kind of biblical scholarship. Once again, a mechanical or simplistic "teach and apply" method of *using* the Bible in ministry, whether in preaching, teaching, or in some other way, is not sufficient. We need to think deeply and implicationally about God, people, and the Bible as we relate to students in the church, the classroom, and in more intimate mentoring contexts.

First of all, in our teaching of the Bible we need to *view* personal change and transformation in the lives of the people to whom we minister as "worship" centered and empowered. We need to *take God seriously* as we approach them. I cannot reach inside someone's life and turn their heart in a different direction, but the Holy Spirit can. He often does this in a situation where people truly "get impressed" with God. This can change how life looks and what is important. It gets their will engaged in what the Holy Spirit wants to do in their life.

Second, we need to *recognize* that, just like us, the people to whom we minister are not made up of just a "brain" to be filled with information, biblical or otherwise. All of the other human capacities with which they have been endowed by God and the tendencies with which they are plagued because of the fall must be taken seriously as well. We need to *take people seriously* as we bring our study to bear upon their lives. Simply depositing truth is not the answer. Truth is basic, but its purpose is to change lives and that means that it has to become more than just intellectual cognition. Just because people "know" something does not necessarily mean that what they know is "touching" them meaningfully.

We are after transformed hearts and lives and *we* cannot *make* that happen! We are totally dependent on God to reach into their life. Therefore, prayer becomes an absolute necessity from our point of view. We must not redefine the task so that we can attain it without the direct "hands on" work of God taking place. As a communicative act, God's word in the Bible has a certain intention that we must not diminish or cheapen.

Third, we need to *help* the people whom we teach to take the Bible seriously. Again, we cannot make this happen, but if we model it in our own scholarship the Holy Spirit can use that too. From a biblical point of view, the Bible is not just *one* of the valid perspectives on life and meaning as the postmodern pluralist would argue. Our goal is to do our scholarship and teach the results of our scholarly work in such a way that our students grow ever more increasingly toward loving God well, loving people well, and living God's word well in their own life and ministry.

First, they, like us, grow to love God well by encountering him regularly, meaningfully, and worshipfully as they are in the text. They become godly. Second, they, like us, love other people well because they are fully engaged on a human level as a godly person and are able to meet them where they are. They are genuine. Third, they, like us, apply God's word well in their own life and ministry as a godly and genuine person; they are subjective, yes, but also well informed when they read and study the Bible. They are illumined by the Holy Spirit.

Conclusion

Finally, in conclusion, let's return to the biblical metanarrative. In my own study of the Bible, attempting to read it in the way described above, I have come to a certain perspective on the overall flow of the biblical message that, for me at least, combines well the need to take God, people, and the Bible itself seriously from the point of view of an overall biblical theology. There is no need for big words or sophisticated theological arguments here. In fact, the more simple and straightforward the language is, the better. Here is how it goes.

First, although the world was created to be a place of "rest" (i.e., peace and purpose) for us, *it* is now a "mess" and so are *we*. We have lost our "rest," and this loss manifests itself in the way we handle life. This is the burden of Gen 1–11, and the effects of these realities are manifest all the way through the rest of scripture as well. Genesis 1–11 is meant to level the ground of our human experience: who we are, the nature of our situation, and how we got ourselves into the mess we are in. One way of talking about the problem we face is that we lack "rest," the kind of rest Jesus invites us to in Matt 11:28–30: "Come to me, all you who are weary and burdened, and I will give you rest. Take my yoke on you and learn from me, because I am gentle and humble in heart, and you will find rest for your souls. For my yoke is easy to bear, and my load is not hard to carry." We all manifest this lack of rest in different ways and down to the very core of our being. We are not in the situation we were originally created to live in. We were created for paradise; we are not there anymore, and we don't like it.

Second, even though we are in this disastrous situation and continue to make it worse because of the many ways we reject God and his design for us and our world, still, he has stayed involved and there *is* a redemptive "rest" to be found amid the "mess." This is what the rest of the Bible is all about, from Gen 12 through Rev 22. Here the focus is on what God has done to help us through the mess in which we find ourselves and back to himself. We can think of this as restoring our rest while we continue to live in the mess. One can recall here the inclusio-like envelope around the Bible as a whole when we compare Gen 1–2 with Rev 21–22—the creation of the heaven and earth, and the new heaven and earth. The paradise, the tree of life, all the freely flowing waters are there again in Rev 21–22. Moreover, there is no more curse, a reflection on Gen 3. By God's grace we are heading back to where we originally came from; in fact, something even better.

Third, from the point of view of our current situation in this in-between age then, our goal in ministry is to work that "rest" down into the hearts and lives of people so that they love God and love people well in spite of the "mess" which we are and in which we live. This is what we are about in biblical scholarship as much as in any other ministry, if our scholarship is truly biblical not only in content but in its intention. In order to accomplish this ministry goal, first, we need to know how to meet people where they are by truly understanding and engaging with them as people. We need to understand people biblically. Second, we need to know how to take them from where they are to where they need to go. We need to be able to help them biblically in terms of working God's "rest" down into their lives even as we ourselves continue to grow in this. On this level, the gospel is always "good news" to everyone, because there are always ways in which the full effect of it has not been worked into our lives.

It is the work of the Holy Spirit to bring the dynamics of this gospel to bear in all levels and dimensions of our lives individually and as a community of faith in this corrupt world. This is his agenda, and his agenda is what we are all about as biblical scholars—if we are truly biblical.

The Holy Spirit and the Arts

Reg Grant

This essay examines the Christian's interaction with the Holy Spirit in the creation of art. We reflect on our shared doxological goal, then consider the difficult question of process, how we are to depend on the Holy Spirit to guide us from concept through production, to help us reach that goal. We consider two utilitarian approaches to dependence before endorsing an organic approach that emphasizes union with the Savior as the source and sustaining influence of our creative work. Finally, we illustrate the difference between subjectivism and objectively-based spirituality in the persons of Thomas Munzer and Martin Luther.

In the beginning of any artistic[1] enterprise, we Christians who also happen to be artists brood over the unformed mass before us in much the same way as the Spirit of God hovered over the chaos at creation. The canvass, the stage, the page, stand empty. The rough-hewn stone squats undraped on the studio floor, awaiting the creator's touch. As God's Spirit brought order out of the confusion, so are we called to transform the emptiness before us—to spread onto the canvass, truth in living colors. To shape the formless stone in a way that will remind the world of the Rock that contains and inspires all form. To compose music that captures the echo of God singing. To direct a play or shoot a film in a way that opens a window into heaven rather than merely holding a mirror up to nature. And we share the Spirit's purpose who, along with the Father and the Son, created the heavens and the earth: we want our art to glorify God.

> "I made the earth, I created the people who live on it. It was me—my hands stretched out the sky, I give orders to all the heavenly lights" (Isa 45:12).

> "The heavens declare God's glory; the sky displays his handiwork" (Ps 19:1).

> "For all things in heaven and on earth were created by him—all things, whether visible or invisible, whether thrones or dominions, whether principalities or powers—all things were created through him and for him.

> He is the head of the body, the church, as well as the beginning, the firstborn from among the dead, so that he himself may become first in all things" (Col 1:16, 18).

I enjoy reading my King James Bible where the Holy Spirit is called the Holy Ghost. I realize the occultish connotation in the word "Ghost" even when capitalized in the middle of a sentence. But it helps me think of him in new ways. I long to be Christ-haunted by the heavenly Muse, our *Holy* Ghost. It is he who not only hovers over us, but actually indwells us, patiently forming our spiritual substance into the image of Christ Jesus even as we try to put a spit shine on a scuffed up world. He lives in us somehow. Never leaves us. Never sleeps. He is here now, aware that I am typing, aware that you are reading. So immediate. So hauntingly available, it seems he should make more of a difference in what I produce. Patience isn't my strong suit, and it may not be yours either. Nor is the humility that is part and parcel of not being God, even though the Lord graciously reminds us of it on a daily basis.

Where God the Holy Spirit expressed the immaterial thought of God perfectly as objective reality (the material universe), we human artists, even though filled with the same creative Spirit, struggle with an imperfect understanding of beauty, imperfect skills, and imperfect tools: is the chisel sharp enough, is the paint the right shade of red, how hard should we strike the key, how much pressure should we exert on the bow? Given our imperfections, how can we ever hope to honor God in our work? It isn't that we don't try hard. In fact, trying so hard is actually part of the problem. Oddly enough, we artists who wish to communicate a worldview consistent with our Christian beliefs often attempt to produce our art using the same process the world uses.

By "process" I do not mean the technical aspects of production. The tools of the trade are available to Christian and non-Christian alike and are amoral. The Christian filmmaker uses the same film stock as the agnostic. The Christian pianist uses the same piano as the atheist. No instrument, no tool has any moral quality in and of itself. These tools will simply serve to translate the artist's immaterial thoughts into something more corporeal and sensate.

Nor do I mean by "process" the discipline required to use these tools effectively. Technical excellence requires disciplined study and rehearsal even among the gifted. By "process" I mean the way in which we draw upon the inner resources that inspire and ultimately guide our exercise. The question before us regards the "how" of art at a deeper level. Not "upon what or whom do we depend?" for the Christian's facile answer is, "the Holy Spirit, of course!" But "how, in what way, do we depend on him?" The temptation for the Christian artist is to depend on the Holy Spirit of God in one of two ways: either as another tool or as a lackey.

The Holy Spirit as Holy Tool

Here, he functions as a sort of magic brush—given by God to make our art "special" in some spiritual sense that we secretly hope will translate into a larger advance, a bigger contract. So our attitude toward the Holy Tool can be as banal, as utilitarian as our attitude toward any of the other useful implements in our bag of tricks. It is a syncretistic business, this blending of a worldly approach with a spiritual purpose, and one that is doomed to produce little of eternal value, and if so, only accidentally. We are no alchemists, though we continue to use the base metals of this world in a vain attempt to create the heavenly gold of the next.

Such a mechanistic view of the Holy Spirit fails to satisfy, and it's no surprise, given the organic union of Vine to branch in John 15. The issue isn't really whether or not we should depend on the Holy Spirit in the artistic endeavor, but "how should we depend on him?" If we look to John 15 for an answer we discover there is no independence at all. There, the branch is either connected in a consistent, vital, life-sustaining union with the vine, or it is dead.

Even when we recognize our own frailty, it is easy to think that if we just open ourselves to the control of God's Spirit, then we will achieve greatness as artists, producing work that will glorify God. Then God reminds us once again that he is, and we are not, sovereign. The degree to which our art will glorify God does *not* vary in direct proportion to our dependence on the Spirit of God in its production. That would make the "success" of our work thoroughly dependent on our own efforts. By depending on him in this way, we may achieve works of art that possess an imaginative resonance otherwise unobtainable. But that doesn't guarantee that God will choose that work to honor himself. He may decide to honor himself through a less "Spirit-dependent" man or woman such as Balaam (Num 22), or he may work through a Spirit-filled person like Bezalel (Exod 31). God can and often does work in spite of us.

While we have no idea of how or if the Lord might choose to glorify himself through our artistic offerings, we still have an obligation to produce our works in a way that would please him. The artistic process must be spiritually based, and spiritually driven if we are to realize a spiritual purpose. We must allow God to produce his art through us—not as if we were limp gloves waiting to be filled by the Divine hand, nor as lifeless instruments waiting to be manipulated, but as children who actually participate with our heavenly Father in a dynamic creative process. And he has given us everything we need to accomplish our purpose.

God, the Master Artisan[2], provides in this phenomenal universe limitless material for contemplation, as well as the material tools fit for the work of composition: palette, brush, chisel, pen, and in the person of the artist, balance, voice, imagination, a sense of timing. Artists learn the discipline of their craft to manipulate these and a host of other tools in a wide variety of media in order to achieve the desired effect—the translation of an immaterial idea into objective reality. Virtually any dedicated individual can gain access to these tools and learn how to use them. One needn't be a Christian to master the techniques, the mechanics of the artisan. It is simply a matter of learning how to draw the brush across the canvass.

But humankind is more than a robot, and art is more than the result of assembly line mechanics. God has breathed into humans the breath of life, and in that breath we have absorbed the image of God in the immaterial essence of soul, spirit, mind, heart, and conscience, each contributing to the development of intellect, emotion, and will. Among all the animals that inhabit the planet, we humans possess the unique ability to think God's thoughts.[3] A man or woman may produce a work of art, but a dog or a canary never will.[4] We are the only ones with a conscience to which God often appeals to exert a profound influence on the will. The degree to which we yield to his appeal is the degree to which we will enjoy blessing and reward. Conversely, the degree to which we resist his appeal to conscience is the degree to which, among all creation, we will suffer loss and shame. I can picture Mark Twain's words chiseled into foundation of the bema of Christ as I stand watching my mound of wood, hay, and stubble consumed by the flames: "Man is the only animal that blushes. Or needs to." The immaterial/spiritual components of humankind, which together make up the *Imago Dei*, are resident in all humans, saved or unsaved.

Where then, does the artist who is a Christian enjoy an advantage over the unsaved artist? In the indwelling Holy Spirit. The very God who formed the world, who brought order out of chaos at creation, also filled men like Bezalel (not a New Testament Christian, but an Old Testament believer) to produce works of art.

> Then Moses said to the Israelites, "See, the LORD has called by name Bezalel son of Uri, the son of Hur, of the tribe of Judah. He has filled him with the Spirit of God—with skill, with understanding, with knowledge, and with all kinds of work, to design artistic designs, to work in gold, in silver, and in bronze, and in cutting stones for their setting, and in cutting wood, to do work in every artistic craft (Exod 35:30-33).

For the artist who is a Christian, and indwelt by God's Spirit, the creative process calls for more than the acquisition of the disciplines of his or her craft. It even calls for more than the supernatural presence of the Holy Spirit. The carnal Christians in Corinth remind us that the mere presence of God's Spirit in the life of the believer is no guarantee of spiritual maturity. Paul reminds us in Eph 5:18 that, as in all the other facets of the Christian life, the creative process requires a consistent, conscious *reliance* on the Holy Spirit.

> "And do not get drunk with wine, which is debauchery, but be filled by the Spirit" (Eph 5:18).

It is interesting that the very next verse considers the righteous effect of such a Spirit-dominated life.

> "speaking to one another in psalms, hymns, and spiritual songs, singing and making music in your hearts to the Lord" (Eph 5:19).

The presence of the Holy Spirit is assumed. Paul's focus is on the Christian's relationship to the Spirit. The first response of a Spirit-controlled Christian, Paul says, is thoroughly artistic and relational. We are to express ourselves to one another and to the Lord through the artistry of music. The words translated "speaking" and "singing" are present active participles, suggesting an ongoing process. The Holy Spirit enables the Christian to celebrate, and thereby exalt God through discourse with other Christians and through private worship ("in your hearts") to the Lord. The content of the musical celebration is dictated by the nature of the controlling Agent. The Holy Spirit inspires (in the non-technical sense) "psalms," "hymns," and "spiritual songs," all terms which denote music that honors the Lord.

The ultimate purpose of the Christian artist, then, as it is for all Christians, is doxological; that is, we are to honor or glorify God in all that we do. We realize that purpose aesthetically, and in the context of relationship as we reveal ourselves through our art to the world.

All art is revelatory. What we reveal and how we reveal it demonstrate our devotion to the discipline of our craft (material technique) and to our awareness of truth (immaterial or spiritual sensitivity). The degree to which material discipline and spiritual sensitivity complement one another in a work of art is the degree to which the artist may achieve greatness *qua* artist, but here we must offer a caveat. Such correspondence may say little or nothing regarding the spiritual maturity of the individual artist. Caravaggio, the 17th century painter, provides a chilling example. His paintings reveal the truth of Christ's deity (in his *Raising of Lazarus*, for example) more powerfully than any other artist of the Baroque period does, and yet he lived a stormy and often dissolute life. Given the piety of the subject and the excellence of the technique, the casual observer would have no clue as to the quality of the artist's relationship with the God he revealed on canvass. Caravaggio's technique was impeccable. His spiritual sensitivity, that is, his ability to discern spiritual truth, was highly developed. It was his unwillingness to submit to the control of God's Spirit in the rest of his life that left him miserable and broken, and finally dead at the age of 36.

We are, in our moments of artistic composition, either under the control of God's Spirit, or under the influence of our own "soulishness" (Jas 3:15), that natural tendency to satisfy the desires of the flesh.

When we submit to the controlling influence of the Holy Spirit, we Christians who are artists function most effectively as intermediaries, as spokespersons, or to use a biblical metaphor, as ambassadors. We are truth-bearers, though our message is at times couched in the poetry rather than the prose of life, and so it may be a bit more difficult to absorb on a first reading/hearing/viewing. At other times it is our privilege to unlock, all at once, the beauty in the everyday treasures of our world, and the viewer finds himself almost overwhelmed in a dynamic rush of truth and beauty. There is truth in a water lily, but who among us, gazing out over a pond full of green on green, unimpressionable and static as the scene before us, has experienced that truth in the same way as Monet? He recreates the fact of the green plants, painting unfocused images that captured an honest and multicolored—in short, a kinetic impression of that truth. Monet, as all artists, allows the audience to participate in the translated event so that they may vicariously experience the truth of the lilies in the same way he experienced it.

This world of common water lilies is the world we seek to reclaim, to recreate, for one simple reason: it is the world we have inherited. Adam lived in a world where he was connected to God (in the creation), then disconnected (through the fall), then reconnected (through the promised redemption in Christ, the last Adam). The world itself, however, remains disconnected and awaits redemption from the curse (Rom 8:22). Paradoxically, there is a need for a kind of detachment (another disconnect) in order for the artist who is a Christian to see the world, not only as it is—on its tired journey back to chaos, but as God wills it to be in the future—a new world taking its first breath.

Our God-given hope provides us a new set of lenses through which we can see these two worlds (the phenomenal, space/time world and the spiritual world) as distinct realities. So the Christian artist is left to discover in a ruined world the blush of beauty he had while virtuous, and which he will regain when redeemed. Ours is a task at once nostalgic and prophetic, and it requires that we work with what we have, i.e., within the limits imposed by our mortality. We cannot create something out of nothing. While God created what is *actual* out of what is *imaginary*, we creative artists must create what is imaginary out of what is actual, and the Holy Spirit works through us to create a work of art.

But then I think, how am I relating to him? If not as a Holy Tool to be picked up and set down at my discretion, then how *should* I relate to him? Like most artists who are Christians, I can honestly say that I depend on the Person of the Holy Spirit to help me. Then it hits me. When I say I depend on the Holy Spirit as a Person to help me, I find myself treating him, not as God, but as if he were a Best Boy on a movie set whose job it is to make me comfortable so that I can do my best work.

The Holy Spirit as Holy Lackey

As spiritually obtuse as it seems, we often exhibit a guarded, almost defensive attitude toward the Holy Spirit's invasion into the creative sphere, into our domain. He is there to help, we insist, not to take over. We expect him to serve us, we remind him, just as Jesus did who came not to be served, but to serve. And isn't the Holy Spirit subservient to the Lord Jesus and the Father?

To use a different metaphor, sometimes we subconsciously assign the Holy Spirit the job of Holy Editor. His touch should be light, and under no circumstances should he attempt a major revision. As a rule, immature artists put up with human editors (in their various incarnations) as necessary contractual evils. For the artist whose soul is wrapped up in his or her work, editors are the cutters of words, the redefiners of vision, the guardians of market-driven standards of mediocrity. It's easy to impute our distrust for human editors (whose motives may be mixed) to the Holy Spirit (whose motives are pure, but which we suspect nonetheless).

A more ominous vision: the Holy Spirit as Divine Executive Producer—the Supreme Suit always on the set during rehearsals. He may be a really nice Guy and all, but if he's always there, looking over our shoulder, how can we really create? He needs to stay in his office and write the checks, dispense the blessings and let us get on with our art. We shudder to think—what happens if, on the next to last stroke of the brush, he decides he doesn't like the chiaroscuro effect? What if he says the invited dress stinks and we should cancel the show and return the advance ticket sales? What if he pulls the plug in dozens of other ways on our artistic creation?

That's the risk we run, we tell ourselves, by allowing him total control, final say, absolute authority. It's a kind of Hobbsian view of the Holy Spirit as despotic monarch, a necessary Governor because without him we spiritually antisocial artists would be throwing paint at each other rather than at the canvass.

And even if we were to seek his guidance, as we seek the guidance of a favorite director, how can we really know it is his voice we are listening to? How can we be sure we are being guided by the Holy Spirit and not by public pressure to conform (the world), our own insecurities (the flesh, or our corrupted/imperfect soul), or the evil one himself (the Unit Production Manager—or the devil, whichever you prefer). The Lord no longer carves out messages in tablets of stone. He doesn't thunder in a voice that shakes mountains or *Paramountains*.

We would settle for a still small voice, a whisper even. But no. We are not told to seek something audible, but we must trust him to lead through his word, the Bible, and through a yielded heart to obey that word. That requires discernment, refined by careful study of the scriptures and long visits with the Lord in prayer. Spiritual discipline. Hard work with a spiritual twist that calls on us to rest in him. But we have such trouble putting the two together. We don't like that tension. We want it to be one way or the other. We either want to work ourselves into an early grave and drag the Holy Spirit in after us, or we want to abandon all responsibility to work and let God dial the phone. Conservative evangelicals fall more easily into the error of works-righteousness than into the error of irresponsible passivity. But that doesn't mean we don't fantasize.

"Life would be so much simpler," we sigh, bone weary, "if we could just shuck our left-brained rational, intellectual robes, and dive buck naked into the right hemisphere of creativity." There's an antiseptic security in an emotional vacuum. There we convince ourselves that spiritual decisions are best made inductively: gather the information, isolate the factors, weight the consequences, and engage the will. And yet, how arrogant to assume that our more intellectual, reductionistic approach to the Spirit-filled life is superior, when in fact that kind of 20th century asceticism leaves us intellectually puffed up and emotionally shriveled at the same time. Still, it's a safe life. Our God is pretty tame most of the time: boxable, predictable, housebroken, servile. The alternative—the idea that the rock-splitting God of the Old Testament might still be lurking in the shadows of the Cross of the gentle Jesus, is too unsettling, too threatening for many of us seeker-sensitive types.

So we stand with the publican in the shadows of the temple, thanking God that He didn't make us a woman or a charismatic, equating total surrender to the control of the Holy Spirit with a knuckles-dragging-the-ground, swinging-from-the-chandeliers, Neanderthal approach to the spiritual life. Why? Because we're scared. Scared of emotions. But, as Howard Hendricks says, "we needn't fear emotions. Emotions are God's gifts. What we should fear is emotionalism, which is emotions out of control."[5] Our irrational fear is that the Holy Spirit might excite in us a fleshly response! So we try to keep him on a leash. We tend his holy fire, and of course wind up quenching him altogether, and living a life that isn't spiritual at all. It is a life thoroughly fleshly and rotten to the core, with only the robes of spirituality to make it respectable in public. We refuse to risk embarrassment. We will protect ourselves at all costs.

But we shall be disappointed if we persist in this childish spirituality. Like children playing at the seashore, we build our theology of the spiritual life on the beach of our own personality, and then we're stunned when it turns out to be nothing but a sandcastle. The cares of this world, or Satan, or God himself will wash it away. If we produce our art in the strength of the flesh, we shouldn't be surprised if it has a fleshly half-life. We need balance between passive dependence on the Holy Spirit and responsible, obedience to his will. Two men from the Reformation will provide illustrations of lives in and out of spiritual balance: Martin Luther and Thomas Munzer.

Luther and Munzer at Spiritual Odds

Here at the end of the twentieth century, the artist who is also a Christian finds himself in somewhat the same position as Luther in the late fifteenth and early sixteenth centuries. Luther confronted a church that claimed a spiritual purpose, but which had become infected with a worldly heart. Historically (and biblically) the church's purpose has been to glorify the Lord through making disciples of the Lord Jesus Christ, and then guiding those believers to spiritual maturity (Matt 28). Instead, the medieval church had decided to glorify God by edifying St. Peter's and making disciples of the clergy. Luther recognized, as we must, that in order fulfill a spiritual mandate, the church had to be reformed. Likewise, we believe it is time for a spiritual reformation in the arts.

The suspicious attitude of many evangelicals toward our charismatic brethren can be summed up in an observation Martin Luther made concerning Thomas Munzer, his more volatile protestant counterpart in the Reformation: Munzer (along with Karlstadt), Luther said, had swallowed the Holy Spirit, "feathers and all."[6] It would be difficult to find two more different men in their views on bibliology, pneumatology, and sanctification. Munzer's sole authority in matters of faith and practice was the inner light given by God's Holy Spirit, and so was subjective in extremis. Luther's far more objective standard of authority was the Bible. Munzer advocated fiery rebellion and swords. Luther pushed for dialogue and the armor of God (at least prior to 1525). If the Reformation had been played out on a baseball diamond and Luther and Munzer had been opposing pitchers, Munzer would have been the finesse pitcher, throwing curves, sliders, and a knuckler that never landed in the same place twice. Luther would have smoked you with a barrage of fastballs—his only pitch. But his accuracy would leave you shaking your head as he repeatedly nipped the outside of the plate for a called third strike.

But lest we see in these two men a clear dichotomy between a "right-brainer" (Munzer) and a "lefty" (Luther) we need to consider a couple of incontrovertible facts: 1) besides being an emotional zealot with a rainbow emblazoned on his flag, Munzer was a linguistic specialist in Latin, Greek, and Hebrew and a recognized scholar of ancient and humanistic literature. He was particularly known for his work in the Old and New Testaments. Doesn't fit the stereotype of the creative artist, does it? 2) Luther, our "typical left-brained dominant, logical, linear, academic" was a musician. Sometimes we forget that he was just as passionate about getting music into the hands of the people as he was in getting the Bible into the vernacular.

The main difference between the two men wasn't their basic personalities. They were cut from the same temperamental cloth. Both were zealots. Both were capable of cruelty and of passion bordering on frenzy. Both were headstrong, with volatile, combustible spirits. Both felt compassion for the struggling peasant-class in Saxony, Thuringia, and beyond. Both were Christians as far as I can tell, though both exhibited plenty of flesh from time to time, and Munzer may have been merely a political opportunist wrapped in a holy shroud. These two fought each other, tried to destroy each other—Munzer, using the weapons of war; Luther, relying on prayer and dialogue. What led one man to pick up a pitchfork and the other to pick up a prayerbook? The issue is one of control. Two different forces controlled these men. It is paradoxical that Munzer, who professed such a dependence on the Holy Spirit to guide him, was ultimately blinded by pride and controlled by his flesh. Luther, I believe was, for the most part, controlled by the Holy Spirit. He "walked in the light" more than Munzer, even though his standard for discerning the will of God was the objective revelation given in scripture rather than Munzer's subjective "inner light."

Now, what do Luther and Munzer have to do with the topic of the Holy Spirit and the arts? Neither man was a champion of the arts as such. Oddly enough, both men were iconoclasts during the High Renaissance, that period when the arts in particular glorified man and during which the humanistic artist began to recast God in his own image. But the Renaissance was a double-edged sword. On one side the Renaissance with its secular humanism elevated and glorified man. But on the other side, as humanism replaced scholasticism as the principle school of thought, men like Luther and Munzer enjoyed the intellectual freedom to explore, exploit, and expunge long held doctrines. Both men used the new intellectual freedom to attack the moral depravity of the corrupt ecclesiastical system they had inherited as well as many humanistic tenets of the Renaissance that gave them the freedom to explore those ideas in the first place.

In other words, both were more than willing to bite the humanistic hand that fed them. Or simply to ignore the hand altogether. While in Rome to appeal a decision in the Observantist/Conventual controversy, Luther expressed little or no interest in seeing any of the great art of the city (Michelangelo was painting the Sistine at the time, less than two modern city blocks away from the debate hall). After the Holy See rejected his appeal, Luther had a lot of time on his hands. At that primitive point in his theological development, he was far more concerned with earning as many indulgences as he could before beginning the six-week hike back to Wittenberg. At the same time, Munzer was too busy whipping up the peasantry to a bloody rebellion to be distracted by the arts.

And yet both men recognized the value of the arts as utilitarian engines to drive their respective causes. Ultimately, Munzer used the arts to manipulate the masses. His dramatic tirades against scripture would have made Billy Sunday blush. On one occasion he threw the Bible down and stomped on it. Munzer understood the importance of visual symbols. His colorful flag was emblazoned with the rainbow, perhaps to signify the overturning of the old order as well as the blessing of God on the new. His fiery oratory was designed to inspire reverential awe and obedience.

In his last great battle against the assembled forces at Frankenhausen he dared the assembled armies of catholic princes to fire on his unarmed peasant army, boasting that he would catch their bullets in his sleeve! These techniques and others betrayed a reliance on theatrical gimmickry to sway an uneducated public. Munzer welcomed the Holy Spirit as the ultimate source of authority, but only he could interpret the Holy Spirit's message rightly. Anyone suspected of disagreeing with Munzer's leadership was automatically guilty of disagreeing with God the Holy Spirit, and that person suffered painful consequences.

Luther on the other hand eagerly sought the illumination of the Spirit in his study of the scriptures. His prayers are saturated with petitions that God would lead him, guide him, direct him in his study of the Bible. Luther was a brilliant debater, and a dynamic preacher, but he also enjoyed tremendous influence as a communicator of God's truth through music. A few scholars have read the translations of his debates with Eck and others. More are familiar with some of his sermons, and, of course, with his translation of the Bible. But the music he composed continues to move and inspire congregations and their leaders, even today. And to teach. Music was for Luther the art of choice. Through music he could educate and build up the hearts of the common people he served. Through music he encouraged his parishioners to obey God's word in the power of the Spirit.

For Munzer, the arts were a tool for touching the masses with the message of God as he received it through visions and dreams and direct command. His own imagination, however, was the *sine qua non* of revelation. For Luther, the arts, and music in particular, were a tool for touching people with the message of God as found in scripture. Each man claimed to rely on the Holy Spirit for guidance, but in the final analysis, Munzer sought to use religion to enhance the mood[7] necessary to advance his own political agenda, while Luther sought to be used by the Holy Spirit to advance God's spiritual agenda. Luther's more objective scriptural basis proved to be more reliable and a stronger safeguard against doctrinal perversion than did Munzer's thoroughly subjective basis. An imaginative use of the arts was a part of the *modus operandi* for both men; however, due to their different approaches to the Holy Spirit, Luther's imagination was essentially different from the Munzer's. Coleridge addresses this difference in his famous definition of imagination:

> The primary imagination I hold to be the living power and prime agent of all human perception, and as a repetition in the finite mind of the eternal act of creation in the infinite I AM. The secondary I consider as an echo of the former, co-existing with the primary in the kind of its agency, and differing only in degree, and in the mode of its operation. It dissolves, diffuses, dissipates, in order to re-create; or where this process is rendered impossible, yet still, at all events, it struggles to idealize and to unify. It is essentially vital, even as all objects (as objects) are essentially fixed and dead.
>
> Fancy, on the contrary, has no other counters to play with but fixities and definites. The fancy is indeed no other than a mode of memory emancipated from the order of time and space; and blended with, and

modified by that empirical phenomenon of the will which we express by the word *choice*.[8]

In distinguishing between the secondary imagination and fancy, Coleridge draws the line between Luther's artistic imagination and that of Munzer. Where Munzer was fenced in by the boundaries of his own fancy, the word of God freed Luther to explore the frontiers of heaven and what Coleridge would call the primary imagination of the infinite *I AM*.

Christian artists in the Reformed tradition, and especially those of us who have been burned by the fires of subjectivism, may tend to shy away from a direct appeal to the Holy Spirit to fill and to guide us in our aesthetic enterprises. Our theology tells us that those "tongues of fire" in Acts are legitimate expressions of an irruptive Spirit, but our experience has emerged from an orthodoxy that, in too many cases, has grown cold. We fear doctrinal error—as if calling on the Spirit means abandoning the word—and that we might wind up with our metaphorical heads on the block as the pitiful Munzer did. That fear, however, will paralyze us into a clinical, bloodless, plastic exposition of life—a rhetorical narrative that would have been better left untold. The word under the influence of the Spirit guards us from that kind of error. May we artists who are Christians embrace the word prayerfully, asking the Holy Spirit to guide us into all truth, to help us to see through deception to truth, and to enable us to render that beauty in a way that will honor the Creator.

The Spirit in the Black Church

Willie O. Peterson

The traditional dispute cessationists have with the charismatics usually ends in a sharp separation, but not so with all evangelicals who are cessationists. Some evangelicals firmly hold to a cessationist position, disallowing the operation of sign gifts for today, but they also fellowship with evangelicals who are charismatics and who argue for the continuation of the sign gifts. This essay presents a plausible understanding of evangelicals who, although cessationists, embrace evangelicals who are charismatics. Finally it addresses the question "Are such cessationists merely a misguided exception; or is the biblical basis for their position sound and thus commendable to all evangelicals who are cessationists?"

Introduction

There they were together on Christian television and there was an obvious comfortable fellowship between them. The scene was the Oak Cliff Bible Fellowship in Dallas, Texas; the characters were Pastor Anthony (Tony) Evans and Pastor Joseph Garlington.

Dr. Evans is a distinguished scholar, theologian, radio preacher, author and noncharismatic pastor. Evans, a graduate of Dallas Theological Seminary, holds both the masters and doctorate in theology. Dallas Seminary is well known for its cessationist views. On the other hand, Pastor Garlington is Senior Pastor of the very successful Covenant Church of Pittsburgh located in Pittsburgh, Pennsylvania. He is internationally known and respected for his leadership within the charismatic movement. His gifted worship ministry has influenced churches of all types and worship styles, charismatic and noncharismatic. But it is inevitable that some one will ask, "How is it that Evans and Garlington are able to come together in light of their opposing views on the Holy Spirit?"

The question could be asked this way, "When would a high profile noncharismatic pastor invite another equally high profile, but charismatic, pastor to lead his cessationist congregation in worship?" The short answer is, "When the noncharismatic cessationist is a black pastor." The type of a comfortable fellowship experience seen between Evans and Garlington has been rather common between noncharismatic blacks and charismatics for a long time. However, I clearly recognize the dilemma the above scenario creates for cessationists. I am a product of the black church and a cessationist. I welcome an opportunity to give what I believe is a plausible explanation.

This essay seeks to wrestle with the question, "What is it about many noncharismatic black Christians' view of the Holy Spirit that allows them to be comfortable worshiping with charismatic Christians?"

This essay paints a generalized picture of a slice of black evangelicals. There are many who would frame the ideas here in a different way than I have and I accept that. But my purpose is to argue that black evangelicals in general relate to the Holy Spirit in a certain way and there is a special reason for that. My objective is to argue that we are comfortable with the Holy Spirit at the existential level as well as at the intellectual level. We see no contradiction in praying for something God promises and not having a rational explanation for how God kept his promise. Instead, experience has conditioned us (and scripture too, when we pay attention) to ask in child-like faith. To keep asking and keep expecting him to graciously answer. Since we are told that his ways are past finding out, why get hung up on not being able to find out? We see no discrepancy when human suffering and brokenness are laid before God in what becomes unanswered prayers, while the capacity of those who prayed to believe God grew stronger.

First, in the black church tradition an authentic encounter with the God of the Bible is synonymous with an experience with the Holy Spirit. Furthermore, this encounter with the Holy Spirit does indeed happen in the context of corporate worship. But it begins long before Sunday in the day-to-day life of the individuals who bring this dynamic to the Sunday morning worship services. Finally, it would be nearly impossible to discuss the topic of the black evangelical church without at least calling attention to the racially hostile environment out of which the black church was born. And this environment has persisted for much of the time since its birth. Otherwise, apart from some understanding of its roots, it is doubtful that one can adequately appreciate the black evangelical church or its contributions. For I am convinced that the black church owes its spiritual power and resilience to black people's struggle for survival. Because the fact is, the church in America has been divided along racial lines since slavery. The "great debate" over the operation of sign gifts has always been much more of a "white Christian" phenomenon than a "black one." For there is a long history of fellowship between noncharismatic blacks with both black and white charismatics.

In the instance of Evans and Garlington, if we grant each of them integrity, then we must conclude that there is something else at work here that goes beyond either their ignorance of the issues, or doctrinal compromise. I will explore these ideas further in this essay as I seek to reconcile noncharismatic blacks worshiping with charismatics.

Both black and white saints are equally flawed sinful creatures, desperately in need of the grace of God. If my portrayal of the black church seems too rosy and uncritical it is only because I wish to make a point. And if I seem somewhat too critical of my white brethren, that is not my intention. Apart from the work of the Holy Spirit, there would be nothing worthy of reporting about either of them.

My Parents Were Devout Christians

My mom and dad were married in October of 1936, and four years later I was born, the oldest of five boys and one girl. The faith of my parents was typical of many older blacks two and three generations removed from slavery whose walk with God would in ways be reminiscent of what some consider the charismatic Christian extremes of today. But living as they did in the crucible of punishing daily experiences, the reality of black Christians' faith was their only real means of survival. To these folks their encounters with the Holy Spirit were not sensational, but they were indispensable.

The Faith of My Parents Was Deeply Rooted in Their Bible Knowledge

I would describe my parents' home as devout and Bible believing. They were by convictions not Pentecostal themselves but they had Pentecostal family members. While neither mom nor dad had much formal education, both were literate and avid Bible readers. My parents' philosophy of life was shaped from start to finish by their detailed knowledge of the Bible and their obedient reverence for it. We were taught to read as children by our parents before entering public school. The Bible was our textbook. Each of us came to personal faith as children at our parents' knees.

In retrospect, I am deeply impressed by the theological sophistication of my simple parents. My theological education consists of three plus earned degrees, each from white conservative evangelical institutions. Nevertheless, I found no glaring doctrinal contradictions between my formal theological training and the biblical convictions instilled in us by my parents as we were growing up during the 40s and 50s in Dallas, Texas.

Over the years they told us many stories about their lives as sharecroppers in rural south Texas. My folks were confronted with many of life's harsh realities for blacks under Jim Crow. Yet, they clearly viewed their hard daily experiences in the light of God's providence and his sovereignty. Mom and dad drew strength from a faith in God's goodness and his absolute power and authority. They saw themselves and their experiences through the biblical characters in the Bible. I grew up in an atmosphere in which the Bible was taken seriously as a survival guide. For white Christians (or blacks for that matter) only familiar with the post-civil rights era it might be a little difficult to imagine this daily struggle just to stay alive in America.

Prayer Was My Parents' Constant Companion

The day-to-day struggles of inequality were a special challenge for black families committed to living by faith. For those families prayer became a constant companion.

We were consistently taught as children to hold no animosity toward whites for their abuses toward blacks. Instead of animus toward whites, we were frequently gathered around mom and dad's bed to pray for those who persecuted us. It was a daily routine for my parents to seek the Holy Spirit's divine intervention in the affairs of their day. If my folks were to be successful in earning a living, God would have to touch the heart of white contractors making them willing to do business with dad's small trucking operation. When a misunderstanding occurred in the context of business dealings, and they did frequently, dad usually suffered whatever loss there might be. I recall on two occasions dad had the same bad experience. One of his better paying contracts was moving materials around the city for a major railroad line in Dallas. Twice on Sundays as our family was preparing to drive off to church my dad was visited at our home by two railroad policemen. Each time instead of going with us to church that Sunday he would have to pay workers to undo a job he had paid them to do earlier in the week. Why? Because as a joke white railroad yard foremen had given dad a bogus work order. Technically my dad was guilty of railroad materials theft. Dad paid his workers wages to retrieve the materials and return them to where they belonged. But dad earned nothing for his efforts because this had been a way for some powerful whites to have a little fun at his expense. I remember how grateful my dad was that the railroad line accepted his explanation and didn't press their technical case against him. The railroad line was definitely in a position to press theft charges against my dad. We children could anticipate that we would be praying for those white foremen that night. When on occasions like this we asked our parents why they loved whites so much they rehearsed for us what the Bible says about loving those who spitefully use you. Dad was absolutely dependent upon the Holy Spirit to negotiate for him. Their confidence in the guidance of the Holy Spirit was evident in the way they would apply to themselves promises made to the disciples. In their situations they took literally such promises as the following: "For it is not you speaking, but the Spirit of your Father speaking through you" (Matt 10:20); or "for the Holy Spirit will teach you at that moment what you must say" (Luke 12:12).

I can recall periods growing up when my dad would stop by home during the day for family prayer. Looking back I can imagine dad might have been asking God for enough work that week to meet his financial obligations. There were times when we were aware of problems in our extended family. We prayed about a marriage that was failing, for an uncle who had a run-in with the law, about a household that was out of work, for some one who was seriously ill. For my mom and dad the Holy Spirit and his power were not an abstraction, nor was he far away in time and place. For them the Holy Spirit came near everyday and made a difference. In their decision-making my parents applied scripture with confidence. In those matters requiring wisdom as to which direction to take, which course of action to follow. In legal matters, in questions about rights of citizenship, like the nation of Israel in Egypt, my parents knew the Holy Spirit was where our help would come from. No area of our family life was exempt from an expectant dependence upon the hand of God.

My Parents Experienced the Living God Every Day

I grew up during a time and amid conditions that required black Christians to expect miracles as the routine way of survival. I repeat. For those unfamiliar with the pre-civil rights era it is not easy to conceive just what a daily struggle it was for blacks to stay alive in America.

When my parents sang on Sunday, "What a friend we have in Jesus," they were reflecting back on the experiences of the week just past. When they quoted the Psalmists and the song writers "I love the Lord, He heard my cry ... as long as I live when trouble rise I will hasten to His throne" they had just gone through such experiences in days prior. "God is our refuge and strength, a very present help in trouble" was more to my parents than just great Hebrew poetry, God was a living reality. He had opened closed doors for the community. The Lord had rescued a helpless neighbor from injustice at the hands of the powerful and the unaccountable. The answers to prayer they were witnessing were victories for individuals otherwise powerless. The black church is inextricably rooted in the context of black struggle. This unique history gives the black church many of its characteristics. For most of the black church's existence the black Christian has lacked the power and privilege enjoyed by the white Christian and as a result has been forced to be much more intentional in relying upon God.

Neighborhood Prayer Bands Were Gatherings Across Denominations

Beyond family prayer, a common institution emerged across black communities everywhere called prayer bands. These prayer bands were not organized around denominational traditions but around the simple confidence that God answers prayer. When trouble invaded our community word went out to the prayer bands. We children often attended the meetings of those prayer bands. Listening to the adults talk to God in prayer we learned about the latest community struggles with inequality. There was prayer about the most recent incidents with the police. God's help was sought for the black community schools that were in a perpetual crisis. There were the out-of-work households needing the Lord to open up jobs for them. There was prayer about the pending trial for a defendant from our community who was facing death in the electric chair. This type of prayer request would likely lead to asking the Lord to help parents to rear their children well. Black parents perceived whites to have such capricious attitudes that it produced in the parents a kind of healthy paranoia. Obedient children would avoid all unnecessary contact with whites for it could only lead to trouble. Dallas was an especially mean-spirited city and whites exercised a near absolute power over blacks. Years later the Kennedy assassination came as no surprise to many in the black Christian community. The silence of evangelical white Christians is still condemned in private conversations by black Christians knowledgeable of the then rampant hateful spirit in our city. When commenting on the moral conscience of Dallas the observations of Leslie were sobering but well placed. "On the surface, at least, integration in Dallas was a brilliant job of execution. It did not, of course, have a moral basis. An appeal to moral values could not have accomplished integration; only an appeal to material values."[1] And blacks who resisted were severely punished one way or another. The pastor of our Baptist church would regularly warn church families that even to associate with civil rights groups was to put their jobs at risk. We knew of people being fired because someone in the family took out a membership in the National Association for the Advancement of Colored People (NAACP). All of us were familiar with stories about black youth, usually males, whose lives were ruined by the false charges of an angry white. I can only imagine the stress mom and dad were under, considering that their children consisted of five sons and one daughter. They felt compelled to interpret each answer to prayer for us. By so doing they were hoping to persuade us to wait upon God instead of ever taking matters into our own hands. They would seldom allow an opportunity to pass, so as to dramatize the futility of trying to fight the system. And there seemed to have been no shortage of failed attempts to challenge that system. Our community grieved with neighbor families when they lost sons to prison and to untimely deaths fighting the system in Dallas. It was considered a proud accomplishment and an answer to prayer when a black family's sons reached adulthood without in some way being permanently marked for life.

My Parents Passed on a Black Christian Tradition of Believing Prayer

My mom and dad had grown up under circumstances even harder than those they reared us under. The important lessons their experiences had taught them about trusting God, they desired to pass on to us. They had a dreadful fear for our very survival in this country. And to them survival was dependent upon how well we learned to rely upon God for each day. Our parents worried that one of their five sons might succumb to the temptation to fight the white system, something tantamount to flirting with death. There was no real difference between the results whether or not they were fighting with legal or illegal means; either way you lose. My parents' point was proven later during the civil rights era as the legal nonviolent protests were plagued by death and violence. Many mostly white liberal Christians stood with the blacks. But how disheartening when prominent conservative white pastors and churches openly opposed equal rights for blacks! No wonder in black Christian homes the daily warnings to frustrated black youth were "You are no match for the absolute power of the white man; leave him to God." As a consequence of these hopeless struggles, our parents were faced with the choices either to despair, or to rely upon God. My own serious faith today is directly related to seeing the living God at work in my parents' lives. I am grateful for their choice.

The Black Tradition of Relying on Prayer Was Not Unique to My Parents

But just how unique were my parents' experiences as compared to their Christian neighbors? According to what I saw and heard at the Baptist church we attended, mom and dad weren't really so unique at all. What I was experiencing in my parents' home was similar to the experiences of other black youth in my community who had Christian parents. These parents were carrying on a black Christian tradition of relying upon the Spirit of God that extends all the way back to the days of slavery. It would matter little whether or not our neighbors were Baptists, Methodists, or Pentecostals. They were Christian people with a good, disciplined understanding of God's word and who, by experience, and believed in the power of prayer.

The Exposure of Slaves to the Bible Doomed Slavery

Blacks were first introduced to the gospel during slavery and the experience left a profound effect upon the institution of slavery. In the same way that no other ethnic American church has developed in a vacuum, neither has the black evangelical church. It should not come as any surprise that some characteristics of the black church can be documented to have their origins in the slave masters' church. Observations such as the following made by these scholars support this suggestion.

> But again it is not easy to tell how much of their 'heathenism' the slaves learned in the whites' churches and at white revival meetings. One Sunday morning … the slaves were permitted to hold their own services before the whites occupied the building. Such a medley of sounds, I never heard before. They exhorted, prayed, sung, shouted, cried, grunted and growled. Poor Souls! They knew no better, for when the other services began the sounds were similar, which the white folks made; and

> the negroes only imitated them and shouted a little louder ... In short, the religion of the slaves was, in essence, strikingly similar to that of the poor, illiterate white men of the antebellum South.[2]

Yet black styles of worship which blacks actually borrowed from whites during slavery are mistakenly labeled today by some as African. Robert Duvall's portrayal of Euliss 'Sonny' Dewey, a white preacher in the movie "Apostle," reminded me that my parents had laughingly told of us about white preachers who preached just the way black preachers did. Mom and Dad said the black shouting in the Spirit was learned from the white preachers. "The tradition of lined hymn singing in the Black church commenced in the early nineteenth century. Its precursor was the psalm-lining of the Calvinists, which was perpetuated in the American colonies by the Puritans... The Black Methodists and Baptists endorsed Watts' hymns, but the Baptists 'blackened' them."[3]

As stated previously, blacks would be totally unaware of "how to do church" prior to the white introduction of "doing church." To be certain, blacks took the idiom or the genre to another level and made it their own. But what we learn here is, that in developing the black church tradition, the slaves imitated the whites. Besides giving blacks their example, whites also, though grudgingly, gave the slaves the scriptures and the scriptures proved to be a much more persuasive influence in the formation of the black church tradition than the example of white Christians. Thus was the beginning of the black and white Christian relationship, deformed from the start.

The Bible Has Profoundly Influenced The Worship of the Black Church

In addition to the white church model, another powerful and important source of influence in the development of the black church as an institution was scripture. Then, within the context of the institutional black church, there is the black Christian experience. This is critical because the black church as an institution depends upon the individual black Christian experience. This is where the scriptures' shaping influence has been most apparent. For the slave, knowledge of the Bible became an indescribably valuable resource. The record shows that even white slave owners recognized the inherent risk and danger in giving slaves the word of God. It was that awareness that led to grudgingly selecting what the slaves should be taught from the Bible. But it was in the purposes of God that the slaves should be taught the scriptures.

The gospel gave the slave a whole new philosophical framework, a different rationale for interpreting his condition. The slave met the God of the Bible and he was totally different from what the slave was accustomed to in his white Christian slave master. The God of the Bible was engaged in facilitating the liberation of the oppressed. The evangelistic preaching of the cross introduced slaves to the theology of man's total depravity and Christ's substitutionary atonement. The slave's God is one who sets the captive free by breaking the chains of spiritual bondage from sin, as well as the chains of physical bondage from slavery. He was a God of impartiality, being not only the Heavenly Father of the white master, but of the slave too. The slaves found a whole new and elevated sense of self-worth through their exposure to the Bible. However, the slave gained something else just as important as higher self-worth; he gained an objective and divine standard by which to form opinions about white Christians. A relationship deformed from the start became even more complicated. As slave conversions began to occur after the introduction of the Bible, that new relationship was gradually affecting everything. This irreversibly altered the slave and slave-master relationship from the perspective of heaven. Slaves now saw God as their final authority, not their master. The slave recognized not only a new accountability to God, but also a powerful new ally in God. There was more going on than cowering docility. It is reasonable to conclude that the ministry of the Holy Spirit was having an ameliorating effect on slaves and slave masters.

I believe out of that convoluted experience, mixing slavery and the Bible, a universal conviction emerged among black Christians: "The Bible can be trusted, but white Christians' interpretation of it cannot be trusted." Some black students of theology have a difficulty with the study of systematic theology. The difficulty is not necessarily their inability to grasp systematic theology. Their problem is a hesitancy to accept a systematic theology organized and articulated according to white cultural bias. This problem is not as restricted to liberal theology as some conservatives might wish to suggest. This ability of blacks and whites to arrive at different interpretations of scripture remains a historic point of division between black and white Christians today. But accepted wisdom says prior experiences do influence one's emphasis even in the scripture. Many whites and blacks view race differently today just as blacks and whites viewed slavery differently during the time of slavery.

Black Christians have had a solemn reverence and love for the scriptures since the time of slavery. This reverence is even found among some blacks who profess no faith in Christ. It's not surprising then that black Christians automatically cast intense suspicions upon Christians appearing to circumvent what the text says. Black Christians in large numbers today continue to be incredulous about white Christians' interpretation of scripture. Those black skeptics believe that whites have ulterior motives and they read the Bible selectively. Whites, according to the skeptics, underscore those portions of the Bible which serve their agenda, but they either ignore, or explain away portions of scripture which reflect unfavorably upon their actions. This might provide a partial answer to why blacks are attending white charismatic churches by the tens of thousands and are mostly avoiding white cessationists churches like the plague. I happen to know personally many such blacks who attend white charismatic churches. But by convictions they are not charismatics. These blacks appear to be less skeptical of white charismatic churches than they are of white cessationists churches. Why? I would speculate that if given an opportunity to survey the opinions of those black laymen, I would guess it would be hard for cessationists churches to explain to those black skeptics why they reject the sign gifts—gifts which are in the Bible. I cannot agree with the logic, but I might understand where these black skeptics were coming from however. Historically, blacks are accustomed to white interpretations of the Bible that are somehow a disadvantage to blacks. The black and white Christian relationship that was crippled during slavery has yet to fully heal. Perhaps a benchmark was established in slavery when white Christians used the Bible to teach slaves to submit to their masters. But on the other hand, blacks read the Bible and saw the promise of liberation.

The institution of the black church owes its origin and existence to slavery and there was no escaping whatever shaping-influence slavery exerted. While the modern version of the black evangelical church is hardly homogeneous, there are undeniable family resemblances. Those observable common practices among black evangelical churches cross denominational traditions. These family resemblances can be largely attributed to a black church tradition of reverence for the examples in scripture. This forceful sway is particularly true of historical narrative texts. The scriptural anecdotes (stories) are particularly authoritative, even when the result has been to embrace theological positions that are contradictory to one another. For example, it is not uncommon for the same person in the same service to affirm and deny the security of the believer.

Through the years the black church has established a reputation as the court of first resort for the poor. This sometimes too aggressive pursuit of advocacy for the poor, in the view of some, involves the church too much in social justice. But most black Christians would see advocacy for the poor as an essential aspect of the gospel. Conservative black preachers are more likely to favor the narrative texts in preaching than the epistolary literature. The story text is much less complicated. The anecdotes provide in story form a pattern or an example to follow. Lessons drawn from the anecdotes are not considered systematic theology by black preachers. Among black evangelical churches the scriptural anecdotes are divinely inspired guides for faith and practice. This reflects a high view of scripture, acknowledging its trustworthiness and authority. Some may wish to quarrel about certain black church interpretations of the scriptures. But there is very little room to deny this historic tradition for devotion to the scriptures in the black church. In past generations older black Christians exhibited a phenomenal knowledge of the Bible. I witnessed that with my own parents. What they lacked in familiarity with other literature they made up for with their thorough Bible knowledge. If in spiritual maturity the Holy Spirit works in conjunction with the word of God, then their powerful walk with God is understandable.

My late-wife's parents were not unlike my own parents, they too were careful students of the scriptures. For almost four decades I enjoyed a wonderful fellowship in the word with them. Until the death of my late mother-in-law (Willie Mae), she and I spoke at least once a week by telephone. My late father-in-law and I have sat up the entire night more than once, discussing the scriptures. He told me that he wished to learn from my formal training. My late mother-in-law's usual inquiry was to ask me about my studying and my preaching. This simple little lady never completed high school, but she had hidden so much of the word in her heart that she could engage me in an extended animated discussion of a passage without holding the text in her hand.

She usually sent me away with a wonderful story-illustration of how God had fulfilled that passage in her life. I marveled that I had twelve years of theological training and yet in the word she was every bit my peer. Her secret was that she believed the word of God to be a living book. She knew the promises in it and understood that they are available to you and me. I can remember how when my late wife and I were barely getting by financially during my student years in the 1960s. Again and again her late mother would repeat the story of some biblical character facing a difficult situation. Then she would say, "Remember how God came to the rescue of that person? Well, the same God that helped that person will help you too." In the years after those days she reminded us of those difficult times and of how faithful God had been to us.

It was my sad honor to give her eulogy in February 1999. She and I had been true soul mates. The days before she died were typical of the way in which she lived in relation to the word of God. In those days before her death, she directed the songs, prayers, and scripture-reading from her sick bed. In the very moments before she passed away that night, I had completed the reading of a long series of promises from God's word. The reading was followed by the singing of her favorite hymns. She opened her eyes, rose up off the pillow, stretched her arms toward heaven, and died peacefully. I was asked by the family to give the eulogy for my late-father-in-law in the following year, July 2000. In March of that next year 2001, my wife died. Thus our family sustained painful losses in three consecutive years.

I have heard numerous stories told about the Bible being the only book many older blacks could read. They could read no other literature. I can't explain that, but I do know that a tradition of devotion to the Bible has served the black church well. For since I believe that one's spiritual maturity is developed, I believe that the Holy Spirit works in conjunction with the word of God.

Black Church Worship Has a Striking Resemblance to That of Israel

The testimony of many whites who seek out the charismatic church is that they love the high-energy worship experience. They often have a sound biblical point. One can easily recognize the influence of the Bible in the worship styles of the black church. There are some definite characteristics of black church worship. Blacks usually object to stereotypes for good reasons. But, if we mean by stereotype "something conforming to a standard pattern," then I am willing to admit to a stereotype of black church worship. I agree with the basic argument of Lincoln and Mamiya in their chapter "The Performed word: Music and the Black Church." They give a persuasive explanation for the origin of what has become known as the traditional black church style of worship.[4] That black church tradition born during slavery was a new institution that never before existed. But I would argue that the ministry of the Holy Spirit had an important role in the formation of the traditional black church style of worship. Neither my parents, nor my slave forefathers would need anyone to explain why the ministry of the Holy Spirit was prominent in the formation of the black worship experience.

The Black Church's High Energy Worship Has Biblical Precedence

Formal corporate worship for black evangelical churches is a high energy celebration experience. Celebration and high energy are basic elements to any black worship experience. Regardless of the denominational tradition, most black evangelicals expect to find these basic elements present and would be disappointed by the absence of either element. Most black worshipers will quickly remind critics and seekers alike that the Bible is the model for this style of worship. The Psalms are just as well loved by black worshipers as they are among other worshipers. The basic elements found in the worship of the Psalms—high energy and celebration—are also found in corporate black worship. Two good examples are Pss 95 and 100. In these Psalms the people of God are exhorted to come before his presence in a spirit of celebration. The Lord's people are exhorted to express joy and gladness—high energy and celebration. In addition to singing they were required to testify to their personal confidence in the faithfulness of God. Allen Ross commenting on Ps 100 says this is "a call for praise and joyful service ... People everywhere ... should shout ... they are not to be subdued in their praise of Him ..."[5] This sounds like the description of a black worship experience.

So the more familiar you are with both the worship of Israel and the black worship experience the more you are able to see a striking resemblance between the black church's high energy celebrative worship and that of Israel in scripture.

Look at Ezra's description of the Jews' worship service when the temple foundation was laid. This could easily refer to the Sunday morning worship of many black churches.

> With antiphonal response they sang, praising and glorifying the LORD: 'For he is good; his loving kindness toward Israel is forever.' All the people gave a loud shout as they praised the LORD when the temple of the LORD was established. Many of the priests, the Levites, and the leaders—older people who had seen with their own eyes the former temple while it was still established—were weeping loudly, and many others raised their voice in a joyous shout. People were unable to tell the difference between the sound of joyous shouting and the sound of the people's weeping, for the people were shouting so loudly that the sound was heard a long way off (Ezra 3:11-13).

John Martin said regarding the Jewish dedication service for the second temple, "The two sounds, the joy and the weeping (from sadness), mingled together and were so loud that they were heard far away."[6] He might well be describing any black church on any Sunday morning.

Summary and Conclusion

Cessationists and Charismatics Have a Common Bond in Jesus Christ

A very basic reason why cessationists can come together with charismatics is a common faith in Jesus Christ. Paul laid down a principle in Romans that teaches Christians to receive one another in spite of differences and without the intention to disagree. Our common faith in the Lord Jesus Christ is a sufficient basis as cessationists to come together with charismatics.

Christ Has Made Christians Different Which Requires Tolerance and Acceptance

In his article, "Worshiping With Your Eyes Wide Open," Towns list six worship styles, pointing out the merits and weaknesses of each one. "Christians worship differently. That's because we are different; different mixtures of spiritual gifts, different callings, different personalities, different backgrounds and different doctrine."[7] But to be different in Christ is no justification for refusing to worship together.

Black people are traditionally tolerant—slow about excluding people—regardless of who they are or what they might be accused of doing. Black Christians are even more accepting of others. We have an unspoken tradition in the black community to champion the underdog. Perhaps as blacks our painful history of experiences with rejection, exclusion, and demonization has conditioned us against being quick to treat others that way. This potential virtue has time and again proven to be a liability, but I don't expect to see it dropped any time soon. The crying need for tolerance and acceptance remains. Perhaps as black Christians we feel more of an emotional need to connect with others than do our white brothers. Maybe we are more willing to admit needing our charismatic brothers as brothers, if not as charismatics. Just watch black Christians in a friendly setting and you will discover that they know how to come together. Everyone's speaking at once. There is hugging, hand and back slapping all over the place.

Personal Tolerance and Acceptance Put to the Test

My own capacity for tolerance and acceptance was put to the test a few years ago when at Christmas my youngest brother announced to the family he was dying of Acquired Immune Deficiency Syndrome, popularly known as AIDS. We were crushed from several directions at once. First, there was the shame that was attached to his admission—years of struggling with the secret sin of homosexuality. Then there was the horror of the accompanying physical pain and suffering before his eventual death.

James was appropriately and convincingly remorseful, ready to courageously accept the consequences of his bad choices. Then it was our turn to respond as a family and as individuals. Being the oldest of our family I was expected to go first, to set the pace. I paused for a few moments—but it seemed like an eternity. I thought about the purpose of the cross. I thought about how Christ's forgiveness was for folks exactly like James and like me. We all wept together sharing the wave of grief that was swept over us by this reality. We then set off to locate for our brother James the best AIDS hospice care available. For the next twenty months we loved James on a daily basis. A couple of times his attending physicians made the comment, "If you were not taking such excellent care of James, he might have died much sooner and cost you much less expense." The tolerance and acceptance we exhibited toward James was not wasted on my own adult children. The conversations they have had with me since then indicate that God used my response to James to increase their appreciation for his grace and forgiveness. The Lord's name is seldom damaged more than when as saints we behave in intolerant and unkind ways toward members of the family that needs us. I think as cessationists and charismatics God has given us a compelling need for each other.

How many of our assumptions as cessationists and charismatics about the presence of the Holy Spirit are misguided? How much is a reflection of our culture and personality? More than many are willing to admit.

When in 1998, my late wife was diagnosed with liver cancer it turned our lives upside down. After being together for nearly forty years this was sobering to say the least. We had friends who were cessationists and friends who were charismatics. There were those praying for my late wife and me who were careful not to embarrass God by asking too much and putting him on the spot. We listened as others ordered God to help us as if somehow he were our opponent. We believed in healing and miracles. But we had no faith in miracle-workers and healers. We were praying for healing by any means God so desired. As time passed we learned so much more about the Lord through that experience. We were blessed by the witness of the Holy Spirit as we walked through that trial. He comforted us during our encounters with our human frailty. We were blessed by the enduring fellowship of the saints, an obvious work of the Holy Spirit. Another evidence for us of the Spirit's presence was his ministry of laying upon other believers a prayer-burden for us. My late wife exhibited such a noticeable peace in spite of her serious medical condition that she was asked repeatedly about that peace as if there were something wrong with it. We believed that her peace came from the Holy Spirit.

"What is it about many noncharismatic black Christians' view of the Holy Spirit that allows them to be comfortable worshiping with charismatic Christians?" The black church has always been comfortable with experiencing the supernatural nature of the work of the Holy Spirit. Noncharismatic blacks and charismatics worship together because they focus on their commonality in Christ, which is much larger than any sign-gifts disagreement between them. The black church may be more predisposed by history and tradition than is the white church to the necessary tolerance and acceptance for worshiping with charismatics. Fellowship is possible for so long as what each believes regarding the operation of the sign-gifts is respected without attempting to impose that view upon each other.

What I have proposed in this essay is a simple idea: the context of struggle has been an indispensable ingredient in forging black evangelical attitudes toward God the Holy Spirit. When black evangelical attitudes toward the Spirit are looked at from that angle, one will understand their reluctance to distance themselves from charismatics.

The Holy Spirit and Our Emotions

David Eckman

Emotions are an ignored reality in much of the Evangelical Church, but it is not so in the Bible. Within the Bible's pages the Trinity manifests a rich emotionality. Within the New Testament the Person of the Spirit not only manifests rich emotions Himself, but is given to the believer to profoundly influence her or his emotional life. As we cooperate with the Spirit and sound spiritual principles, we shall experience an increasingly rich emotional life. The health of our emotions is a critical category of our spiritual life. The why and how of that is explored.

The Significance of Emotions

Why spend our time on the Holy Spirit and emotions? First, emotions are closer to us than air. They are the ever present current within us: they define the inner world and give us continual commentary on the outer world. Awareness of life even starts with emotions. Life demands an understanding of emotions. Setting aside the biblical realities and the evangelical scene, simple existence demands an understanding of the place of emotions. They are closer to us than our skin, than the air we breathe. Emotions are as constant and present as the weather surrounding us. We need to understand and manage them.

Second, emotions come with great intensity. Most of us struggle with our emotions. A thought may be put out of the mind; it is not necessarily so with a fearful emotion. When a person is filled with dread, the source may be a fearful thought or situation, yet the force of the emotions is what makes the individual preoccupied. We cannot flee from our feelings; therefore, we must deal with them.

Third, the evangelical's approach to emotions may be the weakest part of our "system" of spirituality. Note just the differences between charismatics and the Bible movement with reference to emotions. Time after time all of us have heard the biblically-oriented evangelical question the validity of emotions. At the same time the charismatic often elevates emotional experiences to the level of definitive spiritual reality. We desperately need clarity in the area.

Fourth, not only is the place of emotions a significant issue in the evangelical movement, but the place of the emotions is a significant issue within the pages of the Bible. For example, as we shall see, the management of the emotions is critical to the spiritual life. One of the ministries of the Spirit of God is to mold the human ability to have emotions into an instrument for the display of Christ's character. A very practical understanding of the Holy Spirit's role relative to our emotions will lead to a deeper understanding of the spiritual life.

Fifth, with the counseling revolution going on in our circles, clarity is needed concerning the place of emotions. The doorway to the inner life is not the world of dreams as it was with Freud, but among contemporary counselors it is the experience of emotions. Since emotions are where the counselor begins, a proper understanding of them will help define the relationship between the pastor and counselor.

Sixth, whether the counseling revolution occurred or not, pastors in their teaching and leading need to understand the function of emotions. Many view pastors as having nothing to say about the world of emotions. We will see that pastors of all people in the helping professions should have the most to say. The pastor is not playing a pivotal role, however, in the church's understanding of emotions. Many believe that more evangelicals with significant emotional problems are going to Christian and non-Christian counselors rather than their pastors.

According to researchers about one out of twenty pastors still counsels and another one out of twenty trains disciples. Every pastor does counsel in preaching—often very directly—and therefore, also should counsel and disciple individually. In fulfilling these roles he should know intimately the biblical role of emotions. No reason exists that the professional counselor should have a monopoly on the understanding of the world of emotions. The concepts and the material regarding the place of emotions are not that difficult to understand. Freud himself believed that no need existed for the psychiatrist to have a medical degree. In fact, he suggested that the intelligent and insightful lay person could do as well as the medically trained. In the same way pastors can just as easily master the world of emotions. This is especially true because the contents of the Bible constantly address the world of emotions and sometimes address the world of the unconscious.

Seventh, effective preaching demands a clear understanding of emotions. A misconception exists in many places that a deeply emotional sermon striking the congregation with power is, on the face of it, suspect because "it is emotional." That may be a mistaken understanding. Deeply emotional sermons and a strongly felt response may just mean that the preacher has communicated clearly. The emotions exist because both the preacher and the congregation apprehended the perceived existential greatness of what was being taught.

Finally, emotions do not authenticate truth; emotions cannot verify the historicity of the resurrection of Christ or other historical and theological realities. Emotions, however, do authenticate our understanding of the truth. A happy heart is the greatest evidence of the apprehension of spiritual truth. In the Bible, truth is supposed to strike the life with positive emotional force. Truth without effect is an unknown within scripture.

Given the significance of emotions I contend that the Holy Spirit has a fundamental role to play in the emotional life of the Christian. To appreciate this role, three factors must be examined and understood. The first is that we as humans are an analogy of the divine. The reason that we have emotions is that God has emotions. We are made in the image of God, an image that includes a key component of emotions—in short, his emotional image. When we speak of God having emotions, this is not anthropopathic language. We are not saying we are making God in our image. Instead we are in his; therefore, we feel and want.

As we proceed, we will examine the source of our emotional life—God himself. Second, we will see that with the coming of the Holy Spirit into our lives, a richly emotional presence has entered our person. Finally we must learn how to cooperate with this person for our emotional well being.

The Trinity—The Source of Our Emotions

Where do these amazing things called emotions come from? Feelings are the bane and blessing of our existence: a blessing, for example, as they create a profound joy within us as we look upon our children; or a bane as we experience times of grief and loss. At those various times our emotions match the delights and disasters of life. The source of emotions is a surprising place. This ability to feel comes from our being made in the image of God.

A short while back I had a frighteningly interesting experience (more frightening than interesting) of having an ophthalmologist operate on my eye. The procedure was complicated so the operation was at a hospital in an operating room. Stretched out on a gurney I was waiting outside the operating room. Then, an anesthesiologist came over to check on me. We ended up in a conversation. I told him that having a series of eye problems had led me to appreciate how wonderfully our two eyes work together to create the sense of depth. I did not want to lose that, I said.

Then he replied, "Isn't evolution fantastic because a million years ago we had one eye in the middle of our heads, and then it migrated down to our face, and on the way it split in half." Gesturing he placed two hands together on his head and then he slid each hand down to each eye. "That's how we got two eyes," he stated.

Please understand I had been in pain for several weeks and had experienced high levels of stress. I am not as unsubtle as I will now appear.

"That is so stupid," I replied, "that I'm almost forced into believing that God did it." He got the best of the argument because shortly thereafter I was unconscious.

What is true of our bodies is true of our emotions: God did it! Our bodies are repositories of wonder. Within our frame is an unimaginably complex set of abilities. From whistling a tune, to thinking up the splitting of the atom, we are fearfully and wonderfully made. Yet the greatest wonder of all is, all of this is expressed by a moving and flexible pile of chemical and electrical activity. Such is so wonderful that it makes the existence of God reasonable. Not only what we can bring forth is a marvel but what is within is also. Inside of us is a world of emotions, appetites, and imagination.

Our ability to do things without and sense things within exists because God molded clay into an electricochemical masterpiece that makes the complexity of the most advanced computer laughable. What was his model in doing so? The answer is himself. We are flesh and blood expressions of the divine; we are made in his image. If that is so, than the contemplation of ourselves is in some way a basic introduction to deity.

God does have the ability not only to think and to will, but also to feel. The language of the Bible expresses it this way. God is said to have two qualities: he is spirit and he has a soul. The classic statement is John 4:24, "God is spirit." The Greek construction is anarthrous (without the definite article) and emphasizes spirit as a quality. A way of translating the phrase would be, "God as to quality is spirit." Spirit implies self-awareness, reflection, and will. The Hebrew and Greek words for spirit are commonly connected to terms of reflection, intellect, and intention.

God is also described as having a soul. Soul implies sensation, feelings, and appetites. Since he is a sensate being, God has what can be described as a soul. Some erroneously take the language revolving around the word soul and almost turn it into some substance within God or man. I am not suggesting that the soul is a "thing"; rather the soul is best understood as a category of language and psychological observation and not a substance.

> Jer 15:1—"Then said Yahweh to me, 'If Moses and Samuel were standing before me, my **soul** would not be with this people.'"
>
> Isa 1:14—"Your New Moons and appointed Feasts my **soul** hates. They have become a burden to me. I am weary of putting up with them." Note how the strong aversion or dislike is connected with the soul.
>
> Isa 42:1—"Behold, my slave whom I am holding fast, my chosen one. My **soul** delights *in him*. I have placed my spirit upon him." In this verse the soul senses delight.[1]

Notice the collocations or the terms that are found around the word "soul." They are emotionally rich terms like delight, hate, burden, etc. The soul is connected to the experiencing of desiring and feeling.[2]

By its very nature language can generate confusion; this is one of those instances. It is easy to presume that soul and spirit imply substances, a spirit substance and a soul substance. Yet Christians generally understand that God is incorporeal, or is not a body. Instead of God having substance, soul and spirit, these terms may be describing processes within a person. Soul implies that the person has desires and emotions while spirit implies that the person can reflect and be self-observing.

God as the archetype of personhood is therefore the source of emotions. At the center of all reality is a being who feels and thinks. We are a reflection of that deep and wondrous reality. Since the Bible says that we are made in his image, we too feel and think.[3]

Being made in his image is the reason for our emotions and our thoughts. Men and women are similar to animals in having flesh and soul (man—1 Cor 2:11; animals—Gen 7:22; Eccl 3:21-22), but the critical difference is that we are made in the image of God (Gen 1:26-28). The totality of our personhood including our psychological make-up has been molded to be a reflection of the divine. Animals are a whimsical poetic expression of God's artistry; we are expressions of his nature.

Everything about us is a reflection of the deity: we are an analogy of the divine. Yes, we have a soul like God but that is only a part of it. And indeed we have a spirit like God, but it is more than that. Everything about us is an afterthought from and about deity.[4]

Since the Godhead possesses emotions and feels emotions, it is simple deductive logic that the Holy Spirit has emotions. In some senses the Holy Spirit is the emotionally rich member of the Trinity[5] insofar as he is the primary agent of personal interaction with us as human beings. Since the Spirit of God has emotions and is said to interact with humans and be affected emotionally by human activity, that makes our emotional life even more significant.

Lastly the Spirit of God has a direct ministry to our emotional life. This ministry is critical to the quality of the spiritual life. Indeed the implications for the spiritual life and the practice of Christian counseling are endless.

The Emotional Life of the Spirit of God

The emotions that exist within us do follow the pattern of the emotions of God. But God is more than emotions: God is the infinitely deep love and relationships shared among the Three in One. In a number of ways the process of living a godly life is designed to make the believing heart aware of the Trinity. We are called to relate to God as a Father; the Son is the one who saves and protects us. The Father sent Jesus Christ from heaven to earth. After the departure of Jesus Christ to heaven, he sent another Comforter who would be in believers. Those first two persons, in a real sense, are external to the life and consciousness of the believer. It is to our advantage that the Christ outside of us left the disciples, so that the Holy Spirit would come to reside inside of us. Jesus said, "But I tell you the truth, it is to your advantage that I am going away. For if I do not go away, the Advocate will not come to you, but if I go, I will send him to you" (John 16:7). The third member of the Trinity is the one who emphasizes God's ministry to our inner life. Far more so than any other member of the Trinity, the ministry of the Spirit of God is uniquely connected to the emotional life of the believer.[6] Concerning this Jesus also said,

> Then I will ask the Father, and he will give you another Advocate to be with you forever—the Spirit of truth, whom the world cannot accept, because it does not see him or know him. But you know him, because he resides with you and will be in you.

It is the Spirit who directly influences our inner life. Jesus outside a believer is not as effective as the Spirit of God inside a believer. This one conforms those who have trusted Christ to the character of Christ. Such character has a richly emotional component.

It is fascinating that not only does the Spirit of God address our inner life with its never-ending stream of emotions, but the Holy Spirit's experience within us is deeply emotional. Not only is the work of the Spirit emotional; the New Testament emphasizes his emotions. One can see by various portions in the New Testament that his existence among us involves deep responses. This is indicated by his personal reactions.

a. *Deep pain.* Ephesians 4:25-32 contains Paul's admonitions about effective and godly communication, and the abandonment of poor patterns of communication. As he gave his advice, he taught how to deal with strong and powerful emotions. He gave a long list of things that should *not* be done and one of those is not "paining the Holy Spirit." The Holy Spirit is pained when Christians negatively communicate with each other and when they refuse to forgive each other. Paul uses the term λυπέω (*lupeō*), defined by BDAG as "grieve, pain" and which in our popular parlance may be translated "deep pain" to describe the Spirit's experience in response to our sinful behavior. It occurs in the description of Christ's suffering in the Garden (Matt 26:37), "[he] became anguished [λυπεῖσθαι, *lupeisthai*] and distressed." In a sense, we can say that Jesus the Messiah had his passion in the Garden and on the cross, but the Holy Spirit has his continual passion within us.

b. *Desire.* In Jas 4 the author contrasted the life lived for the flesh and the life that was to be lived for God. In v. 4 James forcefully told believers that friendship with the world is a form of adultery. Then I would understand the next verse as a question and an observation: "Or do you think that the Scripture speaks for no purpose? The Spirit that he has made to dwell within us jealously desires us" (Jas 4:5). The Holy Spirit has a strong longing to control the believer's life. The term is used often for the longing of one person for another who is absent (Rom 1:11; Phil 1:8; 2 Tim 1:4). Even though the Holy Spirit is present in our lives, we sometimes go into the dark world of the flesh far from his fellowship.

c. *Jealousy*. The Holy Spirit experiences jealousy as he sees how the believer is caught up with the world (Jas 4:5). Jealousy is an intensely painful and powerful emotion that the conduct of the believer elicits from the Spirit of God.

d. *Unutterable Groaning*. Chapter eight of Romans is Paul's fullest development of the Trinity's ministry within a believer. In this fascinating chapter, spiritual life is described as that which bears the believers through the weakness and sorrow of a fallen world. Romans 8:14 describes what it means to be a Spirit-led individual: the mature believer in Christ is identified by his or her ability to respond to the prompting of the Spirit. This prompting might be emotional inclinations and insights. Over time the believer learns the ability to surrender calmly and expectantly to these impressions. After describing that aspect of maturity, Paul goes on to describe how believers will have to endure sufferings in this life. A large part of maturity will be the challenge of going on in the face of the hurts, harms, and damage caused by others. In doing this Paul points out that a vast network of affliction is going on and the Spirit of God is involved in this symphony of expectant pain.

Romans 8:

8:22 "the whole creation groans" because it has been made pointless and ineffectual due to the rebellion of man.

8:23 "we ourselves groan" as we expectantly await the glorification of our bodies so that we indeed are liberated from the limitations and weaknesses of this life.

8:26 "the Spirit himself intercedes for us with groaning too deep for words."

One of our weaknesses is that we do not know how to pray. So to help us out the Spirit of God intercedes for us. This intercession is unspoken because the Holy Spirit is in deep pain. The same term is used in Acts 7:34 for the children of Israel groaning under the oppression of the Egyptians. The word is the noun-form of the verb found in vv. 22 and 23. The groaning of the Spirit is voiceless so that the one who continually searches the hearts (God) has to know what is the perspective of the Spirit. Romans 8:28 gives the result of this process that all things are worked together for the benefit of the child of God who loves his Father.

As he listens to our prayers the pain is so intense for the Spirit of God that he is reduced to voiceless pain. This again is the passion of the Spirit of God. With great emotion, he who is among us suffers because of us.

The Spirit and Our Emotions

Since the presence of the Spirit is internal, the work of the Spirit of God is emotional. One example will illustrate the point. As the believer is involved in the exercise of faith, the Spirit of God, for example, will supply joy and peace. In the details of a particular text, Rom 15:13, the Spirit is not the only member of the Trinity relating to the Christian. Paul related the believer's emotional life to two members of the Trinity, the Father and the Spirit. The God of hope is supposed to fill (the same word as used in Eph 5:18) the believer with every variety of joy and peace in the process of believing. All of this is to be done by the inherent power of the Holy Spirit. The process of generating these emotions is completely dependent upon the Holy Spirit's work.

Galatians 5 is a longer example of the same reality that the Holy Spirit is involved in a ministry to our emotional life. In Gal 5 Paul has contrasted the dispensation of the Spirit with the law, or more exactly, a corrupted version of the law embraced by the Judaizers. In developing how the believer is to participate in the life of the Spirit, he stated that Christians must walk by the Spirit (Gal 5:16). "Walking," in this context, means to organize our existence around the qualities from the Spirit. This is opposed to making the flesh one's life principle.[7]

As the life is organized around the Spirit, one will also be positively prompted by these qualities (Gal 5:18). These promptings should be followed. As they are followed they will produce wonderfully positive emotions and inner abilities in the life, as indicated by the accompanying vocabulary connected with the fruit of the Spirit: "love, joy, peace, patience, kindness, goodness, faithfulness, gentleness, and self-control ..." (Gal 5:22–23).

Spirituality is a life normally dominated by primary emotions—primary in the sense that these are what Christian existence is founded upon. Note how each term of the fruit of the Spirit carries an emotional connotation.

The work of the Spirit of God in the fruit that he produces is in stark contrast to the works of the flesh (Gal 5:19-21): "…hostilities, strife, jealousy, outbursts of anger, selfish rivalries, dissensions, factions, envying, … and similar things. The contrast to the fruit of the Spirit may be negative and sinful but it is also deeply emotional. The result is that the fruit of the Spirit replaces an emotionally powerful set of opposites. The work of the Spirit is obviously in the arena of the emotions.

This evidence of the emotional impact of the Spirit of God is also found in Eph 5:18 where Paul tells the believers in Ephesus to not get drunk with wine resulting in dissipation and instead to allow the deficits to be filled up by spiritual qualities. These result in singing and gratitude and mutual submission. Both of those experiences have to be profoundly emotional.

Filling emphasizes applying the resources of the Spirit of God to our individual weaknesses. In Eph 5:18 the condition of drunkenness has to be changed to joy and a disciplined life through the filling of the Spirit.

How to Minister to our own Emotions

We now turn our attention to scripture to consider more specifically the outworking of this ministry of the Spirit looking generally at Pauline teaching and concluding with a more detailed examination of Col 3:1-12. This section is important because it underscores the reality that many factors within our lives and the entire Trinity is involved in the Spirit's positive impact upon our emotions.

The management of our emotions involves our imagination (how we reckon; Rom 6:11), our mind (how we set our perspective; Rom 8:5-7), and our ego or self (how we relate to God and people). The terms fall naturally into that order because how we relate to people and to God is based on how we imagine the world to be and God to be, and how we analyze what life presents to us.

Management of our emotions is a by-product of a number of such factors. In New Testament terms the "by-product" nature of emotions is illuminated by the use of fruit and tree imagery. Matthew 7:15-20 and Gal 5:22 underscore the fact that character, the proper use of emotions and our inner life, is a product of a healthy set of spiritual processes or a healthy tree. Seemingly the healthy tree is the identity, perspective, and relationships of the righteous person. This makes the entire process more holistic and fits the biblical and psychological realities well.

What we have to do to gain and maintain spiritual health is as follows:

A. We have to recognize or differentiate what is going on within our emotional life and in the management of our appetites (Gal 5:16-24). This gives us information as to where we are starting from, either with spirituality or carnality.

B. We reckon on how God views us; we control our imagination. This reckoning becomes the basis of our relationship to God as a Father.

C. We have to set our minds on our relationships above; we control our thinking (Rom 8:1-6; Col 3:1-3). The terms used in both Rom 8 and Col 3 refer to perspective.

D. By reckoning we relate to God personally instead of to our appetites (Rom 6:11-12). The focus of a person's inner life can either be the God on the outside or the appetites on the inside. Sadly our appetites many times have far more impact on many of us than God does. The focus of our inner person has to be on God the Father, and our identity before him as found in Christ, and not in our appetites. So no matter the level of pressure from our inward desires, we must freely approach and share ourselves with God.

E. By reckoning we control our memories (Phil 4:8-9). Believers are enjoined to take the positive blessings God brings into our lives and use them as our personal definition and assumption as to what reality is. Oftentimes the fearful and anxious person selectively takes from experience only those things that can be linked to the past trauma and dread. One can just as legitimately take the positive, noble, and happy experiences and have them as the definition of the core of reality.

F. As a result, we experience the primary emotions. Love, joy, and peace can appear and become the stabilizing force in our personality and relationships.

Probably the clearest example of the interplay between emotions and our ability to picture God's view of our identity with Christ, manage a perspective, and relate to God and people is Col 3:1-12. What is of great importance is to notice the sequence of transitional words and phrases that show that the sections of the passage are interconnected and interdependent:

> v. 5: "Therefore…"
>
> v. 8: "But now [you also]…"
>
> v. 12: "Therefore…"

Each new section's application is dependent upon the practice of the preceding portion's principles, with the result that the commands of the third and fourth sections are based upon the practice of all the preceding parts. Notice in the diagram that section D or the last verse is dependent upon the practice of what is in the preceding verses. So the cumulative effect of practicing verses 1-11 allows for the compassion of verse 12.

Colossians 3:1-12

A diagram of this text is as follows:

	Process	Results
3:12 *D*		Allows us to become an other-centered individual that can start a life of ministry.
3:8-11 *A+B+C* = The Ability to Do *D*	We put off the qualities that negatively affect relationships.	Frees of the pain that keeps us from seeing the life and sufferings of others.
3:5-7 *A+B* = The Ability to Do *C*	Putting to death the inward negative moods and appetites that destroy inner peace and joy.	Undercuts the inward atmosphere that negatively affects our relationships.
3:1-4 *A* = Ability to Do *B*	Reckoning God's picture of reality Using a heavenly perspective and Pursuing the heavenly relationship.	Creates a proper foundation to manage moods and appetites.

The entire ethic starts with a picture of the believer's identity with Christ. At the same time, we are to pursue a perspective that is built around heavenly realities and relationships.

Verses 1-4. The believer is encouraged to seek the things above; those things are peace (1:20), reconciliation (1:22), our completeness (2:10), our identification with Christ before God, and holding fast to the Head (2:19). This is very similar to the statement that every variety of spiritual blessings exists for the believer before the Father in heaven.[8] We are to set our perspective around these realities because we have been identified with Christ.

This is an identity hidden from the world but the important reality is that the hiding is God's choice. The all-important one, God, not only intimately knows this identity, he is also the one who has chosen to hide our identity in relationship to him. At the proper time when Christ is revealed to the world, so will our identification be revealed (v. 4). What should control our perspective is the picture that God has of us. In Greek the commands of this section are in the present active indicative. That means that these should be a continual part of the believer's life. We should not allow this exercise to slack, but instead pursuing God as defined by these realities should be continual with us. As we do this, a door will be opened to the management of our inner life.

Verses 5-7. As the relationship to the Father is pursued, we can deal with the moods and desires that are an ever-present problem on this earth. We can actually put them to death as they course through our members. This can only be done though as the previous relationships are sustained and used. We do this by taking the mood or appetite into the Father's presence, and relating the feelings within to him. In doing this we can transition from unbridled appetite to self-control. We can go from great anxiety to great peace. Our identity in Christ gives us permission to be richly personal concerning our internal struggle: seeking the things above deeply affects the way we perceive things and therefore changes the way we feel; setting our perspective properly also has a deeply emotional result.

Verses 8-11. As we deal with the compulsions within through a living relationship with God, we find the ability to deal with our relationships without.

Many of our external relationships are simply lived in reaction to what is going on within. As the Proverb says, with all that we guard, we must guard the heart, for from it are the goings-forth of life (Prov 4:23). Jesus observed that from the abundance of the heart the mouth speaks (Matt 12:34). All three passages—Proverbs, Matthew, and Colossians—are saying the same thing: address what is going on within and it will become the basis for changing how we are acting with people without.

Verse 12. As the three previous practices are learned, the heart finds peace, joy, and love more and more present. With those emotions becoming the environment of the heart, the believer is free to look at people in a new way, sympathetically, and relate to them in a new way as a servant for their good. Without addressing the maelstrom internally, the believer would never notice the needs and problems of the people we must live among. As we manage our inner lives, we are given the opportunity to become other-directed people.

Maturity and this Process

Colossians

3:1-4	3:5-7	3:8-11	3:12
Pursuit of God	Nullifying Inner Moods	Changing Relational Reactions	Ministering to Other People

As a believer matures he or she will spend more and more time ministering to people (v. 12). But throughout the day and at any time, the believer may find himself or herself in need of addressing any of the first three. And the first one should be going on all the time. So it is true that each builds on the previous, but that does not mean that the believer cannot retrogress in this process. What is important to note is that each section is dependent upon the pursuit of God, the perspective set on heavenly values, and the recognition of one's position in Christ. This interplay between our identity (our instinctive, unconscious picture of ourselves), our imagination (how we picture reality and ourselves), and our conscience (our instinctive sense of values) creates the picture and the perspective that we carry into life.

Implications. The preceding carries with it the following implications. Our emotions tell us of our spiritual state. The emotions, by whether they enhance our lives or else they afflict our lives, tell us where we are with God. Spirituality is a life normally dominated by primary emotions. These primary emotions are encapsulated in the fruit of the Spirit (Gal 5:22-23). Each term of the fruit of the Spirit carries an emotional connotation. If love for others is present, along with contentment with life, and a deep sense of well being, that implies that we are being ministered to by the Spirit of God.

Carnality is a life dominated by misused emotions and appetites (Gal 5:19-21). It is a choice for lust rather than God (Rom 6:11-12). If confusion, addictive feelings, and discontent are present, the person's state may certainly be carnal or non-spiritual.

We cannot be spiritually mature without a ministry to our own emotional life. In this text, Col 3:1-12, setting one's mind on things above (vv. 1-2) becomes the first step in the process of controlling one's emotions.

Our emotions tell us *about our thoughts and perspectives.* Our emotions (Col 3:2, 8) may be present before our conscious thoughts. This may be due to the Fall or it may simply be the way we were created. The reason they may be a result of the Fall is that the level of confusion that occurs between the thoughts and emotions may reflect fallen realities (note Paul's connection between confusion and the power of sin with regard to the law in Rom 7:11).

Our emotions are our *true eyes into other people.* Empathetic listening (Col 3:12-13) enables us to experience a similar set of emotions as the person we are listening to. This may lead to a far more profound understanding of the person.

Conclusions

If it is true that the work of the Holy Spirit is involved with our emotions, then the work of the Spirit of God is profoundly psychological. Moreover, even though the Holy Spirit is a divine, mysterious presence, he occupies a strategic place within us. He functions at the confluence of our imagination, perspective, ego, and emotions. At this confluence he works synergistically with us. As we relate to God as a Father through our identity in Christ, deep change takes place through the Spirit of God.

The preceding of course has direct implications concerning the nature of spirituality. Spiritual realities are emotional realities. One cannot say that counseling and psychology deal only with emotional issues. Emotional issues are inexorably intertwined with spiritual issues, for the nature of spirituality is relational and relationships are deeply emotional as even the most cursory examination of the fruit of the Spirit would show. This means that spiritual realities have psychological implications and vice versa.

Spirituality involves nearly everything. In much of evangelicalism, a false spirituality is placed in the space between the intellectual, psychological, physical aspects of humanity. No such space exists. Biblical spirituality is the management of all those aspects in relationship to the reign of the Trinity.

The nature of psychology is such that spiritual implications are everywhere within it. Psychology is filled with spiritual implications. It is not religiously neutral. Psychology addresses the emotional nature of humanity. This also has implications concerning the unitary nature of humanity. Biblically humans are not compartmentalized. Psychologically they are not compartmentalized.

The work of the Spirit is synergistic. It is more than just cooperation with the Spirit; it is cooperation with the Trinity. In prayer we relate to the Father. As we do so we remain confident and conformed to the life of the Son. We are empowered by the Spirit. This empowerment can be sovereign as in his flooding ministry (Luke 1:15, 41, 67; Acts 2:4; 4:8, 31; 9:17; 18:9; overwhelmingly filled) or we can cooperate as in his filling ministry (Acts 14:26; Eph 5:18; filled with character).

As evangelicals we cannot afford to downplay the importance of emotions. The work of the Spirit of God is deeply emotional. Since those realities are so, they carry weighty implications for how Christians should teach and preach and counsel and lead.

The Holy Spirit and the Local Church

Jeff Louie

Jesus is the Lord of his church, and the Spirit of God can work vibrantly among his people. Too often our church life is devoid of the Lord's spiritual dynamism. We become overly dependent upon human wisdom and planning, to such a point that we no longer rely upon the Lord who can deliver us. As we lift up the exalted Christ and depend upon him through worship, prayer and his truth, the majestic working of God will be manifest in the local churches.

The Greatness of God

God is full of might. And though he has the prerogative to manifest his power in any way he desires, the fact that God works to deliver his people spans both Testaments. God transcends this world. He is supernatural. It should not surprise us that our fellowship with him allows glimpses of the divine reality of his greatness. What good is our theology if our knowledge of God is confined to a theoretical understanding that bears no resemblance of our actual faith experience? The scriptures bear testimony that faithful men and women of God were greatly changed and empowered by him. They were always mightier in their works and bolder in their declarations. The Lord gave them ability that went beyond social phenomena or human understanding.

For the New Testament Church, the effect of God's presence should yield a great spiritual dynamism. This potential is greater than during Old Testament times. We have God's forgiveness through the atonement. We have the Spirit who indwells us. The Book of Hebrews describes Jesus as our high priest, who intercedes for our prayers. And we have a triumphant Christ enthroned in heaven. It is of great note that the Old Testament passage most alluded to in the New Testament is Ps 110:1: "Sit down at my right hand until I make your enemies your footstool!" Jesus has authority to conquer; his triumph is certain.

But the triumph of Christ is often lacking in his Church. His manifest power is not seen. At times we seek it, but in the wrong ways, looking for it through some new technique which is biblically unsound. Then there are other approaches that tend to avoid spiritual dynamism by focusing on an intellectualism, or reliance upon human reasoning, or some business model that yields predictable results. There is often a great variance between the spiritual potential in Christ and the spiritual reality of our churches. We need to rekindle our passion for Christ and to fan into flame the Spirit that indwells us. Our strength is found in the spiritual realms and in the power that is found in Christ.

What does a church with a positive spiritual dynamism look like? What are some characteristics of the mighty presence of God within his church? I will present four characteristics. They are not exhaustive, but representative of the Spirit's work in the church. They are: (1) a worship that experiences his presence,

(2) a testimony of his corporate deliverance, (3) a people who are refined, and (4) a manifestation of his might in ministry.

Worship that Experiences His Presence

The Sunday worship is the most common corporate experience of all believers. There is no argument on the importance of worshiping God. But what needs to be discussed is quality of that worship. What is it that God is looking for in worship? This question needs to be addressed, because what is commonly practiced as worship often falls short of what God desires.

All too often, what is understood as good worship is determined by the people who lead the worship. If the music is good, if the sermon is moving, if we have the proper ambiance for the worship experience, then the worship excels. The postmodern age has rejected abstract truth and instead gravitates toward the experience, preferring the music and the ambiance. The modernist goes for the teaching. So we craft our services for the people to evoke a worship experience, great worshipful music that gives praise to God, or powerful preaching that enlightens the mind, or penetrates the soul. We may include a few PowerPoint slides, a video clip, or the strategic dimming of lights. Maybe the topics of the messages can be adapted to draw more people into the worship. But is this all there is to the worship of God?

What is worship? To answer this question we need to look at it from two perspectives: form and function. The form of worship includes music. The Psalms were originally set to melodies. Paul tells us to encourage one another with hymns and spiritual songs (Eph 5:19). The "new song" is echoed in the heavenly presence of God (Rev 5:9; 14:3). Then there is the teaching element. Jesus gave sermons; so did Peter. Teaching is found everywhere in Paul's ministry. The pastor is the teacher (Eph 4:11), and so are the elders of the church (1 Tim 3:2). These are the two major formal ingredients of modern worship, but the function of worship is a quite different issue.

In understanding the function of worship, we need to see what happens when true worship is depicted. A good place to understand the function of worship is the Gospel of Matthew. In this Gospel, there are three clear instances of individuals worshiping Jesus: the Magi who bow before the newborn Christ

(Matt 2:11), the disciples who worship Jesus after seeing his great power in calming a stormy sea (Matt 14:33), and the post-resurrection worship of Jesus (Matt 28:9, 17). In each these three instances, there is no music heard, neither is there a sermon delivered. The *forms* of worship are nowhere to be found, but these three instances are endorsed in the text as genuine expressions of worship of Christ. It is worship without the form, because the worshiper is responding to the realization of Christ's majesty. It is very personal, and the spiritual reflex action is to bow and fall before his presence. Worship in the Gospel of Matthew transcends form. It is about what one truly believes within his soul about the majesty of Christ. This pure worship needs no external assistance.

Besides a personal understanding of the majesty of God, worship has another function, which is to cause us to repent and submit. The worship that God seeks cannot be left on the level of mere words of praise. God is not seeking the words, but the person behind the words. The function of repentance and submission is at the heart of worship. This concept of submission is seen in the temptation of Jesus. Satan wants Jesus to bow and worship him. But how does this temptation work? Jesus is the eternal Son of God. Satan is a high-ranking created angel. Satan can never be intrinsically higher in nature than the Son of God. But the issue is not about who has the greater nature, but who will submit to the other. Worship must include a submission and lordship theme. True worship grapples with the concept of submitting to God through themes of personal confession and repentance. In 1 Cor 14:24–25, Paul relates the process of an unbeliever hearing the words of a prophecy and getting convicted, as the secrets of his heart are opened, with the result that he falls on his face worshiping God, declaring his presence. Prophecy here is not the foretelling of the future, but is the bold forth-telling of our failings and weaknesses in our lives. In this passage, the true worship experience is the humbling experience before a mighty God. Once again, the true essence of worship is not in the form, but in personal understanding of God's majesty and our own fallen nature.

At Sunset Chinese Baptist Church in San Francisco, we are discovering how to go beyond the form of worship and into its reality. In seeking the pure essence of worship, we have rediscovered a simple answer. It is rather primitive. It is through prayer, prayer that is in accordance with the teaching of Jesus.

The final feature of this corporate prayer is based on the Sermon on the Mount. Jesus taught his disciples to go into their "inner room" to pray. Prayer is for God to hear. He tells his followers not to pray like the gentiles who equate effective prayer with wordiness. Rather it is about speaking to the God who already knows all things even before we ask. There is a very personal side to prayer. Privacy before God increases the potential for honesty.

Prayer at Sunset

For many years, I had adopted the usual pattern of Sunday worship. The worship service had a lengthy session of singing, which was then followed by the sermon. The sermon was given the most time, and was the most important component. A small amount of time was given to prayer, which was usually someone saying a prayer on behalf of the congregation. Focus and energy were given to the music and the sermon, and very little to prayer. The thinking was: "if the music is great, and the message is excellent, then people come because it is deemed to be a good worship service."

But I have come to question the premise of this worship pattern. Singing and teaching are important formal elements of corporate worship, but often we stop short of their intended functional goal by not allowing the worshiper time to respond to God personally in repentance, commitment and dependence. Not only do we disallow the worshiper to come to God in personal worship, we can fool worshipers into thinking that excellent worship is determined by the competence of the musicians and preacher, or that the surrounding worship ambiance determines the quality of the worship. The quality of worship that Christ is seeking is not achieved by a handful of gifted individuals leading the worship, but by the personal worship of the total congregation. The form of worship is external, but the essence of worship is an internal matter. It is not the dozen people leading worship that is important; rather, great worship is determined by the hearts of the people sitting in the audience.

In order to focus on the corporate response in worship, we have made a dramatic change in our worship to include much more prayer. We wanted to change the church to have a culture of prayer. We did not want a church with a prayer meeting, but rather a church where everyone prays. We wanted to go beyond the 5 to 10% who come to prayer services; we wanted 100%

All our churches have prayer. But prayer is often given a secon[d] place in our ministries. Prayer may be limited to invocations and be[...] during worship. Sometimes we may add a prayer to introduce the chie[f] worship, the sermon. Sometimes we can add a mid-week prayer mee[ting] only a small percentage of the average Sunday morning congregation a[...] we may include a time of special prayer at the end of the Sunday[...] which prayer warriors pray for those with needs. But prayer needs to[...] the aforementioned variations if we are to realize the spiritual dynami[c] result. Christ's teaching on prayer went beyond the formality, placing[...] element of a believer's personal walk with God. There is no way[...] church can be spiritually revitalized without prayer.

Christ's teaching reveals three transformational characteristics[...] First, it must be a major activity of the church. When Jesus[...] moneychangers out of the temple in Mat 21, he said, "My house wil[l...] house of prayer." Though our churches cannot be equated with tem[ple...] the principle of prayer being at the center of corporate worship can b[e...] we are to have churches that have the spiritual vitality of Christ, pra[yer...] one of the focal points of our ministries, if not the main focus.

Secondly prayer is to be marked by an intimate confession of [...] God. This intimate honesty results in an enjoyment his presence. In [...] Jesus speaks to the church at Laodicea. Here was a church that w[as...] wealthy, but was in total spiritual poverty. Christ demanded that the[...] true spiritual poverty. The passage includes a tragic description of J[esus...] outside his own church, knocking on the door seeking entry, prom[ising...] depth of fellowship. Jesus is seeking an honest recognition of th[e...] before him. We may be wealthy and self-sufficient in this world, bu[t...] our true state. As Jesus is calling the entire church in Laodicea to op[en...] so we need to have our entire congregation open up to him in h[...] problems and weaknesses. We do not need well-crafted prayers.[...] seeking prayers spoken by orators to impress the audience. Rather,[...] prayers of humility by the entire congregation so that we would un[...] we are, so that we do not become impressed with ourselves.

participation. So, we brought the prayer meeting into the Sunday worship. Then it was determined that the worship prayer would not be for people with special needs, or be done by individuals gifted in prayer. Some churches have successful prayer ministries where people with needs come forward at the end of the worship service to be prayed for by those trained for such a service. We wanted to go beyond this, because prayer needed to be done by the entire congregation. I often tell people that it is the people who don't acknowledge their need for prayer who need it the most.

In our Sunday services, prayer is now the most important aspect of our worship. We sing, we teach the word in truth and boldness, but the highlight of our worship is the time set aside for prayer. About 25% of the worship service time is given to prayer and other activities related to personal response. We develop the worship service around prayer, and the staff plans the worship calendar around the focus of prayer.

The manner of our worship prayer can be described as corporate and private. It is corporate because we are praying together. It is private, because people speak to God in their own words. Liturgical prayers have aided many people, but we wanted to focus on the individual response. Liturgical prayers can lose meaning over time, and they cannot reflect the true needs and heart burdens of the individual. Worshipers need to speak in their own words, and not in words we lead them to say. We pattern this time after Christ's Sermon on the Mount teaching of going to one's "inner room" to pray. Prayer must be personal and not for people to hear. People who worship at Sunset know that the prayer is the most powerful aspect of our worship, because at this time the individual worshiper responds to the taught word and personally communes with God in prayer. The taught word of God, intimacy with God, and personal assessment are streams brought together in the quietness of the worship prayer time. Sometimes there is soft music playing in the background. Most of the time there is silence.

As a result, the people greatly enjoy the time of prayer and cherish it. Many people have mentioned that they wished the prayer time were longer. Imagine, people wanting to pray to God more! Prayer is becoming such a major part of our worship experience that a Sunday service without significant time of prayer leaves us spiritually wanting.

When I lead the worship prayer time, it revolves around the major application points of the sermon. I lead them in a theme, and tell them to speak to God in their own words, silently, or in whispers concerning that topic. After a short period of time, I move on to a second topic, and then a third, sometimes a fourth. Everyone is basically praying back the sermon in application. Everyone is assessing his or her own spiritual life. Everyone is repenting. Everyone to telling God about their failures. Everyone is making plans for correction. The prayers are short, intense, and honest. As a result, the time of prayer brings the worship service to a noticeably different plane. It is not about listening to a message, or singing worship songs; it is about the individual worshiper opening a door to speak with God in response to the teaching of his word. There are no gimmicks. It is rather primitive. But the result is dramatic. His presence is felt. We often hear sobbing in the congregation during this time; at times there is a great deal of crying. I often feel weighted down when I lead in corporate private prayer. I often find it difficult to stand, bracing myself on the podium. I have gone on my knees in unrehearsed response when I am humbled by my own silent prayers. It is a strange sense of humbling, for it refreshes rather than discourages. It brings a sense of joy and vitality, because each is brought closer to God.

The prayer themes of personal response, repentance, and commitment are always included in our worship service, but we often include other variations in our corporate prayers. Sometimes we will pray for people going on mission trips. We either have them stand in the aisles and have people surround them in prayer, or have them come forward with the elders praying around them. Having people praying for those serving our Lord is important for the corporate body. All too often our worship lacks the corporate sense of working together for the kingdom of God. We neglect to pray for those who minister in our midst. To combat this tendency, at certain intervals, we pray for each Sunday school teacher, or youth worker, or elder by name in the worship service. I cannot imagine how Christ would be pleased with a church that neglects to uphold corporately her servants and leaders in prayer. We need to learn how to uphold those who serve Jesus in corporate prayer, and need to be reminded that we are part of a larger spiritual community. I remember one Sunday when we sent off about a dozen people at our 8:30 am worship for a summer mission trip. As they stood in the aisles, about 90% of the congregation stood up and surrounded them in prayer. Many of the summer missionaries were moved to tears as well as those doing the praying.

In addition to regularly interceding for those who serve the Lord, we also lead the congregation in intercession for needs of the people. We have times when we collect the names and descriptions of the seriously ill for a month. I sometimes give a sermon on praying for the sick, and then the whole congregation is given strips of paper with various names and descriptions on them. We then pray for them during the worship service. At other times we have collected the names of relatives, friends, and acquaintances who do not know Christ, and we pray that they may one day come to know the Savior. Is it not a spiritual war we are in? Is not the war won in the heavenly places through the power of our Lord? Corporate prayer is transforming us. It reminds us every Sunday of the spiritual reality of God, and our humble dependence upon him. We must not be afraid of this spiritual reality. Personal corporate humility before God transforms. I used to enjoy preaching the most. I still look forward to proclaiming the word of God, but now I deem it a greater honor to lead the people in prayer. I have come to the conclusion that I would much rather have the people talk to God than listen to me. Who am I compared to God?

A Testimony of Corporate Deliverance

Answered prayer can uplift a believer, but when God answers the prayer for a congregation, it invigorates the entire body. Western Christianity often focuses too much on the individual, with an approach of "what God can do for me," as if he were the ultimate self-help guru to solve our problems. God can and does help the individual, but this is so often our central focus that we forget that Jesus stands in the midst of his churches working in them and controlling their destinies. The deliverance of his corporate people manifests his active presence and spiritual favor, and as a result churches with a spiritual dynamism should have stories that testify of it.

A Story of God's Deliverance at Sunset

For many years we at Sunset Chinese Baptist Church have had a major need: more space. For many years now, we have had four Sunday morning worship services. Two of the worship services have overflow viewing areas. People sitting in the halls is not a figure of speech at Sunset. We are very crowded. We needed space, but there was a major obstacle: we are located in the city of San Francisco. Most people don't realize how small this city is. It is only seven by seven miles, and this small area is packed with people. It is difficult to find large parcels of land available. And if a large lot were to become available, the price would be prohibitive for a church.

For many years we looked for a place to expand our ministry: the possible lease of an office building in neighboring Daly City, the purchase of a supermarket, a Christian Scientist church for sale. All these possibilities fell through. Then there was the bid on a furniture store that had been inherited by seven relatives. We were disappointed when the vote by the owners went 4-3 against accepting our bid. In the meantime, we purchased a twelve-unit apartment complex located on a 75 by 100 foot lot across the street from our present church facility. Some churches buy acres; in San Francisco churches buy by the square foot.

With the growing need for space and despite the city's aversion toward such projects, the elders decided to ask the city for permission to tear down the twelve-unit apartment complex to build a new sanctuary. The chance for such approval was highly improbable. The voters of San Francisco had passed Proposition M, which stated that the city would make the preservation of affordable housing a priority for city planning. Apartments were not to be torn down, but were to be preserved. Shortly after we first submitted the building plans we received a call from a city worker with an offer to do us a favor. She had spoken with her colleagues and superiors and got word that the approval of our project was unlikely. So a kind offer was made to refund some of the fees if we decided pull out of the project now. While the offer was appreciated the elders decided to continue.

In soliciting help for the project, we decided to approach two individuals who could assist. One, a building permit expeditor, was well connected with the city planners, with a history of gaining approval for major building projects in the city. He was also a believer and offered to assist without charge. The other individual was the elected supervisor for our district. As a newly elected state assemblyman representing the city he wielded considerable political influence.

With the support of these well-connected and influential individuals we believed that we had a much better chance for approval of the project. The reality was yet another disappointment. They had both talked with the San Francisco city planning commissioners and the word was that the project would be rejected. The building permit expeditor told us we would never get the permit. The politician gave us the same report. As a matter of fact, on the day of the public hearing before the commissioners, the politician told us that the best plan would be to ask for a postponement on the hearing, for it would be better to delay the hearing than to proceed with it and have our plans rejected. The elders conferred and decided to proceed. About two hundred of our members attended the hearing that day. Even though one of our members who attended had by chance known the head Commissioner from public school days, the commissioner told his childhood friend that he couldn't help him. It was a project that was doomed.

At the public hearing many of our members gave testimony in support of the project, from senior citizens to teenagers. They spoke of what we were doing and of what the church meant to them. At the end, the commissioners gave their decision one by one. Each one prefaced his decision by saying that he had come to deny the permit but changed his mind and was voting to grant it. The building permit was unanimously approved. How did this happen? Who changed the minds of the commissioners? We give the glory to our God.

God had brought us through the building permit, but he would also bring us through another aspect of the project: the financing.

I was given an audio CD by a famous pastor in the United States. It was a message on how to raise funds for a building project. It was filled with principles for a successful building campaign. One was to have the head pastor be the chief strategist and promoter. If you want to raise the money, you shouldn't have laymen or secondary pastors do the fund raising; the Senior Pastor has to be the one. Another principle was to prepare for the pledge Sunday with a 90-day preparatory campaign. For three months remind the congregation that the pledge day is coming. Remind them of the vision for the new building, and make the pledge day a big event. Make special coloring books for the children concerning the building project so that everyone would be involved. The final principle I remember from the tape was always to raise funds during a booming economy. Do not raise funds during a recession. These are proven principles. The pastor's church raised a great deal of money.

But in listening to the audio CD, I realized we had done everything wrong, and that it was too late to make any adjustments. The pledges were coming in and the due date for the final pledges was nearing. I had not been the chief strategist for the fund raising. We had formed a committee of laymen to do this task. There was no 90-day preparatory campaign. I just gave two sermons on the topic. There were no coloring books, no t-shirts, no literature. Finally, the fund raising was being done in the midst of the Dot-com bust in northern California and unemployment in our area was the highest in the nation. With such preparatory blunders, how could we ever expect to raise the needed funds?

Despite doing everything "wrong" from a marketing perspective, God was at work. This was clearly his work not just ours. The result of the pledge was remarkable. We raised more money per capita than the church of the well-known leader.

Even in the collection of the funds, we continually saw God's presence. After the pledges, we needed to collect the funds in increments. Our first goal was for $500,000 to be collected by the end of the year. With one Sunday left, we were short $187,000. I didn't think we would reach our goal. On the Monday staff meeting after the first collection goal due date, I asked our administrator what the final total was. The figure was $500,022.

Church growth can often be explained by good planning or other sociological factors. It is strange how church growth seems to always do better in a developing suburban area than in the inner city. Sometimes God works through our planning. But it is when God works despite our plans that brings praise to the name of our Lord, because it reminds us that it is the Spirit and power of God that delivers us. Our new sanctuary is being built as I type this manuscript. Every time I look at the construction, I am reminded of God's deliverance, that it is ultimately not up to man, but up to Christ who sits at the right hand of God.

A People Who Are Refined

One often hears statistics of the high failure rate among seminary graduates once they enter the ministry. One report indicates that 95% of those who enter the ministry will not retire in the ministry. A gloomier study showed that 80% of seminary graduates leave the ministry within two years. Numerous explanations have been proposed for such high rates of failure. Perhaps it is the failure of the seminary training itself. Some argue that there is a disconnect between what is taught and what is actually needed for graduates to succeed in ministry. Perhaps theological education focuses on making the graduates teachers of truth, and does a poorer job of developing them into leaders of people. Others have cited the disillusionment of ministry. Graduates may have an unreasonably high expectation of ministry, but ministries, especially existing ones, have their darker sides which are hidden when the graduate candidates for the position. But the scriptures put forth an alternative to failure. There is the potential to triumph in any given ministry situation by transforming it through the work of the Spirit in his people. We must trust God in his ability to transform the local church. It is the mark of God to transform the "lost cause," be it an individual or an entire church.

I have been a pastor for over twenty years. My first church was in a suburb of Chicago. My present ministry is in San Francisco. When I came to my present ministry fourteen years ago, I can describe it as a church with more infighting than could ever be imagined. Board meetings had a carnal tone to them, as voting could be forecast by alliances rather than by decisions that would promote the cause of Christ. There was the usual territorialism, and then experiences of spiritual backstabbing and personal bouts of emotional depression.

But during the last decade and a half, Sunset has changed and we are now exhibiting a unified peace among the leadership. What happened? What caused the transformation? The answer lies in understanding Revelation chapters 2 and 3, and its teaching that Christ stands in the midst of his churches, determining their destinies. In these seven letters to the churches in Asia Minor, Jesus is the one who can discipline the church, as well as the one who can bless it. The realization that Christ is active in the midst of his churches is just as great a comfort to us as it was to the early Church. Our responsibility is to be faithful to him, for Christ is in ultimate control. We often agonize over difficulties in our churches, or we put great effort in understanding and planning what needs to be done for it to grow. But our task is to remain faithful and uplift Christ. We must always remember that Christ is in control. He will bring things to pass. He transforms.

The transformation in an existing church takes time—years rather than months. The process is slow, but there will be one noticeable change that I will write about, the removal of pride and prideful people. Pride was the cause of Satan's fall, and it is what the Lord hates. It takes many forms in the local church, but the variation that is most deadly is when the pride is exhibited within the leadership of the church. God cannot work with prideful people, because it puts our desires above God, it makes us self-sufficient, and it causes us to be incapable of realizing the weaknesses in our lives. Without an honest confession of our failures before God, we can never be in fellowship with him.

Pride among church leaders is manifested in many ways. Some leaders manifest it by making decisions that benefit themselves. It is not for the good of Christ or the good of the whole church, but the lobbying is driven by selfish motivation. Other leaders manifest pride by their insistence of always being right and their denial of ever being wrong. Over the years, I have graciously confronted many individuals who fall into these categories. Many sound very spiritual minded, but they are not, because they can never see the fault in their own lives. Pride makes repentance impossible. To make matters worse, prideful leaders can be embedded within a ministry, can have many supporters and friends, and they can be skillful in making opponents look bad. I have seen my share of this kind of person.

The solution is twofold. First, we need to take up our responsibility to speak truth in love. We cannot be silent here. A boldness to speak truth is a mark of the Spirit's working throughout scripture. But our truth must be with grace and love. This is a difficult task, because we often go to extremes of a harsh truth without grace, or a graciousness that is devoid of God's righteousness.

Sometimes we fool ourselves into thinking that the end justifies the means. Since few people ever respond in a positive way to a rebuke, why then go through a process of a correction? But people empowered by the Spirit have always been able to speak the truth; it is a mark of the God's presence.

The second part of the solution for spiritual pride within leadership is to trust God that he will do the refining, because we are his church. He has the most at stake. God will definitely intervene.

Over the years, through the process of speaking the truth in love, the church has slowly and steadily been transformed. Some leaders have left for legitimate spiritual reasons, some moved out of the area, but others have moved on because God removed them. We must have the confidence in God that he will defend and refine his church. We often rationalize our need for boldness, because of a fear of the short-term social disruption. But whose church is it anyway? Whose truth are we declaring? It is not my church, or the people's church. Christ holds his church together; he is at the center. Our responsibility is to remain faithful to his teaching.

A Manifestation of His Might in Ministry

We now come to the discussion of the miraculous manifestation of the Spirit in the local church. I have chosen to place this topic at the end of this chapter, not to elevate the miraculous to the highest level of importance. Rather, the placement is to show that it is not the most important characteristic of a church's spiritual dynamism. The miraculous working of God is not an accurate indicator of spiritual maturity. Seek after love and peace. Seek after prayer. Be faithful to God in truth and action; these are more important. The actual worth of miracles is important to understand, as we often place too much value on miracles. We must be reminded of Christ's teaching in Matt 7:22–23, where many come to the Lord proclaiming that they have performed great miracles in his name, only to have Jesus deny even knowing them.

But though the manifestation of the power of God in ministry is not a primary goal, nevertheless, a church with a growing sense of the triumphant and transcendent God can experience it. Although the miraculous spiritual *gifts* may have ceased, this does not mean that *miracles* no longer occur. The power of God is not limited to an association with the spiritual gifts. Miracles occurred in scripture prior to the start of the Church in Acts. And in Jas 5:16, the power of God is connected to prayer rather than giftedness.

I have seen the power of God often in my twenty years of ministry. In retelling them, I do not make the miracles the goal of my spiritual experience or ministry. I would much rather lead a church which emphasizes a true spirit of prayer and worship than one which emphasizes seeing God's miracles in our lives. But though the powerful working of God is not sought after, it is often a natural result of our prayers and the fact that God works in our midst.

On Thursday, February 12, 2004, Gavin Newsom, the Mayor of San Francisco, issued a decree to begin issuing marriage licenses to same-sex partners. It shook and still shakes the nation. In the fall of 2003, I decided to start preaching through the book of Genesis. Ten days after Newsom's decree, the natural order of exposition led to Genesis chapter 18. This is the passage on the sin of Sodom and Gomorrah. I had no problem thinking of an introduction for that sermon. In a few months, our church would play a major role in the San Francisco churches' response to Mayor Newsom's decision. When I gave the sermon, the entire congregation was in awe concerning the timing. I do not know how God coordinates these things, but we should not be surprised that he does.

One Sunday, I was introduced to the fiancée of a member of our church. I frequently meet engaged couples, but this was the only time that I felt compelled to phone the young woman and ask, "Is this an arranged marriage?" Her reply was, "Who told you?" No one told me. As a result a dialogue ensued. The episode had a great ending and she is now happily married. How does one know these things? I am not surprised that God can give such knowledge.

A church member once told me the story of his chronically ill coworker. One day he approached her and said, "In three days you will be well." He had never said such a thing in his life. He was just as surprised as the coworker. He prayed for three days, and on the third day, the coworker became well. When the whole story was told to her, she became a believer in the Lord Jesus Christ. What prompted this man to say such a thing? I am convinced that it was the Spirit of God.

On another occasion a woman came to my office with her mother. This church member had brought her mother because she was extremely bitter at her ex-husband, his friends, and his relatives. The divorce had occurred many years before, but every day she would retell the story of how she was bitterly mistreated. The daughter had heard the same stories over and over again for years. In the office, I heard the facts of the story three times! I told this embittered woman about Christ and about his forgiveness. She accepted Christ's forgiveness, and then I asked her to forgive her tormentors. She agreed. She went through each name, forgiving them. Her demeanor completely changed after the prayer. The daughter told me that this was a turning point in her mother's life. She has not heard her mother bring up the bitter past since. What caused such a quick transformation? Where did this peace come from? It comes from the triumphant Christ who guards our hearts and minds and gives a peace that transcends this world. It is the peace that Paul wrote about in Phil 4.

We have had episodes where demons were cast out, dreams that dramatically changed the path of individuals for the kingdom of God, and times of miraculous recoveries from illness. One incident of healing stands out in my mind as particularly dramatic. The doctors had given up hope on a comatose patient. We prayed and he made an unexpected full recovery. As a result of answered prayer in behalf of this man the whole clan came to the Lord as a result.

In seeing the miraculous side of the ministries, we are not to seek them via unbiblical means. All too often we go beyond that which is scriptural. There have been unsound teachings on spiritual warfare and territorial spirits. There are those who supposedly are gifted in releasing individuals from repressed memory syndrome, empathic healing, and slaying in the spirit. In 1 Thess 5:21 Paul tells us to test all things. We joyously testify of God's power when it is based upon his teaching.

The Spirit of God within the Church

Sunset Chinese Baptist is not a perfect church. Like all churches, we have issues that we still need to deal with. But we have found a passion and a source of strength that gives us great hope and encouragement. Christ is triumphant, sitting at the right hand of God. May we be emboldened by the words of the Apostle Paul, "Now to him who by the power that is working within us is able to do far beyond all that we ask or think, to him be the glory in the church and in Christ Jesus to all generations, forever and ever. Amen" (Eph 3:20–21).

The Holy Spirit in Missions

Donald K. Smith

God is not geographically-biased; the Holy Spirit is equally at work in every part of the world, and not in special ways on traditional mission fields. The arguments that "new" Christians need miracles to undergird their faith is inadequate; the center of the world Christian population is today in Africa, while the Christian population of Europe and North America is statistically declining. The visibility of the Holy Spirit's work in Asia, Africa, Latin America, and the Middle East seems more dependent on an openness to His interventions there than in North America and Europe. It is a matter of human perception, rather than a difference in God's working. Rationalism excludes the invisible spiritual world, thus evidences of the Holy Spirit are seldom perceived. The core issue for man is control - man himself or God. It is the primary work of the Holy Spirit to work within man to give new hearts, to make new creatures that submit to Jesus as Lord. That is the Spirit's great work, not the more visible and striking evidences of His presence.

Why should we find it necessary to talk about the Holy Spirit and *missions*? Does he work in a different manner outside the United States or Europe? Is he more needed when proclaiming the Gospel on the African, Asian, South American continents than in North America or Europe? Mission is not a matter of geography, but of alienation from God. So why do we experience the Holy Spirit differently in Africa than in Europe? In Asia than in America?

In Zimbabwe, a most unusual privilege was extended to me by a "messenger of the gods," an *iwosana*. Would I like to take his picture, wearing the symbols of his office (a python skeleton, tails of certain animals, and the tip of a cow horn full of unknown medicines, suspended on a necklace,)?

"Of course!" I replied.

Three or four weeks later I returned to learn that man was near death. I naturally asked what was wrong—malaria perhaps, or chronic dysentery? "No," the villagers told me. "You took his picture and that offended the spirits for whom he was a messenger." They were surprised at my ignorance in jeopardizing the life of their friend.

When I went to his house, there were three other diviners and "messengers" with him. All of them accusingly told me that my pictures were the problem, so I asked to pray for his healing, in the name of Christ. They did the equivalent of shrugging their shoulders, so I prayed with a sense of real challenge in the spiritual realm. I risked not only my reputation, but the reputation of Christ in that prayer. The man was healed. The presence and power of the Holy Spirit was evident in his glorification of Christ in that confrontation.

Such glimpses of the spirit world and activity of the Holy Spirit are repeatedly given in Africa, South America, and Asia. Far less frequently do we hear of the Holy Spirit's manifestations in North America and Europe. Does that suggest that God is geographically biased? Some have suggested that traditionally "non-Christian" lands need this kind of evidence to reinforce their belief.

But some of these lands traditionally considered non-Christian have a higher percentage of professing Christians than historically "Christian" lands. Today, the population center of the Christian world is not in North America or Europe, but in Africa! There are possibly more believers in mainland China than in the

United States. Churches are multiplying in most of South America, Africa and Asia but the percentage of Christians is static or diminishing in North America and Europe. Former "mission fields" are now sending more missionaries to proclaim his Glory worldwide than the mission-sending lands of the northern hemisphere. The records of the last two decades of the twentieth century show the emptiness, perhaps even the evasiveness, of arguing that the Holy Spirit must work uniquely outside of Europe and North America to undergird the "weaker faith" of those believers.

Deception or Truth?

Evidence of the Holy Spirit's work is not limited to a few untaught people or to a particular theological bias, but is widespread in both space and time, and often objectively verified. "By their fruits you shall know them" and by the lives—and deaths—of a multitude we know that God the Holy Spirit is indeed working in ways that are labeled "remarkable." Of course there are also examples of deceiving and being deceived, and often confusion between what is from the Holy Spirit and what is activity of spirits not from God. Mere "spiritual" interest and "spiritual" manifestations in no way proves that Almighty God is involved.

A Christian college graduate in East Africa very seriously said that you must be careful to dispose of any tissues used to wipe your eyes. "If you do not, an enemy can use the matter from your eyes to bewitch you and cause great trouble!"

In South Africa a young Zulu Christian teacher exclaimed, "Oh no, thank you, I could not eat that rabbit you killed." It was part of a delicious-smelling rabbit stew. When pressed for an explanation, he reluctantly said it was a symbol of his clan—a clan totem. If he ate it, the ancestors and spirits would be very displeased and could cause great trouble for him.

It is possible to dismiss many of these fears as simple superstition, or deception by the spirit mentors of a people. But there are hundreds of other reports that cannot be so easily dismissed.

With startling clarity, a shaman of the Yanomamo (Venezuela) tells of the presence of God's angels, and deliverance by the Spirit of God:

In [the village of] Honey the people worried all the time and talked to Yai Pada, their new spirit. [Yai Pada is the Yanomamo name for Jehovah, the Almighty God. He had been known as the enemy spirit when all Yanomamo were controlled by spirits not from God.] They wanted him to help them fight off their attackers. One morning Spear got out of his hammock at the first light. He couldn't sleep. He had been talking to Yai Pada all night because he was so afraid of Mouth Village. As he stepped from his house onto the wet grass, he saw that Honey Village was surrounded by people, warriors maybe; he wasn't sure. But there were so many of them, big beautiful people in bright white shirts that went down to their feet. Spear could tell that Yai Pada had sent them to protect Honey from all the attacks. But after the sun came up, they were gone. He asked Pepe [a missionary living among the Yanamamo] if Yai Pada had people like that. Pepe said, "I've never seen them, but his book says that he has them and they can protect you."[1]

The shaman, Jungleman, tells of his personal deliverance by Yai Pada from the deception and power of evil spirits:

Just before they (the spirits) killed me, a bright light came. It was so bright that I couldn't see anything. And there was something very warm like I have never felt. A creature stood over me, more dazzling than anyone could ever think. As soon as I felt him, I knew who he was. He was the one we have always called... the unfriendly spirit, the enemy spirit... I have never seen such beautiful light.

I lay on the ground in the cloud of brightness and I saw my whole life, and I saw how completely tricked I had been. I remembered all the things my spirits had told me. Now suddenly in this bright light, I saw that they were all lies. Everything they ever said was a lie. And such clever lies too! All our revenge, every habit, our chest-pounding, all of it was to make us unhappy. I had been used by my spirits for their pleasure.

I've run from this creature of beauty all my life, I thought. No wonder I have nothing...

He (Yai Pada) reached out and grabbed me. I felt so safe ... Then with a big voice the spirit said to my spirits, "Leave him alone. He's mine." They scampered in every direction, like a herd of terrified hogs. And he was right; I was his.[2]

Greed and Fear Overwhelm Rationality

The power of spirits has a firm grip on the thinking of many, so strong that deception can easily be practiced even when spirits are not involved.

A man in Zambia (Central Africa) convinced a clerk that he could use sorcery to triple any amount of money by a "spell," writes Marvin Wolford. "The clerk put [the equivalent of $1400] from a government fund in a special box. After the proper ritual ... it was to be put under the clerk's bed for three weeks. He was told if it were opened before that time then the money would disappear. The clerk couldn't wait so he looked into the box. Of course, all the money was gone. He asked about it. The... man told him that he would actually do it all over again if the clerk would get more government money and promise not to open the box for another three weeks. So the desperate clerk put [the equivalent of $1700] into the box, and the spells were performed again. The case against the clerk was heard in the courts not long afterwards."[3]

How could people be so deceived? It is understandable only by perceiving the binding grip of sorcery and evil spirits, a grip that overwhelms rationality. In such a context, glad response to the ministry of the Holy Spirit can be expected. And those who preach the gospel know that only the power of the Holy Spirit can break the fear of dark powers.

Spiritual gullibility and fear are not restricted to Africa, Asia, or South America, even if such transparent frauds seem to succeed less often. Fear of unknown evil is present in North America and Europe, too. The shaman Jungleman commented on the similarity between the beliefs of the white men they knew and the Yanomamo belief in spirits. "Sometimes they even use the same words!" But more commonly, belief in spirits is denied in North America and Europe, including the activity of the Holy Spirit.

Rationalism Largely Excludes the Holy Spirit

Why, then, does it appear that the Holy Spirit is more active in Asia, Africa, or Latin America than in Europe and North America? Perhaps in the North Atlantic nations evil spirits are not active, or only operate at the margins of society. Yet there is a documented increase in cult activity in those very societies, featuring deceptions similar to that elsewhere, along with self-proclaimed witches, covens, and various forms of spirit worship—the "Mother Goddess," the "life-force" present in the world, and horoscopes.

Some suggest that higher education has made the people less easily deceived—at least concerning evil spirits. That may be true, but in areas of material goods and wealth, deception and confidence tricksters flourish. Ponzi schemes and scams to transfer to "your account" unclaimed millions of dollars left behind by some fallen leader show that greed is universal. Education has not made people less gullible to schemes promising quick riches.

Others suggest that the prevalence of churches and Christians has muted the activity of those spirits that are so fearsome in other parts of the world. If that were true, why is belief in the power of evil spirits pervasive in African nations where professed Christians are 40 to 80% of the total population, and there are more churches per capita than in Europe or North America?

I suggest that the real point is not a difference in the working of the Holy Spirit, but a difference in the working of our human perceptions. Just as our unaided ear cannot detect radio signals nor can our eyes pick up television signals, the untransformed heart is unable and/or unwilling to perceive the Holy Spirit except in ways consistent with our existing understanding. Our ability to perceive anything rests not only on our physical senses but on our previous experience and on our heart belief—our world view.

In Western cultures, reason is considered supreme. The cultural mainstream says that feelings are not to be trusted, and emotion should always be controlled. The Enlightenment paradigm infuses nearly every part of Western life, even our systematic theologies. It leads us to believe that Truth must be found and proved by careful logic, and that logic rests on empirical observations. If "it" cannot be weighed, counted, or measured in some way, "it" does not exist. Reason can only work with verifiable facts, and in that way we know the true and the false. Anything that might exist outside of empirical human experience is irrelevant, and is best simply ignored. This core/heart belief in Western cultures has made it nearly impossible to perceive the genuine working of the Holy Spirit.

Thus, the fundamental reason the ministry of the Holy Spirit seems more visible outside the North Atlantic nations is a matter of perception. We experience what we are conditioned to perceive. Since the dominant paradigm in North Atlantic nations is rationalistic, humanistic, and materialistic, we do not expect to see reality outside the boundaries established by our minds. Man is the measure and reason is the method; thus we are conditioned not to "see" outside that which is tangible—that which can be weighed, measured, counted, and apprehended by the five human senses. Emotional learning/perceiving is distrusted or dismissed, because it is not subject to reason.

Where rationalism is supreme, there is an unwillingness, even an inability, to perceive the spirit world, both the evil and the holy. Differences lie in our perception, not in a chameleon-like God. In the West, we live in a one-dimensional "Flatland" with inability to see in all dimensions. So we look elsewhere, places safely at a distance from our comfort zones, to revel in the evidences of the Holy Spirit's activity in this world.

The Spirit as Power

Initially, I was astonished to learn that my students at a teachers' college in South Africa believed firmly in the reality of the spirit world, the presence of the ancestral spirits, and the validity of dreams. Even with education and church membership, the desire to gain "life force and power" was the major concern, not forgiveness for sin, victory over sin, or even knowing God personally. As South African G. C. Oosthuizen expressed, "The Spirit's activity is not [considered to be] related to moral guidance but rather to vital force."[4]

At the time I served in South Africa, there were some 1500 African-initiated church movements in the country; there are now reputed to be more than 6,000. Virtually all of these independent churches give great emphasis to the Spirit, believing that the Spirit does not manifest himself freely in the mission churches because the missions that originated in the Western world are considered to suppress activity of the Spirit.[5] There are indeed sharp differences concerning the working of the Spirit that divide mission-initiated churches and African-initiated churches. The differences often concern the place of scripture as the norm of Christian experience, the reliability of religious experience stimulated by emotion, and the distinction or lack of it, between the Holy Spirit and the ancestral spirits.

In the absence of scripture as norm, the practice of the Spirit's presence and power may become hopelessly entangled with ancestral reverence or worship. That confusion is also seen among Asian peoples where shamanistic practices have sometimes blended with Christian worship.[6] Teaching of the Word would seem to be the antidote to this silent syncretism. But knowledge of the Word without experience of the Spirit is unpalatable to the African or Asian traditional religionist, so that knowledge may be isolated in a seldom-used "spare room" of life. Quite independently of that knowledge, the spirits' guidance is sought in matters of daily belief and living.

Those who become leaders (in African traditionally-oriented cultures) play a special role in access to the Spirit. Because they are higher in the hierarchy (ladder) of power, and thus closer to the Supreme Spirit, they become the interpreters of the divine and mediators for the people. The ability to see hidden sin and prophesy about the future lies with these leaders, as well as the power to heal, give baptism to open the way for redemption, and determine what liturgy should be followed. They frequently become Messiah figures to their followers— Shembe, Leselinyane, Alice Lenshina, Simon Kimbangu, are some of the familiar names in Africa.

Spirit or spirits?

These religious experiences appear to be Spirit-centered, but do not always distinguish between the spirits.[7] The word of God is often not normative; it is replaced by experiencing spirit-power.

People go into trances, fall on the ground, laugh and cry uncontrollably, speak with strange sounds, and foretell future events. The spirits through possessed individuals can bring disaster to individuals and villages as well as demonstrate protection from dangers with a frequency that is beyond mere chance.[8]

Is God's only answer, "I can do everything you can do, but do it better"? Is the Holy Spirit primarily the emotional side of believing? Is the Holy Spirit only at work when there is evidence of unnatural or supernatural power? So it is correct to ask, What will happen when someone is controlled by the Spirit?

On or In?

The Old Testament speaks of the Spirit acting *upon* people, from the outside... like a storm wind blowing on people. The effect is real and powerful, but not essentially internal. The Spirit "fell upon" as with Ezekiel or Gideon (Ezek 11:5 and Judg 6:34). The Spirit came upon Saul (1 Sam 10:10; 11:6).

In the New Testament the emphasis is on the Holy Spirit *in* us, as in Rom 5:5, "the love of God has been poured out *in* our hearts through the Holy Spirit who was given to us." Romans 8:1-11 emphasizes the Holy Spirit dwelling within. Hebrews 10:16 quotes Jer 31:33 with reference to the New Covenant to show that God makes it internal: "I will put my laws on their hearts, and I will inscribe them on their minds…" The Lord promised that the Spirit would be *in* the believer: "The Spirit of Truth… dwells with you, and shall be in you" (John 14:17), and would flow forth *from* the believer to refresh: "let the one who believes in me drink. Just as the scripture says, 'From within him will flow rivers of living water.' (Now he said this about the Spirit, whom those who believed in him were going to receive.)" (John 7:38-39).

Without biblical teaching and examples to stand on, "we would easily slide into the notion that the Spirit of God is just about feelings, ideas, atmospheres of thought, in which nothing necessarily gets *done*. This is far from the truth."[8] The Holy Spirit is not synonymous with emotion, though his presence and working evokes powerful emotions. The emotions come from ourselves, a proper and blessed response to him, to his working within us. Suppressing emotional responses does not necessarily limit the Spirit's working, but it does rob us of the richness of Christian experience. Many Africans, Asians, and South Americans are unwilling to lose that richness. Discouraged by a dominantly rationalist approach to the gospel, they may wander into areas controlled by unholy spirits.

If emotion is not the primary work of the Spirit, what does he do? He works within, transforming and uniting to Christ. The Holy Spirit is not simply like the attractive clothes a man wears, but like the inner dynamic of the man himself. His work is not primarily to give us emotion in our worship, but to work inwardly—transforming our total lives as we are filled by the Spirit.

The Issue Is Control

The key issue is control. Satan, the deceiving enemy, seeks to control this world and everyone in it. To do that, he must hide the cross, mythologize the resurrection, and limit man's mind to only what can be learned empirically. By so limiting man's rationality, man can be controlled. As C. S. Lewis expressed in *Screwtape Letters*, the enemy's great achievement would be stimulating man to be a "magical materialist."

"Losing control" is literally a fate worse than death for many. A study of assisted-suicide deaths, after the state of Oregon twice approved legislation permitting doctor-assisted suicide, established that uncontrolled physical suffering was reported in only 20% of suicides. Others "appear to be motivated largely by the threat of losing control of their own lives."[9]

Knowledge of the future is coveted—so we can control that future to favor ourselves. As a riddle puts it, "What is worth a million dollars today, but only 25 cents tomorrow?" It is tomorrow's newspaper, worth a million dollars if it could tell us *in advance* what tomorrow would bring so that we could control those events for our benefit.

Attempts to use the spirits for increased control are seen in such non-significant issues as who wins a soccer game, and also at critical points such as protecting soldiers from bullets in battle. Charms "empowered" by a sorcerer—a witchdoctor—are buried in the center of the field before games, and others are carried by players during the game. Sorcerers give magical drinks, skin lotions, or a magical phrase to chant during battle.

The desire to control is an integral part of man. The manner of control is the difference. A culture may attempt to manipulate through emotion, or through spirits by use of spells and charms. Rationalism seeks no less to control, but uses the path of reason to know and control the destiny of self and others. But the Holy Spirit's control is indirect, exalting Christ as Lord, the One who is in control. In daily living, he guides and instructs so that Jesus Christ is in control.

The Holy Spirit is indeed manifest in great explosions of revival and power. But to seek those evidences as the primary work of the Holy Spirit is like seeking the explosion of fireworks on America's Fourth of July as the way to keep America independent. The fireworks are a celebration of what exists. They raise patriotic feelings in many who watch the display. But they have very little to do with the business of winning and maintaining liberty and independence. Freedom is the point, not the celebration.

Fireworks do not solve the issue of control, nor even convince those who would take away independence that they could not win. Victory is won through loyal soldiers controlled by capable generals. Startling manifestations of the Spirit show his power, attracting attention but also sometimes eliciting a desire to manipulate those manifestations, as Simon demonstrated in Acts 8. They may be like fireworks—dramatic and awesome. But essential loyalty has not been changed—it is still self in control.

The truly remarkable work of the Spirit is done in changing individual hearts from self-loyalty to God-loyalty. It is the work of the Holy Spirit to exalt Jesus, to establish his Lordship over the whole earth and everyone on it. For individuals to give glory to Jesus requires a radical transformation in the very core of a woman or man. That is the work of the Spirit which we welcome, and of which we are not afraid.

But in missions we too often look for visible changes, equating them with belief and new life in Christ. This visible part of a culture is behavior, the hundred thousand things that we do, say, and use virtually every day of our lives. It is by no means the whole of culture, though when among people of a different culture we are preoccupied with these differences of mannerisms, speech, foods, clothing—nearly endless differences occupy our attention.

Change at this level is often rapid, a matter of novelty, seeking advantage or enjoyment, or adjusting to new social situations. There is usually little resistance because there is little threat to an individual's sense of self and significance. Even though superficial, changes in behavior may be mistaken for deeper change of the heart—the core commitments on which lives are built.

That innermost or core is called the heart in scripture. The core is made up of "the verities" on which life is built. It determines how we respond to all that surrounds us and places demands on us, from simple survival to satisfying personal relationships. It may be called the "kidney" in some cultures, the "stomach" in others, or even the "liver." Whatever it is labeled, there is an invisible core in an individual and in a specific culture. This deep and closely-guarded core is the determiner of everything else in a person or society. There, and there alone, are resolved the "issues of life." "But the things that come out of the mouth come from the heart, and these things defile a person. For out of the heart come evil ideas, murder, adultery, sexual immorality, theft, false testimony, slander" (Matt 15:18-19). The core, the heart, must be changed.

But How is Change Possible?

We are faced with a deep dilemma. This core is essentially unchangeable after it is established in the first years of life. Not only is the core unchangeable, but it is essentially unchallengeable. There is such deep commitment to the components of the core that a challenge is considered first laughable, then ridiculous. A continued challenge arouses animosity, then rejection. Finally, challenge leads to anger and possibly violence. The challenge must be silenced because it is wrong! If the challenge is seen to be valid, then the innermost being of a person or culture is threatened and may begin crumbling. Self-identity is lost, self-respect is destroyed, and the person/culture is left adrift in a confusing and frightening world.

But entry of the Holy Spirit changes that core, bringing hope and new life. It begins with a new birth. "Jesus replied, 'I tell you the solemn truth, unless a person is born from above, he cannot see the kingdom of God.' ...What is born of the flesh is flesh, and what is born of the Spirit is spirit" (John 3:3, 6). There is no *natural* way by which the heart/core can change or be changed without shattering the individual. Only by the Holy Spirit can make the new birth occur that begins the new life in Christ. And thus is God's promise fulfilled, "I will give you a *new heart*, and I will put a new spirit within you; I will remove the heart of stone from your body and give you a heart of flesh. I will put my spirit within you, and I will make you walk in my statutes and keep my ordinances, and you will do them" (Ezek 36:26-27).

Through personal experience, a thirst and hunger for God may develop. With that deep desire, a choice may be made to seek God's renewal. Then he fulfills his promise and through the new birth he begins the work of growing a member of the family of God. *It is in this miracle of growing transformation that the greatest work of the Holy Spirit among people is seen.* He works in the heart first. "To get at that requires a degree of power greater than anything which... probes the interior of the atom or the depths of space. It would be inconceivable ... that such power could be at work without results that would show up in all directions."[10] Behavioral change certainly results, but is not the cause of transformation.

Even as the basic core of every man is created from birth through approximately the seventh year, so is the new life in Christ created, beginning with the new birth. And with that beginning, the Holy Spirit lives and works within and we are being transformed. Paul sums up the power of his work in us "For now we see in a mirror indirectly, but then we will see face to face" (1 Cor 13:12a). And be like him! It is as we are filled by the Spirit that his work proceeds.

But what does it mean to be filled with the Spirit? "It means to be controlled by the Spirit," responded an African church leader. "If I am controlled by the Spirit, I can be expected to act in ways that are consistent with the very character of God."

The Greatest Work of the Spirit

This is the great work of the Holy Spirit, to give new life and control that transforms the very core of an individual and group. The Spirit exalts Jesus so that he is known and worshiped as Lord of all. Even the sensational acts of the Holy Spirit have only that as their purpose. Concentrating on the actions rather than control is to misunderstand and misuse demonstrations of the Spirit's powerful role. His work is intended to deliver us from both the fear of spirits and the blindness of unrelieved rationalism.

We know the Holy Spirit is the one who reveals and teaches, enabling sinful man to perceive holy Truth. Without his work, mission anywhere is an utter impossibility. Without his work, there would be no deep consciousness of sin, but only a sense of failure. Without his work, there would not be a deep thirsting for God, or for righteousness and salvation. Without the Spirit's work, we would not personally or collectively experience the power of God in transforming us into the likeness of Christ.

The only thing we have to fear in the work of the Holy Spirit is being thrust out of our rationalism and self-control. But as we exchange self-control for

Spirit-control, he will exalt Christ who "will draw all people to myself" (John 12:32). This is the miracle of missions.

The Father, the Son, and the Holy Scriptures?

M. James Sawyer

While the Evangelical tradition has its roots in the Reformation, the tradition associated with mainstream American evangelicalism has been heavily influenced by the Enlightenment through its employment of Common Sense Epistemology. It has often become so thoroughly rationalistic that the existential presence of the Holy Spirit has been all but denied. This essay traces the history of this rationalism within evangelicalism, and contemporary challenges by major evangelical thinkers as to the inadequacy of this rationalism and the need to return to a recognition of the full-orbed existential ministry of the Spirit in the life of the believer.

While the title for this chapter is a bit tongue-in-cheek, it highlights a continuing problem in the mainstream evangelical academic/theological community: an ongoing rationalism that seeks ultimate certainty and assurance of its knowledge in the objective "facts" of the scripture rather than formally recognizing the existential dynamic of the Holy Spirit in the life the believer. While in our piety we stress the necessity of personal conversion and a "personal relationship" with Christ, this stress on objectivity has effectively locked God into the pages of scripture, often reducing knowledge of divine truth to bare *assensus*, effectively cutting off (and at points even denying) the believer the *personal* relationship with God and the witness of the Spirit even in the realm of salvation. The reasons for this propensity are several: a visceral reaction to Pentecostal excesses, a fear factor to the lack of control mechanisms that is associated with the ministry of the Spirit, and the historic epistemological reliance of American Evangelicalism on Scottish Common Sense to frame our outlook on reality.

This study surveys briefly the first two reasons and then 1) focuses on our conservative tendency toward rationalism using both historic and contemporary examples; 2) surveys the underlying reasons that contribute to this rationalism; and 3) concludes with some personal observations. My purpose is to raise for further discussion the question as to whether we need to reconceptualize the way we theologize about the work of the Spirit so that our evangelical academic theologizing reflects more accurately (but not uncritically) the dynamic way the Spirit has been experienced throughout the centuries by the people of God. Or to put it another way, we are seeking an approach from a theological perspective to incorporate the "mysticism of the Spirit" into both the evangelical psyche and its theological matrix in a meaningful way.

The Practical Eschewing of the Spirit by Evangelicalism

The Rise of Pentecostalism

The Azusa Street Revival of 1906 unleashed a new movement in Protestantism, Pentecostalism, which has spread around the globe in the past century and become the dominant form of Protestantism in much of the third world. This dynamic is seen vividly in Latin America. Philip Yancey has quipped that in "Latin America, while the Catholics preached God's 'preferential option for the poor,' the poor embraced Pentecostalism."[1] The Fundamentalist, and later Evangelical, reaction to Pentecostalism was swift and decisive. Pentecostalism insisted on the continuing validity of the "gifts of the Spirit," specifically, tongues, miracles, and prophecy. Many insisted that if one had not received the gift of tongues one was not in fact born again. Pentecostal services stressed the sensational, many of their healings were suspect. Often their "revelations" were so generic as to be meaningless while others contradicted explicit teaching of scripture. Moreover, their prophecies frequently, if not usually, did not come true. Nevertheless old line Pentecostalism found fertile soil and flourished, fostering new denominations like the Assemblies of God, UPC, The Church of God, Cleveland and the like, whose constituency tended to be poor and uneducated.

In 1960 the Charismatic movement was born in Van Nuys California at St. Mark's Episcopal Church through the ministry of Dennis Bennett. This event has been called a "shot heard round the world"[2] ultimately bringing the "gifts of the Spirit" to mainstream denominations and even into Roman Catholicism. In the 1980's the Vineyard Movement or the Third Wave of the Spirit crossed even more traditional boundaries gaining adherents among highly visible mainstream evangelicals.

In 1918 B. B. Warfield attacked the Pentecostal movement in his *Counterfeit Miracles* arguing that the sign gifts had passed out of existence at the end of the apostolic age. Evangelicals have relied on Warfield's work for generations as the foundation for their continuing opposition to the Pentecostal insistence on the continuing validity of the charismata. Over the decades a closely reasoned "cessationist" theology was constructed. That articulation was so associated with Dallas Seminary that many identified opposition to the charismata with dispensationalism.

The characterization of the charismatics and the charismata ranged from skepticism, *ad hoc* exegetical arguments demonstrating the supposed teaching of the text of scripture that the sign gifts had ceased, historical surveys following Warfield that associated periodic historical outbreaks of charismatic type gifts with heterodoxy, to the identification of tongues with demonic inspiration. The reaction among mainstream evangelicals was to focus on the objective authority of the word and to deny the validity of the subjective and unverifiable "gifts" of the Spirit.

Fear and the Dynamic Freedom of the Spirit

In opposition to the anthropotheism of the 19th century, Karl Barth thundered "Let God be God!" He insisted upon the freedom of God. While evangelicals have not (unlike the nineteenth century liberals) sought to find God in cultural progress or philosophical speculation, in our tradition we have often effectively locked God into the pages of the text of scripture. He was free to speak there and then, but not free to speak now. For him to say anything beyond scripture has been understood as a denial of the finality of its message.

There are today some within the evangelical tradition who have recognized this reductionistic rationalism of mainstream evangelicalism and are trying to counteract it without embracing the excesses seen in the Pentecostal/charismatic tradition. For example one evangelical pastor recently acknowledged to his congregation that while the Spirit is sovereign and free, that fact causes many of us, including him, not just anxiety but outright fear—fear of loss of control.

> Our neo-Pentecostal brethren do have a great phrase we must hold on to: "you must be open to the Spirit"... And that is true. We are too much like good Presbyterians, well-educated people who wear our hair nicely and dress very nicely and are called the frozen chosen... We need to have things properly done. It needs to fit our mold or we have issues. I'm like that. But I need to learn that great phrase "To be open to the Spirit." Why is that so hard for me? You know why? I have a fear of freedom.[3]

I am convinced that if we peel away the veneer and rhetoric a major problem that we in ministry have is fear, the fear of the loss of control. Jacques Ellul in *The Subversion of Christianity* asserted that in every generation the Church exchanges the gospel of grace and the freedom of the Spirit for that which is its polar opposite.[4] The outward form of that opposite may be legalism, moralism, or the like. But when one looks beneath the surface the issue is control. The gospel of grace and the ministry of the Spirit produce freedom. The gospel of grace is meant to produce freedom, freedom from the letter that produces death. But we who are in ministry all too often fear freedom. Even the apostle Paul recognized the scandal of grace. In Romans, his objector cries out, "What shall we say then? Are we to remain in sin so that grace may increase?" As Philip Yancey observes, there is a "scent of scandal" surrounding grace.[5] Grace and the freedom of the Spirit go hand in hand.

The Fact of Evangelical Rationalism

"...[O]ne of the banes of modern evangelicalism is rationalism."[6] So says evangelical elder statesman Donald Bloesch. Ultimately the evangelical tradition has its roots in the Reformation, and it continues to preserve that tradition as opposed to the liberalism that grew out of the rationalistic anti-supernaturalism of the Enlightenment. Yet the picture is in fact more complicated than is usually perceived. What is usually not realized is that while liberalism "capitulated to the Enlightenment and lost its message,"[7] conservative evangelicalism was not unaffected by the Enlightenment. We normally trace the development of Enlightenment rationalism as a direct line from Descartes to Locke and Hume who were followed by Immanuel Kant. Kant is recognized as the father of modern thought epistemologically, achieving in the areas of philosophy and epistemology a revolution as profound as the one Copernicus achieved in astronomy. While Copernicus changed the way western civilization thought of the heavens and astronomy, Kant changed the way men thought—period. He introduced phenomenalism as an epistemology. The implications of phenomenalism had tremendous implications for the development of the modern mind.[8] In fact, the origin of the modern mind is often traced to Kant.

The Problem of History: How History and Truth Relate

A key element of the Enlightenment heritage was an identification of *truth* with that which was absolute and non-contingent. In other words, for something to be considered *truth* it had to be true at all times for all people in all places. The Enlightenment project involved, as it were, distilling off all contingencies of any so-called truth until only that which was universal and absolute was left. Such a method in practice deified reason and rational processes and relegated history to the level of a problem, rather than being a source of truth. Gotthold Lessing encapsulated the Enlightenment understanding in his maxim, "The accidental truths of history can never become the proof of the necessary truths of reason."[9]

Like Decartes, Lessing was a mathematician who sought for absolute certainty in the mathematical sense. Since history could not provide first order certainty it could not provide the basis of any systematic thought. Lessing contended that between the certainty of mathematical formulation and the certainty of historical formulations there was an "ugly, broad ditch" across which he (and presumably others) could not jump.[10] The implication for traditional Christianity, based upon the person and work of Jesus Christ in history, was devastating. Enlightenment thinkers understood the truth of religion (Christianity in particular) to be found in its *moral teaching*—adjudged by reason to be true and able to be immediately experienced—rather than in history from which it arose.

In recent years the whole Enlightenment approach has been challenged particularly with reference to the nature of historical knowledge as opposed to the "necessary truths of reason." Key in this challenge is the emergence of the discipline of the Sociology of Knowledge. This "is the study of the way in which the production of knowledge is shaped by the social context of thinkers."[11] While not spoken in precisely these terms, there has long been an implicit recognition of the legitimacy of this concept in the historical disciplines. The question "Do the times make the man or does the man make the times?" reflects at least an awareness of the issue of the larger social context out of which great individuals arise. The theological disciplines have been far slower in recognizing the validity of these insights, but as the observations of Stanley Gundry and J. J. Davis[12] demonstrate, even among evangelicals this is a growing awareness. Likewise, Alister McGrath has observed:

> The exegete brings to the text questions which he or she has been conditioned to ask through his or her experience, social position, political conviction, gender and so forth. The recognition that human thought—whether sociology, theology, ethics, or metaphysics—arises in a specific social context is of fundamental importance to the sociology of knowledge. All social movements, whether religious or secular, including the literature which they produce, involve implicit or explicit ideological perspectives and strategies by which personal experience and social reality may be interpreted and collective needs and interests may be defined and legitimated.[13]

Common Sense: Evangelicalism's Enlightenment Legacy

Nancey Murphy has observed that from an epistemological perspective conservative as well as liberal theology fell under the influence of Enlightenment ways of thinking, although for the conservatives the route was not via Kant but via Scottish Common Sense.[14] What makes this stream more difficult to recognize as Enlightenment thought is that the theology associated with Common Sense Realism is conservative historic orthodox Christianity, and the worldview is decidedly non-philosophical and non-speculative. Common Sense or Scottish Common Sense is given little attention in the surveys of philosophy, despite the fact that it was the dominant philosophy that held together the very fabric of American society for nearly a century.

Scottish Common Sense Realism was popularized in America by John Witherspoon, the sixth President of Princeton University, where he used it as a weapon to vanquish the continuing influence of the idealism of Jonathan Edwards.[15] From Princeton University, the philosophy spread swiftly throughout the land through the higher educational system. The swiftness of its acceptance was due to the fact that Scottish Realism "…contained an immediate conviction of right and wrong, of the reality of the external world, freedom… about which there was no need or warrant for debate or doubt, while its discussion of association, will, and feeling, was lucidity itself, and fitted for our practical country."[16]

There were several key assumptions involved in Common Sense Realism. Among these was the objective tangibility of the world as understood by Newtonian physics. Thomas Reid himself had contended that without this key assumption man was cut off from certain knowledge that could be gained by the inductive method.[17] The ultimate result of this severance would be hopeless skepticism. Secondly, Common Sense posited the reliability of the senses in perceiving reality.[18] By means of one's senses the individual was able to know "the thing in itself." Thirdly, there was a strict subject-object dichotomy. From this distinction flowed the characteristic methodology of Common Sense: empiricism. Truth was to be discovered strictly through the inductive method. The empiricism of the method did not, however, belie a materialism. Common Sense saw the universe ruled by natural law, a law that included moral precepts.[19]

The method assumed that there was objective truth available to man and that such truth was unchanging.[20]

Common Sense Realism was self-consciously employed by the Princeton theologians as they contributed what has come to be recognized as a uniquely American expression of classic Reformed theology. This bent can be seen particularly in the rationalistic apologetics of B. B. Warfield who saw the task of apologetics not as the culmination of the theological disciplines defending conclusions, but as functioning as the *establishing* of truth.[21]

The strict subject-object dichotomy of Common Sense also gave rise to an anti-mystical approach to theology and life, which viewed with suspicion all claims to certainty in matters of faith not grounded in rational processes.

While many examples of Common Sense rationalism could be adduced, four specific examples illustrate the phenomenon.

Common Sense Rationalism & the American Evangelical Community

John Nevin, Philip Schaff, and the Nature of the Eucharist

One historic example of the rationalism within our tradition can be seen in the debate about the nature of the Eucharist during the 1840's. Philip Schaff, a recent emigrant from his native Switzerland to the United States together with American John Nevin became proponents of what became known as "Mercersburg Theology," an articulation of Reformed thought that was then current on the continent.[22] A part of Nevin's and Schaff's theological articulation included an understanding of the Eucharist that followed Calvin, insisting that there was a dynamic personal presence of the Spirit present at the Lord's Supper. Astonishingly this doctrine drew fire from all corners of American Protestantism, including Lutherans! At this point in the nation's history, American Protestants of all stripes operating under the assumptions of a worldview informed by Scottish Common Sense were universally committed to a Zwinglian understanding of the Eucharist as strictly a memorial. Charles Hodge went so far at to associate the Mercersburg doctrine with Roman Catholicism.[23]

The Lordship Salvation Debate

A contemporary issue that demonstrates the underlying rationalism of Evangelicalism is the so-called "Lordship Salvation Debate." This controversy has raged over the past two decades and even spawned a theological society and a journal dedicated to the concept of "free grace," as opposed to Lordship Salvation.

The chief architect of the "free grace" position is Zane Hodges who has articulated his position in two works, *The Hungry Inherit* and *The Gospel Under Siege*. In Hodges and in those who follow him there is an explicit disavowal of the concept of the witness of the Spirit in the life of the believer.[24] As with the Princetonians one finds a decidedly "anti-mystical" tendency that, in effect, strips the Christian life of its relational qualities in order to raise the authority of the scripture as that to which the individual can cling for assurance. In so doing faith is reduced to something close to bare mental assent. The late S. Lewis Johnson, Jr. noted that Hodges "never carefully defines faith."[25] However, in his discussions of faith, his working definition seems often to have reference to *notitia*, and possibly *assensus* but without *fiducia*[26] an assent to facts rather than trust in a person.[27] As his position is worked out he insists that faith can exist without commitment.[28] If pressed, there is a danger of reducing salvation to a kind of magical incantation, or an *ex opere operato*, whereby, for example, the individual repeats the prayer at the end of the Four Laws, with the barest assent to the gospel, and then is considered to be eternally saved, assured by the promises in the scripture.

Canon Rationale For Evangelicals

In about 1988 I had just completed my first article for publication, an examination of the evangelical rationale for the canon of the New Testament.[29] During my research I had discovered, much to my amazement, that the virtually unanimous position of American evangelical theologians and exegetes was that our assurance for the shape of the canon of the New Testament rested ultimately either on the authority of the Church or on the "assured results of higher criticism." This stands in sharp contrast to the heritage flowing from the Reformation that asserts the "witness of the Spirit" as the basis for the final assurance of the canon. I gave a copy of the article to a friend who was then completing his doctoral study. His reaction to my insistence that we return to the Reformer's canon apologetic was, "How is this any different from the Mormon's burning in the bosom?"

The apologetic for the shape of the canon, especially the canon of the New Testament, has been often explored. In the mid-1980's *Christianity Today* devoted a featured series of articles on the subject. That series of articles adopted the classical defense of canon articulated by the Princetonians over a century ago.

The Princetonian explanation of the canon-determination process was made in the context of the Roman Catholic claim that the Church had determined the canon. In this they mirrored the concerns of the Reformers. In contrast to Rome, Charles Hodge contended that the principle for canon-determination in the Old Testament was that those books, and only those, which Christ and his apostles recognized as the written word of God, were entitled to be regarded as canonical.[30] When it came to the canonicity of the New Testament books, the scriptures offer no such christological endorsement. Here echoing the sentiment of the early church, the issue became the primacy of *apostolicity* in canon-determination.[31] Warfield argued that *apostolicity* was a somewhat wider concept than strictly apostolic authorship, although in the early church these two issues were often confounded.[32] "The principle of canonicity was not apostolic authorship," contended Warfield, "but *imposition by the apostles as law*."[33] The practical effect of this subtle distinction is to allow for the inclusion of books such as Mark, Luke, James, Jude, and Hebrews which were not actually penned by the apostles, but were, according to tradition, written under apostolic sanction. Warfield asserted that the canon of scripture was complete when the last book of the New Testament was penned by the apostle John c. A.D. 95. From the divine standpoint the canon of scripture was complete. However, human acceptance of an individual book of that canon hinged upon *"authenticating proof* of its apostolicity."[34]

Elsewhere he concluded:

> We rest our acceptance of the New Testament Scriptures as authoritative thus, not on the fact that they are the product of the revelation-age of the church, for so are many other books which we do

not thus accept; but on the fact *that God's authoritative agents* in founding the church gave them as *authoritative to the church which they founded....* It is clear that prophetic and apostolic origin is the very essence of the authority of the Scriptures.[35]

In yet another place, Warfield explicitly denied that the witness of the Spirit was in any sense direct and supra-rational, insisting that the Spirit works in giving assurance only through rational evidence. Any concept of direct supra-rational assurance was dismissed as "mystic." In so doing he reduced the concept of the witness of the Spirit to a sanctified rationalism.[36]

To demonstrate the logic of canonicity, Warfield took as a test-case the epistle of Second Peter, a book whose canonicity had been repeatedly doubted over the centuries, and proceeded to investigate the provenance of the epistle to prove its canonicity.

Warfield's argument is closely reasoned and rationally convincing. He incisively demolished the arguments of his opponents showing their inadequate basis and contradictory presuppositions. However, even his colleague and friend at Princeton, Francis Landy Patton, in eulogizing Warfield, noted that the rationalism of Warfield's system of logic was built upon probability which precluded the absolute certainty of his conclusions.[37]

In contrast to the Princetonians, Charles Briggs made the classic Reformed doctrine of the Witness of the Spirit the centerpiece of his apologetic for canon.[38] The Princetonians, however, remained unimpressed by Briggs' arguments. C. W. Hodge's reaction to Briggs' position is illustrative of the Princetonian perspective on the necessity of rational certainty in the establishment of the authority of the Bible as divine authority: "...that the canon is determined subjectively by the Christian feeling of the Church, & and not by history, & that it is illogical to prove first Canonicity, & then Inspiration, ...then you have given away the whole historical side of the argument of the Apostolic origin of the Books & of Christianity itself."[39] Certainty of validity of the canon as the word of God, for the Princeton theologians, was established by rational and historical proofs without recourse to the doctrine of the witness of the Spirit in any vital way.[40]

Decision Making and the Will of God

From the perspective of the ordinary individual believer, the question of discovering the will of God for one's life has been viewed mystically and even superstitiously. Interpretation of events for divine messages, asking for signs, setting out fleeces and the like have all been a part of the popular evangelical piety. Over twenty years ago Garry Friesen published his *Decision Making and the Will of God* based upon his Th.D. dissertation research. In this work he boldly challenged the popular piety with sound exegesis and logic and placed explicit scriptural revelation over "impressions" and "leading" and circumstances. Friesen instead put forth a "wisdom" model for determining the will of God for the individual's life, whether the subject be career, school, or marriage. His work has served as a helpful corrective for much of the teaching that was predominantly mystical and confusing. While I believe Friesen has done us a great service and I regularly recommend his book to those struggling with questions regarding the will of God for their lives, I do detect an underlying rationalism communicated as much by what is not said as by what is said. Many have noted that they came away from his presentation with a great disquiet, a disquiet that arises from a tone that implicitly denies that existential dynamic of the Spirit in the life of the believer and substitutes instead a formula (albeit a thoroughly biblical formula) for determining legitimate options in any situation.

J. I. Packer has noted that more foundational to discerning the will of God for the individual is the renewing of the mind taught by Paul:

> But without this renewal, no matter how much thinking we do, and however correct our theological formulations, personal discernment of the will of God will not take place. For the will of God covers not only what we do outwardly as performers, but also how and why we do it from the standpoint of our motives and purposes, and if these inner aspects of action are not as they should be we fall short of the *perfect* (that is, in the Greek, the fully-fashioned and complete) *will of God*, as did the Pharisees in Jesus' day.[41]

While Friesen is clear that God is more interested in who we are than what we do, his lack of development of the foundational theme to which Packer points implicitly contributes to a rationalistic mindset.

The Quest for Certainty of Assurance

Within the evangelical community there remains to this day a quest for absolute *rational* certainty with reference to our beliefs. This reality is vividly illustrated by some of the assertions coming from the Grace Evangelical Society. In his preoccupation with the ability to demonstrate with *absolute certainty* that an individual possesses salvation, for example, society founder Bob Wilkin has tried to demonstrate that a believer can have "100% certainty" that he is saved, without any doubt.[42] This concern reflects a key assertion of Zane Hodges. In this concern one hears the echoes of Calvin who states that faith "requires full and fixed certainty, such as men are wont to have from things experienced and proved."[43] While Wilkin and Hodges reflect the Reformers' perspective that assurance of salvation is the birthright of believers, and is of the essence of faith, they fall far short of endorsing Calvin's insistence that such assurance comes from things "experienced and proved."

Seeing all certainty as of the same type, Wilkin indicates that the level of assurance which the believer may have is akin to the certainty he may have that 2+2=4, mathematical certainty, or the certainty that the sun is shining. That certainty is based on the objective testimony of the word of God.[44] Such a view is at best simplistic. Certainty falls into several categories. (1) Mathematical certainty: In the abstract theoretical and ideal world, we can know things with absolute certainty. There are no contingencies to qualify a reality, thus, there can be certain knowledge in the truest sense. (2) Empirical certainty: This is demonstrated by the scientific method in the real world, as opposed to the ideal world of mathematics. (3) Legal certainty: This involves proof by evidence, given by witnesses. It, however, admits the possibility of error depending upon the truthfulness and credibility of the witnesses. (4) Moral certainty: This is the realm of psychological certainty.[45] It is obvious that nearly all human knowledge outside the realm of mathematics fails the test of absolute certainty. Likewise, salvation is not something that can be analyzed in the test tube; thus it does not fall in the realm of scientific certainty. Salvation falls in the realm of contingent reality, the variety of which cannot be tested. Thus, it is impossible from a psychological perspective to achieve the mathematical level of certainty for which Wilkin seeks. Rightly, he posits the ground of certainty outside the individual, on the basis of the objective word of God. But he neglects the means of certainty, which must take into account the subjective psychological factors of human existence. He posits objectively certain assurance of salvation without recourse to psychological realities—ideal mathematical certainty for an internal psychological reality.

On the other side of the debate we find again a quest for certainty that one is saved. John MacArthur, reacting to the implicit antinomianism of the free grace position adopts a radically different means of assurance of salvation that is ironically as rationalistic as that adopted by the free grace position.

The dynamic of assurance espoused by MacArthur has its roots deep in the tradition of the Puritans and the Scottish Calvinists. The Scots referred to this process as the *Practical Syllogism*. The Puritans called it the *reflex action*.[46] By whatever name, the process is the same. The believer is denied direct access to the Savior for assurance. Instead he must look inside and complete the syllogism. "The Scripture tells me that he who believes shall be saved. If upon examining myself I find fruits of righteousness in my life, I may then complete the syllogism 'But I believe, therefore I shall be saved'."[47] However, such a doctrine lays the ground of assurance solely within ourselves as opposed to relying in any way on the dynamic of a vital relationship with the Holy Spirit "causing the believer to rely more on his own works for assurance, than on the work of Christ on our behalf."[48]

This rationalistic search for certainty is endemic to the evangelical mind and traceable to its Enlightenment roots. The discussions in the latter part of the 20th century have become more sophisticated, and there have been many in our community who have explicitly adopted a "hard foundationalism" as the basis of epistemological certainty.

While many in the mainstream of the evangelical tradition are loathe to acknowledge the crucial role of experience in our theological understanding and even its formulation, in the past two decades a number of evangelical theologians and exegetes in this tradition have broken with its rationalism and embraced the Vineyard movement. Among these are Wayne Grudem, Sam Storms, and Jack Deere. Deere has directly challenged conservative evangelicalism on the point of rationalism. In his *Surprised by the Power of the Spirit*[49] Deere surveys and critiques his own former understanding regarding the cessation of the charismata. He says:

There is one basic reason why Bible-believing Christians do not believe in the miraculous gifts of the Spirit today. It is simply this: *they have not seen them.* Their tradition, of course, supports their lack of belief, but their tradition would have no chance of success if it were not coupled with their lack of *experience* of the miraculous. Let me repeat: Christians do not disbelieve in the miraculous gifts of the Spirit because the Scriptures teach these gifts have passed away. Rather they disbelieve in the miraculous gifts of the Spirit because they have not experienced them.

No Cessationist writer that I am aware of tries to make his case on Scripture alone. All of these writers appeal both to Scripture and to either present or past history to support their case. It often goes unnoticed that this appeal to history either past or present is actually an argument from experience, or better, an argument from the lack of experience.[50]

My point here is not to argue for the continuation of the charismata; rather, it is to look critically at our own apologetic for the cessationist rationale within the evangelical tradition.

Isaac Dorner, reflecting Calvin, argued that spiritual truth made a demand on the soul if certainty were to be attained. Thus, certainty and assurance of spiritual truth were qualitatively different in nature than certainty of all other knowledge. Faith became the *principium cognescendi.* This faith was a product of the personal experience of the presence of God and the medium of his presence. "…Faith has a knowledge of being known by God, and of its existence because of God, and in such a way that it knows God as the one self-verifying and self-subsisting fact…"[51] Thus faith offers a divinely assured certainty since it involves a genuine reciprocal divine communion attested in the human soul. This is not mysticism in the classic sense of the term since this experience of God retains the subject-object dichotomy. The individual does not lose personal identity in the experience of the divine. Rather God, as a person, reaches out to directly touch the soul of the individual and give certain knowledge of himself.

Likewise Dutch Calvinist Abraham Kuyper insisted that the "mysticism of the Spirit is necessary for the theologian."[52] He broadened the basis of the means by which the Holy Spirit might operate from the narrow conception that the scripture *alone* was the divine authority in the construction of theology, noting: "Coordinated under one head, one might say that the Holy Spirit guarantees this organic articulation through the agencies of the Holy Scripture, the Church, and the personal enlightenment of the theologian."[53]

Rationalism, Reality, Truth, and Certainty

Hand in hand with our heritage of rationalism the evangelical tradition has held firmly to the Protestant Scholastic idea that the truth of scripture is communicated in timeless propositions "During that time revelation came to be identified strictly as propositional in nature and timeless/universal in expression. Particularly the historical nature of divine revelation slipped into the background."[54] This period also saw also a "tendency to identify these 'revealed truths' (often rationally deduced via a scholastic theological method) with an expression of the divine mind. And the Spirit was merely an aid to the will in acknowledging that which can be shown as truth on the basis of historical probability."[55] Thomas Torrance observed that theologizing from this time forward succumbed to the "Latin Heresy," i.e., a one-to-one identification with the deposit of faith with a fixed formula handed down from one generation to the next consisting of "irreformable truths" whose verbal expression was seen as identical to the reality rather than pointers to a reality beyond themselves.[56]

Likewise, while they continued to affirm the Reformers' doctrine, the mindset shifted to an Enlightenment framework. God was no longer understood as "utterly different from us. God's omniscience, omnipotence and infinite goodness are the same sorts of qualities we have, differing only in degree."[57]

Key in inculcating this mindset among 20th century evangelical scholars was Gordon Clark. In an age when fundamentalists fled from scholarship, eschewed the laws of logic, and promoted a superpietistic irrationalism, Clark insisted that faith and reason are not antithetical and in so doing laid the foundation for contemporary evangelical scholarship.[58] In his articulation he defended the central role of special revelation in giving the Christian worldview its content.[59] Central in the assertion of special revelation was the *propositional nature not only of revelation but also ultimately of reality.* During his tenure at Wheaton College, Clark influenced a generation of scholars for intellectual engagement with contemporary assaults on Christianity. Among this group of future scholars were many of the future luminaries of Evangelicalism including Carl Henry, E. J. Carnell, Paul K. Jewett, Edmund Clowney and Billy Graham.

Carl Henry has endorsed with approval his mentor's position that propositional revelation is a fundamental category and that "the word *truth* can only be used metaphorically or incorrectly when applied to anything other than a proposition."[60] Ultimately for Clark only propositions are reality. As Hoover has observed:

> Knowledge is always knowledge of the truth and truth, in Clark's view, is a quality of only propositions—that is, only propositions are the sort of thing that can be true (or false). Hence only propositions can be known. But since the range of the real and the range of the knowable coincide— or, alternatively put, since the set of all real objects and the set of all knowables is the same set—then given the doctrine of immediate apprehension, the character of reality itself is propositional, Even God is a proposition because He is thoroughly known to Himself! Hence only propositions exist and Clark's Idealism is a thoroughgoing rationalistic Idealism. No mental entity can be accommodated that is not a proposition.
>
> And fourth, if all reality is propositional, we come to understand Clark's view of how one reality relates to another, Propositions, it would seem, relate only by logic. Propositions are not spatio-temporal objects. They are not facts or events. Unlike spatio-temporal objects, propositions do not occupy space or take up time. Unlike facts, they may be false. And unlike events, propositions do not occur and befall objects. Thus, propositions do not interact causally: they do not affect one another by gravity or electromagnetism, they cannot bump into one another, fall off shelves, or shatter. Clark's propositions, rather, relate by logical implication, and they form, presumably, the one coherent system of truth. As such, Clark's world of "men and things" is held together (sustained) by logic.[61]

This insistence on the propositional nature of all knowledge is seen in Clark's endorsement of an alternate translation of John 1:1: "In the beginning was the logic."[62] Henry posits that the logos of John 1:1 guarantees a universal rational epistemology.[63] The net effect is to reduce the second person of the Trinity to a philosophical principle the contemplation of which grants salvation.

I would insist that salvation comes not from a rational principle but by the historical person of Jesus Christ. While the neo-orthodox reduce revelation to only the personal, the evangelical tradition has adopted a reductionistic view of revelation as simply rational/propositional. Erickson has recognized this impasse concerning the nature of revelation as a false dichotomy and argues instead that revelation is *both* propositional and personal.[64]

This discussion raises the issue of the historical nature of divine revelation. The concept of revelation communicated by Clark and Henry seems to reflect an Enlightenment concept of truth as absolute and unconditioned with all contingencies distilled off. Yet that which sets Christianity apart from other religions and philosophy is a "rootedness" in historical events that are by definition contingent.

Challenges to the Status Quo

With the rise of postmodernism there has been an increasing and explicit tendency by many, particularly in ETS, to rely upon a hard epistemological foundationalism as the bedrock upon which we can build genuine knowledge.[65] Timothy Phillips in the *Journal of the American Scientific Affiliation* concluded that most advocates of inerrancy assume an "epistemological foundationalism," seeing "genuine knowledge" obtainable only from a "foundation of apodictic certitudes." This position is, says Phillips, indefensible—exegetically, theologically, and philosophically.[66] Developing Phillips' idea further Donald Dayton observes:

> ...clearly something like this is at work when the Evangelical Theological Society maintains discipline by requiring annual subscription to only one article of faith: "the Bible alone, and the Bible in its entirety, is the Word of God written, and is therefore inerrant in the autographs." The point is not so much the statement itself as the way it functions in a larger worldview—one that is being increasingly called into question.[67]

Donald Bloesch has undertaken a sustained critique of the idea that revelation is exclusively propositional.

> A proposition... is a truth that is expressed in declarative statements that clearly affirm or deny what is at issue. A narration is a truth that is expressed in the telling of a story and may take the form of poetry as well as prose. Its truth is gleaned through an existential participation in the drama being depicted, so it is more experiential than strictly logical. A propositional truth is immediately accessible to reason whereas a narrational truth can be grasped only by a heightened imagination.

Propositional revelation entails the communication of clear and distinct ideas (à la Decartes). Narrational revelation is the conveyance of insights that can be assimilated only through the obedience of faith. Propositional revelation carries the implication that revelation is exhaustively rational. Narrational revelation presupposes that revelation is polydimemsional—appealing to the will and the affections as well as to reason and logic. Propositional revelation imparts notional knowledge; narrational revelation imparts affectional knowledge.[68]

He is clear that he does not reject propositions.[69] Rather he insists that "Revelation can be expressed in semi-conceptional as well as mythopoetic or narrational language, but in both cases the language is incomplete and awaits further illumination by the Spirit."[70] Likewise in opposition to Clark, Henry, and their followers, he draws a crucial distinction between *truth of being* and *truth of statements*, insisting, "The truth of being takes precedence over the truth of statements, but the latter can transmit the former through the power of the Spirit."[71]

In opposition to the reductionistic tendency of rationalism Bloesch formally invokes the ministry of the Holy Spirit.

Propositions can be gleaned from revelation, but they always point beyond themselves to mysteries that can only be dimly grasped by the enlightened human mind. I affirm both the necessity and the inadequacy of propositions in communicating revelatory truth. Propositions can serve but not exhaust the truth. They can elucidate the truth of the gospel but not secure this truth. Faith terminates not in propositions but in the reality to which they point.[72]

To put it another way, certainty of knowledge cannot ultimately be built on propositional revelation. That certainty must come through the Spirit. Bloesch refers to his understanding as "biblical personalism" which faithfully reproduces the message that resounds in the salvific events and in the scriptural text. "This message, however, does not inhere in the words but must be always spoken anew by the Spirit of God as he reaches out to both struggling saints and lost sinners with the word of life."[73]

"The smell of a cup of coffee" and the Limits of Language

The nature of language to communicate accurately and adequately has in the past century been challenged on two fronts, one theological and the other philosophical. Neo-orthodoxy asserted the personal nature of truth as opposed to the abstract, the timeless and the propositional. On the philosophical front, Wittgenstein's musings about the inability of language to communicate the smell of a cup of coffee powerfully illustrate the fact that language is at best an imperfect vehicle for communication. Wittgenstein further advanced the understanding of the working of language in the communication process with his observations about "language games." While he had early in his career taught a "picture theory of meaning" contending that language always related to the world in the same way, later in his career he repudiated this understanding[74] and instead argued that the use of language is different in different contexts. The utterance "Murder the guy in blue," means something very different in a bank than it does at a baseball game.

This limitation of language has begun to be recognized among evangelicals. In his *Symphonic Theology* Vern Poythress lists "12 Maxims of Symphonic Theology." The first maxim on the list is "Language is not transparent to the world."[75] While we think of language as simply giving us an accurate and adequate means to communicate with others our experience of the world, the actual process is much more complex than we **normally realize.**

> Natural human languages are not simply perfect, invisible glass windows that have no influence on what we see in the world. Nor is there a perfect language available that would be such a perfect window. In particular, no language will enable us to state facts without making any assumptions or without the statements being related to who we are as persons. No special language can free us from having to make crucial judgments on the basis of partial analogies or similarities. No special language can immediately make visible to us the ultimate structure of categories of the universe.
>
> Positively, natural languages are adequate vehicles for human communication and for communication between God and human beings. Some of the features that might be supposed to be imperfections are in fact positive assets. In the Bible, God uses ordinary human language rather than a technically precise jargon. He does not include all the technical, pedantic details that would interest a scholar. By doing so, he speaks clearly to ordinary people, not merely to scholars with advanced technical knowledge.[76]

While there is absolute truth, human grasp of that truth is always partial and perspectivally bound. The discipline of sociology of knowledge has convincingly demonstrated that the human knower is limited in space and time and culture. We might liken TRUTH to a flawless diamond that refracts the light from each of its many facets. However, we can only view the light from a single facet, or a single facet at a time. We recognize truth as it is refracted through the facet at which we gaze, but we err if we globalize that refracted ray of light from one facet in such a way that we deny the validity of the refraction from other facets. Regarding this insight Poythress has stated:

> Among theists, at least, I suppose that no one would deny that human knowledge is relative in these respects… Nevertheless, I do not think that we have always appreciated the consequences of this relativity of our knowledge. We know that truth is absolute—in particular, the truths of the Bible. We allow ourselves, however, to slip over into excessive presumption with regard to our human knowledge. We do not reckon with the fact that our interpretation of the Bible is always fallible. Or if we know a piece of truth, we may erroneously suppose that we know it precisely and exhaustively. The Pharisees doubtless thought that they understood the Sabbath commandment exactly. Therefore they knew that Jesus was breaking the Sabbath. The Pharisees were drawing their boundaries very precisely. They knew, for example, exactly how far they could travel on a Sabbath day without "taking a journey" (i.e., working). But at this point the Pharisees were overconfident and presumptuous. They did not really understand the Old Testament. But let us apply this example to ourselves. We may erroneously suppose that we, in our knowledge, do not really need a background of other, related truths in order to make sense of a certain teaching. We make one truth the basis for a long chain of syllogisms, without considering its context.[77]

Personhood & Relationship

As I mentioned earlier there is a strange dynamic within the evangelical community. A key defining feature of evangelicalism is the insistence that Christianity involves a personal relationship with Jesus Christ. Another key defining element is the final authority of scripture. Within our tradition these are often (perhaps unwittingly) pitted against one another. We must personally trust Christ for salvation, but we learn of God only through scripture.

In asserting the unique authority of the scriptures evangelicals not infrequently stand in danger of denying the validity of experience altogether. Over a century ago Charles Hodge declared that belief of the facts of Christianity, not an experience, made one a Christian.[78] More recently Gordon

Clark explicitly disavowed the relational/experiential aspect of Christianity as contributing to the knowledge of God or things divine: "Here I wish particularly to oppose Dr. MacKay's statement, 'The Christian gospel itself invites the test of daily experience in essentially the same spirit of openness to evidence that animates the enquiring scientist.' This reduction of Christian doctrine to the level of allegedly uninterpreted observation is utterly anti-Christian. Christianity is not based on experience; it is based on a propositional divine revelation, the Holy Scriptures."[79] Likewise John Warwick Montgomery has labeled the hymnist's assertion "You ask me how I know he lives? He lives within my heart" as the evangelical heresy.

The temptation of the Church to gravitate toward propositions over relationship is not new. In Rev 2 the apostle John recounts the words of the glorified Christ, while commending the Ephesians' steadfast adherence to truth insists that this is not enough. Following commendation, he issues words of rebuke and warning: "But I have this against you: You have departed from your first love! Therefore, remember from what high state you have fallen and repent! Do the deeds you did at the first; if not, I will come to you and remove your lampstand from its place—that is, if you do not repent" (Rev 2:4–5).

According to 17th century Anglican divine Jeremy Taylor a purely rational theology understands "by reason," while a spiritual theology understands "by love." In the case of the spiritual theology the theologian "does not only understand the sermons of the spirit, and perceives their meaning; but he pierces deeper, and knows the meaning of the meaning; that is the secret of the Spirit, that which is spiritually discerned, that which gives life to the proposition, and activity to the soul."[80] Or to put it another way, "Our assurance of God's favor toward us lies in our being known by God (1 Cor. 8:3; Gal. 4:9) not in the certainty of human perception in logic."[81]

Concluding Thoughts

Ironically this essay decrying evangelical rationalism has developed in a thoroughly rationalistic manner. In looking at the context of the development of the evangelical mind we have, I believe, seen that in this essay's tongue-in-cheek title there is more truth than most of us would like to admit. American

Evangelicalism has for a variety of reasons been thoroughly rationalistic from the nineteenth century onward. This is all the more amazing when we look just a bit further back historically at our Puritan forefathers and at the dynamic working of the Spirit in the First Great Awakening. In his book *The Log College*,[82] Archibald Alexander, the first professor of Princeton Seminary recounts without even a hint of doubt about their veracity, numerous instances of what would be today considered revelation and miracles. Yet if we hear similar accounts today, many of us may nod condescendingly, sure that we in our theological wisdom know better, or try to persuade those who have seen such incidents that they are mistaken or naïve. Even I, who have wrestled with these issues for years, fall into this category.

A couple, friends from my home church (a non-charismatic Presbyterian Church), Zeus and Charlotte, recently shared such an experience with me. They had gone to Macedonia on a mission trip delivering relief supplies. They carried with them clothing, food, and Bibles. As they distributed supplies one elderly woman was particularly moved. Later as my friends spoke with her in her tent she related that the previous night she had received a revelation from God. She had been visited by an angel who told her that she would shortly be receiving her lifelong dream, a Bible in her language. *"Touched by an Angel"* notwithstanding, my cessationist mind viscerally rebels against such accounts. Yet over the years I have heard far too many such accounts by those whose integrity I trust implicitly. These have caused me to question the hard cessationism in which I was raised.

Certainly, God has told us that scripture gives us a finality of normative revelation. It is not to be added to or subtracted from. Yet may it not be legitimate to make a distinction between normative revelation and divine communication that is *ad hoc* for a specific immediate situation or intimate communion?

I believe that we in the cessationist tradition need to reconceptualize the work of the Spirit in far broader terms than we have in the past. I wonder if we have not become like the dwarfs in C.S. Lewis's *The Last Battle*, so blinded by their own presuppositions that they could not recognize Aslan and his gifts to his children, with the result that they treated them as dung.

I am not arguing here for what we would normally call a non-cessationist position on the charismata. The way this debate has been framed has, I believe, polarized the discussion and obscured critical issues. Among these are the implications of a personal relationship with God, indwelling by the Spirit, the promise of our Lord that he will never leave us or forsake us. Our hymns and devotional literature are filled with testimonies of and exhortations to the personal and the intimate. While admittedly poetic, one well-known hymn still sung by evangelicals proclaims, "He walks with me and He talks with me and He tells me I am his own."

As noted in endnote 78, the Princetonians drove a wedge between theology and piety while not dismissing either. But even in their own day those who read their theological works had a tendency to reduce the faith to the merely propositional. Years ago during my Ph.D. dissertation research I read the correspondence of many of the Northern Presbyterian pastors trained at Princeton. What I found generally was a faith that was reduced to a belief system. We would not call it "dead orthodoxy" for it was a belief system passionately held rather than one to which mere mental assent was given. But it was a form of conservative theology that was cold, hard, defensive, and condemning based upon propositional (theological) truth. It fell far short of the intimate personal relationship described by the authors of the New Testament.

The modern world saw truth only in terms of presuppositions and logic. The result has been a spiritual vacuum not only in the hearts of unbelievers but of many believers as well. The postmodern world has rejected the modern approach to reality and truth and has turned its attention to the "spiritual." Our rhetoric, as noted above has indeed recognized that God desires a personal relationship with us. But in fact that personal relationship has been reduced to a "love letter" from God to us. As important as a love letter may be to those who are separated, it cannot replace the personal give and take, and the intimate sharing of personal presence.

While my wife and I were engaged she spent two months in South America. This was before the days of the Internet and cheap international phone calls. We corresponded nearly every day. As wonderful as it was to get letters from her, that did not begin to compare to the joy it was to meet her at the airport, hold her in my arms and talk face to face with her, and to whisper words of love in her ear.

Barth thundered "Let God be God!" Might we not need to take to heart his rebuke and "Let the Holy Spirit be God!"—a God who is free to act in ways of his choosing as opposed to the boundaries we establish?

Response to
Who's Afraid of the Holy Spirit?

Wayne Grudem

Because the book is so diverse, it is difficult to write an adequate foreword without saying something brief about each of the various chapters, so that is what I have attempted to do in the following comments. It is hard to select a favorite among such excellent essays, but the two that affected my own thinking the most were Dan Wallace's essay, "The Witness of the Spirit in Romans 8:16" and Dick Averbeck's essay, "God, People, and the Bible: The Relationship Between Illumination and Biblical Scholarship." I have known both Dan Wallace and Dick Averbeck as personal friends for many years, and it is a joy to have one's mind persuaded by the writings of such friends.

I came away from Dan Wallace's chapter on Romans 8:16 convinced that "the Spirit himself bears witness with our spirit that we are children of God" (Rom. 8:16) means, and is best translated, "the Spirit himself bears witness *to* our spirit ...." I think I had always thought the verse meant that. I have never thought the verse meant that the Holy Spirit and our spirit *together* bear witness *to* God, for I use the verse as evidence to say "the Spirit works to give us assurance at the subjective level of spiritual and emotional perception" (*Systematic Theology*, p. 644). But I could never quite make sense of the "with" in "bears witness with our spirit," and I thought that "with" was justified by the *sum-* prefix (from *sun-*, "with") in *summartureo*. Wallace shows that this sense is not required and in fact is not correct. I agree with Wallace when he says that the Holy Spirit's "inner witness is both immediate and intuitive. It involves a non-discursive presence that is recognized in the soul" (p. 52).

Dick Averbeck's essay on the relationship between illumination and Biblical scholarship affected me in another way. He argues (rightly, I think) that we must always view the Bible as an act of *communication* between God and his people, and therefore we should always pay attention to the *response* God is seeking from this communication. Specifically, God is seeking people who *relate* better to God and to other people – that is, people who *love* God and others more. Even scholarly research and seminary teaching need to have this goal in mind: to change people's hearts so that they love God and others more. Averbeck goes so far as to say that "the most important exegetical and theological 'tool' that we have is our own 'heart' as it has been shaped by our life experiences and especially by personal encounter with God himself" (p. 159). I had not thought of it this way, but after twenty-eight years of college and seminary teaching, I am inclined to agree with him, and I have resolved to aim more consciously at changing students' hearts in my teaching from now on.

The other chapters were all challenging and stimulating in one way or another. Dan Wallace's first chapter, "The Uneasy Conscience of a Non-Charismatic Evangelical," proposed eleven theses with which I can heartily agree, and which set the tone of the rest of the book. Here he announces several themes that will return throughout the book, such as the fact that we need not just knowledge but relationship with God, that sometimes biblical scholarship can become "bibliolatry" that results in a depersonalization of God, that God is still a God of healing and miracles today, and that "the Spirit often guides me with inarticulate impulses" (p. 12).

I can only smile, however, when Wallace in the beginning of this chapter still uses the category "sign gifts," a category which I totally reject since I see no basis for it at all in Scripture: I think the category is simply a leftover product of earlier cessationist imagination. *All* the gifts of the Spirit are from God and nowhere (in my humble opinion) does the Bible refer to any of them as "sign gifts" that can be put in a special category from the others and then dismissed.

Dick Averbeck's chapter, "The Holy Spirit in the Hebrew Bible and Its Connections to the New Testament," reminded us that the Holy Spirit is like a wind that we cannot always predict or control. Gerald Bray's chapter, "The Spirit and Community: A Historical Perspective," developed a fascinating description of how the pre-Reformation Roman Catholic church assumed that the work of the Holy Spirit was mostly confined to official acts of the priesthood. He wondered if Protestant traditions could ever strike the right balance of seeing the Holy Spirit work both through preaching and governance and through anointed Christians who show holiness of life, because there is always the Puritan tendency to throw out weaker brethren who do not live up to community expectations. At this point I wanted to suggest distinguishing between leaders and all others, a common evangelical practice which allows churches to require higher doctrinal and behavioral standards for those in leadership positions but allows for "weaker" members to participate as some level and not be forced out.

M. James Sawyer's chapter, "The Witness of the Spirit in the Protestant Tradition," documented multiple advocates for the view that the witness of the Holy Spirit in giving assurance of salvation is "an immediate pre-reflective personal experience in the heart of the believer" (p. 73). Supporters for this view included Calvin, Wesley, Edwards, several Puritans, and Abraham Kuyper, all of whom did not limit the witness of the Holy Spirit to rational deduction from observing sanctification in one's own life and concluding that this must indicate that one is saved. I found it interesting that Sawyer categorized both the "free grace" camp (Zane Hodges) and the "Lordship salvation" camp (John MacArthur) as overly rationalistic regarding assurance of salvation. I remained doubtful about one section of Sawyer's chapter, however, in which he discussed differing views about the determination of the canon as held by C. A. Briggs (the Union Seminary professor who was suspended from the Presbyterian Church in 1893 for his attacks on "the dogma of verbal inspiration") and by Charles Hodge, A. A. Hodge, and B. B. Warfield. I find it hard to believe that the Hodges and Warfield disagreed with Chapter 1 of the Westminster Confession, which they were sworn to uphold, where it says that "our full persuasion and assurance of the infallible truth and divine authority thereof [that is, of Scripture], is from the inward work of the Holy Spirit bearing witness by and with the Word in our hearts." Perhaps I am misunderstanding something here. The section was not central to Sawyer's chapter in any case.

I was a bit surprised by the chapter by J. I. Packer, whose friendship, opinions, and doctrinal discernment I esteem so highly. His chapter, "The Ministry of the Holy Spirit in Discerning the Will of God," rightly guarded against some abuses seen in fundamentalism and evangelical pietism, such as cultivating mental passivity as a habit of mind (!) or thinking of God's will as a travel map in which, once one makes a wrong turn, the rest of life is sure to turn out with diminished blessing from God. But what I had hoped for, in addition to these valuable warnings, was a positive word about a moment-by-moment relationship with God the Holy Spirit that is pursued in subjection to the teachings of Scripture and constantly evaluated in light of Spirit-sanctified wisdom. Perhaps he judged that other sections of the book had addressed this topic adequately.

I did not find myself in as much agreement with Timothy Ralston's chapter, "The Spirit's Role in Corporate Worship." While Ralston rightly argued that the Holy Spirit's presence is necessary for genuine worship in both the Old Testament and the New Testament, I thought that his analysis of people's subjective responses in worship was unnecessarily negative, filled with the language of caricature (pp. 132-134). What I would see as people's genuine, heartfelt response to the Holy Spirit's presence in worship Ralston reduced to human, psychological categories that assumed there was no genuine response to the Holy Spirit's presence, and he labeled as sin ("emotional narcissism") something that seems to me to be pure and holy (rejoicing in the manifest presence of God). This chapter seemed to me to be out of character with the rest of the book, although he did hint at the end that perhaps we should "lower the barriers" to the Holy Spirit's functioning in worship "a little bit more" (p. 136).

Reg Grant's interesting chapter, "The Holy Spirit and the Arts," rightly argued that Christians should not fear to appeal to the Holy Spirit to guide in artistic work, but this must always be done in subjection to the objective reality of the Word of God. The implications for writing and leading music, and for producing drama, dance, and the visual arts, are significant.

Willie O. Peterson, "The Spirit in the Black Church," was fascinating and challenging at the same time. What a rich heritage of faith he records among his own parents and grandparents! Because of the harsh oppression of living under slavery and then segregation, black evangelicals for generations have lived in constant dependence on God, and as a result, belief that God would work miracles was a normal and necessary part of life. Peterson points out that non-charismatic black evangelicals still differ from their white counterparts in their suspicion of white cessationist exegesis, their high energy worship style, and their natural sense of fellowship with charismatic black and white churches.

David Eckman's essay, "The Holy Spirit and Our Emotions," rightly argued that the Holy Spirit's sanctifying work should produce in us an increasingly deep and rich emotional life, particularly but not exclusively manifested in love, joy, and peace. I differed with both his use of terms and his exegesis where he spoke of the Holy Spirit experiencing pain (p. 213), but I certainly agreed with his conclusion: "As evangelicals we cannot afford to downplay the importance of emotions. The work of the Spirit of God is deeply emotional" (p. 222).

I thought Jeff Louie's chapter, "The Holy Spirit and the Local Church," was excellent in several ways. He says, "Although the miraculous spectacular *gifts* may have ceased, this does not mean that *miracles* no longer occur" (p. 237), a statement that seems to be one of the major themes of this book. But then Louie goes on to report some examples of what I would describe as the gift of prophecy (p. 238; he, as a good cessationist, does not use this term). He also tells of examples of miraculous healing, dreams that changed the course of individuals' lives, and casting out of demons (p. 239). I began to wonder, how is such a church different from a mature, Bible-based "charismatic" or Vineyard or Assemblies of God church? The differences can be exaggerated if one focuses on stereotypes or caricatures built one-third on reports of abuses from the fringe, one-third on some strange services on TV, and one-third on imagination. But in actual fact, when one has opportunity to participate in and observe responsible, mature examples of evangelical churches where miraculous gifts function (as I have), I doubt that they differ much at all from the church Jeff Louie describes. (But I would hasten to add that, in my opinion, the churches that believe that miraculous gifts [like prophecy, healing, and miracles] continue today have the great advantage of calling these gifts by their biblical names, with the not insignificant benefit of having actual Bible verses that speak directly to what is happening when these gifts are manifested. Does it not seem reasonable that God would provide verses in his Word that speak to these ways the Holy Spirit works in every church?)

Another great strength of this chapter has to do with response to God during worship services. I think all churches of whatever kind could profit greatly from Louie's discussion of the need to allow for worshipers to have time actually to respond to God (in prayer) during the service. He writes, "I used to enjoy preaching the most. I still look forward to proclaiming the word of God, but now I deem it a greater honor to lead the people in prayer" (p. 231).

I agreed with Donald Smith's chapter, "The Holy Spirit in Missions," when he rejected the argument that the Holy Spirit's miraculous work is seen only in foreign mission fields in places previously unreached by the gospel. I also agreed with his warning that Western rationalism often hinders us from perceiving the work of the Holy Spirit (and I would add that it also hinders our faith, consequently diminishing the frequency of God's miraculous answers to prayer). Smith also rightly (in my view) argues that the Holy Spirit's work in people's lives will often be accompanied by strong emotional responses, and that we must remember that the greatest, most important work of the Holy Spirit is changing people's hearts.

The final essay, "The Father, Son, and the Holy Scriptures?" by M. James Sawyer, was exceptionally helpful in returning again to the theme of excessive Western rationalism. Sawyer traces the influence of Scottish Common Sense Realism in American evangelicalism and points out that it too often resulted in reducing the Christian life to belief in a set of *propositions* (in Scripture), and that this led to excluding or viewing with great suspicion any emphasis on personal *relationship* with Christ or personal faith in *Christ himself*. Sawyer, like several others in the book, clearly allows for "divine communication that is *ad hoc* for a specific immediate situation or intimate communication" (p. 278). Once again, I would call this the kind of revelation from the Holy Spirit (1 Cor. 14:30) that leads to prophecies today (1 Cor. 14:29; 1 Thess. 5:20), but whatever it is called, I am thankful when churches allow for and encourage it, because it seems to me to be such an important aspect of our ongoing, personal relationship with God.

What a remarkable book! I expect that its publication will mark a significant turning point in the ongoing debate over the work of the Holy Spirit and spiritual gifts in the church today. It gives articulate expression to a kind of "progressive cessationism" that rightly safeguards the primacy and sufficiency and unique authority of Scripture in guiding our lives today, but that also leaves the door open for Christians to welcome the Holy Spirit to work in ways that have not been seen frequently in cessationist churches. And I think that charismatics, Pentecostals, and other non-cessationists who read this book will be surprised at how much common ground they find with these authors, not least in their evident love for our Lord Jesus Christ.

Wayne Grudem
Research Professor of Bible and Theology
Phoenix Seminary, Phoenix, Arizona
October 2, 2005

Endnotes

The Uneasy Conscience of a Non-Charismatic Evangelical

1. This is what I would call concentric cessationism, as opposed to linear cessationism. That is, rather than taking a chronologically linear approach, this kind of cessationism affirms that as the gospel moves, like the rippling effect of a stone dropping into a pond, in a space-time expanding circle away from first century Jerusalem, the sign gifts will still exist on the cutting edge of that circle. Thus, for example, in third world countries at the time when the gospel is first proclaimed, the sign gifts would be present. This view, then, would allow for these gifts to exist on the frontiers of Christianity, but would be more skeptical of them in the 'worked over' areas.

2. There were twelve apostles at the Light House. We knew each one only by their first name because, as apostle Bob said, "the original apostles only had one name."

3. So much so that as a high school student, during late 60's, I visited the University of California at Irvine to evangelize in a public forum. The occasion was the capturing of UCI and "sit-in" by the SDS (a young socialist group). The school shut down while it was under siege. I sneaked in, hoping to address a group of hundreds of university students about a *greater* revolution than socialism.

4. I must admit, she has that proverbial Irish temperament, too. After over thirty years of living with her, I wouldn't want it any other way.

5. Andy's nick name. Since he was about four years old, he imitated the sounds of the beaker on the PBS program, Sesame Street.

6. The first case reported in America (1934) was so mild, in fact, that the child died before the parents suspected anything worthy of a doctor's attention.

7. Along these lines, see Vern Poythress, "Modern Spiritual Gifts As Analogous To Apostolic Gifts: Affirming Extraordinary Works Of The Spirit Within Cessationist Theology," *Journal of the Evangelical Theological Society* 39 (1996) 72-102, in which he affirmed the miraculous among cessationists. Part of his argument was to note that cessationists in the 19th century sensed God's presence and saw his works in ways that are not nearly as frequent among cessationists today.

8. I am happy to report that Dr. Reg Grant is one of those few Christian artists who teaches at a seminary. He offers two courses on creative writing, and is in charge of a new media arts program at Dallas Seminary. See his stimulating article on the Holy Spirit and the arts in this volume.

The Holy Spirit in the Hebrew Bible and Its Connections to the New Testament

1. The following are good places to begin: Leon J. Wood, *The Holy Spirit in the Old Testament* (Grand Rapids: Zondervan, 1976); Lloyd Neve, *The Spirit of God in the Old Testament* (Tokyo: Seibunsha, 1972); Benjamin Breckinridge Warfield, " The Spirit of God in the Old Testament," in *Biblical and Theological Studies*, ed. Samuel G. Craig (Philadelphia: The Presbyterian and Reformed Pub. Co., 1952); and for special clarity see especially M. V. Van Pelt, W. C. Kaiser, Jr., and D. I. Block, "רוּחַ, *rûah*," in *New International Dictionary of Old Testament Theology and Exegesis*, ed. Willem A. VanGemeren (Grand Rapids: Zondervan, 1997) 3.1073-1078 and the literature cited there.

2. We will discuss this important verse further below.

3. The statistics used in this article are taken from Francis Brown, S. R. Driver, and Charles A. Briggs, *Hebrew and English Lexicon of the Old Testament* (London: Oxford Univ. Press, 1906) 924-926 and Abraham Even-Shoshan, *A New Concordance of the Bible* (Jerusalem: Kiryat Sefer Pub. Hs., 1989) 1063-1066.

4. Consider, e.g., the renderings of Psalm 51:13 "Your holy spirit" and Isa 63:10-11 "His holy spirit" in the *Tanakh* translation of the Jewish Publication Society (1985). Similarly, in Num 11:29b, Moses' remark is handled this way: "Would that all the LORD's people were prophets, that the LORD put His spirit upon them!"

Likewise, in his *The JPS Torah Commentary: Numbers* (Philadelphia: The Jewish Publication Society, 1990) 87, Jacob Milgrom renders 11:17, "I will draw upon the spirit that is upon you," and on p. 90 Moses' statement in v. 29 is translated, "... that the LORD put His spirit upon them!" (See also Milgrom's excursus on ecstatic prophecy and the spirit on pp. 380-383.) However, it should be noted that this translation issue is not limited to exclusively Jewish translations since, for example, the *New Revised Standard Version* (NRSV) renders these passages with "holy spirit" (Psalm 51:11 and Isa 63:10, 11) and "his spirit" (Num 11:29).

5. Israel Abrahams, "God in the Bible," *Encyclopedia Judaica* vol. 7, ed. by Cecil Roth (Jerusalem: Keter Publishing House, 1971) 643.

6. F. W. Horn, "Holy Spirit," translated by Dietlinde M. Elliott in *The Anchor Bible Dictionary*, ed. David Noel Freedman (New York: Doubleday, 1992) 3.264. Although scarred by some non-conservative presuppositions and relatively light treatment of the Old Testament, this article is a very fine concise and well-documented discussion of the evidence regarding the Holy Spirit/holy spirit in the intertestamental and rabbinic sources as well as the New Testament.

7. See, e.g., Warfield, "The Spirit of God in the Old Testament," 149-156; Gary Fredricks, "Rethinking the Role of the Holy Spirit in the Lives of Old Testament

Believers," *Trinity Journal* 9 NS (1988) 81-84; Van Pelt, Kaiser, and Block, "רוּחַ, *rûah*," 1076-1077; and Wood, *The Holy Spirit in the Old Testament*, 16-22 and 64-77.

8. See Peter C. Craigie, *Psalms 1-50*, The Word Biblical Commentary, vol. 19 (Waco: Word, 1983) 262-263 for a brief but very helpful explanation of the relationship between the intent of this verse in Psalm 31 and Jesus' quotation from it on the cross.

9. For those readers who know Greek, the grammar of the expressions for "the spirit of the man" and "the Spirit of God" in v. 11 are exactly the same. They are τὸ πνεῦμα τοῦ ἀνθρώπου (*to pneuma tou anthrōpou*) and τὸ πνεῦμα τοῦ θεοῦ (*to pneuma tou theou*), respectively.

10. From ancient times until today there has been an ongoing dispute among translators and scholars over the proper interpretation of *ruakh 'elohim* in this verse. See the helpful review of the debate in Claus Westermann, *Genesis 1-11: A Commentary*, trans. John J. Scullion S. J. (Minneapolis: Augsburg, 1984) 106-108. He translates "God's wind was moving to and fro . . ." (76). For a helpful discussion favoring "the Spirit of God" see Edward J. Young, "The Interpretation of Genesis 1:2," *Westminster Theological Journal* 23 (1960-61) 174-178. See James K. Hoffmeier, "Some Thoughts on Genesis 1 & 2 and Egyptian Cosmology," *Journal of Ancient Near Eastern Studies* 15 (1983) 44 and the literature cited there favoring "the wind of God." For mediating somewhere between the two positions see Kenneth A Matthews, *Genesis 1-11:26*, New American Commentary, vol. 1A (Nashville: Broadman & Holman, 1996) 134-136.

11. See, e.g., Gordon Wenham, *Genesis 1-15*, Word Biblical Commentary, vol. 1 (Waco: Word, 1987) 2, 16-17, where he translates "the Wind of God hovered" (note the capital W) and takes it to be "a concrete and vivid image of the Spirit of God." As I see it, the main point is that even if "wind of God" were to be the best English rendering in Gen 1:2 (which is still very much in doubt), the expression still indicates that God was actively present in the primeval unformed and unfilled, deep and dark, watery abyss into which God spoke his creative words beginning in Gen 1:3.

12. See the especially helpful treatment of Ezek 37:1-14 in Michael V. Fox, "The Rhetoric of Ezekiel's Vision of the Valley of the Bones," *Hebrew Union College Annual* 51 (1980) 1-15.

13. The close connection here between the four "winds" and the "breath" that gives life to the dry bones causes one to wonder if there is not a similar link between the "windstorm (רוּחַ סְעָרָה, *ruakh se'arah*) coming out of the north" in Ezek 1:4, "the spirit" of the living creatures in 1:12, and "the spirit of the living beings" (probably better rendered 'the spirit of life') that animated the wheels in 1:20. See the discussion in Daniel I. Block, "The Prophet of the Spirit: The Use of *RWH* in the book of Ezekiel," *Journal of the Evangelical Theological Society* 32 (1989) 36-37 and idem, *The Book of Ezekiel: Chapters 1-24*, New International Commentary on the Old Testament (Grand Rapids: Eerdmans, 1997) 101.

14. See the remarks on this issue in D. A. Carson, *The Gospel according to John* (Grand Rapids: Eerdmans, 1991), 188-189.

15. For the relationship between water baptism, purification, repentance, and making disciples see Richard E. Averbeck, "The Focus of Baptism in the New Testament," *Grace Theological Journal* 2 (1981) 265-301.

16. See Gordon D. Fee, *God's Empowering Presence: The Holy Spirit in the Letters of Paul* (Peabody, MA: Hendrickson, 1994) 910-915 for brief remarks on the Holy Spirit in the intertestamental period.

17. For the following discussion I have found certain articles to be especially helpful: Geoffrey W. Grogan, "The Experience of Salvation in the Old and New Testaments," *Vox Evangelica* 5 (1967) 12-17; John Goldingay, "Was the Holy Spirit Active in Old Testament Times? What was New about the Christian Experience of God?" *Ex Auditu* 12 (1996) 14-28; Block, "The Prophet of the Spirit," 40-41; and Fredricks, "Rethinking the Role of the Holy Spirit in the Lives of Old Testament Believers," 81-104.

18. Carson, *The Gospel according to John*, 500-501 and 509-510.

19. See the extensive discussion of the background and interpretation of this passage in Carson, *The Gospel according to John*, 321-329.

20. For a good summary of this matter see Fee, *God's Empowering Presence*, 914-915 and the literature cited there.

The Witness of the Spirit in Romans 8:16: Interpretation and Implications

1. Not all take it this way, of course. Many Reformed scholars have assumed the associative view, but have read the text either as though following the indirect object view, or with the assumption that the Holy Spirit and our spirit combine to witness *to us*. In other words, many have translated the text "with our spirit," but interpreted the text to mean "to our spirit." To some degree, this is sloppy exegesis. But we can understand how they get this. If I say, "The archangel Michael fought with Satan," the preposition certainly does not mean "alongside of Satan"! Yet, many interpreters assume that the same thing is going on in Rom 8:16. One simply has to read their comments to see that they embrace the inner witness view ("to our spirit"), but read it as though it were otherwise ("with our spirit"). The problem with this in English usage has to do with the governing verb. If it implies some tension or contention, then "with" really has the force of "against" ("Michael fought *against* Satan"). But if it implies collaboration, then "with" typically means "alongside of." Even verbs such as "dialogue," in which the tension is subdued, suggest a notion of less than full collaboration: "He dialogued with me on the issue," may or may not involve hostility. It stops short of "alongside." It may be because of such verbs used frequently with "with" that many scholars adopt the "with"

translation in Rom 8:16 but the "to" exegesis. Hence, the data may well be skewed in favor of the "with" view (especially with translations where no explanation is found).

2. Surprisingly, G. I. Williamson's annotations in the *Westminster Confession of Faith for Study Classes* (Philadelphia: Presbyterian and Reformed, 1964) argue this point, but for a slightly different reason (133): "Some have maintained that the Holy Spirit communicates assurance to the soul of the believer immediately, that is, without the use of Scripture. And Romans 8:16 is claimed in support of this view.... It is true that the Spirit himself bears witness. But he bears witness *with* the spirit of man immediately, and not *to* it immediately. In other words God exerts an immediate influence upon the spirit of man, but not by speaking directly to man's spirit apart from Scripture. Rather, the immediate influence is such that man and God speak together...."

3. Gordon D. Fee, *God's Empowering Presence: The Holy Spirit in the Letters of Paul* (Peabody, MA: Hendrickson, 1994) 568. The exact quotation is in the plural because Fee combines the argument of the dative indirect object with that of "a watered down sense" of the verb "('assures our spirits')": "But these are unnecessary expedients that abandon Pauline usage for the sake of a prior theological concern that is not involved here." What Fee never elaborated on, as far as I could see, is what the Pauline usage is that is ignored. If he means lexical usage of this verb, he is clearly wrong (see later discussion). If he means theological usage of Paul's overall meaning, that is something to be construed in the context under consideration. Yet, if so, then isn't Fee guilty of a theological predisposition in this text himself?

4. Ibid., 569.

5. This is Fee's argument (ibid., 567). It can, of course, be nuanced in more than one way. Some may argue that our spirit's testimony *before God* is essential for our own salvation. Others might argue that our spirit combines testimony with the Holy Spirit *before us*.

6. Fee offers other arguments that are not very compelling. For example, he argues by innuendo that the indirect object viewpoint is theologically motivated from the get-go and that therefore it should be rejected: "Disturbed by the supposed theological infelicity of Paul's sentence... some... take the dative as an indirect object..." (568). He pushes hard on Cranfield especially, saying that he has "an extensive argument that manifestly begins with this theological agenda in hand" (ibid.). Yet Fee's theological agenda is hardly less suppressed: "the Spirit has not come to 'take over,' as it were, so that our own human responsibility is diminished" (569). What matters is not whether a particular viewpoint involves presuppositions (for all do), but whether there is evidence in the text to support such a viewpoint.

7. But see the NET Bible: "the Spirit bears witness to our spirit."

8. "Spiritus testimonium reddit spiritui nostro": "The Spirit offers testimony to our spirit."

9. "Der Geist selbst gibt Zeugnis unserm Geist": "The Spirit himself gives testimony to our spirit."

10. Cf. Acts 13:22; 15:8; Rom 10:2; Col 4:13; 1 Tim 6:13; Heb 10:15; 11:4; 1 John 5:9-10; Rev 1:2.

11. 1 John 5:7 is an apparent exception to this, for the Spirit is among the three who bear witness. But the previous verse highlights just the Spirit's testimony ("the Spirit is the one who testifies, because the Spirit is the truth"), suggesting that it is sufficient in itself.

12. Translation is my own.

13. D. B. Wallace, *Greek Grammar beyond the Basics: Exegetical Syntax of the New Testament* (Grand Rapids: Zondervan, 1996) 159.

14. Ibid. The following texts are noted in which the σύν- prefixed verb takes other than a dative of association: Luke 11:48; Acts 6:9; 8:1; 18:7; Rom 7:22; 8:26; 12:2; 1 Cor 4:4; Eph 5:11; Phil 1:27; 2 Tim 1:8; Rev 18:4.

15. In six of its eight occurrences in the NT συμβαίνω takes a dative, none of which are datives of association (Mark 10:32; Acts 3:10; 20:19; 1 Cor 10:11; 1 Peter 4:12; 2 Peter 2:22).

16. This overall assessment is not shared by Strathman in *TDNT* however. Nevertheless, he argues that the force is generally "agree with," but still sees Rom 8:16 as "bear witness to." The problem with this view is that (συμ)μαρτυρέω is not ὁμολογέω. That is, although those texts where he sees "agree with" as the meaning of this verb have a certain plausibility in their contexts, "bear witness to" is equally valid. Further, the semantic domains of these two verbs seem to be quite different, even though in translation they may well look alike.

17. So Moo, *Romans 1-8, loc. cit.,* who nevertheless does not seem to adopt this view here.

18. The translation of Rom 9:1 is my own. In Rom 2:15 no dative is found.

19. Wallace, *Exegetical Syntax,* 143: "Dative of interest typically (but not always) belongs to the larger category of indirect object."

20. μαρτυρέω occurs 76 times in the NT. Eighteen (18) instances take a dative indirect object (John 5:33; 18:37; 1 John 1:2; 3 John 3, 6; Rev 22:18; *incommodi* in Matt 23:31; *commodi* in Luke 4:22; John 3:26, 28; Acts 13:22; 15:8; Acts 22:5; Rom 10:2; Gal 4:15; Col 4:13; Heb 10:15; Rev 22:16); twenty-five (25) instances take a prepositional phrase that emulates a dative of interest, usually *dativus commodi* (περί in John 1:7, 8, 15; 2:25; 5:31, 32 [*bis*], 36, 37, 39; 7:7; 8:13, 14, 18 [*bis*]; 10:25; 15:26; 18:23; 21:24; 1 John 5:9, 10; ἐπί in Acts 14:3; 1 Tim 6:13; Heb 11:4; κατά in 1 Cor 15:15). This leaves thirty-three instances, thirteen of which are passive and thus not easily able to accommodate a dative indirect object (none of the passive forms of this verb

in the NT take a dative or prepositional phrase that emulates it). Thus, of the 63 examples of μαρτυρέω in the NT in the active voice, two thirds of them take a dative direct object or the like. None occurs with a dative of association.

21. Not only this, but μαρτυρέω never occurs with μετά plus the genitive in the NT. However, σύν— verbs that take a dative of association often use this prepositional phrase for the same idea (cf., e.g., συλλαλέω in Matt 17:3 with Mark 9:4; συνεσθίω in Gal 2:12).

22. Cf., e.g., συνανάκειμαι (Matt 19:10; Luke 14:10); συνανάκειμαι (Mark 2:15); συλλαλέω (Mark 9:4; Luke 9:30; 22:4); συναποθνήσκω (Mark 14:31); συναναβαίνω (Mark 15:41; Acts 13:31); συγχαίρω (Luke 1:58; 15:6; Phil 2:17); συναντάω (Luke 9:37; 22:10; Acts 10:25; Heb 7:10); συνεσθίω (Luke 15:2; Acts 10:41; 1 Cor 5:11); συνοδεύω (Acts 9:7); συναναπαύομαι (Rom 15:32); συναναμίγνυμι (1 Cor 5:9; 2 Thess 3:14); συμμερίζω (1 Cor 9:13); συνθάπτω (Col 2:12); συνεγείρω (Col 3:1); συναπόλλυμι (Heb 11:31); συνοικέω (1 Pet 3:7).

23. TLG, or *Thesaurus Linguae Graecae* CD ROM D, is a digitized database of Greek texts from Homer to AD 1453, currently comprising some 57 million Greek words (Los Altos, CA: Packard Humanities Institute, 1993). Produced under the auspices of the Packard Humanities Institute, it is now marketed by the University of California at Irvine. CD ROM E was released in February 2000; it contains 6,625 works from 1,823 authors, and a total count of 76 million words of text. The cover letter to TLG subscribers notes that "This is a significant expansion compared to the 57 million words (from 831 authors and 4,305 works) included in CD ROM D." Nevertheless, the CD ROM D is surely a representative database for the usage of συμμαρτυρέω. Besides TLG, I also examined the first 63 volumes of the *Oxyrhynchus Papyri*, the first two volumes of the Tebtunis papyri, and Packard Humanities Disk #7 containing the Duke University and University of Michigan papyri data. Only one instance was found in the sources outside of TLG. Moulton and Milligan mention an additional two instances (BGU 1.86.41 [AD 155] and PSI 6.696.5 [3rd cent. AD]), bringing the number of which I am aware to 166 instances.

The potential verb forms include συμμαρτυρ—, συνμαρτυρ—, συνεμαρτυρ—, συμμεμαρτυρ—, ξυμμαρτυρ—, ξυνεμαρτυρ—, and ξυμμεμαρτυρ—.

24. It should be noted that a large number of texts are patristic quotations from Paul's three usages of συμμαρτυρέω in Romans, without further comment. These therefore do not contribute to the discussion.

25. The evidence is as follows:

Sixth Century BC

Solon, *Fragment 36*:

συμμαρτυροίη ταῦτ' ἂν ἐν δίκη Χρόνου μήτηρ μεγίστη δαιμόνων
'Ολυμπίων

"May the great mother of the deities of Olympus *bear witness* at the trial of Chronos." There is no dative substantive here; Bauer rightly considered Solon to contain the earliest attestation of συμμαρτυρέω as bearing an intensive force.

Fifth Century BC

Euripides, *Helen of Troy* 1080: Menelaus says to Helen,

καὶ μὴν τάδ᾽ ἀμφίβληστρα σώματος ῥάκη
ξυμμαρτυρήσει ναυτικῶν ἐρειπίων.

"Yes, and these rags wrapped about my body
Shall testify of the salvage from the wreck."

No dative is used; the verb has the intensive force of testifying.

Euripides, *Hippolytus* 286: Nurse to her queen, Phaedra:

ὡς ἂν παροῦσα καὶ σύ μοι ξυμμαρτυρῇς
οἷα πέφυκα δυστυχοῦσι δεσπόταις.

"So stand thou by and *witness unto me*

How true am I to mine afflicted lords." (The translation is that of A. S. Way in the Loeb Classical Library [LCL].) The dative "to me" obviously bears an indirect force.

Euripides, Iphigeneia at Aulis 1158:

συμμαρτυρήσεις ὡς ἄμεμπτος ἦν γυνή

"You testify how blameless a wife she was"

There is no dative; the testimony confirms what she believes, but is not in association with her. (Cf. also in Euripides: with dative substantive which is other than an associative dative: *Fragment* 319; *Comparatio Thesei et Romulii* 6.5; without dative substantive: *Scholia in Hipp* 577.)

Sophocles, *Electra* 1224:

φίλτατον, συμμαρτυρῶ

"I agree [with you]: [it is] a happy [day]."

The context here is minimal, and is poetic (and thus cryptic). Nevertheless, here is a probable instance of an associative συμμαρτυρέω without a dative substantive.

Sophocles, *Philoctetes* 438:

ξυμμαρτυρῶ σοι.

Philoctetes responds to Neoptolemus:

"In that I'll bear thee out." (F. Storr's translation [LCL].)

The force is obviously agreement with someone else. Here the associative and *commodi* uses of the verb shade into one another: "I testify on your behalf" is little different from "I agree with you."

Aelius Aristides, Πρὸς Πλάτωνα περὶ ῥητορικῆς 72.11:

Πλάτωνα αὐτὸν συμμαρτυρῆσαι τῷ λόγῳ

"Plato himself bears witness to the word"

Clearly, this is the indirect usage. (For other fifth century BC texts which confirm the intensifying force of συμμαρτυρέω, cf. Pindar, *Scholia et glossae in Olympia et Pythia* P. 1.87-93; idem, *Scholia* P. 1.87-90; Aelius Aristides, Περὶ τοῦ παραφθέγματος 397.21; idem, *Scholium* 72.7. The first three lack a dative substantive, while the third involves a dative indirect object. All clearly involve an intensifying force for the verb.)

Fifth-Fourth Century BC

Xenophon, *Hellenica* 3.3.2:

συνεμαρτύρησε δὲ ταῦτ' αὐτῷ καὶ ὁ ἀληθέστατος λεγόμενος χρόνος εἶναι.

"And time also, which is said to be the truest witness, gave testimony that the god was right..." (C. L. Brownson's translation [LCL].)

This text is difficult to assess. Like other texts, the associative dative and dative of advantage are close to one another. The αὐτῷ seems to suggest "bore witness *with him* that he was right." However, it could mean "bore witness *for* him."

Xenophon, *Hellenica* 7.1.35:

συνεμαρτύρει δ' αὐτῷ ταῦτα πάντα ὡς ἀληθῆ λέγοι ὁ 'Αθηναῖος Τιμαγόρας...

"And the Athenian, Timagoras, **bore witness** *in his behalf* that all these things which he said were true."

The idea here seems to be closer to indirect object—i.e., he bore witness for him. It crosses over into *dativus commodi*, which in contexts such as this, looks like association, but it still is indirect object. The idea, then, would be "he testified to him."

Isocrates, *Trapeziticus* 42:

Αὐτὸν τοίνυν Πασίων ἔργῳ παρέξομαι τούτοις συμμαρτυροῦντα.

"Pasion himself, moreover—in effect, at least—I will present as corroborating these statements." (LCL translation.) That is, "I will show that Pasion himself has borne witness to [the truth of] these statements." That this is indirect object is evident by the fact that μαρτυροῦντα could easily be substituted here.

Isocrates, *Panegyricus* 31:

τά τε πάλαι ῥηθέντα τοῖς παροῦσιν ἔργοις συμμαρτυρεῖ

"the words spoken long ago confirm the practice of today"

(George Norlin's translation [LCL].)

That is, "the words spoken long ago bear witness to the present deeds." Again, the indirect discourse force is seen in that μαρτυρεῖ could have been substituted.

First-Second Century AD

Josephus, *Antiquities* 19.154:

Κλήμης...μεθίησιν πολλῶν μετ᾽ ἄλλων συγκλητικῶν δικαιοσύνην τῇ πράξει συμμαρτυρῶν καὶ ἀρετὴν τοῖς ἐντεθυμημένοις καὶ πράσσειν μὴ ἀποδεδειλιακόσι.

"Clemens, together with many others of senatorial rank, **bore witness** *to* the justice of *the deed* and *to* the valour of *those who had made the plans* and shown no weakness in the execution of them." (L. H. Feldman's translation [LCL].)

Plutarch, Quomod adulator ab amico interno 64.C:

...γὰρ δεῖ τῷ φίλῳ... συμμαρτυρεῖν

"For it is necessary to support one's friend"

The idea here seems to be more "agree with" than "bear witness to," though it could possibly have the force of "bear witness on behalf of."

Plutarch, Quaestiones convivales 724.C.:

οὐ **συμμαρτυροῦσιν** ὅτι τῆς εἰς τὸ νικᾶν καὶ κρατεῖν δυνάμεως *τῷ θεῷ τούτῳ* πλεῖστον μέτεστιν;

"Do not the dedications of arms and the finest of the battle-spoil and trophies at Pytho **attest** that this god has much influence in the realm of victory and the winning of powers?" (LCL translation.)

The meaning is clearly that the display of evidence strongly attests *to* the god's abilities and record.

Plutarch, *Moralia* 786.F:

οὐ μὴν ἀλλὰ καὶ εὐμενὴς συμμαρτυροῦσα τοῖς ἔργοις...

"Yes, and moreover kindly gratitude, **bearing witness** *to the acts...*"

(I. N. Fowler's translation [LCL].)

Again, a clear instance of indirect object.

Vettius Valens, *Anthologiarum* 9.120:

ἐὰν δέ πως καὶ ὁ τοῦ Διὸς συμμαρτυρήσῃ

"If perhaps the son of Zeus should testify"

No dative substantive here; an intensifying use of the verb.

(Other examples from the first and second centuries AD include: Vettius Valens, *Anthologiarum* 9.61; idem, *Anthologiarum* 9.116. In each of these passages, the datives are other than associative.)

Third-Fourth Century AD

Hippolytus, Commentarium in Danielem 1.19.8:

συμμαρτυρῶν τῇ ἀληθείᾳ

"bearing witness to the truth"

A clear instance of indirect discourse.

Eusebius, Ecclesiastical History 1.11.3:

ὁ δ᾽ αὐτὸς Ἰώσηπος ἐν τοῖς μάλιστα δικαιότατον...τὸν Ἰωάννην, τοῖς περὶ αὐτοῦ κατὰ τὴν τῶν εὐαγγελίων γραφὴν ἀναγεγραμμένοις συμμαρτυρεῖ

"The same Josephus admits that John was peculiarly righteous, and a baptist, *confirming* the testimony recorded in the text of the Gospels concerning him."

This example uses a dative and seems to have a *commodi* force. One must keep in mind that there are sometimes subtle shades of difference between "agree with," "bear witness with," "bear witness to," "bear witness for," and "confirm." However, is it really possible to substitute μυρτυρέω for συμμαρτυρέω here? That seems a stretch, so this instance probably should belong with the associative group.

Eusebius, De laudibus Constantini 16.11:

συμμαρτυρεῖν τῇ ἀληθείᾳ

"bearing witness to the truth"

Eusebius, Supplementa ad quaestiones ad Marinum 22.989:

συμμαρτυρεῖ δὲ αὐτῷ καὶ ὁ ἱερὸς ἀπόστολος ὧδε Κορινθίοις γράφων, ὅτι ὤφθη Κεφᾷ, εἶτα τοῖς ἔνδεκα.

"And the holy apostle also bears witness to him here, in writing to the Corinthians: 'He appeared to Cephas, then to the eleven.'"

Eusebius, Demonstratio evangelica 8.2.123:

αὐτὰ δὴ ταῦτα καὶ ὁ Φίλων συμμαρτυρεῖ

"Philo also testifies of these same things"

(For other fourth-century examples, cf. Eusebius, *De ecclesiastica theologia* 2.2.1; idem, *Praep Evang* 6.8.24; Chrysostom, *In epistulam ad Romanos* 60.428 [these three examples involve datives that are other than associative]. In the following three texts, there is no dative substantive: Basil, *De baptismo libri duo* 31.1561; idem, *Orationes* 31.1684; Chrysostom, *Fragmenta in Jeremiam* 64.905.)

Fifth Century AD

Theodoret, *Eranistes* 87:

> ὁ μέγας Πέτρος τῇ ἀληθείᾳ συμμαρτυρῶν
>
> "the great Peter bearing witness to the truth"

Theodoret, Interpretatio in Jeremiam 81.604:

> πράγματά σου κατηγορεῖ, καὶ τὸ συνειδός σου συμμαρτυρεῖ σοι
>
> "your deeds condemn you, and your conscience bears witness against you"

Theodoret, De providentia orationes decem 83.569:

> ἕτερα, τοῖς προτέροις συμμαρτυροῦντα
>
> other things which bear witness to former things

Theodoret, De incarnatione domini 75.1428:

> Ἰωάννης συμμαρτυρεῖ λέγων· Ἴδε ὁ ἀμνὸς ὁ αἴρων τοῦ κόσμου τὴν ἁμαρτίαν
>
> "John testified saying, "Behold the lamb who takes away the sin of the world"

> Theodoret uses συμμαρτυρέω for John the Baptist's testimony about Jesus in John 1:29. Five times in John chapter 1 μαρτυρέω is used of John's testimony, yet Theodoret here introduces his testimony with a Pauline word. It is evident that it bore the same essential meaning as μαρτυρέω and was selected, in all probability, because of its intensifying force. This instance is significant, too, because there is no dative substantive, and nothing in either Theodoret's context or that of John 1 would suggest an associative notion here.

Sixth Century AD

Simplicius, *In Cat* 8.262:

> τῇ τοιαύτῃ χρήσει συμμαρτυρεῖ
>
> he "bears witness to such great power"

> (Cf. also Simplicius, *in Ph* 9.18 [using a dative indirect object].)

Eighth and Ninth Centuries AD

John Damascene, *De azymis* 95.392:

> Ἰωάννης συμμαρτυρεῖ τῷ λόγῳ
>
> "John bears witness to the word"

> This is followed by a quotation of 1 John 5:7. What is signficant is that the author of the Fourth Gospel and the letters of John uses μαρτυρέω *forty-three* times— more than 50% of all instances in the NT. The concept of John bearing witness to the truth or the word is, therefore, ready at hand. But John Damascene chooses instead to use the verb συμμαρτυρέω even though this verb never appears in John.

It is evident that it bore the same essential meaning as μαρτυρέω and was selected, in all probability, because of its intensifying force. That this is a very late text, however, softens the value of this. Nevertheless, we already saw Theodoret's similar usage three centuries earlier.

(Cf. also John Damascene, *Passio sancti Artemii* 96.1268 for a similar example. In addition, Nicephorus Gregoras, *Historia Romana* 3.361 illustrates the usage of συμμαρτυρέω without a dative substantive.)

Nicephorus Gregoras, *Historia Romana* 3.430:

συμμαρτυρεῖ δ' ἡμῖν καὶ ὁ μέγας ἀπόστολος Παῦλος, λέγων· νῦν μὲν δι' ἐσόπτρου ἐν αἰνίγματι βλέπομεν, τότε δὲ πρόσωπον πρὸς πρόσωπον.

"The great apostle Paul also testifies to us, saying, 'Now we see in a mirror dimly, but then face to face.'"

26. Forty-five of the 166 instances in extant Greek literature were examined. As much as one third of the remaining examples are quotations from Romans without further ado. By my count, at least thirty-eight of the forty-five examples should be labeled "intensive," while two should be labeled "associative," and three are somewhere in between. As well, Moulton-Milligan add two more instances to the associative side of things, bringing that to four. Certainly there are more instances of the associative category (as well as the intensive category), but the pattern is nevertheless clear with the representative texts we have examined.

27. Cranfield, *Romans* (ICC) 1.403.

28. This notion is picked up elsewhere in Paul's writings: cf., e.g., Gal 5:14-25.

29. Other pieces of evidence could be used to show that certainty of our convictions and knowledge of God and his will are directly linked to the presence of the Spirit in our lives. In particular, note the radical difference between the apostles' convictions about the reality of Jesus' resurrection before Pentecost (cf. Matt 28:17 ["they worshiped him, but some doubted"]) and after—even though Jesus went to great lengths to prove to them that he was truly risen from the dead (Acts 1:3).

30. Gregory of Nyssa, *De instituto Christiano* 8,1.73 (δεῖ γὰρ κατὰ τὸ λόγιον Παύλου τὸ πνεῦμα τοῦ θεοῦ συμμαρτυρεῖν τῷ πνεύματι ἡμῶν, ἀλλὰ μὴ τῇ ἡμετέρᾳ κρίσει τὰ ἡμέτερα δοκιμάζεσθαι· οὐ γὰρ φησίν, ὁ ἑαυτὸν συνιστῶν ἐστι δόκιμος ἀλλ' ὃν ὁ κύριος συνίστησιν).

31. Credit is due to M. James Sawyer for this historical summary. The Puritans did not hold to the immediate inner witness, but felt that through the long process of sanctification one came to this. Thus, they both reversed the dwelling and the doing roles of the Spirit and virtually held to a second blessing view of assurance! Warfield and many modern Reformed scholars also hold to a different view, shaped, it seems, by Scottish common sense and the Enlightenment.

The Witness of the Spirit in the Protestant Tradition

1. F. H. Klooster, "Internal Testimony of the Holy Spirit," 564-65 in *Evangelical Dictionary of Theology*, ed. W. Elwell (Grand Rapids: Baker, 1984).

2. These passages include Rom 8:15; 1 John 5:10-12; as well as Gal 4:6.

3. As witnessed in the Reformed confessions.

4. John Calvin, *Institutes of The Christian Religion*, trans. Ford Lewis Battles, 2 vols. (Philadelphia: Westminster, 1977). While modern versions of the *Institutes* are published in two physical volumes, the classic citation is to reference first the book (there are four) the chapter, and finally the paragraph) 1.7.1; 1.7.4.

5. Ibid., 1.7.1.

6. Ibid., 1.7.4.

7. Philip Schaff, *Creeds of Christendom*, 3 vols. (reprint ed; Grand Rapids: Baker, 1977) 3.831.

8. Ibid., 3.362.

9. Ibid., 3.602-3.

10. References to the doctrine are found in the Formula of Concord, Reformed Confessions, the works of Arminius and several Baptist confessions (Klooster, "Internal Testimony of the Holy Spirit", *Evangelical Dictionary of Theology*, 564).

11. Calvin, *Institutes* 3.2.40 (italics added).

12. Lewis Berkhof, *Systematic Theology* (reprint ed; Grand Rapids: Eerdmans, 1979) 508.

13. Ibid.

14. *Institutes* 3.2.15 (italics original).

15. Ibid. (italics added). Significantly, this is exactly the trap into which those who claimed the name of Calvin fell. With their emphasis on limited atonement they could never be sure that Christ had died for them, hence they were forced to look inside at one's works and the essential holiness of one's heart rather than rely upon the promises of scripture and the experience of the Spirit. But even here there was no peace because the doctrine of temporary faith that developed stole the hope of assurance by injecting the question of one's election into the equation: "Perhaps the 'fruit' I see in my life is not that of regeneration but the pre-regenerate work of the Spirit, from which I may fall away." In San Diego in November, 1989, at the Evangelical Theological Society annual meeting, Dr. John MacArthur was asked when a believer could be assured of his salvation; his reply was that such assurance could be had only after death.

16. *Institutes,* 3.11.11 (speaking of Osiander).

17. Ibid., 3.11.11

18. Alister McGrath, "Justification, the New Ecumenical Debate," *Themelios* 13.2 (1988) 145. He continues: "Being justified on the basis of the external righteousness of Christ meant all that needed to be done for an individual's justification had been done by God—and so a believer could rest assured that he had been accepted and forgiven. The Reformers could not see how Trent ensured that the individual was accepted, despite being a sinner. For if the believer possessed perfect righteousness which ensured his justification, he could no longer be a sinner—and yet experience (as well as the penitential system of the Catholic church!) suggested that believers continually sinned. For the Reformers, the Tridentine doctrine of justification was profoundly inadequate, in that it could not account for the fact that the believer was really accepted before God while still remaining a sinner. The Reformers were convinced that Trent taught a profoundly inadequate doctrine of justification as a result. The famous phrase, due to Luther, sums up this precious insight with brilliance and verbal economy: *simul iustus et peccator*, 'righteous and a sinner at the same time.' Luther was one of the few theologians ever to have grasped and articulated the simple fact that God loves us and accepts us just as we are—not as we might be, or will be, but as he finds us."

19. Calvin, *Institutes,* 3.2.39.

20. Ibid.

21. Ibid., 3.2.39.

22. Ibid., 3.2.39.

23. Packer, *Quest for Godliness: the Puritan Vision of the Christian Life* (Wheaton, IL: Crossway Books, 1990) 182.

24. Ibid.

25. Thomas Goodwin, *Works, ed. J. Miller* (James Nicholl: London, 1861) 1.257, quoted by Packer, *Quest for Godliness,* 185 (italics original). This witness is "self-evidencing and self-authenticating and analogous in character to the Spirit's witness to the truth of the gospel" (185).

26. Richard Sibbs, *Works* (Aberdeen : Printed by J. Chalmers for R. Ogle, Holborn; and T. Hamilton, London, 1809) 5.440, quoted by Packer, *Quest for Godliness,* 184.

27. *Institutes,* 3.3.1.

28. Ibid., 3.3.2.

29. M. Charles Bell, *Calvin and Scottish Theology* (Edinburgh: Handsel, 1985) 82.

30. J. I. Packer, "Sola Fide: The Reformed Doctrine of Justification," in *Soli Deo Gloria* (Philadelphia: Presbyterian and Reformed, 1976) 11-12.

31. Isaac August Dorner, *A System of Christian Doctrine* (Edinburgh: T & T Clark, 1897) 2.175.

32. J. I. Packer, *Quest for Godliness,* 180.

33. John Wesley, "A Plain Account of Christian Perfection," *The Works of John Wesley* in the Ages Digital Library version 7 (Rio, WI: Ages Software, 1998) 11.492.

34. Ibid., 179.

35. Ibid., 190-191.

36. Bell summarizing Calvin notes: "If we look to ourselves, we encounter doubt, which leads to despair, and finally our faith is battered down and blotted out. Arguing that our assurance rests in our union with Christ, Calvin stresses that contemplation of Christ brings assurance of salvation, but self-contemplation is 'sure damnation.' For this reason, then, our safest course is to distrust self and look at Christ" (Bell, *Calvin and the Scottish Theology*, 28).

37. Wesley, *Works*, in the Ages Digital Library, version 7 (Rio, WI: Ages Software, 1998) 5.196.

38. Ibid., 193.

39. Wesley's position on the witness of the Spirit sounds amazingly Reformed in its perspective and quite at odds with his equally strident Arminian position taken elsewhere in his writings that one can truly apostatize and lose one's justification and hence one's salvation.

40. Jonathan Edwards, *"A Faithful Narrative of the Suprising Work of God,"* The *Works of Jonathan Edwards*, 2.1084-85 in the Ages Digital Library, version 7 (Rio, WI: Ages Software, 1998).

41. Ibid., 1100-1101.

42. Charles Hodge, *Systematic Theology*, 3 vols. (reprint ed.; Grand Rapids: Eerdmans, 1975) 1.152.

43. Ibid., 1.153. Significantly, Hodge did not address the critical reconstructions of canonical development that were already in vogue even during his own lifetime.

44. Ibid. W. G. T. Shedd, although not a Princetonian by education, succinctly summarized the logic of this position when he stated, "If, as one asserts, 'The great mass of the Old Testament was written by authors whose names are lost in oblivion' it was written by uninspired men… This would be the inspiration of indefinite persons, like Tom, Dick and Harry, whom nobody knows, and not of definite historical persons, like Moses and David, Matthew and John, chosen by God by name and known to men." Cited by C. A. Briggs, *General Introduction to the Study of Holy Scripture* (reprint ed.; Grand Rapids: Baker, 1970) 159.

45. A. A. Hodge, *Commentary on the Confession of Faith* (Philadelphia: Presbyterian Board of Publication, 1926 [First published in 1869]) 51-52.

46. B. B. Warfield, "Review of A. W. Deickhoff, *Das Gepredigte Wort und die Heilige Schrift* and *Das Wort Gottes*," *The Presbyterian Review* 10 (1889) 506 (italics added).

47. Ibid.

48. See *The Westminster Assembly and Its Work* (New York: Oxford University Press, 1931) 212.

49. Briggs, *Whither?*, 82.

50. See "Calvin, the Reformers, and *The Witness of the Spirit*" above.

51. Briggs, *General Introduction to the Study of Holy Scripture*, 142-43.

52. C. W. Hodge to A. A. Hodge, July 6, 1881 (Princeton University: Hodge Papers). (Italics added.)

53. Elsewhere (*Church Unity*, 223-24) he contended that the Reason was to be distinguished from the powers of reasoning "as the more fundamental function of the soul upon which all reasoning depends." To the intellectual faculties, he attributed no ability to attain certainty. The only Reason that can have any measure of religious authority is that of the *moral or religious reason*, the conscience.

54. Briggs, *Church Unity*, 226.

55. See above for the testimony of the Westminster Confession.

56. Briggs, *Whither?*, 73-81. Calvin and the Westminster divines did not totally eschew rational proofs. They did however deny their efficacy to convince a non-believer of the truth of scripture.

57. Briggs himself affirmed the infallibility of the biblical text, but, echoing the language of the Westminster Confession, limited that infallibility to *faith and morals*.

58. *Church Unity*, 161.

59. Ibid., 163.

60. Ibid. (italics added).

61. Ibid. (italics added). In so saying, Briggs placed himself with the Reformers. But he added an important new qualification heretofore unknown, specifically the phrase, "or part of a writing." This would seem to compromise severely his principle of the plenary inspiration of the scriptures, and set each man up as the judge of not only what books were inspired, but also what parts of each individual book. This, however, does not appear to be his intention at this point. Rather, this qualifying phrase was intended to cover situations such as the apocryphal additions to Daniel and Esther. These "parts of books" had not demonstrated by their character that they were inspired, and had thus been rejected by Protestants. Were the principle applied only to whole books, the books would themselves have to be rejected. (This discussion is ignoring, for the sake of argument, textual considerations that prove the spurious nature of the additions in question. In addition, this discussion assumes a positivistic approach to an individual writing taken in isolation from the rest of scripture.)

62. Ibid.

63. Ibid.

64. Ibid., 166.

65. Ibid.

66. Ibid., 167.

67. Ibid.

68. Abraham Kuyper, *Principles of Sacred Theology* (Grand Rapids: Baker, 1980) 624; reprint of *Encyclopedia of Sacred Theology: Its Principles* (New York: Charles Scribner's Sons, 1898).

69. Ibid.

70. Ibid., 556-57.

71. Kuyper sees sin as being at the root of radical individualism: "Sin, and hence unbelief, scatters individualizes and pulverizes; but grace, hence faith, restores life in organic connection, viz. the life of each member of the body." The apprehension of the witness of the Spirit is together with all the saints (Eph 3:18) (*Principles of Sacred Theology*, 553-6, esp. 556).

72. See Kuyper, *Principles of Sacred Theology*, 556.

73. M. James Sawyer, "Evangelicals and the Canon of the New Testament," *Grace Theological Journal* 11.1 (1990) 29-52.

74. See the for example Bob Wilkin's study, "Assurance by Inner Witness? Romans 8:16," http://www.faithalone.org/news/y1993/93march3.html.

75. See M. James Sawyer, "Some Thoughts on Lordship Salvation" delivered at the ETS national meetings in Kansas City, November 1991. This paper is posted on the Biblical Studies Foundation website, http://bible.org/docs/theology/pneuma/ets.htm.

The Ministry of the Spirit in Discerning the Will of God

1. "There are about thirty-five evangelical books in print on this subject (this one makes thirty-six)" (James C. Petty, *Step by Step* [Phillipsburg, NJ: Presbyterian & Reformed, 1999], 9). Among the more useful of these are Petty's own book; Oliver R. Barclay, *Guidance* (London: IVP, 1956); Elisabeth Eliot, *A Slow and Certain Light* (Waco: Word, 1973); Garry Friesen with J. Robin Maxson, *Decision Making and the Will of God* (Portland OR: Multnomah, 1980); M. Blaine Smith, *Knowing God's Will* (Downers Grove, IL: IVP, 1979); Sinclair B. Ferguson, *Discovering God's Will* (Edinburgh: Banner of Truth, 1981); Bruce Waltke, *Finding the Will of God* (Gresham OR: Vision House, 1995); Phillip D. Jensen and Tony Payne, *The Last Word on Guidance* (Homebush West NSW: Anzea [St. Matthias Press], 1991); Dallas Willard, *Hearing God* (Downers Grove, IL: IVP, 1999 [originally, *In Search of Guidance* (Ventura CA: Regal, 1984)]).

2. Waltke, *Finding the Will of God*, 35.

3. For a fuller treatment, see J. I. Packer, *Faithfulness and Holiness: the Witness of J. C. Ryle* (Wheaton, IL: Crossway, 2002) 21-26 and 51-52.

4. Ibid.

5. Ibid., 251.

6. Garth Lean, *On the Tail of a Comet: The Life of Frank Buchman* (Colorado Springs: Helmers & Howard, 1988) 75-76.

7. Petty, *Step by Step*, 165.

8. I echo here some things in my chapter, "Guidance," in *God's Plans for You* (Wheaton, IL: Crossway, 2001) 91.

9. Waltke, *Finding the Will of God*, 360.

The Spirit's Role in Corporate Worship

1. G. Welton Gaddy, *The Gift of Worship* (Nashville: Broadman, 1992) 220.

2. This Latin phrase is the common shorthand for Prosper of Aquitaine's statement (*Indiculus*), *ut legem credendi lex statuat supplicandi*, meaning that while worship practices are predicated on theology, they are even more important to express these beliefs themselves. See Kevin W. Irwin, *Context And Text: Method In Liturgical Theology* (Collegeville: The Liturgical Press, 1994) 4-6.

3. Richard Baxter, "The Savoy Liturgy," in *Liturgies of the Western Church*, Bard Thompson, ed. (New York: William Collins Publishers, 1961) 402.

God, People, and the Bible: The Relationship between Illumination and Biblical Scholarship

1. See, for example, Grant R. Osborne, The Hermeneutical Spiral: A Comprehensive Introduction to Biblical Interpretation (Downers Grove, IL: InterVarsity, 1991) and Walter C. Kaiser, Jr. and Moisés Silva, An Introduction to Biblical Hermeneutics: The Search for Meaning (Grand Rapids: Zondervan, 1994).

2. See Anthony C. Thiselton, *The Two Horizons* (Grand Rapids: Eerdmans, 1980), xix-xx and 10-23 for a basic description of the "two horizons" as a hermeneutical principle. This terminology and the hermeneutical concepts that arise from it derive ultimately from Hans-Georg Gadamer.

3. In effect, Osborne's hermeneutical spiral merges with Thiselton's (*à la* Gadamer's) fusion of the two horizons. For my present description of the principles and procedures involved see Osborne, *The Hermeneutical Spiral*, 370, 386, 411-415, and Thiselton, *The Two Horizons*, 17-23, 439-440, 443-445.

4. Fred H. Klooster, "The Role of the Holy Spirit in the Hermeneutic Process: The Relationship of the Spirit's Illumination to Biblical Interpretation," in *Hermeneutics, Inerrancy, and the Bible*, ed. Earl D. Radmacher and Robert D. Preus (Grand Rapids: Zondervan, 1984), 463-465.

5. Osborne, The Hermeneutical Spiral, 413.

6. Thiselton, *The Two Horizons*, 439.

7. See Anthony C. Thiselton, *New Horizons in Hermeneutics* (Grand Rapids: Zondervan, 1992), 8-10 and 31-35 for helpful remarks on reading the Bible with transforming effect in the life of the reader. However, he says virtually nothing about the importance of the Holy Spirit in bringing about this effect.

8. See Thiselton, *The Two Horizons*, 3-10, and most recently Craig G. Bartholomew, "Uncharted Waters: Philosophy, Theology and the Crisis in Biblical Interpretation ," in Craig Bartholomew, Colin Greene, and Karl Möller, *Renewing Biblical Interpretation* (Grand Rapids: Zondervan, 2000), 1-39 for helpful explanations of the importance of these philosophical discussions for biblical scholars.

9. Kevin J. Vanhoozer, *Is There a Meaning in This Text? The Bible, The Reader, and the Morality of Literary Knowledge* (Grand Rapids: Zondervan, 1998). I am also relying here on his own very helpful earlier summary of his approach in Kevin Vanhoozer, "Introduction: Hermeneutics, Text, and Biblical Theology," in *New International Dictionary of Old Testament Theology & Exegesis*, ed. Willem A. VanGemeren (Grand Rapids: Zondervan, 1997), 14-50.

10. Vanhoozer, *Is There a Meaning in This Text?* 407-431.

11. Vanhoozer, "Introduction: Hermeneutics, Text, and Biblical Theology," 24.

12. Ibid., 19.

13. Colin Brown, *From the Ancient World to the Age of the Enlightenment*. Christianity and Western Thought, vol. 1 (Downers Grove, Illinois: InterVarsity, 1990), 314-315.

14. Vanhoozer, "Introduction: Hermeneutics, Text, and Biblical Theology," 20, 29.

15. Ibid., 21-23. Ed. note: What Vanhooser labels as "biblical positivism" appears historically under the rubric of "Scottish Common Sense" philosophy. See also M. James Sawyer, *The Survivor's Guide To Theology* (Grand Rapids: Zondervan), forthcoming, Ch. 3, "How Do We Know," for a more detailed discussion of *Scottish Common Sense* and Princeton Theology. See also Sidney Ahlstrom "The Scottish Philosophy and American Theology," *Church History* 24 (1955) 257ff; Daryl G. Hart, "The Princeton Mind and the Modern World," *Westminster Theological Journal* 46 (1984) 4; and Nancey Murphy, *Beyond Liberalism and Fundamentalism* (Valley Forge: Trinity Press International), 4-7, 15-19, 32-35.

16. Ibid., 24-26.

17. Ibid., 32-33.

18. Vanhoozer, *Is There a Meaning in This Text?* 428.

19. Ibid., 427.

20. John M. Frame, "The Spirit and the Scriptures," in *Hermeneutics, Authority, and Canon,* ed. D. A. Carson and John D. Woodbridge (Grand Rapids: Zondervan, 1986), 220-225. See in particular Karl Barth, *The Holy Ghost and the Christian Life* (London: Muller, 1938).

21. The few who have written on this subject in the last two or three decades have often lamented the fact that "evangelical scholars are more interested in inspiration than illumination and in the first than in the second horizon" (Clark H. Pinnock, "The Role of the Spirit in Interpretation," *Journal of the Evangelical Theological Society* 36 [1993]: 492). The lack of serious discussion about illumination in standard theological and hermeneutical writings in recent decades and even centuries is also mentioned in Frame, "The Spirit and the Scriptures," 219; Klooster, "The Role of the Holy Spirit," 451; and Art Lindsley, "A Response to: The Role of the Holy Spirit in the Hermeneutic Process," in *Hermeneutics, Inerrancy, and the Bible,* ed. Earl D. Radmacher and Robert D. Preus (Grand Rapids: Zondervan, 1984), 487.

22. See Vanhoozer, *Is There a Meaning in This Text?* 410, 427-429, and Klooster, "The Role of the Holy Spirit," 461-463, 468.

23. See the helpful remarks on this pivotal point and the scriptures that support it in Frame, "The Spirit and the Scriptures," 230-235; Osborne, *The Hermeneutical Spiral,* 341; Pinnock, "The Role of the Spirit in Interpretation," 493-497; and most pointedly in William J. Larkin, Jr., *Culture and Biblical Hermeneutics: Interpreting and Applying the Authoritative Word in a Relativistic Age* (Grand Rapids: Baker, 1988), 288-292.

24. Klooster, "The Role of the Holy Spirit," 457.

25. See Vanhoozer, "Introduction: Hermeneutics, Text, and Biblical Theology," 39 for this definition of the term "metanarrative."

26. See the helpful focus on this in Klooster, "The Role of the Holy Spirit," 454.

27. There has been debate over the meaning of Eph 5:18. Most modern English translations render it "filled with the Spirit," or something very similar, although there is no definite article ("the") and the preposition is most naturally translated "in" (Greek *en*). For a discussion of the interpretation of this passage see Richard E. Averbeck, "Worshiping God in Spirit," in *Authentic Worship: Scripture's Voice, Applying Its Truth,* ed. Herbert W. Bateman (Grand Rapids: Kregel, 2002), 92-94. Ed. Note: For an alternative view of Eph 5:18, see P. T. O'Brien, *The Letter to the Ephesians* (Pillar; Grand Rapids: Eerdmans, 1999) 388-94; H. W. Hoehner, *Ephesians: An Exegetical Commentary* (Grand Rapids: Baker, 2002) 699-705.

28. John Calvin, *Institutes of the Christian Religion*, translated by Henry Beveridge (Grand Rapids: Eerdmans, 1970), 1.37-39. See also Klooster, "The Role of the Holy Spirit," 463.

29. As defective as his view of the inspiration and authority of the Bible is, we need to take this side of Barth's formulation of the Spirit's witness in the reading of scripture seriously (Frame, "The Spirit and the Scriptures," 221-222).

30. "Where Application of God's truth to the heart and life are highly valued the illumination of the Holy Spirit will also be highly valued. Where application to life is given a small place the illumination of the Spirit will be given a small place. We must keep clearly before us that the goal of inspiration and interpretation is application to life" (Lindsley, "A Response to: The Role of the Holy Spirit in the Hermeneutic Process," 491).

The Holy Spirit and the Arts

1. "Art" in this article signifies any work of beauty wrought by the divine will or by human hands, which serves to reveal in objective/sensate form the idea of the artist. The category of art under consideration is limited to the "fine" or "liberal/contemplative" arts (logic, grammar, rhetoric, poetry, sculpture, music, etc.) as differentiated from the "useful" arts (e.g., agriculture, medicine, education, government, war, industrial arts).

2. For the purpose of this article we acknowledge God as divine Artist, though we recognize that any comparison with human artists is merely analogical. The Lord is creative in the absolute sense, calling his creation into being out of nothing, whereas the human artist may be more accurately described as being re-creative in that he must manipulate pre-existing materials in order to give form to his imaginative idea.

3. While Montaigne strains to make a case for the ability of animals to reason alongside man, and thereby to produce sensible art, we would agree with Kant that such references to animals as artists must be metaphorical since "no rational deliberation forms the basis of their labor, [but] we see at once that it is a product of their nature (of instinct), and it is only to their Creator that we ascribe it as art" (Immanuel Kant, *The Critique of Judgement*, trans. Creed Meredith, in *Great Books of the Western World*, 42.523 [Chicago: Encyclopaedia Britannica, 1990]).

4. "A spider conducts operations that resemble those of a weaver, and a bee puts to shame many an architect in the construction of her cells. But what distinguishes the worst architect from the best of bees is this, that the architect raises his structure in imagination before he erects it in reality. At the end of every labour process, we get a result that already existed in the imagination of the labourer at its commencement. He not only effects a change of form in the material on which he works, but he also realizes a purpose of his own that gives the law to his *modus operandi*, and to which he must subordinate his will" (Karl Marx, *Capital*, edited by Frederich Engels, in *Great Books of*

the Western World, Robert Maynard Hutchins, ed. 50.85 [Chicago: Encyclopaedia Britannica, 1990]).

5. Class notes, Dallas Seminary, 1977.

6. "Against the Heavenly Prophets in the Matter of Images and Sacraments." Luther's Works. Vol. 40. (Philadelphia, PA: Fortress Press, 1958) 83.

7. I am indebted to Gregory Wolfe in his brief exposition of Coleridge for the idea of "enhancement" as used here ("Editorial Statement: Image Vs. Fancy," *Image: a Journal of the Arts & Religion* 7 [Fall 1994] 3).

8. Samuel Taylor Coleridge, *Biographia Literaria or, Biographical sketches of my literary life and opinions.* ed. by James Engell and W. Jackson Bate (London: Routledge & Kegan Paul, 1983) I:295-296.

The Spirit in the Black Church

1. Warren Leslie, *Dallas: Public and Private* (Dallas: Southern Methodist University Press, 1998) 73-74.

2. Hart M. Nelsen, Raytha L. Yokley, and Anne K. Nelsen, *The Black Church in America* (New York: Basic Books, 1971) 61.

3. C. Eric Lincoln and Lawrence H. Mamiya, *The Black Church in the African Experience* (Durham and London: Duke University Press, 1990) 354-355.

4. C. Eric Lincoln and Lawrence H. Mamiya, *The Black Church in the African Experience* (Durham and London: Duke University Press, 1990) 346-381.

5. Allen P. Ross, "Psalms," in, *The Bible Knowledge Commentary*, edited by John F. Walvoord and Roy B. Zuck (Wheaton, IL: Victor Books, 1985) 865-866.

6. John Martin, "Ezra," in *The Bible Knowledge Commentary* 680.

7. Elmer Towns, "Worshiping With Your Eyes Wide Open," *Worship Leader* 6.4 (July-August 1997) 22.

The Holy Spirit and Our Emotions

1. The translation of these texts is my own from the Hebrew.

2. When I had Professor James Barr as a supervisor at Oxford, in a private conversation with me he aptly pointed out that dictionaries do not give meanings to words, only contexts. It is in the contexts that soul is used that we see it is used to represent the process of feeling and wanting.

3. Making God richly emotional does not negate his divine attributes; his omniscience, omnipotence, and sovereignty are intact but deeply enriched. He is not a desiccated philosopher, but a passionate lover and ruler.

4. Walther Eichrodt, *Theology of the Old Testament* (Philadelphia: Westminster, 1961-67) 2.122-130; J. Barton Payne, *Theology of the Older Testament* (Grand Rapids: Zondervan, 1962) 226-227; Hans Walter Wolff, *Anthropology of the Old Testament* (Philadelphia: Fortress, 1974) 159-162.

5. "Karl Barth has called the expansion in [Genesis 1] v. 27b a 'definitive explanation' of the text of v. 27a. Men are to be allowed to complement themselves in love... They are the image of God in that together they are one ... men can only fulfil the commission as the image of God given to them in their creation by turning towards one another and by complementing one another, like man and wife" (Wolff, *Anthropology*, 162). When Yahweh spoke to the other with him, he was communicating in relationship (Gen. 1:26). God intended to make mankind in "... image." To do this adequately he had to make two (Gen. 1:27). So that two communicating Beings were "imaged" by two communicating human beings. Man—man and woman—made in the image of God and man as "soul" underscore twin truths. Individuals are created to be in relationships and the quality of those relationships will be felt in the soul.

6. Paul begins his description of the fruit of the Spirit, i.e., the byproduct of his ministry in the heart of the believer, in Gal 5:22-23 in terms of emotions: love, joy, peace.

7. "To walk" (περιπατέω, *peripateō*) is a most general term for the principles that should hold sway over our lives. Scripture teaches that the believer should walk or order the affairs of his or her life around love (Eph 5:2); we should live in a way worthy of the calling (Eph 4:1; Col 1:10), not the way the gentiles arrange their lives (Eph 4:17), as children of light (Eph 5:8), carefully (Eph 5:15), as [we] have received the Lord (Col 2:6), in a new kind of life (Rom 6:4), not according to the flesh (Rom 8:4), as called of God (1 Cor 7:17). What this means is that when this verb for walking is used, it indicates that the entirety of one's life should be dominated by the characteristic cited. This is equivalent to the Hebrew term הלך, *halakh.*

8. Eph 1:3; this is noted in Cleon L. Rogers Jr. and Cleon L. Rogers III, *The New Linguistic and Exegetical Key to the New Testament* (Grand Rapids: Zondervan, 1998) 434.

The Holy Spirit in Missions

1. Mark Ritchie, *Spirit of the Rain Forest* (Chicago: Island Lake Press, 1996) 122.

2. Ibid., 227-8.

3. Marvin Wolford, *Free Indeed from Sorcery and Bondage* (San Rafael, CA: Pathway Press, 1999).

4. G. C. Oosthuizen, Post-Christianity in Africa: A Theological and Anthropological Study (Grand Rapids, MI, Eerdmans, 1968).

5. Ibid., 122-3.

6. Note the highly controversial presentation by Chung Hyun Kyung at the World Council of Churches Assembly in 1991 in which she identified the Holy Spirit with other spirits recognized in traditional religions: "Come, Holy Spirit—Renew the Whole Creation" in *Signs of the Spirit: Official Report of the Seventh Assembly of the WCC, Canberra, 1991.*

7. "A major concern at Canberra was to establish criteria for discerning the Spirit among the many spirits. Two were put forward...1) The Holy Spirit 'points to the cross and resurrection and witnesses to the Lordship of Christ,' 2) The Holy Spirit produces the fruit of the Spirit..." (Kirsteen Kim, "Spirit or 'Spirits'," *Missiology* 32.3 [July 2004] 358).

8. "Joseph Osei-Bonsu from Ghana draws attention to the fact that many African Christians are more Spirit-centered than Christ-centered, particularly because of the 'endemic and chronic fear of evil spirits' against which the Holy Spirit provides protection" (Kirsteen, "Spirit or 'Spirits'," 352). Allan Anderson makes the same point in *Bazalwane: African Pentecostals in South Africa* (Pretoria, South Africa: University of South Africa, 1992) 20.

9. "Suicide: Patients fear losing control," *The Oregonian*, February 24, 2000 (Portland, OR) A13.

10. John Peck, *The Holy Spirit* (Eastbourne, England: Kingsway Publications, 1979) 21.

The Father, the Son, and the Holy Scriptures?

1. Philip Yancey, "Would Jesus Worship Here?" *Christianity Today*, February 7, 2000. (http://www.christianitytoday.com/ct/2000/002/38.152.html)

2. Dennis J. Bennett *In Touch and Emotionally Free*, http://www.emotionallyfree.org/dennis.htm.

3. Ed Blake, sermon preached to San Ramon (Evangelical) Presbyterian Church, January 26, 2003.

4. Jacques Ellul, *The Subversion of Christianity*, translated by Geoffrey W. Bromiley (Grand Rapids: Eerdmans, 1986). Chapter 2 (19-51) particularly surveys these exchanges from an historical perspective.

5. Philip Yancey, *What is so Amazing about Grace?* (Grand Rapids: Zondervan, 1997) 139.

6. Donald Bloesch, *The Holy Spirit: Works and Gifts* (Downers Grove, IL: InterVarsity, 2000) 34.

7. Bernard Ramm, *After Fundamentalism* (San Francisco: Harper & Row, 1983) 15-20.

8. For and introductory discussion of these developments see Trevor Hart, *Faith Thinking* (Downers Grove: InterVarsity, 1995) 23-70.

9. Gotthold Lessing, *Lessing's Theological Writings,* tr. H. Chadwick, (Stanford: Stanford University Press, 1957) 53.

10. Ibid., 55.

11. "The early sociology of knowledge (M. Kearl) was dominated by the ideas of Karl Marx and Karl Mannheim, who defined the subject as the relation between knowledge and a social base. Branches of the sociology of knowledge include the sociology of literature and science. How do social institutions influence literary forms or writers? How do scientists decide what counts as knowledge? To what extent are different types of Knowledge socially constructed?

Different types of knowledge (e.g., religious, scientific, political, everyday) are understood to grow differentially within varying social environments. Are there cultural differences in rationality? How does social power, especially when embodied in institutional practices, shape knowledge?

The sociology of knowledge examines how types of social organization make the ordering of knowledge possible. There is less focus on the differing social locations and interests of individuals or groups. How do different social and cultural environments produce different knowledge systems? The social modification of knowledge may occur through processes such as knowledge production, knowledge encoding, knowledge transmission, decoding, storage of knowledge, and decision making and combinations of the previous. This causal connection between knowledge and society is seen as reciprocal—society affects knowledge and knowledge affects society" (description of the discipline of Sociology of Knowledge posted by the sociology department of the University of Texas San Antonio: http://colfa.utsa.edu/Sociology/masters/topics.html#Sociology%20of%20Knowledge)

12. Stanley Gundry, in his presidential address to the Evangelical Theological Society ("Evangelical Theology, Where Should We Be Going?" *Journal of the Evangelical Theological Society* 22 [1979] 11), stated:

> I wonder if we recognize that all theology represents a contextualization, even our own theology? We speak of Latin American liberation theology, black theology, or feminist theology; but without the slightest second thought we will assume that our own theology is simply theology, undoubted, in its purest form. Do we recognize that the versions of evangelical theology held to by most of the people in this room are in fact North American, white and male and that they reflect and/or address those values and concerns?

Likewise John Jefferson Davis ("Contextualization and the Nature of Theology" in *The Necessity of Systematic Theology,* 2nd ed., J. J. Davis, ed. [Grand Rapids: Baker, 1978] 177) has noted:

...if systematic theology is essentially a "biblical theology" that merely repeats and arranges the statements and categories of Scripture, then which biblical theology is the really biblical one? The Lutheran? The Reformed? The Wesleyan? The dispensational? The very variety of theological systems within the evangelical tradition alone, all claiming an equally high regard for the authority of Scripture, is in itself an indication that there are factors beyond the text itself which shape the Gestalt of the system. In no case does the exegete or theologian come to the text completely free of presuppositions. We can to a degree become more critically aware of our presuppositions, but we cannot eliminate them entirely. There is an inescapable element of personal judgment which shapes the theologian's vision, just as it does the artist's or scientist's.

13. Alister McGrath, *Genesis of Doctrine* (Oxford: Blackwell, 1990) 89-90.

14. Nancey Murphy, *Beyond Liberalism and Fundamentalism* (Valley Forge: Trinity, 1996) 4-7.

15. Stephen Douglas Bennett, "Thomas Reid and the Scottish School of Common Sense Philosophy: Historically and Philosophically Considered" (Th.M. thesis, Dallas Theological Seminary, 1980) 47-50.

16. G. Stanley Hall, "On the History of American College Textbooks and Teaching in Logic, Ethics, Psychology and Allied Subjects," Proceedings of the American Antiquarian Society, n.s., 9 (1893-94) 158. Quoted by Martin Terrance, *The Instructed Vision, Scottish Common Sense Philosophy and The Origins of American Fiction* (Bloomington, IN: Indiana University Press, 1961) 3.

17. See Thomas Reid, *Essays on the Intellectual Powers of Man* (London: Macmillan, 1941) 389-91.

18. Ibid., 186.

19. Reid balanced his empiricism with an emphasis on intuition that gave his epistemology a dualistic bent. In addition, he was adamant about the limits of empirical inquiry; induction could not answer ultimate questions concerning first causes (Bennett, "Thomas Reid," 62; cf. Reid, *Essays*, 399-400).

20. Reid, *Essays*, 338-39; 384-86. Cf. Daryl G. Hart, "The Princeton Mind in the Modern World," *Westminster Theological Journal* 46 (1984) 4.

21. B. B. Warfield, "Apologetics," *Studies In Theology* (reprint ed.; Grand Rapids: Baker, 1981) 3. He viewed the primary task of apologetics, not as "the defense, not even the vindication, but the *establishment*... of that knowledge of God which Christianity professes to embody and seeks to make efficient in the world..." (italics added.)

22. The Mercersburg Theology admittedly incorporated elements of romanticism and idealism, then current on the continent.

23. "In time, the Reformed rationalism and sacramental theology of Turretin permeated the ranks of much of American Presbyterianism. However, at Columbia Theological Seminary in South Carolina, the Professor of Theology, James Henley Thornwell, and the Professor of Church History and Polity, John B. Adger, employed Calvin's *Institutes* as the text for theology and ecclesiology with the result that many Southern ministers were Calvinistic in their sacramental theology.

"These two strains of Reformed sacramental theology came into conflict when John Nevin published his controversial *The Mystical Presence* in June 1846. Nevin, professor of theology of the seminary of the German Reformed Church at Mercersburg, Pennsylvania, had been much influenced by German philosophy, especially that of Hegel, and also by the High Church movement of the nineteenth century. Nevin had been a student of Charles Hodge at Princeton but later repudiated Hodge's sacramental theology. He sought to demonstrate the historical decline of the doctrine of the Supper that had occurred in the Reformed churches and also to revive Calvin's doctrine which had been codified in the Belgic Confession, one of the symbols of the German Reformed Church. Hodge responded to Nevin's volume in 1848 in a long article in the Princeton Review. (Charles Hodge, "Doctrine of the Reformed Church on the Lord's Supper", *The Biblical Repertory and the Princeton Review*, 20 [April 1848]: 227-77.)

"First, he tried to demonstrate that the symbols of the Reformed churches did not contain the high doctrine of the Supper that was set forth by Calvin in the *Institutes*. Next, he made the incredible assertion that Calvin's true opinion, pertaining to the nature of Christ's presence in the Supper, was to be found not in the *Institutes* but in the Consensus Tigurinus, a symbol that was framed for the purpose of uniting the Swiss churches. He implied that the view set forth in the *Institutes* was intended by Calvin to be a mediating position in order to conciliate the Lutherans. Finally, he refuted Nevin's theory of the Supper with its Hegelian overtones" (*Brian Nicholson*, "Calvin's Doctrine of the Spiritual Presence of Christ in the Lord's Supper," *Antithesis* 2.2 (May/June 1991) (© Covenant Community Church [OPC] of Orange County, 1991) (http://www.reformed.org/webfiles/antithesis/v2n2/ant_v2n2_presence.html)

24. Rom 8:16. The central passage upon which the doctrine of the witness of the Spirit is built is said by some to refer to the fact that the Spirit bears witness *with* our spirit to God, not that the Spirit bears witness *to* our spirit in any sort of experiential way. Although I am not aware of whether Hodges has put this in print, Dr. Bob Wilkin, President of the Grace Evangelical Society, made this very point in the interaction after his paper, "Assurance: That You May Know" delivered at the National ETS meetings in New Orleans, November, 1990. See Daniel B. Wallace's essay in this volume, "Romans 8:16 and the Witness of the Spirit."

25. S. Lewis Johnson, Jr., "How Faith Works," *Christianity Today*, September 22, 1989, 23.

26. *Notitia* refers to factual knowledge; *assensus* is assent to facts; *fiducia* is personal trust.

27. For example, he states of the woman at the well that she "received this saving *truth* in faith" (Zane Hodges, *Absolutely Free* [Grand Rapids: Zondervan, 1989] 42). The point here is that he describes faith as trust in facts, rather than trust in a person who was in fact in her presence. Concerning faith, Millard Erickson has noted: "...the type of faith necessary for salvation involves both believing that and believing in, or assenting to facts and trusting in a person. It is vital to keep these two together. Sometimes in the history of Christian thought one of the aspects of faith has been so strongly emphasized as to make the other seem insignificant" (*Christian Theology* [Grand Rapids: Baker, 1989] 940).

28. See, for example, *The Gospel Under* Siege, 14.

29. M. James Sawyer, "Evangelicals and the Canon of the New Testament," *Grace Theological Journal* 11.1 (1990) 29-52.

30. Charles Hodge, *Systematic Theology*, 3 vols. (reprint ed.; Grand Rapids: Eerdmans, 1975) 1.152.

31. F. F. Bruce discusses surveys the concept of apostolicity in the early church and documents numerous mentions of this factor as being a primary criterion in canon determination. He also mentions other issues related to apostolicity which were mentioned by some patristic writers as offering evidence that a book was indeed canonical (*The Canon of Scripture* [Downers Grove, IL: InterVarsity, 1988], 256-269, especially 256-258). R. Laird Harris, surveying the same material, insists that the sole criterion was apostolic authorship (*Inspiration and Canonicity of the Bible* [Grand Rapids: Zondervan, 1957, 1969], 219-245, especially 244-245).

32. B. B. Warfield, "The Formation of the Canon of The New Testament," *The Inspiration and Authority of the Bible* (reprint ed.; Philadelphia: Presbyterian and Reformed, 1970) 415.

33. Ibid.

34. Ibid. (italics added).

35. B. B. Warfield, "Review of A. W. Deickhoff, *Das Gepredigte Wort und die Heilige Schrift* and *Das Wort Gottes*," *The Presbyterian Review* 10.506 (1889) (italics added).

36. See *The Westminster Assembly and Its Work* (New York: Oxford University Press, 1931) 212.

37. F. L. Patton, "Benjamin Breckinridge Warfield," *The Princeton Theological Review* 19 (1921) 369-91.

Norman Kraus (*The Principle of Authority in the Theology of B. B. Warfield, William Adams Brown, and Gerald Birney Smith* [Ph.D. dissertation, Drew University, 1961] 270) rightly observes concerning Warfield's use of reason:

> His "evidence," on his own admission, did not amount to demonstration, and yet he sought to escape the logical consequences of this admission by claiming that "probable" evidence though different in kind from "demonstrable evidence" is nonetheless objective, rational, and capable of establishing certainty of conviction. Thus he claimed that the probable evidence which he had produced was of such a quantity and quality as to overwhelmingly establish the rational ground for and force mental assent to the message and authority of Scripture. But in the final analysis, *he was unable to close the gap between probability and absolute certainty with a rational demonstration of mathematical quality*... And as long as the gap between probability and demonstration remains, there also remains the necessity of a subjective and volitional response to the appeal of truth before there can be certainty [italics added].

38. See M. J. Sawyer, "Evangelicals and the Canon of the New Testament," *Grace Theological Journal* 11:1 (Spring 1990) 29-52

39. C. W. Hodge to A. A. Hodge, July 6, 1881, *Hodge Papers* (Princeton University). (Italics added.)

40. With reference to the Westminster Confession doctrine of the witness of the Spirit Warfield stated:

> "...the inward work of the Holy Spirit bearing witness by and with the Word in our hearts."

> This beautiful statement of the Confession has sometimes of late been strangely misunderstood.... A man needs a preparation of the spirit [*sic*], as well as an *exhibition of the evidences*, in order to be persuaded and enabled to yield faith and obedience. If this be not true the whole Reformed system falls with it. It is then neither to be misunderstood as *mysticism*, on the one hand, *as if the "testimony of the Holy Spirit" were expected to work faith in the Word apart from or even against evidences* (Warfield, *Westminster Assembly*, 212. [italics added]).

41. J. I. Packer, "The Ministry of The Spirit In Discerning the Will of God," in this volume.

42. Bob Wilkin, "Assurance: That You May Know," delivered at the national Evangelical Theological Society meeting in New Orleans, November, 1990.

43. Calvin, *Institutes* 3.2.15.

44. He bases this position on texts such as 1 John 5:11-13: "And this is the testimony: God has given us eternal life, and this life is in his Son. The one who has the Son has this eternal life; the one who does not have the Son of God does not have this

eternal life. I have written these things to you who believe in the name of the Son of God so that you may know [εἰδῆτε] that you have eternal life."

45. "Psychological certainty may be justified or unjustified, as in the belief that the moon reflects light or is made of green cheese. Propositional certainty is never justified or unjustified; it simply obtains or does not obtain, someone must have made sure or become justifiably certain of the proposition. Thus certainty of propositions requires psychological certainty plus its justification" (*Encyclopedia of Philosophy* [New York: Macmillian, 1967] 2.67. See also Thomas C. Oden, *The Living God* [San Francisco: Harper & Row, 1987] 382-404, and Otto Weber, *Foundations of Dogmatics* [Grand Rapids: Eerdmans, 1988] 195-198).

46. Contrast this to Calvin who states unequivocally that we know that we are saved by a direct act of faith, rather than a reflex act! Cf., e.g., John Calvin, *Concerning the Eternal Predestination of God* (London: James Clark, 1961) 130-131.

47. Bell, *Calvin and Scottish Theology*, 82. Bell, summarizing Calvin, notes: "If we look to ourselves, we encounter doubt, which leads to despair, and finally our faith is battered down and blotted out. Arguing that our assurance rests in our union with Christ, Calvin stresses that contemplation of Christ brings assurance of salvation, but self-contemplation is 'sure damnation.' For this reason, then, our safest course is to distrust self and look at Christ" (28).

48. Ibid., 98.

49. Jack Deere, *Surprised by the Power of the Spirit* (Grand Rapids: Zondervan, 1993).

50. Ibid., 55-56.

51. Isaac August Dorner, *A System of Christian Doctrine* (Edinburgh: T & T Clark, 1897) 2.175.

52. Abraham Kuyper, *Principles of Sacred Theology* (reprint ed.; Grand Rapids: Baker, 1980) 624.

53. Ibid.

54. Donald Bloesch, *The Holy Spirit*, 36.

55. Bloesch, *The Holy Spirit*, 36. Note above the Princetonians' apologetic for canon.

56. Thomas F. Torrance, *Karl Barth, Biblical and Evangelical Theologian* (Edinburgh: T. & T. Clark, 1990) 221-222. See also Bloesch, *The Holy Spirit*, 36, and C. Fitzsimmons Allison, *The Cruelty of Heresy* (Harrisburg, PA: Morehouse) 20.

57. William Placher, *The Domestication of Divine Transcendence* (Louisville, KY: Westminster/John Knox, 1996) 87.

58. Ronald Nash, "Gordon H. Clark," in *Handbook of Evangelical Theologians,* Walter A. Elwell ed. (Grand Rapids: Baker, 1993) 182-83.

59. Ibid., 183-84.

60. Carl F. H. Henry, *God, Revelation and Authority* (Waco: Word, 1979) 3.429.

61. David P. Hoover, "Gordon Clark's Extraordinary View of Men & Things," IBRI Research Report No. 22, 1984 (posted at: http://ibri.org/22gordonclark1.html).

Similarly McDowell comments of Clark's work, "The trouble primarily is caused by the fact that Clark imagines truth and meaning, or knowledge, in propositional terms, and therefore fails to comprehend performative utterance…. 'Knowledge and meaning always have the form of a proposition'" [149; cf. 150] John C. McDowell, "Review: *Karl Barth's Theological Method,* 2nd ed (Jefferson, MD: Trinity Foundation, 1997)." Posted on *John McDowell's Theology and Philosophy Page:* http://www.geocities.com/johnnymcdowell/ Review_Clark.htm.

62. P. Andrew Sandlin, "A Conflict of Apologetic Visions," *The Chalcedon Report,* December 2000 (http://www.chalcedon.edu/report/2000dec/sandlin_conflict.shtml).

> God's revelation to man is religiously holistic, not reductionistically rational. We are not saved by ideas; we are saved by union with Christ communicated, to be sure, in the propositional ideas of the Bible.

63. Ibid.

64. Millard Erickson, *Christian Theology* (Grand Rapids: Baker, 1983) 1.196.

65. See Nancey Murphy, *Beyond Liberalism and Fundamentalism* (Valley Forge: Trinity, 1996) 15-19.

66. Timothy Phillips, "The Argument for Inerrancy: An Analysis," *Journal of the American Scientific Affiliation* vol 31 (June, 1979) 80-88 (http://www.asa3.org/ASA/PSCF/1979/JASA6-79Phillips.html).

67. Donald Dayton, "'The Battle for the Bible' Rages On" *Theology Today* 37 (April 1980) 82 (http://theologytoday.ptsem.edu/apr1980/v37-1-article6.htm).

68. Bloesch, *Holy Spirit,* 39-40.

69. Ibid., 40

70. Ibid., 40: "…Although truth is not a property of propositions, propositions can attest truth."

71. Ibid., 44.

72. Ibid.

73. Ibid., 46-47.

74. With reference to the concept of language games Wittgenstein argued that if one actually looks to see how language is used, the variety of linguistic usage becomes clear.

"Words are like tools, and just as tools serve different functions, so linguistic expressions serve many functions. Although some propositions are used to picture facts, others are used to command, question, pray, thank, curse, and so on. This recognition of linguistic flexibility and variety led to Wittgenstein's concept of a language game and to the conclusion that people play different language games. The scientist, for example, is involved in a different language game than the theologian. Moreover, the meaning of a proposition must be understood in terms of its context, that is, in terms of the rules of the game of which that proposition is a part. The key to the resolution of philosophical puzzles is the therapeutic process of examining and describing language in use" (*Microsoft Encarta*, s.v. "Wittgenstein, Ludwig Josef Johann," http://encarta.msn.com /encyclopedia_761565894/Wittgenstein.html).

75. Vern Poythress, *Symphonic Theology* (Grand Rapids: Zondervan, 1987) 69.

76. Ibid.

77. Ibid., 46-47.

78. Charles Hodge, as representative of the Princetonian position, displayed a great antipathy for any emphasis on the subjective nature of Christianity. At one point he stated: "The idea that Christianity is a form of feeling, a life, and not a system of doctrines is contrary to the faith of all Christians. Christianity always has a creed. A man who believes certain doctrines is a Christian" (*Biblical Repertory and Princeton Review* 29 [1857] 693). C. R. Jeschke states of the Princetonians ("The Briggs Case: The Focus of a Study in Nineteenth Century Presbyterian History," Ph.D. Dissertation, University of Chicago, 1967," 56):

> The strict compartmentalization of formal theology and the life of piety that came to prevail at Princeton reflected in part the growing irrelevance of traditional modes of thought and inherited statements of faith for the needs of the church in a rapidly changing world. The fact that Hodge and his colleagues, like most of their contemporaries, were unaware of the sickness in the theological body, only permitted the condition to worsen, and heightened the reaction of the patient to the cure, when its true condition was finally diagnosed.

Andrew Hoffecker has challenged this perception of the Princetonians, contending that those who make such assertions ignore the wealth of devotional material left by Alexander, Charles Hodge, and Warfield (*Piety and the Princeton Theologians* [Grand Rapids: Baker, 1981]). Despite Hoffecker's defense of the Princetonians themselves, it is not too much to say that many even among the Old School read only the theological material of the Princetonians. This fact contributed to a cold creedal orthodoxy among a significant contingent of the Old School with its stress on pure doctrine. Even the great Greek grammarian Basil L. Gildersleeve, himself a Princeton graduate, decried the "baleful influence of Princeton" stating that there was from there "very little hope of a generous vivifying force" (Letter from Gildersleeve to Charles Augustus Briggs, *Briggs Transcripts,* 5.470 (Twelve ledger books hand-copied by Emilie Grace Briggs comprising a transcription of Charles Briggs' personal correspondence, Union Theological Seminary Library).

79. Gordon H. Clark "Behaviorism & Christianity," This article has been taken from *Against the World: The Trinity Review, 1978–1988,* Copyright © 1996 John W. Robbins. It is published by The Trinity Foundation, P.O. Box 68, Unicoi, TN 37692. (http://www.cfcnb.org/1999wia/aug1999.htm)

80. Jeremy Taylor, *Selected Works,* ed. Thomas K. Carroll (New York: Paulist, 1990) 374, 371.

81. Bloesch, *Holy Spirit,* 47.

82. Archibald Alexander, *The Log College* (reprint ed., London: Banner of Truth Trust, 1968).

Printed in the United States
39176LVS00003B/91-336